P9-CCX-371

POPOL

The Mayan Book
of the Dawn of Life

REVISED EDITION

Translated by

DENNIS TEDLOCK

with commentary based on the
ancient knowledge of the modern Quiché Maya

VUH

A TOUCHSTONE BOOK

Published by Simon & Schuster
New York   London   Toronto   Sydney

Are k'u wa' nu tak'alib'al, nu presenta
chikiwach ri nantat, comon chuchkajawib'
much'ulik ulew, much'ulik poqlaj, much'ulik baq.

TOUCHSTONE
Rockefeller Center
1230 Avenue of the Americas
New York, NY 10020

Copyright © 1985, 1996 by Dennis Tedlock
All rights reserved,
including the right of reproduction
in whole or in part in any form.

TOUCHSTONE and colophon are registered trademarks
of Simon & Schuster Inc.

Designed by Irving Perkins Associates, Inc.

Manufactured in the United States of America

20 19 18

Library of Congress Cataloging-in-Publication Data
Popul Vuh. English.
Popol Vuh: the Mayan book of the dawn of life / translated by Dennis Tedlock; with
commentary based on the ancient knowledge of the modern Quiché Maya.—Rev. ed.
p. cm.
Translated from the Quiché.
"A Touchstone book."
Includes bibliographical references and index.
1. Popol Vuh.   2. Quiché Indians—Religion.
3. Quiché mythology.
I. Tedlock, Dennis, 1939–   .   II. Title.
F1465.P813   1996   299'.784—dc20   95-46822   CIP
ISBN-13: 978-0-684-81845-0
ISBN-10:   0-684-81845-0
Special acknowledgment is due to Donna Serwinowski
for her excellent editorial assistance
in the preparation of this edition.

CONTENTS

Part Four

Part Five

11

ILLUSTRATIONS

PREFACE

THE POPOL VUH TELLS THE STORY of the emergence of light in the darkness, from primordial glimmers to brilliant dawns, and from rainstorms as black as night to days so clear the very ends of the earth can be seen. A revised edition of this translation of the Popol Vuh has become necessary because the world of Mayan studies is itself a constantly brightening one. Advances in the understanding of Mayan languages, literature, art, history, politics, and astronomy have required changes in the introduction, notes, commentaries, glossary, and illustrations. There are also changes in the translation itself, some of them subtle refinements and others that readers of the previous edition may find surprising. And finally, an index has been added.

Newly available sources on Mayan languages have made it possible to give meaning to proper names that were left untranslated before. For example, Xbaquiyalo, the wife of Seven Macaw, now becomes Egret Woman. The temptresses Xtah and Xpuch are now Lust Woman and Wailing Woman, and they stand revealed as the predecessors of a dangerous phantom known all the way from Guatemala to northern New Mexico by her Spanish name, La Llorona. And Tecum, Keeper of the Mat in the ninth generation of Quiché lords, becomes Black Butterfly.

In other cases new sources have made it possible to correct errors of translation that were caused by imprecise spellings or slips of the pen in the Popol Vuh manuscript, which often leave words and phrases open to multiple interpretations. What was once "the emergence of all the sky-earth" now becomes "the lighting of all the sky-earth," a reference to the astronomical aspect of the story. The name of the first human woman, given as Celebrated Seahouse in the previous edition, now changes to Red Sea Turtle. The term for the rubber used by the hero twins to heal a falcon's eye is no longer "sorrel gum" but rather "blood of sacrifice." And the image of the god Hacauitz is no longer located "above a great red river" but rather "at the top of a great pyramid."

Other refinements have resulted from discussions with Quiché linguist and literary scholar Enrique Sam Colop, who recently completed his

15

dissertation on Mayan poetics. For example, he has conclusively shown that various translators (including myself) have misread the phrase *saq petenaq ch'aqa palo,* which is one of several titles of the Popol Vuh. My previous version was "The Light That Came from Across the Sea," but the actual meaning of *ch'aqa,* in the present context, calls for the rendition given in the present edition, which is "The Light That Came from *Beside* the Sea." Corrected in this way, the phrase becomes one of a number of clues that converge to indicate that the east coast of Yucatán was the region where Quiché ancestors acquired the hieroglyphic Popol Vuh, or some part of it, on a pilgrimage.

Advances in the understanding of ancient Mayan art have made it clearer than ever that many of the characters and events in the Popol Vuh have a very deep past and were well known among the lowland Maya. This has made it possible to add more than forty new illustrations to the new edition, using images from carved reliefs in stucco and stone, from engraved bones and shells, and from painted vases and books. Now we can see Blood Gatherer sending away his pregnant daughter; we can see Hunahpu and Xbalanque talking things over, or Hunahpu playing ball with a lord of Xibalba, or a lord of Xibalba playing ball with the head of Hunahpu, or Xbalanque playing the role of the moon.

The continuing decipherment of Mayan hieroglyphic texts is another source of new light for the Popol Vuh, including the astronomical aspects of the story it tells. At times the astronomy is quite explicit, but the narrators often content themselves with allusions whose meaning is left to knowledgeable readers. Such is the case with their account of the cataclysm that ended the world preceding this one, where they mention that hearthstones came shooting out of a kitchen fireplace. Mayan fireplaces have three hearthstones arranged in a triangle, and we know that the contemporary Quiché have a hearthstone constellation consisting of a triangle of three stars in Orion. The authors of the Popol Vuh might well be telling us the origin story of this constellation, but they never come right out and say so. This is where their Mayan predecessors come to the rescue, writers who worked at Palenque and Quiriguá many centuries before them. Those writers clearly state that at the end of the world before this one, three hearthstones marked out a new place for themselves in the sky.

Some of the earthly places whose locations remained uncertain in the previous edition have emerged from the mists to take their places on the map. There is growing evidence that for at least a part of Quiché history, the great eastern city that figures in Part Four of the Popol Vuh was the place whose ruins are known today as Copán, located straight east of the

Quiché capital and just across the border in Honduras. Another place that is no longer misty is the mountain named *Pan Paxil* or "Split Place" (previously translated "Broken Place"), which turns out to be well known to the present-day Mam Maya under the name *Paxal*. It is located in the far western highlands of Guatemala, near the Mexican border and just south of the Pan-American Highway. The Mam, like the writers of the Popol Vuh, say that corn originated from the split in that mountain.

A reexamination of the ways in which the European invaders of Mesoamerica conducted themselves has led to a reinterpretation of the Popol Vuh passage that describes the hanging of the Quiché kings. It is now evident that this was not hanging by the neck but rather hanging by the wrists, the method of torture favored by Europeans at the time. Pedro de Alvarado, acting in accordance with the European belief that people who are tortured will make truthful statements, forced Three Deer and Nine Dog to confess that they had plotted against him and then used their confession as a justification for burning them at the stake. What most struck the authors of the Popol Vuh was not the execution but the means of interrogation. Accordingly, the translation no longer states that the kings "were hanged by the Castilian people," which appears to refer to execution, but rather that they "were tortured by the Castilian people."

In 1988, Mayan scholars and educators in Guatemala established the Academia de las Lenguas Mayas de Guatemala. The long-range goals of the members of the Academia include the introduction of the reading and writing of Mayan languages in the public schools of Guatemala. Their first practical task was to institute reforms in the alphabetic writing of Mayan languages; for the first time ever, all the orthographic decisions were made by native speakers of the languages in question. In the present edition of this book I retain old spellings only for proper names appearing in the Popol Vuh manuscript and other early documents, or for direct citations of such sources. Otherwise I have been guided by the decisions of the Academia de las Lenguas Mayas.

The opportunities for the field work, library research, and writing that went into the original edition of this book and the present revision came during an era that may yet survive all the recent efforts to shut it down. A Fellowship for Independent Study and Research from the National Endowment for the Humanities, a grant from the Translations Program at the National Endowment for the Humanities, and a sabbatical leave from Boston University made the first edition possible. The time for work on this new one was provided by a Fellowship in Pre-Columbian Studies at Dumbarton Oaks in Washington, D.C., and by a sabbatical leave from the State University of New York at Buffalo. May we all see a

17

time when the understanding of other languages, literatures, and cultures is more highly valued than ever.

My greatest debt in preparing this new edition of the Popol Vuh is to Barbara Tedlock, as scholar, artist, colleague, soul mate, and wife of many more years than most couples we know. All this while she has been writing her own accounts of Mayan peoples and places and times. We have made return visits to the Quiché, but we have also ventured onto new ground with the Achí of Rabinal, the Kekchí in the Alta Verapaz and Belize, and the Mopán of San Antonio Toledo in Belize.

I remain grateful to Andrés Xiloj Peruch of Momostenango, who not only traveled with me through the Quiché text of the Popol Vuh but taught Barbara Tedlock and myself how to read dreams, omens, and the rhythms of the Mayan calendar. Today he continues as the mother-father or spiritual head of his lineage, and recently he accepted a new burden, becoming the mother-father for all the people of his district of Momostenango. As a diviner he is, by profession, an interpreter of difficult texts. From the moment he first saw the Quiché text of the Popol Vuh, he was intrigued by its patterns of darkness and light. His insights shine throughout the old edition and they continue to shine in this new one.

From the beginning of our work on the Popol Vuh, Xiloj felt certain that if one only knew how to read it perfectly, borrowing the knowledge of the lords of the days, the moist breezes, and the distant lightning, it should reveal everything under the sky and on the earth, all the way out to the four corners. As a help to my own reading and pondering of the book, he suggested an addition to the prayer that daykeepers recite when they go to public shrines. It goes like this:

> Make my guilt vanish,
> Heart of Sky, Heart of Earth;
> do me a favor,
> give me strength, give me courage
> in my heart, in my head,
> since you are my mountain and my plain;
> may there be no falsehood and no stain,
> and may this reading of the Popol Vuh
> come out clear as dawn,
> and may the sifting of ancient times
> be complete in my heart, in my head;
> and make my guilt vanish,
> my grandmothers, grandfathers,

18

and however many souls of the dead there may be,
you who speak with the Heart of Sky and Earth,
may all of you together give strength
to the reading I have undertaken.

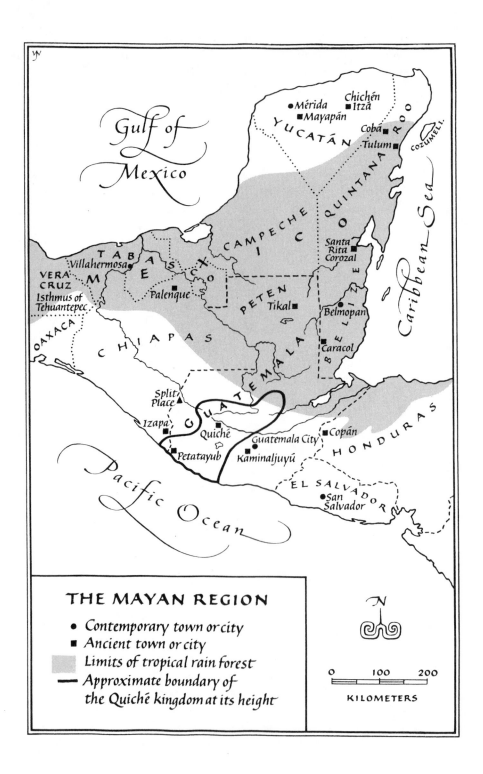

Gulf of
Mexico

Chichén
Mérida ● Itzá
■ Mayapán
Y U C A T Á N Cobá ●
Tulum ■
COZUMEL

C A M P E C H E Q U I N T A N A R O O Caribbean Sea

T A B A S C O Santa
Villahermosa● Rita
M É X I C O Corozal ■
VERA
CRUZ
Isthmus of Palenque● P E T E N Belmopan ●
Tehuantepec Tikal ■ B E L I Z E
OAXACA C H I A P A S Caracol ■
G U A T E M A L A
Split
Place ▲ Copán ■
Izapa ■ Quiché ■ Guatemala City ● H O N D U R A S
■ Kaminaljuyú ●
Petatayub
E L S A L V A D O R
San
Salvador ●
Pacific Ocean

THE MAYAN REGION

- ● Contemporary town or city
- ■ Ancient town or city
- Limits of tropical rain forest
- — Approximate boundary of
  the Quiché kingdom at its height

N

0   100   200
KILOMETERS

INTRODUCTION

THE FIRST FOUR HUMANS, the first four earthly beings who were truly articulate when they moved their feet and hands, their faces and mouths, and who could speak the very language of the gods, could also see everything under the sky and on the earth. All they had to do was look around from the spot where they were, all the way to the limits of space and the limits of time. But then the gods, who had not intended to make and model beings with the potential of becoming their own equals, limited human sight to what was obvious and nearby. Nevertheless, the lords who once ruled a kingdom from a place called Quiché, in the highlands of Guatemala, once had in their possession the means for overcoming this nearsightedness, an *ilb'al*, a "seeing instrument" or a "place to see"; with this they could know distant or future events. The instrument was not a telescope, not a crystal for gazing, but a book.

The lords of Quiché consulted their book when they sat in council, and their name for it was Popol Vuh or "Council Book." Because they obtained the book (or some section of it) on a pilgrimage that took them down from the highlands to the Atlantic shore, they called it "The Light That Came from Beside the Sea." Because the book told of events that happened before the first true dawn, and of a time when their ancestors hid themselves and the stones that contained the spirit familiars of their gods in forests, they also called it "Our Place in the Shadows." And because it told of the rise of the morning star and the sun and moon, and foretold the rise and radiant splendor of the Quiché lords, they called it "The Dawn of Life."

Those who wrote the version of the Popol Vuh we know today do not give us their personal names, but rather call themselves "we" in its opening pages and "we who are the Quiché people" later on. In contemporary usage "the Quiché people" are an ethnic group in Guatemala, consisting of all those who speak the particular Mayan language that itself has come to be called Quiché; they presently number close to a million and occupy most of the former territory of the kingdom whose development is described in the Popol Vuh. To the west and northwest of them are other Mayan peoples, speaking other Mayan languages, who extend across the Mexican border into the highlands of Chiapas and down into the Gulf coastal plain of Tabasco. To the east and northeast still other Mayans extend just across the borders of El Salvador and Honduras, down into the lowlands of Belize, and across the peninsula of Yucatán. These are the peoples, with a total population of more than six million today, whose ancestors developed what has become known to the outside world as Mayan civilization.

The roots of Mayan civilization may lie in the prior civilization of the Olmecs, which was flowering on the Gulf coastal plain of Veracruz and Tabasco by about 1200 B.C. A more immediate antecedent is the Izapan culture, which ran along the western and southern edges of the Mayan world and reached inside that world at the highland site of Kaminaljuyú, on the west side of what is now Guatemala City. Beginning in the first century B.C., Izapan stone monuments display an iconography and writing system similar to the ones that emerge later in the sites archaeologists designate as properly Mayan. This emergence took place during the period they call the Early Classic (A.D. 300–600), and it was centered in the lowland rain forest that separates the mountain pine forest of Chiapas and Guatemala from the low and thorny scrub forest of northern Yucatán. Swamps were drained and trees were cleared to make way for intensive cultivation. Hieroglyphic texts in great quantity were sculpted in stone and stucco, painted on pottery and plaster, and inked on long strips of paper that were folded like screens to make books.

During the Early Classic period lords from Teotihuacan, the great city of the central Mexican highlands, took control of Kaminaljuyú and established political and trade relationships with such lowland Mayan cities as Tikal. The Late Classic period (A.D. 600–900) opened with the collapse of Teotihuacan and its outpost at Kaminaljuyú, and it saw the establishment of a Mayan presence at Xochicalco and Cacaxtla in central Mexico. In the lowland rain forest, such Mayan cities as Palenque, Tikal, and Caracol rose to their greatest glory, and Chichén Itzá was founded in the north. The southernmost city was Copán, located in the foothills of the highlands rather than in the rain forest. Its rise to prominence coincided with the decline of Kaminaljuyú, and it has recently been revealed that its rulers claimed descent from the royal line of Teotihuacan.

As the Late Classic period drew to a close, the Mayan communities that had carved out a place for themselves in the rain forest, along with Copán, were caught in a deepening vortex of overpopulation, environ-

22

mental degradation, malnutrition, and warfare. At the same time, they were being bypassed by a developing sea-trade network that reached all the way around Yucatán from Tabasco to Honduras. By A.D. 900, the political and economic strength of the larger city-states had broken under the strain. From that time until the European invasion, the remaining inhabitants of the rain forest lived in smaller towns along the shores of lakes, rivers, and estuaries. The greater part of the Maya population was now divided between two areas that had been on the periphery during Classic times, one in northern Yucatán and the other in the southern highlands. The Late Postclassic (from A.D. 1200 to the European invasion) saw the rise of the kingdom of Mayapán in the north and that of Quiché in the south, both of them tribute-collecting conquest states that followed Chichén Itzá in giving mythic prominence to a divine king named Plumed Serpent. At the core of each of these states was an alliance of noble lineages that was largely Mayan but included Mexicans whose native language was Nahua. The heads of these lineages, whatever their places of origin, resided in the capital, surrounded by fortifications.

Carved inscriptions were no longer a major feature of Mayan monuments and buildings during the Postclassic period, but writing and painting flourished on plastered walls and the pages of books. This is especially evident for sites located on or near the east coast of Yucatán, from the island of Cozumel and the mainland sites of Cobá, Tancah, and Tulum in the north down to Santa Rita Corozal in Belize. The illustrations in three of the surviving Mayan books, the ones now known as the Madrid, Paris, and Dresden codices, have strong ties in both style and content to the wall art of this region. Cortés and his men saw many books when they landed on Cozumel, and there is good evidence that the loot they took away with them included the Dresden Codex. The writing in Postclassic books, as compared with Classic writing, shows an increased reliance on phonetic signs, including the use of distinctly Mayan signs to spell out words borrowed from Nahua.

The European invasion of the Mayan world began during the sixteenth century, and so did a long history of Mayan resistance that continues right down to the broadcast news of our own day. Backed by means of persuasion that included gunpowder, instruments of torture, and the threat of eternal damnation, the invaders established a monopoly on virtually all major forms of visible public expression, whether in drama, architecture, sculpture, painting, or writing. In the highlands, when they realized that textile designs carried complex messages, they even at-

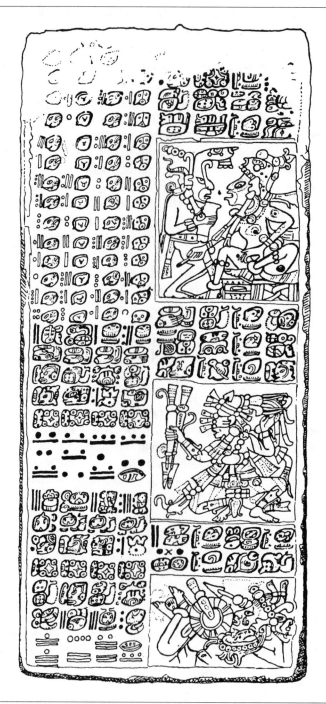

DRAWING BY CARLOS A. VILLACORTA

tempted to ban the wearing of Mayan styles of clothing. Hundreds of hieroglyphic books were burned by missionaries, but they were still in use as late as the end of the seventeenth century in Yucatán and the beginning of the eighteenth in highland Guatemala. Only four books are known to have survived to the present day, including the three that found their way to Madrid, Paris, and Dresden long ago. A fourth was recovered in 1966 from looters who had found it in a dry cave in Chiapas.

But the survival of ancient Mayan literature was not dependent on the survival of its outward forms. Just as Mayan peoples learned to use the symbolism of Christian saints as masks for ancient gods, so they learned to use the Roman alphabet as a mask for ancient texts. There was no little justice in the fact that it was the missionaries themselves, the burners of the ancient books, who first introduced Mayans to alphabetic writing. What they wanted their pupils to write was translations of Christian prayers, sermons, and catechisms into Mayan languages, but very little time passed before some Mayans found political and religious applications for alphabetic writing that suited their own purposes. These independent writers have left a literary legacy that is both more extensive than the surviving hieroglyphic corpus and more open to understanding. Their most notable works, created as alphabetic substitutes for hieroglyphic books, are the Chilam Balam or "Jaguar Translator" books of Yucatán and the Popol Vuh of Guatemala.

The authors of the alphabetic Popol Vuh were members of the three lordly lineages that had once ruled the Quiché kingdom: the Cauecs, the Greathouses, and the Lord Quichés. They worked in the middle of the sixteenth century, and the scene of their writing was the town of Quiché, northwest of what is now Guatemala City. The east side of this town, on flat land, was new in their day, with low buildings in files on a grid of streets and a tall church on a central plaza. The west side, already in

---

THE PAGES OF BOOKS: *This is a page from the Maya hieroglyphic book known as the Dresden Codex, dating from the fifteenth century. The left-hand column describes the movements of Venus during one of five different types of cycles reckoned for that planet. The right-hand column describes the auguries for the cycle and gives both pictures and names for the attendant deities. In the top picture the seated figure is Hunahpu, called Hun Ahaw in Yucatán. In the middle picture is the god who currently accounts for Venus itself, holding a dart thrower in his left hand and darts in his right. In the bottom picture is his victim, whose shield has been pierced by a dart.*

THE ONLY SURVIVING COPY: *The first page of the alphabetic version of the Popol Vuh, as copied by Francisco Ximénez in Chichicastenango; the Quiché text is on the left and his Spanish translation is on the right.*

PHOTO COURTESY NEWBERRY LIBRARY

ruins, was on fortified promontories above deep canyons, with pyramids and palaces clustered around multiple plazas and courtyards. The buildings of the east side displayed broad expanses of blank stone and plaster, but the ruined walls of the west side bore tantalizing traces of multicolored murals. What concerned the authors of the new version of the Popol Vuh was to preserve the story that lay behind the ruins.

During the early colonial period the town of Quiché was eclipsed, in both size and prosperity, by the neighboring town of *Chuwi La'* or "Nettles Heights," otherwise known as Chichicastenango. The residents of this rising town included members of the Cauec and Lord Quiché lineages, and at some point a copy of the alphabetic Popol Vuh found its way there. Between 1701 and 1703, a friar named Francisco Ximénez happened to get a look at this manuscript while he was serving as the parish priest. He made the only surviving copy of the Quiché text of the Popol Vuh and added a Spanish translation (see the illustration on the opposite page). His work remained in the possession of the Dominican order until after Guatemalan independence, but when liberal reforms forced the closing of all monasteries in 1830, it was acquired by the library of the University of San Carlos in Guatemala City. Carl Scherzer, an Austrian physician, happened to see it there in 1854, and Charles Etienne Brasseur de Bourbourg, a French priest, had the same good fortune a few months later. In 1857 Scherzer published Ximénez' Spanish translation under the patronage of the Hapsburgs in Vienna, members of the same royal lineage that had ruled Spain at the time of the conquest of the Quiché kingdom, and in 1861 Brasseur published the Quiché text and a French translation in Paris. The manuscript itself, which Brasseur spirited out of Guatemala, eventually found its way back across the Atlantic from Paris, coming to rest in the Newberry Library in 1911. The town graced by this library, with its magnificent collection of Native American texts, is not in Mesoamerica, but it does have an Indian name: Chicago, meaning "Place of Wild Onions."

The manuscript Ximénez copied in the place called "Nettles Heights" may have included a few illustrations and even an occasional hieroglyph, but his version contains nothing but solid columns of alphabetic prose. Mayan authors in general made only sparing use of graphic elements in their alphabetic works, but nearly every page of the ancient books combined writing (including signs meant to be read phonetically) and pictures. In Mayan languages the terms for writing and painting were and are the same, the same artisans practiced both skills, and the patron deities of both skills were twin monkey gods bearing two different names for the same day, translatable as One Monkey and One Artisan. In the books made under the patronage of these twin gods there is a dialectical relationship between the writing and the pictures: the writing not only records words but sometimes offers pictorial clues to its meaning. As for the pictures, they not only depict what they mean but have elements that can be read as words.

At times the writers of the alphabetic Popol Vuh seem to be describing pictures, especially when they begin new episodes in narratives. In passages like the following, the use of sentences beginning with phrases like "this is" and the use of verbs in the Quiché equivalent of the present tense cause the reader to linger, for a moment, over a lasting image:

> This is the great tree of Seven Macaw, a nance, and this is the food of Seven Macaw. In order to eat the fruit of the nance he goes up the tree every day. Since Hunahpu and Xbalanque have seen where he feeds, they are now hiding beneath the tree of Seven Macaw, they are keeping quiet here, the two boys are in the leaves of the tree.

It must be cautioned, of course, that word pictures painted by storytellers, in Quiché or in any other language, need not have physical counterparts in the world outside the mind's eye. But the present example has an abruptness that suggests a sudden still picture from a story already well under way rather than a moving picture unfolded in the course of the events of that story. The narrators do not describe how the boys arrived "in the leaves of the tree"; the opening scene is already complete, waiting for the blowgun shot that comes in the next sentence, where the main verb is in the Quiché equivalent of the past tense and the still picture gives way to a moving one.

The writing of words in ancient Mayan books was done by means of a script that combines logographic and phonetic principles. Logographic signs, which stand for entire words and sometimes carry pictorial clues to their meaning, are most often used for such common items as day names. Mayan phonetic signs proceed syllable by syllable, with each sign corresponding to a consonant and vowel in combination or (less often) a vowel alone. Where a spelling problem was created by a syllable that had a single vowel bracketed by two consonants, the conventional solution was to treat it as if it were two syllables, each containing one of the consonants, and leave it up to the reader to avoid pronouncing the second vowel sound. This and other syllabic conventions sometimes affected the spelling choices Mayan writers made when they later used the Roman alphabet. For example, if the authors of the Popol Vuh had written in a purely alphabetic manner, they might have spelled the Quiché name of

Macaw House, one of the first four women created by the gods, as Cakixha. What they did instead was to treat its three syllables as if they were four, spelling it Cakixaha (Ca-ki-xa-ha).

More than any other Mayan book, whether hieroglyphic or alphabetic, the Popol Vuh tells us something about the conceptual place of books in the pre-Columbian world. The writers of the alphabetic version explain why the hieroglyphic version was among the most precious possessions of Quiché rulers:

> They knew whether war would occur; everything they saw was clear to them. Whether there would be death, or whether there would be famine, or whether quarrels would occur, they knew it for certain, since there was a place to see it, there was a book. "Council Book" was their name for it.

When "everything they saw was clear to them" the Quiché lords were recovering the vision of the first four humans, who at first "saw everything under the sky perfectly." That would mean that the Popol Vuh made it possible, once again, to sight "the four sides, the four corners in the sky, on the earth," the corners and sides that mark the earth and serve as reference points for the movements of celestial lights.

If the ancient Popol Vuh was like the surviving hieroglyphic books, it contained systematic accounts of cycles in astronomical and earthly events that served as a complex navigation system for those who wished to see and move beyond the present. In the case of a section dealing with the planet Venus, for example, there would have been tables of rising and setting dates, pictures of the attendant gods, and brief texts outlining what these gods did when they first established the pattern for the movements of Venus. When the ancient readers of the Popol Vuh took the roles of diviners and astronomers, seeking the proper date for a ceremony or a momentous political act, we may guess that they looked up specific passages, pondered their meanings, and rendered an opinion. But the authors of the alphabetic Popol Vuh tell us that there were also occasions on which readers offered "a long performance and account" whose subject was the lighting of the whole *kajulew* or "sky-earth," which is the Quiché way of saying "world." If a divinatory reading or pondering was a way of recovering the depth of vision enjoyed by the first four humans, a long performance, in which readers may well have covered every major subject in the entire book, was a way of recovering the full cosmic sweep of that vision.

If the authors of the alphabetic Popol Vuh had transposed the ancient Popol Vuh directly, on a glyph-by-glyph basis, they might have produced a text that would have made little sense to anyone but a fully trained diviner and performer. What they did instead was to quote what readers of the ancient book would say when they gave long performances, telling the full story that lay behind the charts, pictures, and plot outlines of the ancient book. Lest we miss the fact that they are quoting, they periodically insert such phrases as "This is the account, here it is," or "as it is said." At one point they themselves become performers, *speaking directly to us* as if we were members of a live audience rather than mere readers. When they introduce the first episode of a long cycle of stories about the gods who prepared the sky-earth for human life, they propose that we all drink a toast to the heroes.

At the beginning of their book, the authors delicately describe the difficult circumstances under which they work. When they tell us that they are writing "amid the preaching of God, in Christendom now," we can catch a plaintive tone only by noticing that they make this statement immediately after asserting that their own gods "accounted for everything—and did it, too—as enlightened beings, in enlightened words." What the authors propose to write down is what Quichés call the *Ojer Tzij*, the "Ancient Word" or "Prior Word," which has precedence over "the preaching of God." They have chosen to do so because "there is no longer" a Popol Vuh, which makes it sound as though they intend to re-create the original book solely on the basis of their memory of what they have seen in its pages or heard in the long performance. But when we remember their complaint about being "in Christendom," there remains the possibility that they still have the original book but are protecting it from possible destruction by missionaries. Indeed, their next words make us wonder whether the book might still exist, but they no sooner raise our hopes on this front than they remove the book's reader from our grasp: "There is the original book and ancient writing, but the one who reads and assesses it has a hidden identity." Here we must remember that the authors of the alphabetic Popol Vuh have chosen to remain anonymous; in other words, they are hiding their identities. If they are protecting anyone with their enigmatic statements about an inaccessible book or an anonymous reader, it could well be themselves.

The authors begin their narrative in a world that has nothing but an empty sky above and a calm sea below. The action gets under way when the gods who reside in the primordial sea, named Maker, Modeler, Bearer, Begetter, Heart of the Lake, Heart of the Sea, and Sovereign Plumed Serpent, are joined by gods who come down from the primordial sky, named Heart of Sky, Heart of Earth, Newborn Thunderbolt, Sudden Thunderbolt, and Hurricane. These two groups engage in a dialogue,

THE EMERGENCE OF THE EARTH FROM THE WATER: *Lake Atitlán, called* Najachel *in Quiché, with the volcanoes of Cerro de Oro (in the middle distance) and San Pedro (beyond). The contemporary Quichés of Momostenango reckon this as the lake of the south, one of four sacred lakes that mark the four sides of their world.*

PHOTO BY THE AUTHOR

and in the course of it they conceive the emergence of the earth from the water and the growth of plants and people on its surface. They wish to set in motion a process they call the "sowing" and "dawning," by which they mean several different things at once. There is the sowing of seeds in the earth, whose sprouting will be their dawning, and there is the sowing of the sun, moon, and stars, whose difficult passage beneath

31

the earth will be followed by their own dawning. Then there is the matter of human beings, whose sowing in the womb will be followed by their emergence into the light at birth, and whose sowing in the earth at death will be followed by dawning when their souls become sparks of light in the darkness.

For the gods, the idea of human beings is as old as that of the earth itself, but they fail in their first three attempts (all in Part One of the present translation) to transform this idea into a living reality. What they want is beings who will walk, work, and talk in an articulate and measured way, visiting shrines, giving offerings, and calling upon their makers by name, all according to the rhythms of a calendar. What they get instead, on the first try, is beings who have no arms to work with and can only squawk, chatter, and howl, and whose descendants are the animals of today. On the second try they make a being of mud, but this one is unable to walk or turn its head or even keep its shape; being solitary, it cannot reproduce itself, and in the end it dissolves into nothing.

Before making a third try the gods decide, in the course of a further dialogue, to seek the counsel of an elderly husband and wife named Xpiyacoc and Xmucane. Xpiyacoc is a divine matchmaker and therefore prior to all marriage, and Xmucane is a divine midwife and therefore prior to all birth. Like contemporary Quiché matchmakers and midwives, both of them are *ajq'ij* or "daykeepers," diviners who know how to interpret the auguries given by thirteen day numbers and twenty day names that combine to form a calendrical cycle lasting 260 days. They are older than all the other gods, who address them as grandparents, and the cycle they divine by is older than the longer cycles that govern Venus and the sun, which have not yet been established at this point in the story. The question the younger gods put to them here is whether human beings should be made out of wood. Following divinatory methods that are still in use among Quiché daykeepers, they give their approval. The wooden beings turn out to look and talk and multiply themselves something like humans, but they fail to time their actions in an orderly way and forget to call upon the gods in prayer. Hurricane brings a catastrophe down on their heads, not only flooding them with a gigantic rainstorm but sending monsters to attack them. Even their own dogs, turkeys, tools, and houses rise against them, taking vengeance for past mistreatment. Their only descendants are the monkeys that inhabit the forests today.

At this point the gods who have been working on the problem of making human beings will need only one more try before they solve it, but the authors of the Popol Vuh postpone the telling of this episode,

DIVINATORY METHODS THAT ARE STILL IN USE: *A divination in progress on top of the mountain called Tohil's Place. At left is the client, Lucas Pacheco Benítez, himself a daykeeper. Spread out on the stone at lower right is the paraphernalia of the daykeeper who is divining for him, set up for a counting of days. Burning in the background are offerings of candles and copal incense.*

PHOTO BY BARBARA TEDLOCK

turning their attention to stories about two generations of heroic deities whose triumphs make the sky-earth a safer place for human habitation. First come the twin sons of Xpiyacoc and Xmucane, named One Hunahpu and Seven Hunahpu, together with Blood Moon, the daughter of a lord of the underworld named Blood Gatherer. In the second generation come her twin sons, Hunahpu and Xbalanque, jointly fathered by One and Seven Hunahpu. Both generations of twins are players of the Mesoamerican ball game, in which the rubber ball (an indigenous American invention) is hit with a yoke-shaped device worn on one side of the body, riding just under the arm or resting on the hip. In addition to being ballplayers, One and Seven Hunahpu occupy themselves by gambling with dice, whereas Hunahpu and Xbalanque go out hunting with blowguns.

The adventures of the sons, daughter-in-law, and grandsons of Xpiyacoc and Xmucane are presented in two different cycles, with the episodes divided between the cycles more on the basis of where they take place in space than when they take place in time. The first cycle deals entirely with adventures on the face of the earth, while the second, though it has two separate aboveground passages, deals mainly with adventures in the underworld, a region named Xibalba or "Place of Fear." If the events of these two cycles were combined in a single chronological sequence, the aboveground episodes might alternate with those below, with the heroes descending into the underworld, emerging on the earth again, and so forth. These sowing and dawning movements of the heroes, along with those of their supporting cast, prefigure the present-day movements of the sun, moon, planets, and stars.

Hunahpu and Xbalanque are the protagonists of the first of the two hero cycles (presented in Part Two), and their enemies are a father and his two sons, all of them pretenders to lordly power over the affairs of the earth. Hurricane, or Heart of Sky, is offended by this threesome, and it is he who sends Hunahpu and Xbalanque against them. The first to get his due is the father, named Seven Macaw, who claims to be both the sun and moon. In chronological terms this episode overlaps with the story of the wooden people (at the end of Part One), since Seven Macaw serves as their source of celestial light and has his downfall at the same time they do. The twins shoot him while he is at his meal, high up in a fruit tree, breaking his jaw and bringing him down to earth. Later they persuade a pair of curers, an elderly couple named Great White Peccary and Great White Coati, to give him the reverse of a face-lift, pulling out his teeth and removing the metal disks from around his eyes. His earthly descendants are scarlet macaws, with broken, toothless jaws and bare white cheeks that turn red when they get excited. He himself remains as the seven stars of the Big Dipper, and his wife, Chimalmat, corresponds to a circle of northern stars that includes the arc of the Little Dipper. In mid-July, when he is already falling from his tree as the night begins, he opens the hurricane season, and in mid-October, when he almost gets back up the tree before morning, he closes it. It was his first fall, brought on by the blowgun shot of Hunahpu and Xbalanque, that opened the way for the great flood that brought down the wooden people. Just as Seven Macaw only pretended to be the sun and moon, so the wooden people only pretended to be human.

Hunahpu and Xbalanque next take on Zipacna, the elder of Seven Macaw's two sons, a crocodilian monster who claims to be the maker of mountains. But first comes an episode in which Zipacna has an encounter with the gods of alcoholic drinks, the Four Hundred Boys. Alarmed by Zipacna's great strength, these boys trick him into digging a deep hole and try to crush him by dropping a great log down behind him. He survives, but he waits in the hole until they are in the middle of a drunken victory celebration and then brings their own house down on top of them. At the celestial level they become the stars called Motz, the Quiché name for the Pleiades, and their downfall corresponds to early-evening settings of these stars. At the earthly level, among contemporary Quichés, the Pleiades symbolize a handful of seeds, and their disappearance in the west marks the proper time for the sowing of crops.

Zipacna meets his own downfall when Hunahpu and Xbalanque set out to avenge the Four Hundred Boys. At a time when Zipacna has gone without food for several days, they set a trap for him by making a device that appears to be a living, moving crab. Having placed this artificial crab in a tight space beneath an overhang at the bottom of a great mountain, they show him the way there. Zipacna goes after the crab with great passion, and his struggles to wrestle himself into the right position to consummate his hunger become a symbolic parody of sexual intercourse. When the great moment comes the whole mountain falls on his chest (which is to say he ends up on the bottom), and when he heaves a sigh he turns to stone.

Finally there comes the demise of the younger son of Seven Macaw, named Earthquake, who bills himself as a destroyer of mountains. In his case the lure devised by Hunahpu and Xbalanque is the irresistibly delicious aroma given off by the roasting of birds. They cast a spell on the bird they give him to eat: just as it was cooked inside a coating of earth, so he will end up covered by earth. They leave him buried in the east, opposite his elder brother, whose killing of the Four Hundred Boys associates him with the west (where the Pleiades may be seen to fall beneath the earth). Seven Macaw, as the Big Dipper, is of course in the north. He is near the pivot of the movement of the night sky, whereas his two sons make the earth move—though they cannot raise or level whole mountains in a single day as they once did.

Having accounted for three of the aboveground episodes in the lives of Hunahpu and Xbalanque, the Popol Vuh goes back a generation to tell the story of their twin fathers, One Hunahpu and Seven Hunahpu (at the beginning of Part Three). This is the point at which the authors treat us as if we were in their very presence, introducing One Hunahpu by saying, "Let's drink to him." As the story opens, One Hunahpu is married to Egret Woman and they have twin sons named One Monkey and One Artisan. One and Seven Hunahpu sometimes play ball with these two boys, and a messenger from Hurricane, a falcon, sometimes comes to watch them. The boys become practitioners of all sorts of arts and crafts, including flute playing, singing, writing, carving, jewelry making, and metalworking. At some point Egret Woman dies, but we are not told how; that leaves Xmucane, the mother of One and Seven Hunahpu, as the only woman in the household.

The ball court of One and Seven Hunahpu lies in the east, at a place called Great Hollow with Fish in the Ashes. Their ball playing offends the lords of Xibalba, who dislike hearing noises above their subterranean domain. The head lords are named One Death and Seven Death, and under them are other lords who specialize in causing such maladies as lesions, jaundice, emaciation, edema, stabbing pains, and sudden death from vomiting blood. One and Seven Death decide to challenge One and Seven Hunahpu to come play ball in the court of Xibalba, which lies at the western edge of the underworld. They therefore send their messengers, who are monstrous owls, to the Great Hollow. One and Seven Hunahpu leave One Monkey and One Artisan behind to keep Xmucane entertained and follow the owls over the eastern edge of the world. The way is full of traps, but they do well until they come to the Crossroads, where each of four roads has a different color corresponding to a different direction. They choose the Black Road, which means, at the terrestrial level, that their journey through the underworld will take them from east to west. At the celestial level, it means that they were last seen in the black cleft of the Milky Way when they descended below the eastern horizon; to this day the cleft is called the Road of Xibalba.

Entering the council place of the lords of Xibalba is a tricky business, beginning with the fact that the first two figures seated there are mere manikins, put there as a joke. The next gag that awaits visitors is a variation on the hot seat, but after that comes a deadly serious test. One and Seven Hunahpu must face a night in Dark House, which is totally black inside. They are given a torch and two cigars, but they are warned to keep these burning all night without consuming them. They fail this test, so their hosts sacrifice them the next day instead of playing ball with them. Both of them are buried at the Place of Ball Game Sacrifice, except that the severed head of One Hunahpu is placed in the fork of a tree that stands by the road there. Now, for the first time, the tree bears fruit, and it becomes difficult to tell the head from the fruit. This is the origin of the calabash tree, whose fruit has the character of a human skull when dried and hollowed.

Blood Moon, the maiden daughter of a Xibalban lord named Blood Gatherer, goes to marvel at the calabash tree. The skull of One Hunahpu, animated by both brothers, now spits in her hand and makes her pregnant with Hunahpu and Xbalanque. A voice comes from the skull, explaining to her that henceforth a father's face will survive in his son, even after his own face has rotted away and left nothing but bone. After six moons, when Blood Moon's father notices that she is pregnant, he demands to know who is responsible. She answers that "there is no man whose face I've known," which is literally true. He orders the owl messengers of Xibalba to cut her heart out and bring it back in a bowl; armed with the White Dagger, the instrument of sacrifice, they take her away. But she persuades them to spare her, devising a substitute for her heart in the form of a congealed nodule of sap from a croton tree. The lords heat the nodule over a fire and are entranced by the aroma; meanwhile the owls show Blood Moon to the surface of the earth. As a result of this episode it is destined that the lords of Xibalba will receive offerings of incense made from croton sap rather than human blood and hearts. At the astronomical level Blood Moon corresponds to the moon, which appears in the west at nightfall when it begins to wax, just as she appeared before the skull at the Place of Ball Game Sacrifice when she became pregnant.

Once she is out of the underworld, Blood Moon goes to Xmucane and claims to be her daughter-in-law, but Xmucane resists the idea that her own sons could be responsible for Blood Moon's pregnancy. She puts Blood Moon to a test, sending her to get a netful of corn from the garden that One Monkey and One Artisan have been cultivating. Blood Moon finds only a single clump of corn plants there, but she produces a whole netful of ears by pulling out the silk from just one ear. When Xmucane sees the load of corn she goes to the garden herself, wondering whether Blood Moon has stripped it bare. On the ground at the foot of the clump of plants she notices the imprint of the carrying net, which she reads as a sign that Blood Moon is indeed pregnant with her own grandchildren.

To understand how Xmucane is able to interpret the sign of the net we must remember that she knows how to read the auguries of the Mayan calendar, and that one of the twenty day names that go into the making of that calendar is "Net." Retold from a calendrical point of view, the story so far is that Venus rose as the morning star on a day named Hunahpu, corresponding to the ball playing of Xmucane's sons, One and Seven Hunahpu, in the east; then, after being out of sight in Xibalba, Venus reappeared as the evening star on a day named Death, corresponding to the defeat of her sons by One and Seven Death and the placement of One Hunahpu's head in a tree in the west. The event that is due to come next in the story is the rebirth of Venus as the morning star, which should fall, as she already knows, on a day named Net. When she sees the imprint of the net in the field, she takes it as a sign that this event is coming near and that the sons born to Blood Moon will make it possible.

When Hunahpu and Xbalanque are born they are treated cruelly by their jealous half-brothers, One Monkey and One Artisan, and even by their grandmother. They never utter a complaint, but keep themselves happy by going out every day to hunt birds with their blowguns. Eventually they get the better of their brothers by sending them up a tree to get birds that failed to fall down when they were shot. They cause the tree to grow tall enough to maroon their brothers, whom they transform into monkeys. When Xmucane objects they give her four chances to see the faces of One Monkey and One Artisan again, calling them home with music. They warn her not to laugh, but the monkeys are so ridiculous she cannot contain herself; finally they swing up and away through the treetops for good. One Monkey and One Artisan, both of whose names refer to a single day on the divinatory calendar, correspond to the planet Mars, whose period is thereafter reckoned by that day, and their temporary return to the house of Xmucane corresponds to the retrograde motion of Mars. They are also the gods of arts and crafts, and they probably made their first journey through the sky during the era of the wooden people, who were the first earthly beings to make and use artifacts and who themselves ended up as monkeys.

With their half-brothers out of the way, Hunahpu and Xbalanque decide to clear a garden plot of their own, but when they return to the chosen spot each morning they find that the forest has reclaimed it. By hiding themselves at the edge of the plot one night, they discover that the animals of the forest are restoring the cleared plants by means of a chant. They try to grab each of these animals in turn, but they miss the puma and jaguar completely, break the tails off the rabbit and deer, and finally get their hands on the rat. In exchange for his future share of stored crops, the rat reveals to them that One and Seven Hunahpu left a set of ball game equipment tied up under the rafters of their house, and he agrees to help them get it down. At home the next day, Hunahpu and Xbalanque get Xmucane out of the house by claiming her chili stew has made them thirsty; she goes after water but is delayed when her water jar springs a leak. Then, when Blood Moon goes off to see why Xmucane has failed to return, the rat cuts the ball game equipment loose and the twins take possession of it.

When Hunahpu and Xbalanque begin playing ball at the Great Hollow they disturb the lords of Xibalba, just like their fathers before them. Once again the lords send a summons, but this time the messengers go to Xmucane, telling her that the twins must present themselves in seven days. She sends a louse to relay the message to her grandsons, but the louse is swallowed by a toad, the toad by a snake, and the snake by a falcon. The falcon arrives over the ball court and the twins shoot him in the eye. They cure his eye with rubber stripped from their ball, which is why this particular species of falcon (the so-called laughing falcon) now has a black patch around the eye. The falcon vomits the snake, who vomits the toad, who still has the louse in his mouth, and the louse recites the message, quoting what Xmucane told him when she quoted what the owls told her when they quoted what the lords of Xibalba told them to say.

Having been summoned to the underworld, Hunahpu and Xbalanque go to take leave of their grandmother, and in the process they demonstrate a harvest ritual that Quichés follow to this day. They "plant" ears of corn in the center of her house, in the attic; these ears are neither to be eaten nor used as seed corn but are to be kept as a sign that corn remains alive throughout the year, even between the drying out of the plants at harvest time and the sprouting of new ones after planting. They tell their grandmother that when a crop dries out it will be a sign of their death, but that the sprouting of a new crop will be a sign that they live again.

The twins play a game with language when they instruct their grandmother; only now, instead of a quotation swallowed up inside other quotations we get a word hidden within other words. The secret word is *Aj*, one of the twenty day names; the twins point to it by playing on its sounds rather than simply mentioning it. When they tell their grandmother that they are planting corn ears (*aj*) in the house (*ja*), they are making a pun on the name *Aj* in the one case and reversing its sound in the other. The play between *Aj* and *ja* is familiar to contemporary Quiché daykeepers, who use it when they explain to clients that the day *Aj* is portentous in matters affecting households. If the twins planted their corn ears in the house on this day, then their expected arrival in Xibalba, seven days later, would fall on the day named Hunahpu. This fits the Mayan Venus calendar perfectly: whenever Venus rises as the morning star on a day named Net, corresponding to the appearance of Hunahpu and Xbalanque on the earth, its next descent into the underworld will always fall on a day named Hunahpu.

Following in the footsteps of their fathers, Hunahpu and Xbalanque descend the road to Xibalba, but when they come to the Crossroads they do things differently. They send a spy ahead of them, a mosquito, to learn the names of the lords. He bites each one of them in turn; the first two lords reveal themselves as mere manikins by their lack of response, but the others, in the process of complaining about being bitten, address each other by name, all the way down the line. When the twins themselves arrive before the lords, they ignore the manikins (unlike their fathers) and address each of the twelve real lords correctly. Not only that, but they refuse to fall for the hot seat, and when they are given a torch and two cigars to keep lit all night, they trick the lords by passing off a macaw's tail as the glow of the torch and by putting fireflies at the tips of their cigars.

The next day Hunahpu and Xbalanque play ball with the Xibalbans, something their fathers did not survive long enough to do. The Xibalbans insist on putting their own ball into play first, though the twins protest that this ball, which is covered with crushed bone, is nothing but a skull. When Hunahpu hits it back to the Xibalbans with the yoke that rides on his hip, it falls to the court and reveals the weapon that was hidden inside it. This is nothing less than the White Dagger, the same instrument of sacrifice the owls were supposed to use on Blood Moon; it twists its way all over the court, but it fails to kill the twins.

The Xibalbans consent to use the rubber ball belonging to the twins in a further game; this time four bowls of flower petals are bet on the outcome. After playing well for a while the twins allow themselves to lose, and they are given until the next day to come up with the petals. This time they must spend the night in Razor House, which is full of voracious stone blades that are constantly looking for something to cut. In exchange for a promise that they will one day have the flesh of animals as their food, the blades stop moving. This leaves the boys free to attend to the matter of the petals; they send leaf-cutting ants to get them from the very gardens of the lords of Xibalba. The ground-dwelling birds who guard this garden, poorwills and whippoorwills, are so oblivious that they fail to notice that their own tails and wings are being trimmed along with the flowers. The lords, who are aghast when they receive bowls filled with the petals of their own flowers, split the birds' mouths open, giving them the wide gape that birds of the nightjar family have today.

Next, the hero twins survive stays in Cold House, which is full of drafts and falling hail; Jaguar House, which is full of hungry, brawling jaguars; and a house with fire inside. After these horrors comes Bat House, full of moving, shrieking bats, where they spend the night squeezed up inside their blowgun. When the house grows quiet and Hunahpu peeks out from the muzzle, one of the bats swoops down and takes his head off. The head ends up rolling on the ball court of Xibalba, but Xbalanque gives his brother a temporary replacement in the form of a carved squash. While he is performing this head transplant the eastern sky reddens with

CONTEMPORARY QUICHÉ DAYKEEPERS: *All the adults in this picture are day-keepers; in addition, the woman is a midwife, the man wearing a hat is a matchmaker, and the man at right is a singer and prayer maker. The man bending over toward the child is Andrés Xiloj.*

PHOTO BY THE AUTHOR

the dawn, and a possum, addressed in the story as "old man," makes four dark streaks along the horizon. Not only the red dawn but the possum and his streaks are signs that the time of the sun (which has never before been seen) is coming nearer. In the future a new solar year will be brought in by the old man each 365 days; the four streaks signify that only four of the twenty day names—Deer, Tooth, Thought, and Wind—will ever correspond to the first day of a solar year. Contemporary Quiché daykeepers continue to reckon the solar dimension of the Mayan calendar; in the year 2000, for example, they will expect the old man to arrive on February 25, which will fall on One Thought.

Once Hunahpu has been fitted out with a squash for a head, he and Xbalanque are ready to play ball with the Xibalbans again. When the lords send off Hunahpu's original head as the ball, Xbalanque knocks it out of the court and it lands among a group of ball bags. Hidden among the bags is a rabbit, and when it runs away the lords mistake it for the bouncing ball. While they chase it Xbalanque retrieves the head, puts it

41

back on Hunahpu's shoulders, and then puts the squash among the bags, pretending to find the ball there. Now the squash is put into play, but it wears out and splatters its seeds on the court, revealing to the lords of Xibalba that they have been played for fools. The game played with the squash, like the games played with the bone-covered ball and with Hunahpu's severed head, corresponds to an appearance of Venus in the west, the direction of evening and death. If these events were combined in chronological order with those that take place entirely above ground, they would probably alternate with the episodes in which the twins defeat One Monkey and One Artisan, Seven Macaw, Zipacna, and Earthquake, with each of these latter episodes corresponding to an appearance of Venus in the east, the direction of morning and life.

At this point we are ready for the last of the episodes that prefigure the cycles of Venus and prepare the way for the first rising of the sun. Knowing that the lords of Xibalba plan to burn them, Hunahpu and Xbalanque instruct two seers named Xulu and Pacam as to what they should say when the lords seek advice as to how to dispose of their remains. This done, the twins cheerfully accept an invitation to come see the great stone pit where the Xibalbans are roasting the ingredients for an alcoholic beverage. The lords challenge them to a contest in which the object is to leap clear across the pit, but the boys cut the deadly game short and jump right in. Thinking they have triumphed, the Xibalbans follow the advice of Xulu and Pacam, grinding the bones of the boys and spilling the powder into a river.

After five days Hunahpu and Xbalanque reappear as catfish; the day after that they take human form again, only now they are disguised as vagabond dancers and actors. They gain great fame as illusionists, their most popular acts being the ones in which they set fire to a house without burning it and perform a sacrifice without killing the victim. The lords of Xibalba get news of all this and invite them to show their skills at court; they accept with pretended reluctance. The climax of their performance comes when Xbalanque sacrifices Hunahpu, rolling his head out the door, removing his heart, and then bringing him back to life. One and Seven Death go wild at the sight of this and demand that they themselves be sacrificed. The twins oblige—and, as might already be imagined, these final sacrifices are real ones. Hunahpu and Xbalanque now reveal their true identities before all the inhabitants of the underworld. They declare that henceforth the offerings received by Xibalbans will be limited to incense made of croton sap and to animals, and that Xibalbans will limit their attacks on future human beings to those who have weaknesses or guilt.

At this point the narrators take us back to the twins' grandmother, telling us what she has been doing all this time. She cries when the season comes for corn plants to dry out, signifying the death of her grandsons, and rejoices when they sprout again, signifying rebirth. She burns incense in front of ears from the new crop and thus completes the establishment of the custom whereby humans keep consecrated ears in the house, at the center of the stored harvest. Then the scene shifts back to Hunahpu and Xbalanque, who are about to establish another custom.

Having made their speech to the defeated Xibalbans, the twins go to the Place of Ball Game Sacrifice with the intention of reviving Seven Hunahpu, whose head and body still lie buried there. The full restoration of his face depends on his own ability to pronounce the names of all the parts it once had, but he gets no further than the mouth, nose, and eyes, which remain as notable features of skulls. They leave him there, but they promise that human beings will keep his day (the one named Hunahpu), coming to pray where his remains are. To this day, Hunahpu days are set aside for the veneration of the dead, and graveyards are called by the same word (*jom*) as the ball courts of the Popol Vuh.

At the astronomical level the visit of Hunahpu and Xbalanque to Seven Hunahpu's grave signals the return of a whole new round of Venus cycles, starting with a morning star that first appears on a day named Hunahpu. As for the twins themselves, they rise as the sun and moon. Contemporary Quichés regard the full moon as a nocturnal equivalent of the sun, pointing out that it has a full disk, is bright enough to travel by, and goes clear across the sky in the same time it takes the sun to do the same thing. Most likely the twin who became the moon is to be understood specifically as the full moon, whereas Blood Moon, the mother of the twins, would account for other phases of the moon.

With the ascent of Hunahpu and Xbalanque the Popol Vuh returns to the problem the gods confronted at the beginning: the making of beings who will walk, work, talk, and pray in an articulate manner. The account of their fourth and final attempt at a solution is a flashback, since it takes us back to a time when Seven Macaw had already seen his downfall but the real sun had yet to appear. As we have already seen, the gods failed when they tried using mud and then wood as the materials for the human body, but now they get news of a mountain filled with yellow corn and white corn, discovered by the fox, coyote, parrot, and crow (at the beginning of Part Four). Xmucane grinds the corn from this mountain very finely, and the flour, mixed with the water she rinses her hands with, provides the substance for human flesh, just as the ground bone thrown in the river by the Xibalbans becomes the substance for the rebirth of

THEY ARE CALLED "MOTHER-FATHERS": *Andrés Xiloj (at left), who read through the Popol Vuh text with the present translator and provided numerous comments, is himself a mother-father, or patrilineage head. He is shown here at his house in Momostenango, with his son Anselmo and his daughter-in-law Manuela.*

PHOTO BY THE AUTHOR

her grandsons. The first people to be modeled from the corn dough are four men named Jaguar Quitze, Jaguar Night, Not Right Now, and Dark Jaguar. They are the first four heads of Quiché patrilineages; as in the case of the men who occupy such positions today, they are called "mother-fathers," since in ritual matters they serve as symbolic androgynous parents to everyone in their respective lineages.

This time the beings shaped by the gods are everything they hoped for and more: not only do the first four men pray to their makers, but they have perfect vision and therefore perfect knowledge. The gods are alarmed that beings who were merely manufactured by them should have divine powers, so they decide, after their usual dialogue, to put a fog on human eyes. Next they make four wives for the four men, and from these couples come the leading Quiché lineages. Red Sea Turtle becomes the wife of Jaguar Quitze, who founds the Cauec lineage; Prawn House becomes the wife of Jaguar Night, who founds the Greathouse lineage; and Water Hummingbird becomes the wife of Not Right Now, who founds the Lord Quiché lineage. Dark Jaguar is also given a wife, Macaw House, but they have no male children. Other lineages also come into being, and they all begin to multiply until they form whole tribes.

All these early events in human history take place in darkness, and all the different tribes wander about and grow weary as they go on watching and waiting for the rising of Venus as the morning star, to be followed by the sun. Jaguar Quitze, Jaguar Night, Not Right Now, and Dark Jaguar decide to change their situation by going eastward to a city that is somehow already there. What they seek is elevation to noble rank and the right to establish themselves as lords over an earthly domain. Petitioners from many different tribes converge on the city, speaking a variety of languages. The authors of the Popol Vuh describe some of them as rustic "mountain people," including the Quichés and their closest Mayan relatives: Rabinals, Cakchiquels, and "those of the Bird House" (Tzutuhils).

The Popol Vuh gives the eastern city names that reach deep into the Mesoamerican past, calling it Tulan Zuyua, Seven Caves, Seven Canyons. From other Mayan authors we learn that this city had a western twin that shared the name Tulan, which means "Place of Cattails" in Nahua. A new reading of the inscriptions at Copán reveals that Mayans knew this name as long ago as the Classic period, and that they applied it to the great western city whose ruins are known today as Teotihuacan. Their closest contact with the world of that city, while it was still in its glory, was through its eastern outpost at Kaminaljuyú, which is a likely candidate for the eastern city of the Popol Vuh.

By specifying that their Tulan was the one named Zuyua, the authors of the Popol Vuh further indicate its eastern position. When other Mayan authors mention both members of an east-west pair of cities, they reserve this name for the eastern one. Whatever language it came from, Zuyua came to mean "twisted" or "deceptive" in Yucatec Maya and referred to riddles that pretenders to lordly positions were required to answer. As for the names Seven Caves and Seven Canyons, they evoke both cities. At Teotihuacan, the Pyramid of the Sun rises directly above a cave whose main shaft and side chambers add up to seven, while Kaminaljuyú is located on a tableland that falls away into multiple canyons.

During their stay in the eastern city, the Quiché ancestors are given patron deities. Among these the first in rank is Tohil, patron of the Cauecs and two lesser lineages, the Tams and Ilocs. Next comes Auilix, god of the Greathouses, and then Hacauitz, god of the Lord Quichés. It is not known what language was spoken at Kaminaljuyú, but the names of all three of these gods are of Cholan origin, belonging to the same

45

branch of the Mayan family as the inscriptions at Copán. Tohil, who stands on one leg, provides fire, and thirsts for blood, is very much like the one-legged patron deity of Classic Maya rulers, whose image takes the form of a scepter.

Tohil introduces the element of riddling into the story. When a great hailstorm puts out the fires of all the visitors to the city, he makes himself into a fire drill on behalf of the Quichés, pivoting on one leg and using his sandal as the drill socket. Members of other tribes, shivering with cold, beg for a little of his fire, but he refuses to let them have it unless they promise to embrace him someday, allowing themselves to be suckled. Not realizing that he is speaking the twisted language of Zuyua, they agree to this. When the time comes for the Quiché lords to subjugate the members of these tribes, being "suckled" by Tohil will mean having their hearts cut out as a sacrifice to him. Only the Cakchiquels, who get their fire by sneaking past everyone else in the smoke, escape this fate.

The Cakchiquel version of the visit to the city weaves in threads that seem to belong to the Late Classic period, when Teotihuacan had fallen and Copán had replaced Kaminaljuyú as the greatest city of the Mayan highlands. Two details point straight to Copán itself. First, we are told that the lords of the city had a bat as their insignia. Second, just as the Cakchiquel visitors to the city were passing through its gate, they heard one of the world's most dramatic bird cries, that of the brown-backed solitaire. It happens that the hieroglyphic emblem of the rulers of Copán features the profiled head of a leaf-nosed bat and spells out the word *xwukpi*, the term for the brown-backed solitaire in the Mayan language

---

THE HEAD OF A BAT: *The heraldic emblem of the lords of the Classic Maya city of Copán, with the profile of a leaf-nosed bat facing left at the center. The bat's head, itself a hieroglyph, forms the first syllable of a phrase that continues to the right of the bat's mouth and runs clockwise around its head from there. The first full word is* xwukpi, *a term for the brown-backed solitaire and the name of the ruling lineage of Copán; then comes the title of the ruler himself,* ch'ul pop ahaw, *"Lord of the Holy Council."*

DRAWING BY THE AUTHOR

that was spoken there. A further clue that may point to Copán appears in the Popol Vuh, where the Quiché ancestors continue to watch for the first appearance of the morning star after they leave the city, an act that turns their gaze back toward the east. It happens that the inscriptions of Copán give more attention to Venus than those of any other major Classic Maya site.

When Jaguar Quitze, Jaguar Night, Not Right Now, and Dark Jaguar leave the eastern city, they pack the gods they were given on their backs. Singing a song in which they lament the loss of a cosmopolitan life, they begin their search for a place to found their own kingdom. Eventually they pass Great Hollow with Fish in the Ashes, the location of the eastern ball court where the sons and grandsons of Xmucane once played. Moving westward and a little south, they reach a mountain called Place of Advice, not very far south of the site where they will one day reach their greatest glory. Still with them at this point, having accompanied them all the way from the city, are the Rabinals, Cakchiquels, and Bird House people.

Up on the mountain, Jaguar Quitze, Jaguar Night, Not Right Now, and Dark Jaguar observe a great fast together with their wives, Red Sea Turtle, Prawn House, Water Hummingbird, and Macaw House. During the fast Tohil, Auilix, and Hacauitz speak to them, asking to be given hiding places so that they will not be captured by enemies of the Quichés. After a search through the highland pine forest, the three gods are hidden at places that are named after them. At first they are put beneath arbors decorated with bromeliads and hanging mosses, Tohil on a mountain and Auilix in a canyon, but Hacauitz, on his own mountain, is eventually put at the top of a great pyramid. The Cauecs, Greathouses, and Lord Quichés all wait for the approaching dawn on the mountain of Hacauitz; the Tams and Ilocs wait on nearby mountains; while peoples other than the Quichés wait at more distant places. When, at last, they all see the "sun carrier," or the morning star, they give thanks by burning the incense they have kept for this occasion, ever since they left the city.

At this point we reach the moment in the account of human affairs that corresponds to the final event in the account of the lives of the gods: the Sun himself rises. On just this one occasion he appears as an entire person, so hot that he dries out the face of the earth. His heat turns Tohil, Auilix, and Hacauitz to stone, along with such pumas, jaguars, and snakes as there were at the time. A diminutive god called White Sparkstriker escapes petrification by going into the shade of the trees, becoming the keeper of the stone animals. He remains to this day as a

47

gamekeeper, with volcanic concretions, fulgurites, and meteorites that resemble animals in his personal care. He may be encountered in forests and caves, or on dark nights and in dreams; he appears in contemporary masked dramas dressed entirely in red, the color of dawn.

At first the Quichés rejoice when they see the sunrise, but then they remember their "brothers," the members of other tribes who were with them at the eastern city. They sing their lament again, wondering where their brothers might be at this very moment. In effect, the coming of the first sunrise reunites the tribes despite the fact that they remain widely separated in space. As the Popol Vuh has it, "There were countless peoples, but there was just one dawn for all tribes." What makes such a vision of unity possible is the possession of a common calendar. All Mesoamerican peoples shared the 260-day calendar whose auguries were first read by Xpiyacoc and Xmucane, and they used its rhythms to measure off those of the sun, and moon, and planets.

Having seen the first sunrise from the mountain of Hacauitz, the Quichés eventually build a citadel there. Wherever Hacauitz may have been, it is mentioned in a Late Classic inscription at the lowland site of Seibal. At first, even while the people of other tribes are becoming thickly settled and can be seen traveling the roads in great numbers, the Quichés remain rustic and rural, gathering the larvae of yellow jackets, wasps, and bees for food and staying largely out of sight. When they go before the petrified forms of Tohil, Auilix, and Hacauitz, they burn bits of pitchy bark and wildflowers as substitutes for refined incense, and they offer blood drawn from their own bodies. The three gods are still able to speak to them, but only by appearing in spirit form. Tohil tells them to augment their offerings with the blood of deer and birds taken in the hunt, but they grow dissatisfied with this arrangement and begin to cast eyes on the people they see walking by in the roads. From hiding places on

---

HACAUITZ: *A four-part glyph from Stele 8 at Seibal, carved during the ninth century. It refers to the place of origin of a lord from elsewhere than Seibal, reading* ha- *(upper left)* -ka- *(lower left)* -witz- *(upper right)* -il *(lower right);* hakawitzil *means "from Hacauitz."*

DRAWING BY LINDA SCHELE

mountain peaks, they begin imitating the cries of the coyote, fox, puma, and jaguar.

Finally Tohil reminds his followers that members of other tribes once promised to embrace him, allowing him to suckle. Now the Quichés begin to seize people they find out walking alone or in pairs, taking them away to cut them open before Tohil, Auilix, and Hacauitz and then rolling their heads out onto the roads. At first the lords who rule the victimized tribes think these deaths are the work of wild animals, but then they suspect the worshippers of Tohil, Auilix, and Hacauitz and attempt to track them down. Again and again they are foiled by rain, mist, and mud, but they do discover that the three gods, whose spirit familiars take the form of adolescent boys, have a favorite bathing place. They send two beautiful maidens, Lust Woman and Wailing Woman, to wash clothes there, instructing them to tempt the boys and yield to any advances. They warn the maidens to return with proof of the success of their mission, which must take the form of presents from the boys.

Contrary to plan, the three Quiché gods fail to lust after Lust Woman and Wailing Woman, but they do agree to provide them with presents. They give them three cloaks, one brocaded with the figure of a jaguar by Jaguar Quitze, another with an eagle by Jaguar Night, and the third with swarms of yellow jackets and wasps by Not Right Now. When the maidens return the enemy lords are so pleased with the cloaks that they cannot resist trying them on. All is well until the brocaded wasps of the third cloak turn into real ones. Lust Woman and Wailing Woman are spurned; despite their failure to tempt Tohil, Auilix, and Hacauitz they become the first prostitutes, or what Quichés call "barkers of shins." As for the enemy lords, they resolve to make war, launching a massive attack on the Quiché citadel at Hacauitz.

The enemy warriors come at night in order to get as far as possible without resistance, but they fall into a deep sleep on the road. The Quichés not only strip them of all the metal ornaments on their weapons and clothes, but pluck out their eyebrows and beards as well. They press on the next day, determined to recover their losses, but the Quichés are well prepared. What the enemy lookouts see all around the citadel of Hacauitz is a wooden palisade; visible on the parapet are rows of warriors, decked out with the very metal objects that were stolen during the night. What the lookouts do not see is that these warriors are mere wooden puppets, and that behind the palisade, on each of its four sides, is a large gourd filled with yellow jackets and wasps, put there at the suggestion of Tohil. As for the Quichés on the inside, what they see, once the attack begins, is more than twenty-four thousand warriors converging on them, bristling with weapons and shouting continuously. But Tohil has made them so confident that they treat the attack as a great spectacle, bringing their women and children up on the parapet to see it. When they release the yellow jackets and wasps their enemies drop their weapons and attempt to flee, so badly stung they hardly even notice the blows they receive from conventional Quiché weapons. The survivors become permanent payers of tribute to the Quiché lords.

After their great victory, Jaguar Quitze, Jaguar Night, Not Right Now, and Dark Jaguar begin preparing, with complete contentment, for what they know to be their approaching death. They sing the lament they last sang at the first sunrise, and then they explain to their wives and successors that "the time of our Lord Deer" has come around again. This is a reference to the transition from one solar year to another, in particular from a year ruled by Lord Wind, beginning on a day named Wind, to a year whose first day will be Deer. Lord Wind rules from a western mountain, while Lord Deer rules from an eastern one. The Quiché forefathers choose the passage to the easterly year to announce that they intend to return to the east. Jaguar Quitze leaves behind a sacred object called the "Bundle of Flames," a sort of cloth-wrapped ark with mysterious contents, as a "sign of his being." Neither he nor the others are ever seen again, but their descendants burn incense before the Bundle of Flames in remembrance of them, just as Xmucane burned incense before the ears of corn in remembrance of Hunahpu and Xbalanque.

The Quiché lords of the second generation, following the instructions of their fathers, go eastward on a pilgrimage (at the beginning of Part Five). Unlike their fathers, they do this with the intention of returning in the flesh. Noble Two goes on behalf of the Cauec lineage, Noble Acutec represents the Greathouses, and Noble Lord represents the Lord Quichés. Here the authors of the Popol Vuh have foreshortened time; an alternative Quiché account puts these same individuals not in the second but in the fourth generation. In any case they go all the way down to the lowlands, and at some point they cross a "sea," or what is described in other accounts as both a lake and a sea, on a stone causeway. This would be one of the ancient stone causeways of Yucatán, perhaps the one that ran northward across a lake on its way to Cobá. No name is given for their destination, but when they get there they come before the ruler of a large kingdom. He gives them the royal titles Keeper of the Mat and Keeper of the Reception House Mat, the one belonging to a head of state and the other to an overseer of tribute collection. Both of these titles go to the Cauecs, but other sources add that the Greathouse and Lord Quiché lineages also receive titles at this time, with the position of

Lord Minister (ranking third) going to one and that of Herald (ranking fourth) to the other.

The titles bestowed on the pilgrims are venerable Mayan ones, yet the ruler who bestows them is called by the Nahua name Nacxit. In Yucatec accounts this is one of the names of the god-king Plumed Serpent, who established himself at Chichén Itzá at some time during the transition from the Classic to the Postclassic period, but it was used by later rulers as well. The Nacxit of the Popol Vuh does not give his Quiché visitors patron deities, as did the rulers of the eastern city visited by their fore-fathers, but rather gives them canopies, thrones, musical instruments, cosmetics, and ornaments that serve as emblems of lordship. Where the names of the patron deities were Cholan, the foreign words in the list of emblems are either Yucatec, as in the case of a gourd container of tobacco called *k'us b'us,* or Nahua, as in the case of a food bowl called *kaxkon* (from *caxcomulli*). Somewhere along the way, when the pilgrims are "beside the sea," they also acquire "the writing of Tulan, the writing of Zuyua." This would be the hieroglyphic Popol Vuh, or at least the part of it known as "The Light That Came from Beside the Sea." It seems likely that the coast in question was the eastern one of Yucatán, which was not only a source of books but famous for its places of pilgrimage as well.

When Noble Two, Noble Acutec, and Noble Lord return from their pilgrimage, their sovereignty is recognized not only by the Quichés them-selves, but by the Rabinals, Cakchiquels, and Bird House people as well. Only now do the Quiché lords begin to have what the Popol Vuh calls "fiery splendor." It seems likely that their pilgrimage was conceived as a reenactment of the adventures of Hunahpu and Xbalanque in Xibalba, who had only the planet Venus to their credit when they first descended in the east at the Great Hollow, but who eventually returned with the greater splendor of the sun and full moon.

Eventually the Quichés leave Hacauitz and settle at a succession of other sites. The Popol Vuh mentions only one of these by name, Thorny Place, settled at some point after the deaths of Noble Two, Noble Acutec, and Noble Lord. This move temporarily takes the Quichés back in the direction from which they came, to a point between Place of Advice and the Great Hollow. When they move again two generations later, they resume their original trajectory and go farther west than ever before. With Noble Sweatbath as Keeper of the Mat and Iztayul as Keeper of the Reception House Mat, they found the citadel of Bearded Place, directly across a canyon to the south of the site that later becomes their greatest citadel.

At Bearded Place there is great harmony among the Cauecs, Greathouses, and Lord Quichés; these three lineages, each with its own palace, are tied together through intermarriage. At Thorny Place women were married off in exchange for modest favors and gifts, but now, at Bearded Place, wedding arrangements are accompanied by elaborate feasting and drinking. The only disturbance during this period comes from the Ilocs, who first try to get Iztayul involved in a plot to assassinate Noble Sweatbath and then go so far as to mount a direct attack on Bearded Place. They are defeated, and some of their own number are sacrificed before the gods of their intended victims. The Cauec, Greathouse, and Lord Quiché lineages now gain greater and greater power, defeating some tribes in direct attacks and terrorizing still others by having them witness the sacrifice of prisoners of war.

In the next generation the Keeper of the Mat takes the name Plumed Serpent, while the Keeper of the Reception House Mat is Noble Sweatbath, named after the previous Keeper of the Mat. They build a new and larger citadel across the canyon from Bearded Place, at Rotten Cane. The three leading lineages, faced with increased numbers and torn by quarrels over inflation in the costs of marriage, break apart into smaller groups. The Cauecs divide into nine segments, the Greathouses into nine, and the Lord Quichés into four, with each of these segments headed by a titled lord and occupying its own palace. In addition, the inhabitants of Rotten Cane include the Zaquics, a lineage not previously mentioned in the Popol Vuh, divided into two segments but occupying only a single palace, making twenty-three palaces in all. Along with all these palaces, Rotten Cane is provided with three pyramids that bear the temples of Tohil, Auilix, and Hacauitz, ranged around a central plaza; elsewhere is a fourth pyramid for Corntassel, the god of the Zaquics.

The Popol Vuh identifies Plumed Serpent, who holds the titles of both Keeper of the Mat and Keeper of the Reception House Mat during at least part of his reign at Rotten Cane, as "a true lord of genius." He has the power to manifest his personal spirit familiars, putting on performances in which he transforms himself into a snake, an eagle, a jaguar, or a puddle of blood, climbing to the sky or descending to Xibalba. As the Popol Vuh explains it, his displays are "just his way of revealing himself," but they have the effect of terrorizing the lords of other tribes. The next Quiché lords to manifest genius, coming two generations later, are Quicab, who serves as Keeper of the Mat, and Cauizimah, who serves as Keeper of the Reception House Mat. Under their rule the dominion of the Quichés reaches its greatest extent. Where Plumed Serpent gained power through spectacular displays of shamanic skill, Quicab now gains

PYRAMIDS THAT BEAR THE TEMPLES: *At left is one of the pyramids of Iximché, a site whose buildings are far better preserved than those of Rotten Cane. When the Cakchiquels ended their allegiance with the Quichés, two generations after the founding of Rotten Cane, Iximché became their capital. To the right of the pyramid is a long platform on which a palace once stood. Major structures, here and at Rotten Cane, were covered with plaster (fragments of which are visible in the picture) and painted with polychrome murals.*

PHOTO BY THE AUTHOR

it by conquest, extending the kingdom southwestward as far as the present-day border of Mexico. Not content with merely overpowering the citadels of surrounding peoples, he sends out loyal vassals, called

53

"guardians of the land" or "lookout lineages," to serve as forces of occupation. The stationing of these guardians is conceived as analogous to the construction of a palisade; they turn the entire Quiché kingdom into one great fortress.

During this period the settlement at the center of the Quiché kingdom embraced a cluster of four citadels, with Rotten Cane at the focal point. Together with the ordinary houses that occupied the lower or less defensible land around them, these four sites made up a larger town that took the name Quiché. It was perhaps the most densely built-up area that had existed in highland Guatemala since the Early Classic, and it took on the stature of the place where Noble Two, Noble Acutec, and Noble Lord had gone to receive the titles and emblems of truly glorious lordship. Five generations after their pilgrimage a new conferring of titles took place, only now it was not pilgrims but the heads of the leading lookout lineages who were ennobled, and it happened not under the authority of Nacxit, lord of a distant and ever more mythic domain, but under Quicab, who ruled from Quiché.

The town of Quiché not only took on the status of the place visited by the pilgrims who received titles from Nacxit, but of the eastern city visited by their forefathers as well. When the founders of the ruling Quiché lineages and their closest allies left that city before the first sunrise, they had come away with tribal gods whose names were "meant to be in agreement," and they were "in unity" when they passed the Great Hollow and convened at Place of Advice. Now, in this latter day, "the word came from just one place" again, and the allies convened in a town and "came away in unity" again, but this time they came away "having heard, there at *Quiché,* what all of them should do." It was probably during this period that the Quiché lords went so far as to have an artificial cave constructed directly beneath Rotten Cane, a cave whose main shaft and side chambers add up to seven. Not content with honoring the memory of the eastern city, they brought the Seven Caves of Teotihuacan, the greatest of all the ancient cities, to the time and place of their own greatest glory.

It is in the course of explaining the greatness of lords like Plumed Serpent and Quicab that the writers of the alphabetic Popol Vuh tell us how its hieroglyphic predecessor was put to use, serving as a way of seeing into distant places and times. Greatness also came to the lords through their participation in religious retreats. For long periods they would stay in the temples, praying, burning incense, letting their own blood, sleeping apart from their wives, and abstaining not only from meat but from corn products, eating nothing but the fruits of various trees. The shortest fast lasted 180 days, corresponding to half the 360-day cycle (separate from the solar year) that was used in keeping chronologies of historical events, and another lasted 260 days, or one complete run of the cycle whose days were counted by Xpiyacoc and Xmucane when they divined for the gods. The longest fast, 340 days, corresponded to a segment of the Mayan Venus calendar, beginning with the departure of Venus as the morning star and continuing through its stay in the underworld and its period of reappearance as the evening star, leaving just eight days to go before its rebirth as the morning star. This fast probably commemorated the heroic adventures of Hunahpu and Xbalanque in Xibalba, the long darkness endured by the first generation of lords as they watched for the first appearance of the morning star, and perhaps the lowland pilgrimage undertaken by Noble Two, Noble Acutec, and Noble Lord.

The Quiché lords sought identification with the very gods, not only in their pilgrimages, shamanic feats, limitless vision, and long fasts, but in the requirements they set for their subjects. Just as the gods needed human beings to nurture them with offerings, so human lords required subjects to bring them tribute. As the Popol Vuh points out, the "nurture" required by the Quiché lords consisted not only of the food and drink that were prepared for them, but of turquoise, jade, and the iridescent blue-green feathers of the quetzal. Such precious objects as these were considered the ultimate fruits of the blue-green world of earth and sky.

Near the end, the Popol Vuh lists all the noble titles held by the various segments of the Cauec, Greathouse, and Lord Quiché lineages (in rank order), and it gives the names of those who held the highest titles (in the order of their succession). In the case of the two leading segments of the Cauec lineage, those whose heads held the titles of Keeper of the Mat and Keeper of the Reception House Mat, the text lists four generations after Quicab and Cauizimah, who were in the seventh generation, without comment. Then, in the twelfth generation, the names Three Deer and Nine Dog are followed by two sentences whose combination of gravity and brevity gives the reader a chill. The first is, "And they were ruling when Tonatiuh arrived," Tonatiuh or "he who goes along getting hot" being the name given by the Aztecs to Pedro de Alvarado, the man whose forces destroyed Rotten Cane in 1524. And the second sentence about Three Deer and Nine Dog is simply, "They were tortured by the Castilian people." Alvarado, convinced that they had plotted against him, hung them by their wrists as an aid to interrogation. Afterward he had them executed, but what struck the authors of the Popol Vuh was the torture.

In the thirteenth generation of Cauecs the Popol Vuh lists Black Butterfly and Tepepul, who were "tributary to the Castilian people." Then, at the end of the list of Cauec generations, come the first lords who adopted Spanish names, Juan de Rojas and Juan Cortés, the living holders of the titles of Keeper of the Mat and Keeper of the Reception House Mat when the alphabetic Popol Vuh was written. Today Quichés ideally list either nine or thirteen generations when they invoke their ancestors in prayer; from this we can see that the thirteen generations of lords named as preceding Juan de Rojas and Juan Cortés need not be taken as constituting an exhaustive genealogy, but may rather be the names these two men were using in their current prayers.

By giving us the names of Quiché lords who were alive while they were writing, the authors of the alphabetic Popol Vuh also give us the means for dating their work. They could not have finished it any later than 1558, since by that year the name of Juan de Rojas is missing from documents he would have signed had he still been among the living. And since they mention Pedro de Robles of the Greathouse lineage as the current Lord Minister, they could not have finished any earlier than 1554, at which time his predecessor was still in office. During this same period Juan Cortés, whose duties as Keeper of the Reception House Mat would have included tribute collection had he served before the coming of Alvarado, worked constantly to restore tribute rights to the lordly lineages of the town of Quiché. In 1557 he went all the way to Spain to press his case, and it could be that he took a copy of the alphabetic Popol Vuh with him. He continued to make claims when he returned to Guatemala in 1558, prompting a missionary to warn Philip II that "this land is new and not confirmed in the faith," and that Cortés, "son of idolatrous parents, would need to do very little to restore their ceremonies and attract their former subjects to himself." Quiché rights to collect tribute never were restored, but over the next thirty years Juan Cortés did take a considerable role in appointing and installing the leaders of various towns that had once been under Quiché rule.

By the time the authors of the Popol Vuh have finished listing noble titles and the names of the persons who held them, they are only a few sentences away from finishing their work. At this point they single out one of the lesser titles for further discussion, a move that seems anticlimactic until we realize that they are giving us a clue to their own identity. Without naming any individuals, they point out that each of the three leading lineages included one lord bearing the title of Master of Ceremonies. Here we may recall that when the authors introduced the story of One Hunahpu, they themselves proposed a toast to the reader. If we look for masters of ceremonies among the contemporary Quiché we find the professional matchmakers, who preside over the feasts where marriage arrangements are completed. If our mysterious authors were themselves the three Masters of Ceremonies, and if their duties included speaking at wedding banquets, that would help explain why they took a special interest in marriage customs when they recounted the life and times of successive Quiché citadels. Indeed, they specifically noted the point at which feasting and drinking first became a part of the negotiations for a bride.

The authors give us one final clue to their identity when they tell us that the three Masters of Ceremonies are "Mothers of the Word" and "Fathers of the Word." The combination of "Mother" and "Father" suggests the contemporary daykeepers called mother-fathers, who serve as the ritual heads of patrilineages; it is from their ranks that matchmakers are drawn. Moreover, matchmakers are admired above all other public performers for their eloquence. The focus on "the Word," coming as it does near the very end of a work whose opening line promised to give us the "Ancient Word," suggests that the Word parented by the Masters of Ceremonies and the Word written down in the alphabetic Popol Vuh are one and the same. If so, we know who one of the writers was. As of 1554, the current Master of Ceremonies for the Cauecs was a man named Cristóbal Velasco.

At the end of their work the authors repeat the enigma they presented near the beginning, allowing us to wonder whether the hieroglyphic Popol Vuh might still exist somewhere, only now they say it has been "lost" instead of telling us that the reader is hiding his identity. They close on a note of reassurance, asking us, in effect, to accept what they have written without demanding a closer look at their sources, since "everything has been completed here concerning Quiché," meaning the place named Quiché. Then, lest we forget their difficult circumstances, they add the phrase, "which is now named Santa Cruz," or "Holy Cross." Here again they take us back to the beginning, where they told us, "We shall write about this now amid the preaching of God, in Christendom now."

Today, even when Quiché daykeepers go to a remote mountaintop shrine, sending up great clouds of incense for multitudes of deities and ancestors, they sometimes begin and end by running through an "Our Father" and a "Hail Mary" and crossing themselves. It is as if the alien eye and ear of the conqueror were present even under conditions of solitude and required the recitation of two spells, one to ward them off for a while and the other to readmit their existence. Between these protective spells daykeepers are left to enter, in peace, a world whose obligations they know to be older than those of Christianity, obligations to the mountains and plains where they continue to live and to all those who have ever lived there before them. So it is with the authors of the Popol Vuh, who mention Christendom on the first page, Holy Cross on the last page, and open up the whole sky-earth, vast and deep, within.

Perhaps the most remarkable thing about the Popol Vuh, considered in its entirety, is the vast temporal sweep of its narrative. It begins in darkness, with a world inhabited only by gods, and continues all the way past the dawn into the time of the humans who wrote it. The surviving Mayan hieroglyphic books abound with gods, but they seem to stop short of dealing directly with the acts of mortals. The Dresden book does have one page that shifts the action to the human sphere, but the following pages were torn off at some time in the past. If we wish to find hieroglyphic texts that have the same proportion between divine and human affairs as the alphabetic Popol Vuh, we must leave the time and place in which it was written and go a thousand years back and hundreds of miles away to the Classic Maya site of Palenque, down in the rain forest.

At Palenque, in the sanctuary of each of the three temples in what is now known as the Cross Group, is a stone tablet bearing a hieroglyphic narrative. In each case the text is divided into two panels, one of which begins with the deeds of gods, and the other of which ends with the deeds of human lords whose own scribes were the authors of the inscriptions. In the middle of this narrative, where the reader passes from one panel to the other, is a transition from divine to human characters. So also with the Popol Vuh: about halfway through, the reader comes to a transition between what might be called "myth" and "history" (at the end of Part Three). The characters in the narrative are still divine at this point, but they are described as performing rituals for the veneration of ripened corn and deceased relatives, rituals that are meant to be followed by future humans rather than by ancient gods. After this episode, in which the gods act like people, comes another in which people act like gods (at the beginning of Part Four). The people in question are the first four humans, the ones who saw and understood everything in the sky-earth. Once their perfect vision has been taken away the narrative begins to sound more like history as it moves along, though human characters continue to aspire to deeds of divine proportions.

We tend to think of myth and history as being in conflict with each other, but the authors of the inscriptions at Palenque and the alphabetic text of the Popol Vuh treated the mythic and historical parts of their narratives as belonging to a single, balanced whole. By their sense of proportion, the Egyptian Book of the Dead would need a second half devoted to human deeds in the land of the living, and the Hebrew Testament would need a first half devoted to events that took place before the fall of Adam and Eve. In the case of ancient Chinese literature, the Book of Changes, which is like the Popol Vuh in being subject to divinatory interpretation, would have to be combined with the Book of History in a single volume.

To this day the Quiché Maya think of dualities in general as complementary rather than opposed, interpenetrating rather than mutually exclusive. Instead of being in logical opposition to one another, the realms of divine and human actions are joined by a mutual attraction. If we had an English word that fully expressed the Mayan sense of narrative time, it would have to embrace the duality of the divine and the human in the same way the Quiché term *kajulew* or "sky-earth" preserves the duality of what we call the "world." In fact we already have a word that comes close to doing the job: *mythistory*, taken into English from Greek by way of Latin. For the ancient Greeks, who set about driving a wedge between the divine and the human, this term became a negative one, designating narratives that should have been properly historical but contained mythic impurities. For Mayans, the presence of a divine dimension in narratives of human affairs is not an imperfection but a necessity, and it is balanced by a necessary human dimension in narratives of divine affairs. At one end of the Popol Vuh the gods are preoccupied with the difficult task of making humans, and at the other humans are preoccupied with the equally difficult task of finding the traces of divine movements in their own deeds.

The difference between a fully mythistorical sense of narrative time and the European quest for pure history is not reducible to a simple contrast between cyclical and linear time. Mayans are always alert to the reassertion of the patterns of the past in present events, but they do not expect the past to repeat itself exactly. Each time the gods of the Popol Vuh attempt to make human beings they get a different result, and except for the solitary person made of mud, each attempt has a lasting result rather than completely disappearing into the folds of cyclical time. Later, when members of the second generation of Quiché lords go on a pilgrimage that takes them into the lowlands, their journey is not described as a literal repetition of the journey of Hunahpu and Xbalanque to Xibalba, nor even as a retracing of the journey of the human founders of the ruling Quiché lineages, but is rather allowed its own character as a unique event, an event that nevertheless carries constant echoes of the past. The effect of these events, like others, is cumulative, and it is a specifically human capacity to take each of them into account separately while at the same time recognizing that they double back on one another.

In theory, if we who presently claim to be human were to forget our efforts to find the traces of divine movements in our own actions, our fate should be something like that of the wooden people in the Popol Vuh. For them, the forgotten force of divinity reasserted itself by inhabiting their own tools and utensils, which rose up against them and drove them from their homes. Today they are swinging through the trees.

> On the holy day Eight Monkey
> in the year Eleven Thought,
> June 22, 1984,
> Menotomy, Massachusetts

> On the holy day One Hunahpu
> in the year Nine Tooth,
> July 24, 1995,
> East Aurora, New York

PART
ONE

THIS IS THE BEGINNING OF THE ANCIENT WORD, here in this place called Quiché. Here we shall inscribe, we shall implant the Ancient Word, the potential and source for everything done in the citadel of Quiché, in the nation of Quiché people.

And here we shall take up the demonstration, revelation, and account of how things were put in shadow and brought to light by

> the Maker, Modeler,
> named Bearer, Begetter,
> Hunahpu Possum, Hunahpu Coyote,
> Great White Peccary, Coati,
> Sovereign Plumed Serpent,
> Heart of the Lake, Heart of the Sea,
> plate shaper, bowl shaper, as they are called,
> also named, also described as
> the midwife, matchmaker
> named Xpiyacoc, Xmucane,
> defender, protector,
> twice a midwife, twice a matchmaker,

as is said in the words of Quiché. They accounted for everything—and did it, too—as enlightened beings, in enlightened words. We shall write about this now amid the preaching of God, in Christendom now. We shall bring it out because there is no longer

> a place to see it, a Council Book,
> a place to see "The Light That Came from
>   Beside the Sea,"
> the account of "Our Place in the Shadows."
> a place to see "The Dawn of Life,"

as it is called. There is the original book and ancient writing, but the one who reads and assesses it has a hidden identity. It takes a long performance and account to complete the lighting of all the sky-earth:

> the fourfold siding, fourfold cornering,
> measuring, fourfold staking,
> halving the cord, stretching the cord

in the sky, on the earth,
the four sides, the four corners, as it is said,
by the Maker, Modeler,
mother-father of life, of humankind,
giver of breath, giver of heart,
bearer, upbringer in the light that lasts
of those born in the light, begotten in the light;
worrier, knower of everything, whatever there is:
sky-earth, lake-sea.

THIS IS THE ACCOUNT, here it is:

Now it still ripples, now it still murmurs, ripples, it still sighs, still hums, and it is empty under the sky.

Here follow the first words, the first eloquence:

There is not yet one person, one animal, bird, fish, crab, tree, rock, hollow, canyon, meadow, forest. Only the sky alone is there; the face of the earth is not clear. Only the sea alone is pooled under all the sky; there is nothing whatever gathered together. It is at rest; not a single thing stirs. It is held back, kept at rest under the sky.

Whatever there is that might be is simply not there: only the pooled water, only the calm sea, only it alone is pooled.

Whatever might be is simply not there: only murmurs, ripples, in the dark, in the night. Only the Maker, Modeler alone, Sovereign Plumed Serpent, the Bearers, Begetters are in the water, a glittering light. They are there, they are enclosed in quetzal feathers, in blue-green.

Thus the name, "Plumed Serpent." They are great knowers, great thinkers in their very being.

SOVEREIGN PLUMED SERPENT: *Here he is seated, holding a snake in his hand. On his back he wears a quetzal bird, with its head behind his, its wings at the level of his shoulders, and its tail hanging down to the ground. From the Dresden Codex.*

DRAWING BY KARL TAUBE

And of course there is the sky, and there is also the Heart of Sky. This is the name of the god, as it is spoken.

And then came his word, he came here to the Sovereign Plumed Serpent, here in the blackness, in the early dawn. He spoke with the Sovereign Plumed Serpent, and they talked, then they thought, then they worried. They agreed with each other, they joined their words, their thoughts. Then it was clear, then they reached accord in the light, and then humanity was clear, when they conceived the growth, the generation of trees, of bushes, and the growth of life, of humankind, in the blackness, in the early dawn, all because of the Heart of Sky, named Hurricane. Thunderbolt Hurricane comes first, the second is Newborn Thunderbolt, and the third is Sudden Thunderbolt.

So there were three of them, as Heart of Sky, who came to the Sovereign Plumed Serpent, when the dawn of life was conceived:

"How should the sowing be, and the dawning? Who is to be the provider, nurturer?"

"Let it be this way, think about it: this water should be removed, emptied out for the formation of the earth's own plate and platform, then should come the sowing, the dawning of the sky-earth. But there will be no high days and no bright praise for our work, our design, until the rise of the human work, the human design," they said.

And then the earth arose because of them, it was simply their word that brought it forth. For the forming of the earth they said "Earth." It arose suddenly, just like a cloud, like a mist, now forming, unfolding.

THE HEART OF SKY, NAMED HURRICANE: *Here he peers out from among swirls of smoke and flame (or clouds and lightning) that come from the obsidian mirror on his own forehead. From a Late Classic vase from the lowlands.*

DRAWING BY KARL TAUBE

THUNDERBOLT: *A lowland Maya* Chak *or*
Thunderbolt god, holding a lightning-
striking axe in his left hand and a
representation of the sound of thunder in his
right. From the Dresden Codex.

DRAWING BY CARLOS A. VILLACORTA

Then the mountains were separated from the water, all at once the great mountains came forth. By their genius alone, by their cutting edge alone they carried out the conception of the mountain-plain, whose face grew instant groves of cypress and pine.

And the Plumed Serpent was pleased with this:

"It was good that you came, Heart of Sky, Hurricane, and Newborn Thunderbolt, Sudden Thunderbolt. Our work, our design will turn out well," they said.

And the earth was formed first, the mountain-plain. The channels of water were separated; their branches wound their ways among the mountains. The waters were divided when the great mountains appeared.

Such was the formation of the earth when it was brought forth by the Heart of Sky, Heart of Earth, as they are called, since they were the first to think of it. The sky was set apart, and the earth was set apart in the midst of the waters.

Such was their plan when they thought, when they worried about the completion of their work.

Now they planned the animals of the mountains, all the guardians of the forests, creatures of the mountains: the deer, birds, pumas, jaguars, serpents, rattlesnakes, fer-de-lances, guardians of the bushes.

A Bearer, Begetter speaks:

"Why this pointless humming? Why should there merely be rustling beneath the trees and bushes?"

66

"Indeed—they had better have guardians," the others replied. As soon as they thought it and said it, deer and birds came forth.

And then they gave out homes to the deer and birds:

"You, the deer: sleep along the rivers, in the canyons. Be here in the meadows, in the thickets, in the forests, multiply yourselves. You will stand and walk on all fours," they were told.

So then they established the nests of the birds, small and great:

"You, precious birds: your nests, your houses are in the trees, in the bushes. Multiply there, scatter there, in the branches of trees, the branches of bushes," the deer and birds were told.

When this deed had been done, all of them had received a place to sleep and a place to stay. So it is that the nests of the animals are on the earth, given by the Bearer, Begetter. Now the arrangement of the deer and birds was complete.

A ND THEN THE DEER AND BIRDS WERE TOLD by the Maker, Modeler, Bearer, Begetter:

"Talk, speak out. Don't moan, don't cry out. Please talk, each to each, within each kind, within each group," they were told—the deer, birds, puma, jaguar, serpent.

"Name now our names, praise us. We are your mother, we are your father. Speak now:

> 'Hurricane,
> Newborn Thunderbolt, Sudden Thunderbolt,
> Heart of Sky, Heart of Earth,
> Maker, Modeler,
> Bearer, Begetter,'

speak, pray to us, keep our days," they were told. But it didn't turn out that they spoke like people: they just squawked, they just chattered, they just howled. It wasn't apparent what language they spoke; each one gave a different cry. When the Maker, Modeler heard this:

"It hasn't turned out well, they haven't spoken," they said among themselves. "It hasn't turned out that our names have been named. Since we are their mason and sculptor, this will not do," the Bearers and Begetters said among themselves. So they told them:

"You will simply have to be transformed. Since it hasn't turned out well and you haven't spoken, we have changed our word:

67

JUST LET YOUR FLESH BE EATEN: *A turkey (left) and deer (right) caught in bent-tree snares. From the Madrid Codex.*

DRAWING BY CARLOS A. VILLACORTA

"What you feed on, what you eat, the places where you sleep, the places where you stay, whatever is yours will remain in the canyons, the forests. Although it turned out that our days were not kept, nor did you pray to us, there may yet be strength in the keeper of days, the giver of praise whom we have yet to make. Just accept your service, just let your flesh be eaten.

"So be it, this must be your service," they were told when they were instructed—the animals, small and great, on the face of the earth.

And then they wanted to test their timing again, they wanted to experiment again, and they wanted to prepare for the keeping of days again. They had not heard their speech among the animals; it did not come to fruition and it was not complete.

And so their flesh was brought low: they served, they were eaten, they were killed—the animals on the face of the earth.

AGAIN THERE COMES AN EXPERIMENT WITH THE HUMAN WORK, the human design, by the Maker, Modeler, Bearer, Begetter:

"It must simply be tried again. The time for the planting and dawning is nearing. For this we must make a provider and nurturer. How else can we be invoked and remembered on the face of the earth? We have already made our first try at our work and design, but it turned out that they didn't keep our days, nor did they glorify us.

"So now let's try to make a giver of praise, giver of respect, provider, nurturer," they said.

So then comes the building and working with earth and mud. They made a body, but it didn't look good to them. It was just separating, just crumbling, just loosening, just softening, just disintegrating, and just dissolving. Its head wouldn't turn, either. Its face was just lopsided, its

68

face was just twisted. It couldn't look around. It talked at first, but senselessly. It was quickly dissolving in the water.

"It won't last," the mason and sculptor said then. "It seems to be dwindling away, so let it just dwindle. It can't walk and it can't multiply, so let it be merely a thought," they said.

So then they dismantled, again they brought down their work and design. Again they talked:

"What is there for us to make that would turn out well, that would succeed in keeping our days and praying to us?" they said. Then they planned again:

"We'll just tell Xpiyacoc, Xmucane, Hunahpu Possum, Hunahpu Coyote, to try a counting of days, a counting of lots," the mason and sculptor said to themselves. Then they invoked Xpiyacoc, Xmucane.

T HEN COMES THE NAMING OF THOSE WHO ARE THE MIDMOST SEERS: the "Grandmother of Day, Grandmother of Light," as the Maker, Modeler called them. These are names of Xpiyacoc and Xmucane.

When Hurricane had spoken with the Sovereign Plumed Serpent, they invoked the daykeepers, diviners, the midmost seers:

"There is yet to find, yet to discover how we are to model a person, construct a person again, a provider, nurturer, so that we are called upon and we are recognized: our recompense is in words.

> Midwife, matchmaker,
> our grandmother, our grandfather,
> Xpiyacoc, Xmucane,
> let there be planting, let there be the dawning
> of our invocation, our sustenance, our recognition
> by the human work, the human design,
> the human figure, the human form.
> So be it, fulfill your names:
> Hunahpu Possum, Hunahpu Coyote,
> Bearer twice over, Begetter twice over,
> Great Peccary, Great Coati,
> lapidary, jeweler,
> sawyer, carpenter,
> plate shaper, bowl shaper,
> incense maker, master craftsman,
> Grandmother of Day, Grandmother of Light.

You have been called upon because of our work, our design. Run your hands over the kernels of corn, over the seeds of the coral tree, just get it done, just let it come out whether we should carve and gouge a mouth, a face in wood," they told the daykeepers.

And then comes the borrowing, the counting of days; the hand is moved over the corn kernels, over the coral seeds, the days, the lots.

Then they spoke to them, one of them a grandmother, the other a grandfather.

This is the grandfather, this is the master of the coral seeds: Xpiyacoc is his name.

And this is the grandmother, the daykeeper, diviner who stands behind others: Xmucane is her name.

And they said, as they set out the days:

> "Just let it be found, just let it be discovered,
> say it, our ear is listening,
> may you talk, may you speak,
> just find the wood for the carving and sculpting
> by the builder, sculptor.
> Is this to be the provider, the nurturer
> when it comes to the planting, the dawning?
> You corn kernels, you coral seeds,
> you days, you lots:
> may you succeed, may you be accurate,"

they said to the corn kernels, coral seeds, days, lots. "Have shame, you up there, Heart of Sky: attempt no deception before the mouth and face of Sovereign Plumed Serpent," they said. Then they spoke straight to the point:

"It is well that there be your manikins, woodcarvings, talking, speaking, there on the face of the earth."

"So be it," they replied. The moment they spoke it was done: the manikins, woodcarvings, human in looks and human in speech.

This was the peopling of the face of the earth:

They came into being, they multiplied, they had daughters, they had sons, these manikins, woodcarvings. But there was nothing in their hearts and nothing in their minds, no memory of their mason and builder. They just went and walked wherever they wanted. Now they did not remember the Heart of Sky.

And so they fell, just an experiment and just a cutout for humankind. They were talking at first but their faces were dry. They were not yet

70

developed in the legs and arms. They had no blood, no lymph. They had no sweat, no fat. Their complexions were dry, their faces were crusty. They flailed their legs and arms, their bodies were deformed.

And so they accomplished nothing before the Maker, Modeler who gave them birth, gave them heart. They became the first numerous people here on the face of the earth.

Again there comes a humiliation, destruction, and demolition. The manikins, woodcarvings were killed when the Heart of Sky devised a flood for them. A great flood was made; it came down on the heads of the manikins, woodcarvings.

The man's body was carved from the wood of the coral tree by the Maker, Modeler. And as for the woman, the Maker, Modeler needed the hearts of bulrushes for the woman's body. They were not competent, nor did they speak before the builder and sculptor who made them and brought them forth, and so they were killed, done in by a flood:

There came a rain of resin from the sky.

There came the one named Gouger of Faces: he gouged out their eyeballs.

There came Sudden Bloodletter: he snapped off their heads.

There came Crunching Jaguar: he ate their flesh.

There came Tearing Jaguar: he tore them open.

He gouged out their eyeballs: *A human eye in the beak of a king vulture, still attached by the optic nerve. From the Madrid Codex.*

DRAWING BY CARLOS A. VILLACORTA

They were pounded down to the bones and tendons, smashed and pulverized even to the bones. Their faces were smashed because they were incompetent before their mother and their father, the Heart of Sky, named Hurricane. The earth was blackened because of this; the black rainstorm began, rain all day and rain all night. Into their houses came the animals, small and great. Their faces were crushed by things of wood and stone. Everything spoke: their water jars, their tortilla griddles, their plates, their cooking pots, their dogs, their grinding stones, each and every thing crushed their faces. Their dogs and turkeys told them:

"You caused us pain, you ate us, but now it is *you* whom *we* shall eat." And this is the grinding stone:

"We were undone because of you.

> Every day, every day,
> in the dark, in the dawn, forever,
> r-r-rip, r-r-rip,
> r-r-rub, r-r-rub,
> right in our faces, because of you.

This was the service we gave you at first, when you were still people, but today you will learn of our power. We shall pound and we shall grind your flesh," their grinding stones told them.

And this is what their dogs said, when they spoke in their turn:

"Why is it you can't seem to give us our food? We just watch and you just keep us down, and you throw us around. You keep a stick ready when you eat, just so you can hit us. We don't talk, so we've received nothing from you. How could you not have known? You *did* know that we were wasting away there, behind you.

"So, this very day you will taste the teeth in our mouths. We shall eat you," their dogs told them, and their faces were crushed.

And then their tortilla griddles and cooking pots spoke to them in turn:

"Pain! That's all you've done for us. Our mouths are sooty, our faces are sooty. By setting us on the fire all the time, you burn us. Since *we* felt no pain, *you* try it. We shall burn you," all their cooking pots said, crushing their faces.

The stones, their hearthstones were shooting out, coming right out of the fire, going for their heads, causing them pain. Now they run for it, helter-skelter.

They want to climb up on the houses, but they fall as the houses collapse.

They want to climb the trees; they're thrown off by the trees.

THEIR HEARTHSTONES WERE SHOOTING OUT: *According to Classic Maya inscriptions, three hearthstones entered the sky and formed a new constellation at the end of the world that preceded the present one. The glyph at left (from a stele at Quiriguá) reads* yax ox tunal, *"new three-stone place," and repeats the sign for "stone"* (tun) *three times; the glyph at right (from a stele at Toniná) adds signs for smoke and flames to the stones.*

DRAWING BY KARL TAUBE

They want to get inside caves, but the caves slam shut in their faces.

Such was the scattering of the human work, the human design. The people were ground down, overthrown. The mouths and faces of all of them were destroyed and crushed. And it used to be said that the monkeys in the forests today are a sign of this. They were left as a sign because wood alone was used for their flesh by the builder and sculptor.

So this is why monkeys look like people: they are a sign of a previous human work, human design—mere manikins, mere woodcarvings.

THIS WAS WHEN THERE WAS JUST A TRACE OF EARLY DAWN on the face of the earth, there was no sun. But there was one who magnified himself; Seven Macaw is his name. The sky-earth was already there, but the face of the sun-moon was clouded over. Even so, it is said that his light provided a sign for the people who were flooded. He was like a person of genius in his being.

"I am great. My place is now higher than that of the human work, the human design. I am their sun and I am their light, and I am also their months.

"So be it: my light is great. I am the walkway and I am the foothold of the people, because my eyes are of metal. My teeth just glitter with jewels, and turquoise as well; they stand out blue with stones like the face of the sky.

"And this nose of mine shines white into the distance like the moon.

Since my nest is metal, it lights up the face of the earth. When I come forth before my nest, I am like the sun and moon for those who are born in the light, begotten in the light. It must be so, because my face reaches into the distance," says Seven Macaw.

It is not true that he is the sun, this Seven Macaw, yet he magnifies himself, his wings, his metal. But the scope of his face lies right around his own perch; his face does not reach everywhere beneath the sky. The faces of the sun, moon, and stars are not yet visible, it has not yet dawned.

And so Seven Macaw puffs himself up as the days and the months, though the light of the sun and moon has not yet clarified. He only wished for surpassing greatness. This was when the flood was worked upon the manikins, woodcarvings.

And now we shall explain how Seven Macaw died, when the people were vanquished, done in by the mason and sculptor.

PART
TWO

Here is the beginning of the defeat and destruction of the day of Seven Macaw by the two boys, the first named Hunahpu and the second named Xbalanque. Being gods, the two of them saw evil in his attempt at self-magnification before the Heart of Sky. So the boys talked:

"It's no good without life, without people here on the face of the earth."

"Well then, let's try a shot. We could shoot him while he's at his meal. We could make him ill, then put an end to his riches, his jade, his metal, his jewels, his gems, the source of his brilliance. Everyone might do as he does, but it should not come to be that fiery splendor is merely a matter of metal. So be it," said the boys, each one with a blowgun on his shoulder, the two of them together.

And this Seven Macaw has two sons: the first of these is Zipacna, and the second is the Earthquake. And Chimalmat is the name of their mother, the wife of Seven Macaw.

And this is Zipacna, this is the one to build up the great mountains: Fireplace, Hunahpu, Cave by the Water, Xcanul, Macamob, Huliznab, as the names of the mountains that were there at the dawn are spoken. They were brought forth by Zipacna in a single night.

And now this is the Earthquake. The mountains are moved by him; the mountains, small and great, are softened by him. The sons of Seven Macaw did this just as a means of self-magnification.

"Here am I: I am the sun," said Seven Macaw.

"Here am I: I am the maker of the earth," said Zipacna.

THE BOYS TALKED: *Hunahpu (left) and Xbalanque (right). The latter, known as Yax Balam in lowland Maya texts, has patches of jaguar skin on his face and body. Classic Maya painting from the cave at Naj Tunich, Guatemala.*

DRAWING BY KARL TAUBE

"As for me, I bring down the sky, I make an avalanche of all the earth," said Earthquake. The sons of Seven Macaw are alike, and like him: they got their greatness from their father.

And the two boys saw evil in this, since our first mother and father could not yet be made. Therefore deaths and disappearances were planned by the two boys.

Aɴᴅ ʜᴇʀᴇ ɪs ᴛʜᴇ sʜᴏᴏᴛɪɴɢ ᴏꜰ Sᴇᴠᴇɴ Mᴀᴄᴀᴡ ʙʏ ᴛʜᴇ ᴛᴡᴏ ʙᴏʏs. We shall explain the defeat of each one of those who engaged in self-magnification.

This is the great tree of Seven Macaw, a nance, and this is the food of Seven Macaw. In order to eat the fruit of the nance he goes up the tree every day. Since Hunahpu and Xbalanque have seen where he feeds, they are now hiding beneath the tree of Seven Macaw, they are keeping quiet here, the two boys are in the leaves of the tree.

And when Seven Macaw arrived, perching over his meal, the nance, it was then that he was shot by Hunahpu. The blowgun shot went right to his jaw, breaking his mouth. Then he went up over the tree and fell flat on the ground. Suddenly Hunahpu appeared, running. He set out to

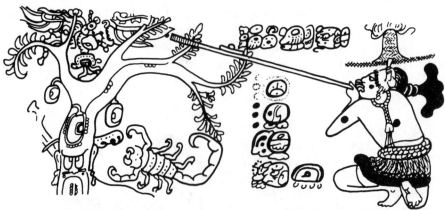

Hᴇ ᴡᴀs sʜᴏᴛ ʙʏ Hᴜɴᴀʜᴘᴜ: *Seven Macaw is perched at the top of the tree at left. Xbalanque is hidden behind its trunk, with only his pawlike hand showing just below the fruit that dangles from the base of the tree's right limb. Hunahpu, with his blowgun on target, crouches at right, shaded by a straw hat. From a Classic Maya vase.*

DRAWING BY KARL TAUBE

78

grab him, but actually it was the arm of Hunahpu that was seized by Seven Macaw. He yanked it straight back, he bent it back at the shoulder. Then Seven Macaw tore it right out of Hunahpu. Even so, the boys did well: the first round was not their defeat by Seven Macaw.

And when Seven Macaw had taken the arm of Hunahpu, he went home. Holding his jaw very carefully, he arrived:

"What have you got there?" said Chimalmat, the wife of Seven Macaw.

"What is it but those two tricksters! They've shot me, they've dislocated my jaw. All my teeth are just loose, now they ache. But once what I've got is over the fire—hanging there, dangling over the fire—then they can just come and get it. They're real tricksters!" said Seven Macaw, then he hung up the arm of Hunahpu.

Meanwhile Hunahpu and Xbalanque were thinking. And then they invoked a grandfather, a truly white-haired grandfather, and a grandmother, a truly humble grandmother—just bent-over, elderly people. Great White Peccary is the name of the grandfather, and Great White Coati is the name of the grandmother. The boys said to the grandmother and grandfather:

"Please travel with us when we go to get our arm from Seven Macaw; we'll just follow right behind you. You'll tell him:

'Do forgive us our grandchildren, who travel with us. Their mother and father are dead, and so they follow along there, behind us. Perhaps we should give them away, since all we do is pull worms out of teeth.' So we'll seem like children to Seven Macaw, even though *we're* giving *you* the instructions," the two boys told them.

"Very well," they replied.

After that they approached the place where Seven Macaw was in front

---

GREAT WHITE PECCARY: *A white-lipped peccary wearing a cloth headdress. From the Dresden Codex.*

DRAWING BY CARLOS A. VILLACORTA

of his home. When the grandmother and grandfather passed by, the two boys were romping along behind them. When they passed below the lord's house, Seven Macaw was yelling his mouth off because of his teeth. And when Seven Macaw saw the grandfather and grandmother traveling with them:

"Where are you headed, our grandfather?" said the lord.

"We're just making our living, your lordship," they replied.

"Why are you working for a living? Aren't those your children traveling with you?"

"No, they're not, your lordship. They're our grandchildren, our descendants, but it is nevertheless *we* who take pity on *them*. The bit of food they get is the portion we give them, your lordship," replied the grandmother and grandfather. Since the lord is getting done in by the pain in his teeth, it is only with great effort that he speaks again:

"I implore you, please take pity on me! What sweets can you make, what poisons can you cure?" said the lord.

"We just pull the worms out of teeth and we just cure eyes. We just set bones, your lordship," they replied.

"Very well, please cure my teeth. They really ache, every day. It's insufferable! I get no sleep because of them—and my eyes. They just shot me, those two tricksters! Ever since it started I haven't eaten because of it. Therefore take pity on me! Perhaps it's because my teeth are loose now."

"Very well, your lordship. It's a worm, gnawing at the bone. It's merely a matter of putting in a replacement and taking the teeth out, sir."

"But perhaps it's not good for my teeth to come out—since I am, after all, a lord. My finery is in my teeth—and my eyes."

"But then we'll put in a replacement. Ground bone will be put back in." And this is the "ground bone": it's only white corn.

"Very well. Yank them out! Give me some help here!" he replied.

And when the teeth of Seven Macaw came out, it was only white corn that went in as a replacement for his teeth—just a coating shining white, that corn in his mouth. His face fell at once, he no longer looked like a lord. The last of his teeth came out, the jewels that had stood out blue from his mouth.

And when the eyes of Seven Macaw were cured, he was plucked around the eyes, the last of his metal came off. Still he felt no pain; he just looked on while the last of his greatness left him. It was just as Hunahpu and Xbalanque had intended.

And when Seven Macaw died, Hunahpu got back his arm. And Chimalmat, the wife of Seven Macaw, also died.

Such was the loss of the riches of Seven Macaw: only the doctors got the jewels and gems that had made him arrogant, here on the face of the earth. The genius of the grandmother, the genius of the grandfather did its work when they took back their arm: it was implanted and the break got well again. Just as they had wished the death of Seven Macaw, so they brought it about. They had seen evil in his self-magnification.

After this the two boys went on again. What they did was simply the word of the Heart of Sky.

AND HERE ARE THE DEEDS OF ZIPACNA, the first son of Seven Macaw.

"I am the maker of mountains," says Zipacna.

And this is Zipacna, bathing on the shore. Then the Four Hundred Boys passed by dragging a log, a post for their hut. The Four Hundred Boys were walking along, having cut a great tree for the lintel of their hut.

And then Zipacna went there, he arrived where the Four Hundred Boys were:

"What are you doing, boys?"

THIS IS ZIPACNA, BATHING ON THE SHORE: *With bands of sky above and water below, this lowland version of Zipacna takes the form of a caiman. From a Classic Maya vase.*

DRAWING BY KARL TAUBE

"It's just this log. We can't lift it up to carry it."

"I'll carry it. Where does it go? What do you intend to use it for?"

"It's just a lintel for our hut."

"Very well," he replied.

And then he pulled it, or rather carried it, right on up to the entrance of the hut of the Four Hundred Boys.

"You could just stay with us, boy. Do you have a mother and father?"

"Not so," he replied.

"We'd like some help tomorrow in cutting another one of our logs, a post for our hut."

"Good," he replied.

After that the Four Hundred Boys shared their thoughts:

"About this boy: what should we do with him?"

"We should kill him, because what he does is no good. He lifted that log all by himself. Let's dig a big hole for him, and then we'll throw him down in the hole. We'll say to him:

'Why are you spilling dirt in the hole?' And when he's wedged down in the hole we'll wham a big log down behind him. Then he should die in the hole," said the Four Hundred Boys.

And when they had dug a hole, one that went deep, they called for Zipacna:

"We're asking you to please go on digging out the dirt. We can't go on," he was told.

"Very well," he replied.

After that he went down in the hole.

"Call out when enough dirt has been dug, when you're getting down deep," he was told.

"Yes," he replied, then he began digging the hole. But the only hole he dug was for his own salvation. He realized that he was to be killed, so he dug a separate hole to one side, he dug a second hole for safety.

"How far is it?" the Four Hundred Boys called down to him.

"I'm digging fast. When I call up to you, the digging will be finished," said Zipacna, from down in the hole. But he's not digging at the bottom of the hole, in his own grave; rather, the hole he's digging is for his own salvation.

After that, when Zipacna called out, he had gone to safety in his own hole. Then he called out:

"Come here, take the dirt, the fill from the hole. It's been dug. I've really gone down deep! Can't you hear my call? As for your call, it just echoes down here, it sounds to me as if you were on another level, or two levels away," said Zipacna from his hole. He's hidden in there, he calls out from down in the hole.

Meanwhile, a big log is being dragged along by the boys.

And then they threw the log down in the hole.

"Isn't he there? He doesn't speak."

"Let's keep on listening. He should cry out when he dies," they said among themselves. They're just whispering, and they've hidden themselves, each one of them, after throwing down the log.

And then he did speak, now he gave a single cry. He called out when the log fell to the bottom.

"Right on! He's been finished!"

"Very good! We've done him in, he's dead."

"What if he had gone on with his deeds, his works? He would've made himself first among us and taken our place—we, the Four Hundred Boys!" they said. Now they enjoyed themselves:

"On to the making of our sweet drink! Three days will pass, and after three days let's drink to dedicate our hut—we, the Four Hundred Boys!" they said. "And tomorrow we'll see, and on the day after tomorrow we'll see whether or not ants come from the ground when he's stinking and rotting. After that our hearts will be content when we drink our sweet drink," they said. But Zipacna was listening from the hole when the boys specified "the day after tomorrow."

And on the second day, when the ants collected, they were running, swarming. Having taken their pickings under the log, they were everywhere, carrying hair in their mouths and carrying the nails of Zipacna. When the boys saw this:

"He's finished, that trickster! Look here how the ants have stripped him, how they've swarmed. Everywhere they carry hair in their mouths. It's his nails you can see. We've done it!" they said among themselves.

But this Zipacna is still alive. He just cuts the hair off his head and chews off his nails to give them to the ants.

And so the Four Hundred Boys thought he had died.

After that, their sweet drink was ready on the third day, and then all the boys got drunk, and once they were drunk, all four hundred of those boys, they weren't feeling a thing.

After that the hut was brought down on top of them by Zipacna. All of them were completely flattened. Not even one or two were saved from among all the Four Hundred Boys. They were killed by Zipacna, the son of Seven Macaw.

Such was the death of those Four Hundred Boys. And it used to be said that they entered a constellation, named Hundrath after them, though perhaps this is just a play on words.

And this is where we shall explain the defeat of Zipacna by the two boys, Hunahpu and Xbalanque.

NOW THIS IS THE DEFEAT AND DEATH OF ZIPACNA, when he was beaten by the two boys, Hunahpu and Xbalanque.

What now weighed heavily on the hearts of the two boys was that the Four Hundred Boys had been killed by Zipacna.

It's mere fish and crabs that Zipacna looks for in the waters, but he's eating every day, going around looking for his food by day and lifting up mountains by night.

Next comes the counterfeiting of a great crab by Hunahpu and Xbalanque.

And they used bromeliad flowers, picked from the bromeliads of the forests. These became the forearms of the crab, and where they opened were the claws. They used a flagstone for the back of the crab, which clattered.

After that they put the shell beneath an overhang, at the foot of a great mountain. Meauan is the name of the mountain where the defeat took place.

After that, when the boys came along, they found Zipacna by the water:

"Where are you going, boy?" Zipacna was asked.

"I'm not going anywhere. I'm just looking for my food, boys," Zipacna replied.

"What's your food?"

"Just fish and crabs, but there aren't any that I can find. It's been two days since I stopped getting meals. By now I can't stand the hunger," Zipacna told Hunahpu and Xbalanque.

"There *is* that crab that's down in the canyon. A really big crab! Perhaps you might manage to eat her. We were just getting bitten. We wanted to catch her, but we got scared by her. If she hasn't gone away you could catch her," said Hunahpu and Xbalanque.

"Take pity on me, please come point her out, boys," said Zipacna.

"We don't want to, but you go ahead. You can't miss her. Just follow the river, and you go straight on over there below a great mountain. She's clattering there at the bottom of the canyon. Just head on over there," said Hunahpu and Xbalanque.

"But won't you please take pity on me? What if she can't be found, boys? If you come along I'll show you a place where there are plenty of birds. Please come shoot them, I know where they are," Zipacna replied. They consented. He went ahead of the boys.

"What if you can't catch the crab? Just as we had to turn back, so will you. Not only didn't we eat her, but all at once *she* was biting *us*. We were entering face down, but when she got scared we were entering on our back. We just barely missed reaching her then, so you'd better enter on your back," he was told.

"Very well," Zipacna replied, and then they went on. Now Zipacna had company as he went. They arrived at the bottom of the canyon.

The crab is on her side, her shell is gleaming red there. In under the canyon wall is their contrivance.

"Very good!" Zipacna is happy now. He wishes she were already in his mouth, so she could really cure his hunger. He wanted to eat her, he just wanted it face down, he wanted to enter, but since the crab got on top of him with her back down, he came back out.

"You didn't reach her?" he was asked.

"No indeed—she was just getting on top with her back down. I just barely missed her on the first try, so perhaps I'd better enter on my back," he replied.

After that he entered again, on his back. He entered all the way—only his kneecaps were showing now! He gave a last sigh and was calm. The great mountain rested on his chest. He couldn't turn over now, and so Zipacna turned to stone.

Such, in its turn, was the defeat of Zipacna by the two boys, Hunahpu and Xbalanque. He was "the maker of mountains," as his previous pronouncements had it, the first son of Seven Macaw. He was defeated beneath the great mountain called Meauan, defeated by genius alone. He was the second to magnify himself, and now we shall speak what is spoken of another.

A̲ND THE THIRD TO MAGNIFY HIMSELF IS THE SECOND SON OF SEVEN MACAW, NAMED EARTHQUAKE.

"I am the breaker of mountains," he said. But even so, Hunahpu and Xbalanque defeated the Earthquake. Then Hurricane spoke, Newborn Thunderbolt, Sudden Thunderbolt; he spoke to Hunahpu and Xbalanque:

"The second son of Seven Macaw is another one, another who should be defeated. This is my word, because what they do on the face of the earth is no good. They are surpassing the sun in size, in weight, and it should not be that way. Lure this Earthquake into sitting down over there in the east," Hurricane told the two boys.

"Very well, your lordship. There is more to be done. What we see is no good. Isn't it a question of your position and your eminence, sir, Heart of Sky?" the two boys said when they responded to the word of Hurricane.

Meanwhile he presses on, this Earthquake, breaker of mountains. Just by lightly tapping his foot on the ground he instantly demolishes the mountains, great and small. When he met up with the two boys:

"Where are you going, boy?" they asked Earthquake.

"I'm not going anywhere. I just scatter the mountains, and I'm the one who breaks them, in the course of the days, in the course of the light," he said when he answered. Then the Earthquake asked Hunahpu and Xbalanque:

"Where did you come from? I don't know your faces. What are your names?" said Earthquake.

"We have no names. We just hunt and trap in the mountains. We're just orphans, we have nothing to call our own, boy. We're just making our way among the mountains, small and great, boy. And there's one great mountain we saw that's just growing right along. It's rising really high! It's just swelling up, rising above all the other mountains. And there weren't even one or two birds to be found, boy. So how could it be that you destroy all mountains, boy?" Hunahpu and Xbalanque said to Earthquake.

"It can't be true you saw the mountain you're talking about. Where is it? You'll see me knock it down yet. Where did you see it?"

"Well, it's over there in the east," said Hunahpu and Xbalanque.

"Good. Lead the way," the two boys were told.

"Not so. You take the middle. Stay here between us—one of us at your left, the other at your right hand—because of our blowguns. If there are birds, we'll shoot," they said. They enjoy practicing their shooting.

And this is the way they shoot: the shot of their blowguns isn't made of earth—they just blow at the birds when they shoot, to the amazement of the Earthquake.

And then the boys made fire with a drill and roasted the birds over the fire. And they coated one of the birds with plaster, they put gypsum on it.

"So this is the one we'll give him when he's hungry, and when he

86

THE BOYS MADE FIRE WITH A DRILL: *Two figures turn a fire drill while sparks fly up from the wooden platform where the point of the drill is inserted. They are seated beside a road, marked by footprints. From the Madrid Codex.*

DRAWING BY CARLOS A. VILLACORTA

savors the aroma of our birds. That will be victory, since we've covered his bird with baked earth. In earth we must cook it, and in earth must be his grave—if the great knower, the one to be made and modeled, is to have a sowing and dawning," said the boys.

"Because of this, the human heart will desire a bite of meat, a meal of flesh, just as the heart of the Earthquake will desire it," Hunahpu and Xbalanque said to each other. Then they roasted the birds and cooked them until they were brown, dripping with fat that oozed from the backs of the birds, with an overwhelmingly fragrant aroma.

And this Earthquake wants to be fed, his mouth just waters, he gulps and slurps with spittle and saliva because of the fragrance of the birds. So then he asked:

"What are you eating? I smell a truly delicious aroma! Please give me a little bit," he said. And when they gave a bird to Earthquake, he was as good as defeated.

After he had finished off the bird, they went on until they arrived in the east, where the great mountain was.

Meanwhile, Earthquake had lost the strength in his legs and arms. He couldn't go on because of the earth that coated the bird he'd eaten. So now there was nothing he could do to the mountain. He never recovered; he was destroyed. So then he was bound by the two boys; his hands were bound behind him. When his hands had been secured by the boys, his ankles were bound to his wrists.

After that they threw him down, they buried him in the earth.

Such is the defeat of Earthquake. It's Hunahpu and Xbalanque yet again. Their deeds on the face of the earth are countless.

And now we shall explain the birth of Hunahpu and Xbalanque, having first explained the defeat of Seven Macaw, along with Zipacna and Earthquake, here on the face of the earth.

PART THREE

AND NOW WE SHALL NAME THE NAME OF THE FATHER OF HUN-AHPU AND XBALANQUE. Let's drink to him, and let's just drink to the telling and accounting of the begetting of Hunahpu and Xbalanque. We shall tell just half of it, just a part of the account of their father. Here follows the account.

These are the names: One Hunahpu and Seven Hunahpu, as they are called.

And these are their parents: Xpiyacoc, Xmucane. In the blackness, in the night, One Hunahpu and Seven Hunahpu were born to Xpiyacoc and Xmucane.

And this One Hunahpu had two children, and the two were sons, the firstborn named One Monkey and the second named One Artisan.

And this is the name of their mother: she is called Egret Woman, the wife of One Hunahpu. As for Seven Hunahpu, he has no wife. He's just a partner and just secondary; he just remains a boy.

They are great thinkers and great is their knowledge. They are the midmost seers, here on the face of the earth. There is only good in their being and their birthright. They taught skills to One Monkey and One Artisan, the sons of One Hunahpu. One Monkey and One Artisan became flautists, singers, and writers; carvers, jadeworkers, metalworkers as well.

And as for One and Seven Hunahpu, all they did was throw dice and play ball, every day. They would play each other in pairs, the four of them together. When they gathered in the ball court for entertainment a falcon would come to watch them, the messenger of Hurricane, Newborn Thunderbolt, Sudden Thunderbolt. And for this falcon it wasn't far to the earth here, nor was it far to Xibalba; he could get back to the sky, to Hurricane, in an instant.

The four ballplayers remained here on the face of the earth after the mother of One Monkey and One Artisan had died. Since it was on the road to Xibalba that they played, they were heard by One Death and Seven Death, the lords of Xibalba:

"What's happening on the face of the earth? They're just stomping and shouting. They should be summoned to come play ball here. We'll defeat them, since we simply get no deference from them. They show no respect, nor do they have any shame. They're really determined to run right over us!" said all of Xibalba, when they all shared their thoughts, the ones named One and Seven Death. They are great lawgivers.

AND THESE ARE THE LORDS OVER EVERYTHING, each lord with a commission and a domain assigned by One and Seven Death:

There are the lords named Scab Stripper and Blood Gatherer. And this is their commission: to draw blood from people.

Next are the lordships of Demon of Pus and Demon of Jaundice. And this is their domain: to make people swell up, to make pus come out of their legs, to make their faces yellow, to cause jaundice, as it is called. Such is the domain of Demon of Pus and Demon of Jaundice.

Next are the lords Bone Scepter and Skull Scepter, the staff bearers of Xibalba; their staffs are just bones. And this is their staff-bearing: to reduce people to bones, right down to the bones and skulls, until they die from emaciation and edema. This is the commission of the ones named Bone Scepter and Skull Scepter.

Next are the lords named Demon of Filth and Demon of Woe. This is their commission: just to give people a sudden fright whenever they have filth or grime in the doorway of the house, the patio of the house. Then they're struck, they're just punctured till they crawl on the ground, then die. And this is the domain of Demon of Filth and Demon of Woe, as they are called.

Next are the lords named Wing and Packstrap. This is their domain: that people should die in the road, just "sudden death," as it is called. Blood comes to the mouth, then there is death from vomiting blood. So to each of them his burden, the load on his shoulders: just to strike people on the neck and chest. Then there is death in the road, and then

---

PEOPLE SHOULD DIE IN THE ROAD: *A Xibalban (right) stabs a merchant god (left) on a road (indicated by the footprints). From the Madrid Codex.*

DRAWING BY KARL TAUBE

they just go on causing suffering, whether one is coming or going. And this is the domain of Wing and Packstrap.

Such are those who shared their thoughts when they were piqued and driven by One and Seven Hunahpu. What Xibalba desired was the gaming equipment of One and Seven Hunahpu: their kilts, their yokes, their arm guards, their panaches and headbands, the costumes of One and Seven Hunahpu.

And this is where we shall continue telling of their trip to Xibalba. One Monkey and One Artisan, the sons of One Hunahpu, stayed behind. Their mother died—and, what is more, they were to be defeated by Hunahpu and Xbalanque.

AND NOW FOR THE MESSENGERS OF ONE AND SEVEN DEATH:
"You're going, you Military Keepers of the Mat, to summon One and Seven Hunahpu. You'll tell them, when you arrive:

' "They must come," the lords say to you. "Would that they might come to play ball with us here. Then we could have some excitement with them. We are truly amazed at them. Therefore they should come," say the lords, "and they should bring their playthings, their yokes and arm guards should come, along with their rubber ball," say the lords,' you will say when you arrive," the messengers were told.

THESE MESSENGERS OF THEIRS ARE OWLS:
The great horned owl appears as a bird of omen in lowland Maya art, serving as the messenger of the merchant lord of Xibalba. From the Dresden Codex.

DRAWING BY KARL TAUBE

And these messengers of theirs are owls: Shooting Owl, One-legged Owl, Macaw Owl, Skull Owl, as the messengers of Xibalba are called.

There is Shooting Owl, like a point, just piercing.

And there is One-legged Owl, with just one leg; he has wings.

And there is Macaw Owl, with a red back; he has wings.

And there is also Skull Owl, with only a head alone; he has no legs, but he does have wings.

There are four messengers, Military Keepers of the Mat in rank.

And when they came out of Xibalba they arrived quickly, alighting above the ball court where One and Seven Hunahpu were playing, at the ball court called Great Hollow with Fish in the Ashes. The owls, arriving in a flurry over the ball court, now repeated their words, reciting the exact words of One Death, Seven Death, Demon of Pus, Demon of Jaundice, Bone Scepter, Skull Scepter, Scab Stripper, Blood Gatherer, Demon of Filth, Demon of Woe, Wing, Packstrap, as all the lords are named. Their words were repeated by the owls.

"Don't the lords One and Seven Death speak truly?"

"Truly indeed," the owls replied. "We'll accompany you.

'They're to bring along all their gaming equipment,' say the lords."

"Very well, but wait for us while we notify our mother," they replied.

And when they went to their house, they spoke to their mother; their father had died:

"We're going, our dear mother, even though we've just arrived. The messengers of the lord have come to get us:

' "They should come," he says,' they say, giving us orders. We'll leave our rubber ball behind here," they said, then they went to tie it up under the roof of the house. "Until we return—then we'll put it in play again."

They told One Monkey and One Artisan:

"As for you, just play and just sing, write and carve to warm our house and to warm the heart of your grandmother." When they had been given their instructions, their grandmother Xmucane sobbed, she had to weep.

"We're going, we're not dying. Don't be sad," said One and Seven Hunahpu, then they left.

A FTER THAT ONE AND SEVEN HUNAHPU LEFT, guided down the road by the messengers.

And then they descended the road to Xibalba, going down over the edge of a steep slope, and they descended until they came to the mouth where the canyons change, the ones named Rustling Canyon, Gurgling Canyon.

They passed through there, then they passed through Scorpion Rapids. They passed through countless scorpions but they were not stung.

And then they came to water again, to blood: Blood River. They crossed but did not drink. They came to a river, but a river filled with pus. Still they were not defeated, but passed through again.

And then they came to the Crossroads, but here they were defeated, at the Crossroads:

Red Road was one and Black Road another.

White Road was one and Yellow Road another.

There were four roads, and Black Road spoke:

"I am the one you are taking. I am the lord's road," said the road. And they were defeated there: this was the Road of Xibalba.

And then they came to the council place of the lords of Xibalba, and they were defeated again there. The ones seated first there are just manikins, just woodcarvings dressed up by Xibalba. And they greeted the first ones:

"Morning, One Death," they said to the manikin. "Morning, Seven Death," they said to the woodcarving in turn.

So they did not win out, and the lords of Xibalba shouted out with laughter over this. All the lords just shouted with laughter because they had triumphed; in their hearts they had beaten One and Seven Hunahpu. They laughed on until One and Seven Death spoke:

"It's good that you've come. Tomorrow you must put your yokes and arm guards into action," they were told.

"Sit here on our bench," they were told, but the only bench they were offered was a burning-hot rock.

THE LORDS OF XIBALBA SHOUTED OUT WITH LAUGHTER: *This lowland Maya death lord, whose skull and joints have no flesh on them, sits on a throne made of bones. From the Dresden Codex.*

DRAWING BY CARLOS A. VILLACORTA

So now they were burned on the bench; they really jumped around on the bench now, but they got no relief. They really got up fast, having burned their butts. At this the Xibalbans laughed again, they began to shriek with laughter, the laughter rose up like a serpent in their very cores, all the lords of Xibalba laughed themselves down to their blood and bones.

"Just go in the house. Your torch and cigars will be brought to your sleeping quarters," the boys were told.

After that they came to the Dark House, a house with darkness alone inside. Meanwhile the Xibalbans shared their thoughts:

"Let's just sacrifice them tomorrow. It can only turn out to be quick; they'll die quickly because of our playing equipment, our gaming things," the Xibalbans are saying among themselves.

This ball of theirs is just a spherical knife. White Dagger is the name of the ball, the ball of Xibalba. Their ball is just ground down to make it smooth; the ball of Xibalba is just surfaced with crushed bone to make it firm.

A ND One and Seven Hunahpu went inside Dark House.

And then their torch was brought, only one torch, already lit, sent by One and Seven Death, along with a cigar for each of them, also already lit, sent by the lords. When these were brought to One and Seven Hunahpu they were cowering, here in the dark. When the bearer of their torch and cigars arrived, the torch was bright as it entered; their torch and both of their cigars were burning. The bearer spoke:

" 'They must be sure to return them in the morning—not finished,

A CIGAR: *A lowland Maya god producing a shower of sparks with a cigar. From the Dresden Codex.*

DRAWING BY CARLOS A. VILLACORTA

but just as they look now. They must return them intact,' the lords say to you," they were told, and they were defeated. They finished the torch and they finished the cigars that had been brought to them.

And Xibalba is packed with tests, heaps and piles of tests.

This is the first one: the Dark House, with darkness alone inside.

And the second is named Rattling House, heavy with cold inside, whistling with drafts, clattering with hail. A deep chill comes inside here.

And the third is named Jaguar House, with jaguars alone inside, jostling one another, crowding together, with gnashing teeth. They're scratching around; these jaguars are shut inside the house.

Bat House is the name of the fourth test, with bats alone inside the house, squeaking, shrieking, darting through the house. The bats are shut inside; they can't get out.

And the fifth is named Razor House, with blades alone inside. The blades are moving back and forth, ripping, slashing through the house.

These are the first tests of Xibalba, but One and Seven Hunahpu never entered into them, except for the one named earlier, the specified test house.

And when One and Seven Hunahpu went back before One and Seven Death, they were asked:

"Where are my cigars? What of my torch? They were brought to you last night!"

"We finished them, your lordship."

"Very well. This very day, your day is finished, you will die, you will disappear, and we shall break you off. Here you will hide your faces: you are to be sacrificed!" said One and Seven Death.

And then they were sacrificed and buried. They were buried at the Place of Ball Game Sacrifice, as it is called. The head of One Hunahpu was cut off; only his body was buried with his younger brother.

"Put his head in the fork of the tree that stands by the road," said One and Seven Death.

And when his head was put in the fork of the tree, the tree bore fruit. It would not have had any fruit, had not the head of One Hunahpu been put in the fork of the tree.

This is the calabash, as we call it today, or "the skull of One Hunahpu," as it is said.

And then One and Seven Death were amazed at the fruit of the tree. The fruit grows out everywhere, and it isn't clear where the head of One Hunahpu is; now it looks just the way the calabashes look. All the Xibalbans see this, when they come to look.

The state of the tree loomed large in their thoughts, because it came about at the same time the head of One Hunahpu was put in the fork. The Xibalbans said among themselves:

"No one is to pick the fruit, nor is anyone to go beneath the tree," they said. They restricted themselves; all of Xibalba held back.

It isn't clear which is the head of One Hunahpu; now it's exactly the same as the fruit of the tree. Calabash came to be its name, and much was said about it. A maiden heard about it, and here we shall tell of her arrival.

AND HERE IS THE ACCOUNT OF A MAIDEN, the daughter of a lord named Blood Gatherer.

And this is when a maiden heard of it, the daughter of a lord. Blood Gatherer is the name of her father, and Blood Moon is the name of the maiden.

And when he heard the account of the fruit of the tree, her father retold it. And she was amazed at the account:

"I'm not acquainted with that tree they talk about. ' "Its fruit is truly sweet!" they say,' I hear," she said.

Next, she went all alone and arrived where the tree stood. It stood at the Place of Ball Game Sacrifice:

"What? Well! What's the fruit of this tree? Shouldn't this tree bear something sweet? They shouldn't die, they shouldn't be wasted. Should I pick one?" said the maiden.

And then the bone spoke; it was here in the fork of the tree:

BLOOD MOON IS THE NAME OF THE MAIDEN: *The lowland Maya moon goddess sits on a platform that represents the sky, and receives an offering. Her lunar identity is revealed in part by the crescent-shaped object she wears tucked under her arm and curving up behind her back to touch her shoulder. From the Dresden Codex.*

DRAWING BY CARLOS A. VILLACORTA

"Why do you want a mere bone, a round thing in the branches of a tree?" said the head of One Hunahpu when it spoke to the maiden. "You don't want it," she was told.

"I do want it," said the maiden.

"Very well. Stretch out your right hand here, so I can see it," said the bone.

"Yes," said the maiden. She stretched out her right hand, up there in front of the bone.

And then the bone spit out its saliva, which landed squarely in the hand of the maiden.

And then she looked in her hand, she inspected it right away, but the bone's saliva wasn't in her hand.

"It is just a sign I have given you, my saliva, my spittle. This, my head, has nothing on it—just bone, nothing of meat. It's just the same with the head of a great lord: it's just the flesh that makes his face look good. And when he dies, people get frightened by his bones. After that, his son is like his saliva, his spittle, in his being, whether it be the son of a lord or the son of a craftsman, an orator. The father does not disappear, but goes on being fulfilled. Neither dimmed nor destroyed is the face of a lord, a warrior, craftsman, orator. Rather, he will leave his daughters and sons. So it is that I have done likewise through you. Now go up there on the face of the earth; you will not die. Keep the word. So be it," said the head of One and Seven Hunahpu—they were of one mind when they did it.

This was the word Hurricane, Newborn Thunderbolt, Sudden Thunderbolt had given them. In the same way, by the time the maiden returned to her home, she had been given many instructions. Right away something was generated in her belly, from the saliva alone, and this was the generation of Hunahpu and Xbalanque.

And when the maiden got home and six months had passed, she was found out by her father. Blood Gatherer is the name of her father.

A ND AFTER THE MAIDEN WAS NOTICED BY HER FATHER, when he saw that she was now with child, all the lords then shared their thoughts —One and Seven Death, along with Blood Gatherer:

"This daughter of mine is with child, lords. It's just a bastard," Blood Gatherer said when he joined the lords.

"Very well. Get her to open her mouth. If she doesn't tell, then sacrifice her. Go far away and sacrifice her."

TAKE HER AWAY FOR SACRIFICE: *The merchant lord of the underworld (the lowland Maya equivalent of Blood Gatherer) sends away the moon goddess. Sitting on his hat is his owl messenger. From the Dresden Codex.*

DRAWING BY CARLOS A. VILLACORTA

"Very well, your lordships," he replied. After that, he questioned his daughter:

"Who is responsible for the child in your belly, my daughter?" he said.

"There is no child, my father, sir; there is no man whose face I've known," she replied.

"Very well. It really is a bastard you carry! Take her away for sacrifice, you Military Keepers of the Mat. Bring back her heart in a bowl, so the lords can take it in their hands this very day," the owls were told, the four of them.

Then they left, carrying the bowl. When they left they took the maiden by the hand, bringing along the White Dagger, the instrument of sacrifice.

"It would not turn out well if you sacrificed me, messengers, because it is not a bastard that's in my belly. What's in my belly generated all by itself when I went to marvel at the head of One Hunahpu, which is there at the Place of Ball Game Sacrifice. So please stop: don't do your sacrifice, messengers," said the maiden. Then they talked:

"What are we going to use in place of her heart? We were told by her father:

'Bring back her heart. The lords will take it in their hands, they will satisfy themselves, they will make themselves familiar with its composition. Hurry, bring it back in a bowl, put her heart in the bowl.' Isn't that what we've been told? What shall we deliver in the bowl? What we want above all is that you should not die," said the messengers.

"Very well. My heart must not be theirs, nor will your homes be here. Nor will you simply force people to die, but hereafter, what will be truly yours will be the true bearers of bastards. And hereafter, as for One and

Seven Death, only blood, only nodules of sap, will be theirs. So be it that these things are presented before them, and not that hearts are burned before them. So be it: use the fruit of a tree," said the maiden. And it was red tree sap she went out to gather in the bowl.

After it congealed, the substitute for her heart became round. When the sap of the croton tree was tapped, tree sap like blood, it became the substitute for her blood. When she rolled the blood around inside there, the sap of the croton tree, it formed a surface like blood, glistening red now, round inside the bowl. When the tree was cut open by the maiden, the so-called cochineal croton, the sap is what she called blood, and so there is talk of "nodules of blood."

"So you have been blessed with the face of the earth. It shall be yours," she told the owls.

"Very well, maiden. We'll show you the way up there. You just walk on ahead; we have yet to deliver this apparent duplicate of your heart before the lords," said the messengers.

And when they came before the lords, they were all watching closely:

"Hasn't it turned out well?" said One Death.

"It has turned out well, your lordships, and this is her heart. It's in the bowl."

"Very well. So I'll look," said One Death, and when he lifted it up with his fingers, its surface was soaked with gore, its surface glistened red with blood.

"Good. Stir up the fire, put it over the fire," said One Death.

After that they dried it over the fire, and the Xibalbans savored the aroma. They all ended up standing here, they leaned over it intently. They found the smoke of the blood to be truly sweet!

THE OWLS WENT TO SHOW THE MAIDEN THE WAY OUT: *Flying above the moon goddess (and thus appearing above the earth ahead of her) is the owl messenger of the merchant god of the underworld. From the Dresden Codex.*

DRAWING BY CARLOS A. VILLACORTA

And while they stayed at their cooking, the owls went to show the maiden the way out. They sent her up through a hole onto the earth, and then the guides returned below.

In this way the lords of Xibalba were defeated by a maiden; all of them were blinded.

And here, where the mother of One Monkey and One Artisan lived, was where the woman named Blood Moon arrived.

AND WHEN BLOOD MOON CAME TO THE MOTHER OF ONE MONKEY AND ONE ARTISAN, her children were still in her belly, but it wasn't very long before the birth of Hunahpu and Xbalanque, as they are called.

And when the woman came to the grandmother, the woman said to the grandmother:

"I've come, my lady. I'm your daughter-in-law and I'm your child, my lady," she said when she came here to the grandmother.

"Where do you come from? As for my little babies, didn't they die in Xibalba? And these two remain as their sign and their word: One Monkey and One Artisan are their names. So if you've come to see my children, get out of here!" the maiden was told by the grandmother.

"Even so, I really am your daughter-in-law. I am already his, I belong to One Hunahpu. What I carry is his. One Hunahpu and Seven Hunahpu are alive, they are not dead. They have merely made a way for the light to show itself, my mother-in-law, as you will see when you look at the faces of what I carry," the grandmother was told.

And One Monkey and One Artisan have been keeping their grandmother entertained: all they do is play and sing, all they work at is writing and carving, every day, and this cheers the heart of their grandmother.

And then the grandmother said:

"I don't want you, no thanks, my daughter-in-law. It's just a bastard in your belly, you trickster! These children of mine who are named by you are dead," said the grandmother.

"Truly, what I say to you is so!"

"Very well, my daughter-in-law, I hear you. So get going, get their food so they can eat. Go pick a big netful of ripe corn ears, then come back—since you are already my daughter-in-law, as I understand it," the maiden was told.

"Very well," she replied.

After that, she went to the garden; One Monkey and One Artisan had a garden. The maiden followed the path they had cleared and arrived

ALL THEY WORK AT IS WRITING: *Two monkey scribes sit on either side of a thick screen-fold book, discussing a page they have opened. The scribe on the left holds a writing instrument in his hand. From a Late Classic Maya vase.*

DRAWING BY STEPHEN D. HOUSTON

there in the garden, but there was only one clump, there was no other plant, no second or third. That one clump had borne its ears. So then the maiden's heart stopped:

"It looks like I'm a sinner, a debtor! Where will I get the netful of food she asked for?" she said. And then the guardians of food were called upon by her:

> "Come on out, rise up now, come on out, stand up now:
> Thunder Woman, Yellow Woman,
> Cacao Woman and Cornmeal Woman,
> thou guardian of the food of One Monkey, One Artisan,"

said the maiden.

And then she took hold of the silk, the bunch of silk at the top of the ear. She pulled it straight out, she didn't pick the ear, and the ear reproduced itself to make food for the net. It filled the big net.

And then the maiden came back, but animals carried her net. When she got back she went to put the pack frame in the corner of the house, so it would look to the grandmother as if she had arrived with a load.

And then, when the grandmother saw the food, a big netful:

"Where did that food of yours come from? You've leveled the place! I'm going to see if you've brought back our whole garden!" said the grandmother.

And then she went off, she went to look at the garden, but the one clump was still there, and the place where the net had been put at the foot of it was still obvious.

And the grandmother came back in a hurry, and she got back home, and she said to the maiden:

"The sign is still there. You really are my daughter-in-law! I'll have to keep watching what you do. These grandchildren of mine are already showing genius," the maiden was told.

Now this is where we shall speak of the birth of Hunahpu and Xbalanque.

AND THIS IS THEIR BIRTH; WE SHALL TELL OF IT HERE.

Then it came to the day of their birth, and the maiden named Blood Moon gave birth. The grandmother was not present when they were born; they were born suddenly. Two of them were born, named Hunahpu and Xbalanque. They were born in the mountains, and then they came into the house. Since they weren't sleeping:

"Throw them out of here! They're really loudmouths!" said the grandmother.

After that, when they put them on an anthill, they slept soundly there. And when they removed them from there, they put them in brambles next.

And this is what One Monkey and One Artisan wanted: that they should die on the anthill and die in the brambles. One Monkey and One Artisan wanted this because they were rowdy and flushed with jealousy. They didn't allow their younger brothers in the house at first, as if they didn't even know them, but even so they flourished in the mountains.

And One Monkey and One Artisan were great flautists and singers, and as they grew up they went through great suffering and pain. It had cost them suffering to become great knowers. Through it all they became flautists, singers, and writers, carvers. They did everything well. They simply knew it when they were born, they simply had genius. And they were the successors of their fathers who had gone to Xibalba, their dead fathers.

Since One Monkey and One Artisan were great knowers, in their hearts they already realized everything when their younger brothers

104

came into being, but they didn't reveal their insight because of their jealousy. The anger in their hearts came down on their own heads; no great harm was done. They were decoyed by Hunahpu and Xbalanque, who merely went out shooting every day. These two got no love from the grandmother, or from One Monkey and One Artisan. They weren't given their meals; the meals had been prepared and One Monkey and One Artisan had already eaten them before they got there.

But Hunahpu and Xbalanque aren't turning red with anger; rather, they just let it go, even though they know their proper place, which they see as clear as day. So they bring birds when they arrive each day, and One Monkey and One Artisan eat them. Nothing whatsoever is given to Hunahpu and Xbalanque, either one of them. All One Monkey and One Artisan do is play and sing.

And then Hunahpu and Xbalanque arrived again, but now they came in here without bringing their birds, so the grandmother turned red:

"What's your reason for not bringing birds?" Hunahpu and Xbalanque were asked.

"There are some, our dear grandmother, but our birds just got hung up in a tree," they said, "and there's no way to get up the tree after them, our dear grandmother, and so we'd like our elder brothers to please go with us, to please go get the birds down," they said.

"Very well. We'll go with you at dawn," the elder brothers replied.

Now they had won, and they gathered their thoughts, the two of them, about the fall of One Monkey and One Artisan:

"We'll just turn their very being around with our words. So be it, since they have caused us great suffering. They wished that we might die and disappear—we, their younger brothers. Just as they wished us to be slaves here, so we shall defeat them there. We shall simply make a sign of it," they said to each other.

And then they went there beneath a tree, the kind named yellow tree, together with the elder brothers. When they got there they started shooting. There were countless birds up in the tree, chittering, and the elder brothers were amazed when they saw the birds. And not one of these birds fell down beneath the tree:

"Those birds of ours don't fall down; just go throw them down," they told their elder brothers.

"Very well," they replied.

And then they climbed up the tree, and the tree began to grow, its trunk got thicker.

After that, they wanted to get down, but now One Monkey and One

Artisan couldn't make it down from the tree. So they said, from up in the tree:

"How can we grab hold? You, our younger brothers, take pity on us! Now this tree looks frightening to us, dear younger brothers," they said from up in the tree. Then Hunahpu and Xbalanque told them:

"Undo your pants, tie them around your hips, with the long end trailing like a tail behind you, and then you'll be better able to move," they were told by their younger brothers.

"All right," they said.

And then they left the ends of their loincloths trailing, and all at once these became tails. Now they looked like mere monkeys.

After that they went along in the trees of the mountains, small and great. They went through the forests, now howling, now keeping quiet in the branches of trees.

Such was the defeat of One Monkey and One Artisan by Hunahpu and Xbalanque. They did it by means of their genius alone.

And when they got home they said, when they came to their grandmother and mother:

"Our dear grandmother, something has happened to our elder brothers. They've become simply shameless, they're like animals now," they said.

"If you've done something to your elder brothers, you've knocked me down and stood me on my head. Please don't do anything to your elder brothers, my dear grandchildren," the grandmother said to Hunahpu and Xbalanque. And they told their grandmother:

"Don't be sad, our dear grandmother. You will see the faces of our elder brothers again. They'll come, but this will be a test for you, our dear grandmother. Will you please not laugh while we test their destiny?" they said.

And then they began playing. They played "Hunahpu Monkey."

AND THEN THEY SANG, THEY PLAYED, THEY DRUMMED. When they took up their flutes and drums, their grandmother sat down with them, then they played, they sounded out the tune, the song that got its name then. "Hunahpu Monkey" is the name of the tune.

And then One Monkey and One Artisan came back, dancing when they arrived.

And then, when the grandmother looked, it was their ugly faces the grandmother saw. Then she laughed, the grandmother could not hold

DANCING WHEN THEY
ARRIVED: *A monkey scribe
dances with a mirror in his
right hand. From a Late
Classic Maya vase.*

DRAWING BY KARL TAUBE

back her laughter, so they just left right away, out of her sight again, they went up and away in the forest.

"Why are you doing that, our dear grandmother? We'll only try four times; only three times are left. We'll call them with the flute, with song. Please hold back your laughter. We'll try again," said Hunahpu and Xbalanque.

Next they played again, then they came back, dancing again, they arrived again, in the middle of the patio of the house. As before, what they did was delightful; as before, they tempted their grandmother to laugh. Their grandmother laughed at them soon enough. The monkeys looked truly ridiculous, with the skinny little things below their bellies and their tails wiggling in front of their breasts. When they came back the grandmother had to laugh at them, and they went back into the mountains.

"Please, why are you doing that, our dear grandmother? Even so, we'll try it a third time now," said Hunahpu and Xbalanque.

Again they played, again they came dancing, but their grandmother held back her laughter. Then they climbed up here, cutting right across the building, with thin red lips, with faces blank, puckering their lips, wiping their mouths and faces, suddenly scratching themselves. And when the grandmother saw them again, the grandmother burst out laughing again, and again they went out of sight because of the grandmother's laughter.

107

SUDDENLY SCRATCHING
THEMSELVES: *This spider
monkey has his genitals
showing, or what the Popol
Vuh calls "the skinny little
things below their bellies."
From a Late Classic Maya
vase.*

DRAWING BY THE AUTHOR

"Even so, our dear grandmother, we'll get their attention."

So for the fourth time they called on the flute, but they didn't come back again. The fourth time they went straight into the forest. So they told their grandmother:

"Well, we've tried, our dear grandmother. They came at first, and we've tried calling them again. So don't be sad. We're here—we, your grandchildren. Just love our mother, dear grandmother. Our elder brothers will be remembered. So be it: they have lived here and they have been named; they are to be called One Monkey and One Artisan," said Hunahpu and Xbalanque.

So they were prayed to by the flautists and singers among the ancient people, and the writers and carvers prayed to them. In ancient times they turned into animals, they became monkeys, because they just magnified themselves, they abused their younger brothers. Just as they wished them to be slaves, so they themselves were brought low. One Monkey and One Artisan were lost then, they became animals, and this is now their place forever.

Even so, they were flautists and singers; they did great things while they lived with their grandmother and mother.

ND NOW THEY BEGAN TO ACT OUT THEIR SELF-REVELATION before their grandmother and mother. First they made a garden:

"We'll just do some gardening, our dear grandmother and mother," they said. "Don't worry. We're here, we're your grandchildren, we're the successors of our elder brothers," said Hunahpu and Xbalanque.

And then they took up their axe, their mattock, their hoe; each of them went off with a blowgun on his shoulder. They left the house having instructed their grandmother to give them their food:

"At midday bring our food, dear grandmother," they said.

"Very well, my dear grandchildren," said their grandmother.

After that, they went to their gardening. They simply stuck their mattock in the ground, and the mattock simply cultivated the ground.

And it wasn't only the mattock that cultivated, but also the axe. In the same way, they stuck it in the trunk of a tree; in the same way, it cut into the tree by itself, felling, scattering, felling all the trees and bushes, now leveling, mowing down the trees.

Just the one axe did it, and the mattock, breaking up thick masses, countless stalks and brambles. Just one mattock was doing it, breaking up countless things, just clearing off whole mountains, small and great.

And then they gave instructions to that creature named the mourning dove. They sat up on a big stump, and Hunahpu and Xbalanque said:

"Just watch for our grandmother, bringing our food. Cry out right away when she comes, and then we'll grab the mattock and axe."

"Very well," said the mourning dove.

This is because all they're doing is shooting; they're not really doing any gardening.

And as soon as the dove cries out they come running, one of them grabbing the mattock and the other grabbing the hoe, and they're tying up their hair.

One of them deliberately rubs dirt on his hands; he dirties his face as well, so he's just like a real gardener.

And as for the other one, he deliberately dumps wood chips on his head, so he's like a real woodcutter.

Once their grandmother has seen them they eat, but they aren't really doing their gardening; she brings their food for nothing. And when they get home:

"We're really ready for bed, our dear grandmother," they say when they arrive. Deliberately they massage, they stretch their legs, their arms in front of their grandmother.

And when they went on the second day and arrived at the garden, it had all grown up high again. Every tree and bush, every stalk and bramble had put itself back together again when they arrived.

"Who's been picking us clean?" they said.

And these are the ones who are doing it, all the animals, small and great: puma, jaguar, deer, rabbit, fox, coyote, peccary, coati, small birds, great birds. They are the ones who did it; they did it in just one night.

After that, they started the garden all over again. Just as before, the ground worked itself, along with the woodcutting.

And then they shared their thoughts, there on the cleared and broken ground:

"We'll simply have to keep watch over our garden. Then, whatever may be happening here, we'll find out about it," they said when they shared their thoughts. And when they arrived at the house:

"How could we get picked clean, our dear grandmother? Our garden was tall thickets and groves all over again when we got there a while ago, our dear grandmother," they said to their grandmother and mother. "So we'll go keep watch, because what's happening to us is no good," they said.

After that, they wound everything up, and then they went back to the clearing.

And there they took cover, and when they were well hidden there, all the animals gathered together, each one sat on its haunches, all the animals, small and great.

And this was the middle of the night when they came. They all spoke when they came. This is what they said:

"Arise, conjoin, you trees!
Arise, conjoin, you bushes!"

they said. Then they made a great stir beneath the trees and bushes, then they came nearer, and then they showed their faces.

The first of these were the puma and jaguar. The boys tried to grab them, but they did not give themselves up. When the deer and rabbit came near they only got them by the tail, which just broke off: the deer left its tail in their hands. When they grabbed the tail of the deer, along with the tail of the rabbit, the tails were shortened. But the fox, coyote, and peccary, coati did not give themselves up. All the animals went by in front of Hunahpu and Xbalanque.

110

So NOW THERE WAS FIRE IN THEIR HEARTS, because they didn't catch them. And one more came, the last one now, jumping as he came, then they cut him off. In their net they caught the rat.

And then they grabbed him and squeezed him behind the head. They tried to choke him; they burned his tail over a fire. Ever since the rat's tail got caught, there's been no hair on his tail, and his eyes have been the way they are since the boys tried to choke him, Hunahpu and Xbalanque.

"I will not die by your hand! Gardening is not your job, but there is something that is," said the rat.

"Where is what is ours? Go ahead and name it," the boys told the rat.

"Will you let me go then? My word is in my belly, and after I name it for you, you'll give me my morsel of food," said the rat.

"We'll give you your food, so name it," he was told.

"Very well. It's something that belonged to your fathers, named One Hunahpu and Seven Hunahpu, who died in Xibalba. What remains is their gaming equipment. They left it up under the roof of the house: their kilts, their wrist guards, their rubber ball. But your grandmother doesn't take these down in front of you, because this is how your fathers died."

"You know the truth, don't you!" the boys told the rat.

There was great joy in their hearts when they got word of the rubber ball. When the rat had named it they gave the rat his food, and this is his food: corn kernels, squash seeds, chili, beans, pataxte, cacao. These are his.

"If anything of yours is stored or gets wasted, then gnaw away," the rat was told by Hunahpu and Xbalanque.

"Very well, boys. But what will your grandmother say if she sees me?" he said.

"Don't be fainthearted. We're here. We know what our grandmother needs to be told. We'll set you up under the corner of the roof right away. When that's taken care of you'll go straight to where the things were left, and we'll look up there under the roof, but it's our stew we'll be looking at," they told the rat when they gave him his instructions.

Hunahpu and Xbalanque made their plans overnight and arrived right at noon, and it wasn't obvious that they had a rat with them when they arrived. One of them went right inside the house when he reached it, while the other went to the corner of the house, quickly setting up the rat. And then they asked their grandmother for their meal:

"Just grind something for our stew, we want chili sauce, our dear grandmother," they said.

After that, she ground chili for their stew. A bowl of broth was set out in front of them, but they were just fooling their grandmother and mother. They had emptied the water jar:

"We're really parched! Bring us a drink," they told their grandmother.

"Yes," she said, then she went, and they kept on eating. They weren't really hungry; they just put on false appearances.

And then they saw the rat reflected in their chili sauce: here was the rat loosening the ball that had been left in the peak of the roof. When they saw him in the chili sauce they sent a mosquito, that creature the mosquito, similar to a gnat. He went to the water, then he punctured the side of the grandmother's jar. The water just gushed out from the side of her jar. She tried, but she could not stop up the side of her jar.

"What has our grandmother done? We're choking for lack of water, our parched throats will do us in," they told their mother, then they sent her there.

After that, the rat cut the ball loose. It dropped from beneath the roof, along with the yokes, wrist guards, kilts. These were taken away then; they went to hide them on the road, the road to the ball court.

After that, they went to join their grandmother at the water, and their grandmother and mother were unable to stop up the side of the jar, either one of them.

After that, the boys arrived, each with his blowgun. When they arrived at the water:

"What have you done? We got weary at heart, so we came," they said.

"Look at the side of my jar! It cannot be stopped," said their grandmother, and they quickly stopped it up.

And they came back together, the two of them ahead of their grandmother.

In this way, the matter of the rubber ball was arranged.

Happy now, they went to play ball at the court. So they played ball at a distance, all by themselves. They swept out the court of their fathers.

And then it came into the hearing of the lords of Xibalba:

"Who's begun a game again up there, over our heads? Don't they have any shame, stomping around this way? Didn't One and Seven Hunahpu die trying to magnify themselves in front of us? So, you must deliver another summons," they said as before, One and Seven Death, all the lords.

"They are hereby summoned," they told their messengers. "You are to say, on reaching them:

' "They must come," say the lords, "We would play ball with them here. In seven days we'll have a game," say the lords,' you will say when you arrive," the messengers were told.

And then they came along a wide roadway, the road to the house of the boys, which actually ended at their house, so that the messengers came directly to their grandmother. As for the boys, they were away playing ball when the messengers of Xibalba got there.

" 'Truly, they are to come,' say the lords," said the messengers of Xibalba. So then and there the day was specified by the messengers of Xibalba:

" 'In seven days our game will take place,' " Xmucane was told there.

"Very well. They'll go when the day comes, messengers," said the grandmother, and the messengers left. They went back.

So now the grandmother's heart was broken:

"How can I send for my grandchildren? Isn't it really Xibalba, just as it was when the messengers came long ago, when their fathers went to die?" said the grandmother, sobbing, at home by herself.

After that a louse came down where it could be seen, and then she picked it up and put it in her hand, and the louse moved around with fits and starts.

"My grandchild, perhaps you might like to take my message, to go where my grandchildren are, at the ball court," the louse was told when he went as a message bearer:

" 'A messenger has come to your grandmother,' you will say. ' "You are to come:

'In seven days they are to come,' say the messengers of Xibalba," says your grandmother,' you will say," the louse was told.

Then he went off, and he went in fits and starts, and sitting in the road was a boy named Tamazul, the toad.

"Where are you going?" said the toad to the louse.

"My word is contained in my belly. I'm going to the two boys," said the louse to Tamazul.

"Very well. But I notice you're not very fast," the louse was told by the toad. "Wouldn't you like me to swallow you? You'll see, I'll run bent over this way, we'll arrive in a hurry."

TAMAZUL, THE TOAD: *Trailing down the back of this toad is a piece of skin he is shedding. From a Late Classic Maya vase.*

DRAWING BY KARL TAUBE

"Very well," said the louse to the toad.

After that, when he had been united with the toad, the toad hopped. He went along now, but he didn't run.

After that, the toad met a big snake named Zaquicaz:

"Where are you going, Tamazul boy?" the toad was asked next by Zaquicaz.

"I'm a messenger. My word is in my belly," the toad next said to the snake.

"But I notice you're not fast. Listen to me, I'll get there in a hurry," said the snake to the toad.

"Get going," he was told, so then the toad was next swallowed by Zaquicaz. When snakes get their food today they swallow toads.

So the snake was running as he went, then the snake was met from overhead by a laughing falcon, a large bird. The snake was swallowed up by the falcon, and then he arrived above the court. When hawks get their food, they eat snakes in the mountains.

And when the falcon arrived he alighted on the rim of the ball court. Hunahpu and Xbalanque were happy then, they were playing ball when the falcon arrived.

So then the falcon cried out:

"Wak-ko! Wak-ko!"

said the falcon as he cried.

"Who's crying out there? Come on! Our blowguns!" they said. And they shot the falcon, landing their blowgun shot right in his eye. Wobbling, he fell down and they went right there to grab him, then they asked him:

"What are you after?" they said to the falcon.

"My word is contained in my belly. But heal my eye first, then I'll name it," said the falcon.

"Very well," they said.

Next they took a bit of rubber off the surface of the ball, then they put it on the falcon's eye. "Blood of sacrifice" was their name for it. As soon as he was treated by them, the falcon's vision became good again.

"So name it," they said to the falcon, and then he vomited a big snake.

"Speak up," they said next to the snake.

"Yes," he said next, then he vomited the toad.

"What's your errand? Tell it," the toad was told next.

"My word is contained in my belly," the toad said next, and then he tried to throw up, but there was no vomit, he just sort of drooled. He was trying, but there was no vomit.

After that, he had to be kicked by the boys.

"You trickster!" he was told, then they kicked him in the rear, and they crushed the bones of his rear end with their feet. When he tried again, he just sort of spit.

And then they pried the toad's mouth open, it was opened by the boys. They searched his mouth, and the louse had simply stuck in the toad's teeth, it was right there in his mouth. He hadn't swallowed it, but had only seemed to swallow.

And such was the defeat of the toad. It's not clear what kind of food they gave him, and because he didn't run he became mere meat for snakes.

"Tell it," the louse was told next, so then he named his word:

"Boys, your grandmother says:

'Summon them. A message came for them:

"From Xibalba comes the messenger of One and Seven Death:

THEY PUT IT ON THE FALCON'S EYE:
*The laughing falcon, alone among the
hawks and falcons of Mesoamerica, has
black feathers around the eye.*

DRAWING BY THE AUTHOR

' "In seven days they are to come here. We'll play ball. Their gaming equipment must come along: rubber ball, yokes, arm guards, kilts. This will make for some excitement here," say the lords,' is the word that came from them," ' says your grandmother. So your grandmother says you must come. Truly your grandmother cries, she calls out to you to come."

"Isn't it the truth!" the boys said in their thoughts. When they heard it they left at once and got to their grandmother, but they went there only to give their grandmother instructions:

"We're on our way, dear grandmother. We're just giving you instructions. So here is the sign of our word. We'll leave it with you. Each of us will plant an ear of green corn. We'll plant them in the center of our house. When the corn dries up, this will be a sign of our death:

'Perhaps they died,' you'll say, when it dries up. And when the sprouting comes:

'Perhaps they live,' you'll say, our dear grandmother and mother. From now on, this is the sign of our word. We're leaving it with you," they said, then they left.

Hunahpu planted one and Xbalanque planted another. They were planted right there in the house: neither in the mountains nor where the earth is damp, but where the earth is dry, in the middle of the inside of their house. They left them planted there, then went off, each with his own blowgun.

T HEY WENT DOWN TO XIBALBA, quickly going down the face of a cliff, and they crossed through the change of canyons. They passed right through the birds—the ones called throng birds—and then they crossed Pus River and Blood River, intended as traps by Xibalba. They did not step in, but simply crossed over on their blowguns, and then they went on over to the Crossroads. But they knew about the roads of Xibalba: Black Road, White Road, Red Road, Green Road.

And there they summoned that creature named the mosquito. Having heard that he's a spy, they sent him ahead:

"Bite them one by one. First bite the first one seated there, then bite every last one of them, and it will be yours alone to suck the blood of people in the roads," the mosquito was told.

"Very well," replied the mosquito, then he took Black Road and stopped at the two manikins, or woodcarvings, that were seated first. They were all dressed up, and he bit the first of them. It didn't speak, so he bit again. When he bit the one seated second, again it didn't speak,

THAT CREATURE NAMED THE MOSQUITO: *In this drawing from a Late Classic Maya vase, the mosquito wears its weapon on the front of its headdress and dribbles blood from its anus.*

DRAWING BY KARL TAUBE

and then he bit the third one, the one seated third actually being One Death.

"Yeow!" each one said as he was bitten.

"What?" each one replied.

"Ouch!" said One Death.

"What is it, One Death?"

"Something's bitten me."

"It's—ouch! There's something that's bitten me," the one seated fourth said next.

"What is it, Seven Death?"

"Something's bitten me." The one seated fifth spoke next:

"Ow! Ow!" he said.

"What, Scab Stripper?" Seven Death said to him.

"Something's bitten me," he said next. The one seated sixth was bitten:

"Ouch!"

"What is it, Blood Gatherer?" Scab Stripper said to him.

"Something's bitten me," he said next. Then the one seated seventh was bitten:

"Ouch!" he said next.

"What is it, Demon of Pus?" Blood Gatherer said to him.

"Something's bitten me," he said next. The one seated eighth was bitten next:

117

"Ouch!" he said next.

"What is it, Demon of Jaundice?" Demon of Pus said to him next.

"Something's bitten me," he said next. Then the one seated ninth was bitten next:

"Ouch!" he said.

"What is it, Bone Scepter?" Demon of Jaundice said to him.

"Something's bitten me," he said next. Then the one seated tenth in order was bitten next:

"Ouch!"

"What is it, Skull Scepter?" said Bone Scepter.

"Something's bitten me," he said next. Then the one seated eleventh was bitten next:

"Ouch!" he said next.

"What is it, Wing?" Skull Scepter said to him next.

"Something's bitten me," he said next. Then the one seated twelfth was bitten next:

"Ouch!" he said next.

"What, Packstrap?" he was asked next.

"Something's bitten me," he said next. Then the one seated thirteenth was bitten next:

"Ouch!"

"What is it, Bloody Teeth?" Packstrap said to him.

"Something's bitten me," he said next. Then the one seated fourteenth was bitten next:

"Ouch! Something's bitten me," he said next.

"Bloody Claws?" Bloody Teeth said to him next.

And such was the naming of their names, they named them all among themselves. They showed their faces and named their names, each one named by the one ranking above him, and naming in turn the name of the one seated next to him. There wasn't a single name they missed, naming every last one of their names when they were bitten by the hair that Hunahpu had plucked from his own shin. It wasn't really a mosquito that bit them. It went to hear all their names for Hunahpu and Xbalanque.

After that Hunahpu and Xbalanque went on, and then they came to where the Xibalbans were:

"Bid the lords good day," said someone who was seated there. It was a deceiver who spoke.

"These aren't lords! These are manikins, woodcarvings!" they said as they came up.

And after that, they bid them good morning:

"Morning, One Death.   Morning, Seven Death.
Morning, Scab Stripper.   Morning, Blood Gatherer.
Morning, Demon of Pus.   Morning, Demon of Jaundice.
Morning, Bone Scepter.   Morning, Skull Scepter.
Morning, Wing.   Morning, Packstrap.
Morning, Bloody Teeth.   Morning, Bloody Claws,"

they said when they arrived, and all of their identities were accounted for. They named every one of their names; there wasn't a single name they missed. When this was required of them, no name was omitted by them.

"Sit here," they were told. They were wanted on the bench, but they didn't want it:

"This bench isn't for us! It's just a stone slab for cooking," said Hunahpu and Xbalanque. They were not defeated.

"Very well. Just get in the house," they were told.

And after that, they entered Dark House. They were not defeated there. This was the first test they entered in Xibalba, and as far as the Xibalbans were concerned they were as good as defeated.

F IRST THEY ENTERED DARK HOUSE.

And after that, the messenger of One Death brought their torch, burning when it arrived, along with one cigar apiece.

" 'Here is their torch,' says the lord. 'They must return the torch in the morning, along with the cigars. They must return them intact,' say the lords," the messenger said when he arrived.

"Very well," they said, but they didn't burn the torch—instead, something that looked like fire was substituted. This was the tail of the macaw, which looked like a torch to the sentries. And as for the cigars, they just put fireflies at the tips of those cigars, which they kept lit all night.

"We've defeated them," said the sentries, but the torch was not consumed—it just looked that way. And as for the cigars, there wasn't anything burning there—it just looked that way. When these things were taken back to the lords:

"What's happening? Where did they come from? Who begot them and bore them? Our hearts are really hurting, because what they're doing to us is no good. They're different in looks and different in their very being," they said among themselves. And when they had summoned all the lords:

"Let's play ball, boys," the boys were told. And then they were asked by One and Seven Death:

"IT'S JUST A SKULL": *In this game the ball (just right of center) is marked with a skull in profile. From the mouths of the two players at left and the one at extreme right comes speech (resembling curling smoke), probably in the form of taunts like the ones hurled back and forth in the Popol Vuh. The first player to the left of the ball holds the severed head of the first player to the right, whose neck sprouts serpents (representing spurts of blood) and a squash vine (recalling an episode in which a squash serves as Hunahpu's head). From a relief panel in the great ball court at Chichén Itzá.*

"Where might you have come from? Please name it," Xibalba said to them.

"Well, wherever did we come from? We don't know," was all they said. They didn't name it.

"Very well then, we'll just go play ball, boys," Xibalba told them.

"Good," they said.

"Well, this is the one we should put in play, here's our rubber ball," said the Xibalbans.

"No thanks. This is the one to put in, here's ours," said the boys.

"No it's not. This is the one we should put in," the Xibalbans said again.

"Very well," said the boys.

"After all, it's just a decorated one," said the Xibalbans.

"Oh no it's not. It's just a skull, we say in return," said the boys.

"No it's not," said the Xibalbans.

"Very well," said Hunahpu. When it was sent off by Xibalba, the ball was stopped by Hunahpu's yoke.

And then, while Xibalba watched, the White Dagger came out from inside the ball. It went clattering, twisting all over the floor of the court.

120

DRAWING FROM ALFRED M. TOZZER, *CHICHEN ITZA AND ITS CENOTE OF SACRIFICE:* PHOTO BY HILLEL BURGER © 1984 BY THE
PRESIDENT AND FELLOWS OF HARVARD COLLEGE

"What's that!" said Hunahpu and Xbalanque. "Death is the only thing
you want for us! Wasn't it *you* who sent a summons to us, and wasn't it
your messenger who went? Truly, take pity on us, or else we'll just
leave," the boys told them.

And this is what had been ordained for the boys: that they should have
died right away, right there, defeated by that knife. But it wasn't like
that. Instead, Xibalba was again defeated by the boys.

"Well, don't go, boys. We can still play ball, but we'll put yours into
play," the boys were told.

"Very well," they said, and this was the time for their rubber ball, so
the ball was dropped in.

And after that, they specified the prize:

"What should our prize be?" asked the Xibalbans.

"It's yours for the asking," was all the boys said.

"We'll just win four bowls of flowers," said the Xibalbans.

"Very well. What kinds of flowers?" the boys asked Xibalba.

"One bowl of red petals, one bowl of white petals, one bowl of yellow
petals, and one bowl of whole ones," said the Xibalbans.

"Very well," said the boys, and then their ball was dropped in. The
boys were their equals in strength and made many plays, since they only

THEIR BALL WAS DROPPED IN: *Hunahpu (left) and a member of the Xibalba team (right) jointly hold a ball up with their arm guards just before putting it into play; the latter wears a trophy head on his back. From a relief carved on a stone ball-court marker at Copán.*

DRAWING BY BARBARA FASH

had very good thoughts. Then the boys gave themselves up in defeat, and the Xibalbans were glad when they were defeated:

"We've done well. We've beaten them on the first try," said the Xibalbans. "Where will they go to get the flowers?" they said in their hearts.

"Truly, before the night is over, you must hand over our flowers and our prize," the boys, Hunahpu and Xbalanque, were told by Xibalba.

"Very well. So we're also playing ball at night," they said when they accepted their charge.

AND AFTER THAT, THE BOYS NEXT ENTERED RAZOR HOUSE, the second test of Xibalba.

And this is when it was ordained that they be cut clear through with knives. It was intended to be quick, intended that they should die, but they did not die. They spoke to the knives then, they instructed them:

"This is yours: the flesh of all the animals," they told the knives, and they no longer moved—rather, each and every knife put down its point.

And this is how they stayed there overnight, in Razor House. Now they summoned all the ants:

> "Cutting ants, conquering ants, come now,
> all of you fetch all of them for us:
> flowers in bloom, prizes for lords."

"Very well," they replied. Then all the ants went to get the flowers, the plantings of One and Seven Death, who had already given instructions to the guardians of the flowers of Xibalba:

"Would you please watch our flowers? Don't let them get stolen. We've defeated these boys, so won't they come looking for the prize they owe us? Don't sleep tonight."

"Very well," they replied, but the guardians of the plants never knew a thing. Their only inclination was to stretch their mouths wide open, going from one perch to another in the trees and plants, repeating the same song:

> "Whip-poor-will! Whip-poor-will!"

one of them says as he cries.

> "Poor-willow! Poor-willow!"

says the other as he cries, the one named poorwill.

The two of them are the guards of the garden, the garden of One and Seven Death, but they don't notice the ants stealing what's under their guard, swarming, carrying away loads of flowers, coming to cut down the flowers in the trees, gathering these together with the flowers beneath the trees, while the guards just stretch their mouths wide open, not noticing the nibbling at their own tails, the nibbling at their own wings. The severed flowers rain down into the gathering and bunching here below, so that four bowls of flowers are easily filled, an acrobatic performance that lasts till dawn.

After that the messengers, the pages, arrive:

" 'They are to come,' says the lord: 'They must bring our prizes here right away,' " the boys were told.

"Very well," they said. Having loaded up the flowers, four bowls of them, they left and came before the lord, or lords, who received the flowers with pained looks.

With this, the Xibalbans were defeated. The boys had sent mere ants; in just one night the ants had taken the flowers and put them in the bowls.

With this, all the Xibalbans looked sick, they paled at the sight of the flowers.

After that, they summoned the flower guards:

"How did you allow our flowers to get stolen? These are *our* flowers! Here! Look!" the guards were told.

"We took no notice, your lordship, though our tails are the worse for it," they said.

And then their mouths were split wide, their payment for the theft of what was under their guard.

Such was the defeat of One and Seven Death by Hunahpu and Xbalanque, on account of which the whippoorwills got gaping mouths. Their mouths gape to this day.

Now after that, when the ball was dropped in, they just played to a tie. When they finished the game they made an arrangement with each other:

"At dawn again," said Xibalba.

"Very well," said the boys, then they were finished.

A ND NOW THEY ENTERED COLD HOUSE. There are countless drafts, thick-falling hail inside the house, the home of cold. They diminished the cold right away by shutting it out. The cold dissipated because of the boys. They did not die, but were alive when it dawned.

So, although Xibalba had wanted them to die there, they did not, but were alive when it dawned. They came out when the pages arrived and the guards left.

"Why haven't they died?" said the rulers of Xibalba. Again they were amazed at the feats of the boys, Hunahpu and Xbalanque.

S O NEXT THEY ENTERED JAGUAR HOUSE, the jaguar-packed home of jaguars:

"Don't eat *us*. There *is* something that should be yours," the jaguars were told.

With that, they scattered bones before the animals.

After that, the jaguars were wrestling around there, over the bones.

"So they've made good work of them, they've eaten their very hearts. Now that the boys have given themselves up, they've already been transformed into skeletons," said the sentries, all of them finding it sweet. But they hadn't died; they were well. They came out of Jaguar House.

"What sort of people are they? Where did they come from?" said all the Xibalbans.

So NEXT THEY ENTERED THE MIDST OF THE FIRE, a house of fire with only fire alone inside. They weren't burned by it, just toasted, just simmered, so they were well when it dawned. Although it had been ordained that they be quickly killed in there, overcome, they weren't, and instead it was the Xibalbans who lost heart over this.

Now THEY WERE PUT INSIDE BAT HOUSE, with bats alone inside the house, a house of snatch-bats, monstrous beasts, their snouts like knives, the instruments of death. To come before these is to be finished off at once.

When they were inside they just slept in their blowgun; they were not bitten by the members of the household. But this is where they gave one of themselves up because of a snatch-bat that came down, he came along just as one of them showed himself. They did it because it was actually what they were asking for, what they had in mind.

And all night the bats are making noise:

"Eek-eek! Eek-eek!"

they say, and they say it all night.

Then it let up a little. The bats were no longer moving around. So there, one of the boys crawled to the end of the blowgun, since Xbalanque said:

"Hunahpu? Can you see how long it is till dawn?"

"Well, perhaps I should look to see how long it is," he replied. So he kept trying to look out the muzzle of the blowgun, he tried to see the dawn.

SNATCH-BATS, MONSTROUS BEASTS: *The design on the bat's wings represents plucked-out eyes; the scroll-like forms issuing from his mouth are his shrieks. From a Late Classic Maya vase in the Chamá style, found in the same region as the Great Hollow where Hunahpu and Xbalanque descended into Xibalba.*

DRAWING BY THE AUTHOR

And then his head was taken off by a snatch-bat, leaving Hunahpu's body still stuffed inside.

"What's going on? Hasn't it dawned?" said Xbalanque. No longer is there any movement from Hunahpu. "What's this? Hunahpu hasn't left, has he? What have you done?" He no longer moves; now there is only heavy breathing.

After that, Xbalanque despaired:

"Alas! We've given it all up!" he said. And elsewhere, the head meanwhile went rolling onto the court, in accordance with the word of One and Seven Death, and all the Xibalbans were happy over the head of Hunahpu.

After that, Xbalanque summoned all the animals: coati, peccary, all the animals, small and great. It was at night, still nighttime when he asked them for their food:

"Whatever your foods are, each one of you: that's what I summoned you for, to bring your food here," Xbalanque told them.

"Very well," they replied, then they went to get what's theirs, then indeed they all came back.

HIS HEAD WAS TAKEN OFF: *Hunahpu stands headless with his arms bound. From the Dresden Codex.*

DRAWING BY CARLOS A. VILLACORTA

There's the one who only brought his rotten wood.

There's the one who only brought leaves.

There's the one who only brought stones.

There's the one who only brought earth, on through the varied foods of the animals, small and great, until the very last one remained: the coati. He brought a squash, bumping it along with his snout as he came.

And this became a simulated head for Hunahpu. His eyes were carved right away, then brains came from the thinker, from the sky. This was the Heart of Sky, Hurricane, who came down, came on down into Bat House. The face wasn't finished any too quickly; it came out well. His strength was just the same, he looked handsome, he spoke just the same.

And this is when it was trying to dawn, reddening along the horizon:

"Now make the streaks, man," the possum was told.

"Yes," said the old man. When he made the streaks he made it dark again; the old man made four streaks.

XBALANQUE SUMMONED ALL THE ANIMALS: *Here he brings a hummingbird to him. Around his mouth and on his back and thigh are patches of jaguar skin. From the Dresden Codex.*

DRAWING BY CARLOS A. VILLACORTA

127

THE POSSUM: *Bringing in a new year that begins on the day named E or Eb, a possum uses a backpack to carry the patron deity assigned to such years. There are four kinds of year in all, corresponding to the four streaks made by the possum who comes to the aid of Xbalanque. Drawing from the Dresden Codex.*

DRAWING BY CARLOS A. VILLACORTA

"Possum is making streaks," people say today, ever since he made the early dawn red and blue, establishing its very being.

"Isn't it good?" Hunahpu was asked.

"Good indeed," he replied. His head was as if it had every bone; it had become like his real head.

After that, they had a talk, they made arrangements with each other:

"How about not playing ball yourself? You should just make lots of threats, while I should be the one to take all the action," Xbalanque told him. After that, he gave instructions to a rabbit:

"Your place is there above the court, on top. Stay there among the ball bags," the rabbit was told by Xbalanque, "until the ball comes to you, then take off while I get to work," the rabbit was told. He got his instructions while it was still dark.

After that, when it dawned, both of them were just as well as ever.

And when the ball was dropped in again, it was the head of Hunahpu that rolled over the court:

> "We've won! You're done!
> Give up! You lost!"

they were told. But even so Hunahpu was shouting:

"Punt the head as a ball!" he told them.

"Well, we're not going to do them any more harm with threats," and with this the lords of Xibalba sent off the ball and Xbalanque received it, the ball was stopped by his yoke, then he hit it hard and it took off, the

128

IT WAS THE HEAD OF
HUNAHPU: *A member of the
Xibalba team goes down on one
knee and returns the ball with
his thigh, protected by a leather
kilt. The ball bears the name of
Hunahpu. From a relief carved
on an Early Classic Maya
ball-court marker from La
Esperanza, Chiapas.*

DRAWING BY THE AUTHOR

ball passed straight out of the court, bouncing just once, just twice, and stopping among the ball bags. Then the rabbit took off hopping, then they went off in pursuit, then all the Xibalbans went off, shouting, shrieking, they went after the rabbit, off went the whole of Xibalba.

After that, the boys got Hunahpu's head back. Then Xbalanque planted the squash; this is when he went to set the squash above the court.

So the head of Hunahpu was really a head again, and the two of them were happy again. And the others, those Xibalbans, were still going on in search of the ball.

After that, having recovered the ball from among the bags, the boys cried out to them:

"Come back! Here's the ball! We've found it!" they said, so they stopped. When the Xibalbans got back:

"Have we been seeing things?" they said. Then they began their ball game again, and they made equal plays on both sides again.

After that, the squash was punted by Xbalanque. The squash was wearing out; it fell on the court, bringing to light its light-colored seeds, as plain as day right in front of them.

"How did you get ahold of that? Where did it come from?" said Xibalba.

With this, the masters of Xibalba were defeated by Hunahpu and Xbalanque. There was great danger there, but they did not die from all the things that were done to them.

129

Aᴺᴰ ʜᴇʀᴇ ɪᴛ ɪs: ᴛʜᴇ ᴇᴘɪᴛᴀᴘʜ, ᴛʜᴇ ᴅᴇᴀᴛʜ ᴏꜰ Hᴜɴᴀʜᴘᴜ ᴀɴᴅ Xʙᴀʟᴀɴǫᴜᴇ.

Here it is: now we shall name their epitaph, their death. They did whatever they were instructed to do, going through all the dangers, the troubles that were made for them, but they did not die from the tests of Xibalba, nor were they defeated by all the voracious animals that inhabit Xibalba.

After that, they summoned two midmost seers, similar to readers. Here are their names: Xulu, Pacam, both knowers.

"Perhaps there will be questions from the lords of Xibalba about our death. They are thinking about how to overcome us because we haven't died, nor have we been defeated. We've exhausted all their tests. Not even the animals got us. So this is the sign, here in our hearts: their instrument for our death will be a stone oven. All the Xibalbans have gathered together. Isn't our death inevitable? So this is your plan, here we shall name it: if you come to be questioned by them about our death, once we've been burned, what will you say, Xulu, and you, Pacam? If they ask you:

'Wouldn't it be good if we dumped their bones in the canyon?'

'Perhaps it wouldn't be good, since they would only come back to life again,' you will say.

'Perhaps this would be good: we'll just hang them up in a tree,' they'll say to you next.

'Certainly that's no good, since you would see their faces,' you will say, and then they'll speak to you for the third time:

'Well, here's the only good thing: we'll just dump their bones in the river.' If that's what they ask you next:

'This is a good death for them, and it would also be good to grind their bones on a stone, just as hard corn is refined into flour, and refine each of them separately, and then:

'Spill them into the river,
sprinkle them on the water's way,
among the mountains, small and great,'

you will say, and then you will have carried out the instructions we've named for you," said little Hunahpu and Xbalanque. When they gave these instructions they already knew they would die.

130

THIS IS THE MAKING OF THE OVEN, the great stone oven. The Xibalbans made it like the places where the sweet drink is cooked, they opened it to a great width.

After that, messengers came to get the boys, the messengers of One and Seven Death:

" 'They must come. We'll go with the boys, to see the treat we've cooked up for them,' say the lords, you boys," they were told.

"Very well," they replied. They went running and arrived at the mouth of the oven.

And there they tried to force them into a game:

"Here, let's jump over our drink four times, clear across, one of us after the other, boys," they were told by One Death.

"You'll never put that one over on us. Don't we know what our death is, you lords? Watch!" they said, then they faced each other. They grabbed each other by the hands and went head first into the oven.

And there they died, together, and now all the Xibalbans were happy, raising their shouts, raising their cheers:

"We've really beaten them! They didn't give up easily," they said.

After that they summoned Xulu and Pacam, who kept their word: the bones went just where the boys had wanted them. Once the Xibalbans

WALKING ON STILTS: *A figure from the Madrid Codex.*

DRAWING BY CARLOS A. VILLACORTA

had done the divination, the bones were ground and spilled in the river, but they didn't go far—they just sank to the bottom of the water. They became handsome boys; they looked just the same as before when they reappeared.

A ND ON THE FIFTH DAY THEY REAPPEARED. They were seen in the water by the people. The two of them looked like catfish when their faces were seen by Xibalba. And having germinated in the waters, they appeared the day after that as two vagabonds, with rags before and rags behind, and rags all over too. They seemed unrefined when they were examined by Xibalba; they acted differently now.

It was only the Dance of the Poorwill, the Dance of the Weasel, only Armadillos they danced.

Only Swallowing Swords, only Walking on Stilts now they danced.

They performed many miracles now. They would set fire to a house, as if they were really burning it, and suddenly bring it back again. Now Xibalba was full of admiration.

Next they would sacrifice themselves, one of them dying for the other, stretched out as if in death. First they would kill themselves, but then they would suddenly look alive again. The Xibalbans could only admire what they did. Everything they did now was already the groundwork for their defeat of Xibalba.

And after that, news of their dances came to the ears of the lords, One and Seven Death. When they heard it they said:

"Who are these two vagabonds? Are they really such a delight? And is their dancing really that pretty? They do everything!" they said. An account of them had reached the lords. It sounded delightful, so then they entreated their messengers to notify them that they must come:

" ' "If only they'd come make a show for us, we'd wonder at them and marvel at them," say the lords,' you will say," the messengers were told. So they came to the dancers, then spoke the words of the lords to them.

"But we don't want to, because we're really ashamed. Just plain no. Wouldn't we be afraid to go inside there, into a lordly house? Because we'd really look bad. Wouldn't we just be wide-eyed? Take pity on us! Wouldn't we look like mere dancers to them? What would we say to our fellow vagabonds? There are others who also want us to dance today, to liven things up with us, so we can't do likewise for the lords, and likewise is not what we want, messengers," said Hunahpu and Xbalanque.

132

Even so, they were prevailed upon: through troubles, through torments, they went on their tortuous way. They didn't want to walk fast. Many times they had to be forced; the messengers went ahead of them as guides but had to keep coming back. And so they went to the lord.

AND THEY CAME TO THE LORDS. Feigning great humility, they bowed their heads all the way to the ground when they arrived. They brought themselves low, doubled over, flattened out, down to the rags, to the tatters. They really looked like vagabonds when they arrived.

So then they were asked what their mountain and tribe were, and they were also asked about their mother and father:

"Where do you come from?" they were asked.

"We've never known, lord. We don't know the identity of our mother

THEY DANCED THE ARMADILLO: *This dancer wears a scaly armadillo mask, plays a flute, and shakes a rattle. From a Late Classic Maya vase in the Chamá style, found in the same region as the Great Hollow where Hunahpu and Xbalanque descended into the Xibalba.*

DRAWING BY THE AUTHOR

133

THEN THEY TOOK HOLD OF A HUMAN
SACRIFICE: *The aged merchant god of
the underworld sits on a dais in his palace, with his owl messenger perched on
his hat. The women around the platform are all of noble rank; one of them
turns to watch the performance to the
left, in which two masked dancers
(probably Hunahpu and Xbalanque in
disguise) carry out a human sacrifice.
The left-hand dancer is applying an axe
to the back of the neck of the victim.
From a Late Classic Maya vase in the
Princeton University Art Museum.*

and father. We must've been small when they died," was all they said.
They didn't give any names.

"Very well. Please entertain us, then. What do you want us to give you
in payment?" they were asked.

"Well, we don't want anything. To tell the truth, we're afraid," they
told the lord.

"Don't be afraid. Don't be ashamed. Just dance this way: first you'll
dance to sacrifice yourselves, you'll set fire to my house after that, you'll
act out all the things you know. We want to be entertained. This is our
heart's desire, the reason you had to be sent for, dear vagabonds. We'll
give you payment," they were told.

So then they began their songs and dances, and then all the Xibalbans
arrived, the spectators crowded the floor, and they danced everything:
they danced the Weasel, they danced the Poorwill, they danced the
Armadillo. Then the lord said to them:

"Sacrifice my dog, then bring him back to life again," they were told.

"Yes," they said.

134

DRAWING REPRODUCED BY PERMISSION OF MICHAEL D. COE AND THE GROLIER CLUB

When they sacrificed the dog
   he then came back to life.
And that dog was really happy
   when he came back to life.
Back and forth he wagged his tail
   when he came back to life.

And the lord said to them:

"Well, you have yet to set my home on fire," they were told next, so then they set fire to the home of the lord. The house was packed with all the lords, but they were not burned. They quickly fixed it back again, lest the house of One Death be consumed all at once, and all the lords were amazed, and they went on dancing this way. They were overjoyed.

And then they were asked by the lord:

"You have yet to kill a person! Make a sacrifice without death!" they were told.

SACRIFICE YET AGAIN, EVEN DO IT TO YOURSELVES!: *At left is Hunahpu disguised as a Thunderbolt god, about to swing a lightning-striking axe; the catfish barbel on his cheek recalls the episode in which he and his brother appeared as catfish. Playfully waiting to have his head cut off is a prostrate Xbalanque, no longer limited to wearing a few patches of jaguar skin but rather appearing as a parody of himself. Next (from left to right) are a skeletal Xibalban who dances with delight, a dog who wags his tail (having survived his own decapitation), and a firefly bearing a torch (from the Dark House episode). From a Late Classic Maya vase in the Metropolitan Museum of Art.*

"Very well," they said.

And then they took hold of a human sacrifice.

And they held up a human heart on high.

And they showed its roundness to the lords.

And now One and Seven Death admired it, and now that person was brought right back to life. His heart was overjoyed when he came back to life, and the lords were amazed:

"Sacrifice yet again, even do it to yourselves! Let's see it! At heart, that's the dance we really want from you," the lords said now.

"Very well, lord," they replied, and then they sacrificed themselves.

A ND THIS IS THE SACRIFICE OF LITTLE HUNAHPU BY XBALANQUE. One by one his legs, his arms were spread wide. His head came off, rolled far away outside. His heart, dug out, was smothered in a leaf, and all the Xibalbans went crazy at the sight.

136

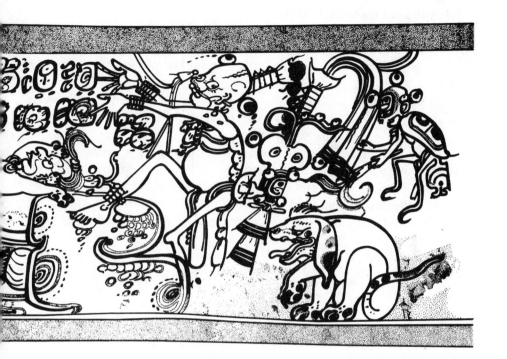

DRAWING REPRODUCED BY PERMISSION OF MICHAEL D. COE AND THE GROLIER CLUB

So now, only one of them was dancing there: Xbalanque.

"Get up!" he said, and Hunahpu came back to life. The two of them were overjoyed at this—and likewise the lords rejoiced, as if they were doing it themselves. One and Seven Death were as glad at heart as if they themselves were actually doing the dance.

And then the hearts of the lords were filled with longing, with yearning for the dance of little Hunahpu and Xbalanque, so then came these words from One and Seven Death:

"Do it to us! Sacrifice us!" they said. "Sacrifice both of us!" said One and Seven Death to little Hunahpu and Xbalanque.

"Very well. You ought to come back to life. What is death to you? And aren't we making you happy, along with the vassals of your domain?" they told the lords.

And this one was the first to be sacrificed: the lord at the very top, the one whose name is One Death, the ruler of Xibalba.

And with One Death dead, the next to be taken was Seven Death. They did not come back to life.

And then the Xibalbans were getting up to leave, those who had seen the lords die. They underwent heart sacrifice there, and the heart sacrifice was performed on the two lords only for the purpose of destroying them.

As soon as they had killed the one lord without bringing him back to life, the other lord had been meek and tearful before the dancers. He didn't consent, he didn't accept it:

"Take pity on me!" he said when he realized. All their vassals took the road to the great canyon, in one single mass they filled up the deep abyss. So they piled up there and gathered together, countless ants, tumbling down into the canyon, as if they were being herded there. And when they arrived, they all bent low in surrender, they arrived meek and tearful.

Such was the defeat of the rulers of Xibalba. The boys accomplished it only through wonders, only through self-transformation.

AND THEN THEY NAMED THEIR NAMES, they gave themselves names before all of Xibalba:

"Listen: we shall name our names, and we shall also name the names of our fathers for you. Here we are: we are little Hunahpu and Xbalanque by name. And these are our fathers, the ones you killed: One Hunahpu and Seven Hunahpu by name. And we are here to clear the road of the torments and troubles of our fathers. And so we have suffered all the troubles you've caused us. And so we are putting an end to all of you. We're going to kill you. No one can save you now," they were told. And then all the Xibalbans got down on the ground and cried out:

"Take pity on us, Hunahpu and Xbalanque! It is true that we wronged your fathers, the ones you name. Those two are buried at the Place of Ball Game Sacrifice," they replied.

"Very well. Now this is our word, we shall name it for you. All of you listen, you Xibalbans: because of this, your day and your descendants will not be great. Moreover, the gifts you receive will no longer be great, but reduced to scabrous nodules of sap. There will be no cleanly blotted blood for you, just griddles, just gourds, just brittle things broken to pieces. Further, you will only feed on creatures of the meadows and clearings. None of those who are born in the light, begotten in the light will be yours. Only the worthless will yield themselves up before you. These will be the guilty, the violent, the wretched, the afflicted. Wherever the blame is clear, that is where you will come in, rather than just making sudden attacks on people in general. And you will hear petitions over headed-up sap," all the Xibalbans were told.

Such was the beginning of their disappearance and the denial of their worship.

> Their ancient day was not a great one,
> these ancient people only wanted conflict,
> their ancient names are not really divine,
> but fearful is the ancient evil of their faces.
>
> They are makers of enemies, users of owls,
> they are inciters to wrongs and violence,
> they are masters of hidden intentions as well,
> they are black and white,
> masters of stupidity, masters of perplexity,

as it is said. By putting on appearances they cause dismay.

Such was the loss of their greatness and brilliance. Their domain did not return to greatness. This was accomplished by little Hunahpu and Xbalanque.

AND THIS IS THEIR GRANDMOTHER, CRYING AND CALLING OUT IN FRONT OF THE EARS OF GREEN CORN they left planted. Corn plants grew, then dried up.

And this was when they were burned in the oven; then the corn plants grew again.

And this was when their grandmother burned something, she burned copal before the ears of green corn as a memorial to them. There was happiness in their grandmother's heart the second time the corn plants sprouted. Then the ears were deified by their grandmother, and she gave them names: Middle of the House, Middle of the Harvest, Living Ears of Green Corn, Bed of Earth became their names.

And she named the ears Middle of the House, Middle of the Harvest, because they had planted them right in the middle of the inside of their home.

And she further named them Bed of Earth, Living Ears of Green Corn, since the ears had been placed up above an earthen floor.

And she also named them Living Ears of Green Corn, because the corn plants had grown again. So they were named by Xmucane. They had been left behind, planted by Hunahpu and Xbalanque, simply as a way for their grandmother to remember them.

And the first to die, a long time before, had been their fathers, One Hunahpu and Seven Hunahpu. And they saw the face of their father again, there in Xibalba. Their father spoke to them again when they had defeated Xibalba.

THEIR FATHER IS PUT BACK TOGETHER BY THEM: *Hunahpu (left) and Xbalanque (right) resurrect their father. He takes the form of a maize god in lowland Maya art, here emerging (or sprouting) from a cleft in the back of a turtle (the earth). From a Late Classic Maya bowl.*

DRAWING BY KARL TAUBE

AND HERE THEIR FATHER IS PUT BACK TOGETHER BY THEM. They put Seven Hunahpu back together; they went to the Place of Ball Game Sacrifice to put him together. He had wanted his face to become just as it was, but when he was asked to name everything, and once he had found the name of the mouth, the nose, the eyes of his face, there was very little else to be said. Although his mouth could not name the names of each of his former parts, he had at least spoken again.

And so it remained that they were respectful of their father's heart, even though they left him at the Place of Ball Game Sacrifice:

"You will be prayed to here," his sons told him, and his heart was comforted. "You will be the first resort, and you will be the first to have your day kept by those who will be born in the light, begotten in the light. Your name will not be lost. So be it," they told their father when they comforted his heart.

"We merely cleared the road of your death, your loss, the pain, the suffering that were inflicted upon you."

And such was the instruction they gave when all the Xibalbans had been finally defeated. And then the two boys ascended this way, here into the middle of the light, and they ascended straight on into the sky, and the sun belongs to one and the moon to the other. When it became light within the sky, on the face of the earth, they were there in the sky.

THE MOON TO THE OTHER:
The lowland Maya Jaguar
Moon Lord, enclosed by a
lunar crescent. From an Early
Classic conch shell trumpet.

DRAWING BY LINDA SCHELE

And then the Four Hundred Boys climbed up, the ones who were killed by Zipacna.

And so they came to accompany the two of them, they became the sky's own stars.

PART
FOUR

Aᴺᴰ ʜᴇʀᴇ ɪꜱ ᴛʜᴇ ʙᴇɢɪɴɴɪɴɢ ᴏꜰ ᴛʜᴇ ᴄᴏɴᴄᴇᴘᴛɪᴏɴ ᴏꜰ ʜᴜᴍᴀɴꜱ, and of the search for the ingredients of the human body. So they spoke, the Bearer, Begetter, the Makers, Modelers named Sovereign Plumed Serpent:

"The dawn has approached, preparations have been made, and morning has come for the provider, nurturer, born in the light, begotten in the light. Morning has come for humankind, for the people of the face of the earth," they said. It all came together as they went on thinking in the darkness, in the night, as they searched and they sifted, they thought and they wondered.

And here their thoughts came out in clear light. They sought and discovered what was needed for human flesh. It was only a short while before the sun, moon, and stars were to appear above the Makers and Modelers. Split Place, Bitter Water Place is the name: the yellow corn, white corn came from there.

And these are the names of the animals who brought the food: fox, coyote, parrot, crow. There were four animals who brought the news of the ears of yellow corn and white corn. They were coming from over there at Split Place, they showed the way to the split.

Tʜᴇ ʏᴇʟʟᴏᴡ ᴄᴏʀɴ ᴀɴᴅ
ᴡʜɪᴛᴇ ᴄᴏʀɴ ᴡᴇʀᴇ ɢʀᴏᴜɴᴅ:
*This woman is rubbing a
hand stone ("mano") over a
grinding stone ("metate") that
has stone feet. From a Late
Classic Maya bowl.*

DRAWING BY THE AUTHOR

And this was when they found the staple foods.

And these were the ingredients for the flesh of the human work, the human design, and the water was for the blood. It became human blood, and corn was also used by the Bearer, Begetter.

And so they were happy over the provisions of the good mountain, filled with sweet things, thick with yellow corn, white corn, and thick with pataxte and cacao, countless zapotes, anonas, jocotes, nances, matasanos, sweets—the rich foods filling up the citadel named Split Place, Bitter Water Place. All the edible fruits were there: small staples, great staples, small plants, great plants. The way was shown by the animals.

And then the yellow corn and white corn were ground, and Xmucane did the grinding nine times. Food was used, along with the water she rinsed her hands with, for the creation of grease; it became human fat when it was worked by the Bearer, Begetter, Sovereign Plumed Serpent, as they are called.

After that, they put it into words:

> the making, the modeling of our first mother-father,
> with yellow corn, white corn alone for the flesh,
> food alone for the human legs and arms,
> for our first fathers, the four human works.

It was staples alone that made up their flesh.

T HESE ARE THE NAMES OF THE FIRST PEOPLE WHO WERE MADE AND MODELED.

This is the first person: Jaguar Quitze.

And now the second: Jaguar Night.

And now the third: Not Right Now.

And the fourth: Dark Jaguar.

And these are the names of our first mother-fathers. They were simply made and modeled, it is said; they had no mother and no father. We have named the men by themselves. No woman gave birth to them, nor were they begotten by the builder, sculptor, Bearer, Begetter. By sacrifice alone, by genius alone they were made, they were modeled by the Maker, Modeler, Bearer, Begetter, Sovereign Plumed Serpent. And when they came to fruition, they came out human:

They talked and they made words.

They looked and they listened.

They walked, they worked.

They were good people, handsome, with looks of the male kind. Thoughts came into existence and they gazed; their vision came all at once. Perfectly they saw, perfectly they knew everything under the sky, whenever they looked. The moment they turned around and looked around in the sky, on the earth, everything was seen without any obstruction. They didn't have to walk around before they could see what was under the sky; they just stayed where they were.

As they looked, their knowledge became intense. Their sight passed through trees, through rocks, through lakes, through seas, through mountains, through plains. Jaguar Quitze, Jaguar Night, Not Right Now, and Dark Jaguar were truly gifted people.

And then they were asked by the builder and mason:

"What do you know about your being? Don't you look, don't you listen? Isn't your speech good, and your walk? So you must look, to see out under the sky. Don't you see the mountain-plain clearly? So try it," they were told.

And then they saw everything under the sky perfectly. After that, they thanked the Maker, Modeler:

> "Truly now,
> double thanks, triple thanks
> that we've been formed, we've been given
> our mouths, our faces,
> we speak, we listen,
> we wonder, we move,
> our knowledge is good, we've understood
> what is far and near,
> and we've seen what is great and small
> under the sky, on the earth.
> Thanks to you we've been formed,
> we've come to be made and modeled,
> our grandmother, our grandfather,"

they said when they gave thanks for having been made and modeled. They understood everything perfectly, they sighted the four sides, the four corners in the sky, on the earth, and this didn't sound good to the builder and sculptor:

"What our works and designs have said is no good:

'We have understood everything, great and small,' they say." And so the Bearer, Begetter took back their knowledge:

"What should we do with them now? Their vision should at least reach nearby, they should see at least a small part of the face of the earth, but what they're saying isn't good. Aren't they merely 'works' and 'designs' in their very names? Yet they'll become as great as gods, unless they procreate, proliferate at the sowing, the dawning, unless they increase."

"Let it be this way: now we'll take them apart just a little, that's what we need. What we've found out isn't good. Their deeds would become equal to ours, just because their knowledge reaches so far. They see everything," so said

> the Heart of Sky, Hurricane,
> Newborn Thunderbolt, Sudden Thunderbolt,
> Sovereign Plumed Serpent,
> Bearer, Begetter,
> Xpiyacoc, Xmucane,
> Maker, Modeler,

as they are called. And when they changed the nature of their works, their designs, it was enough that the eyes be marred by the Heart of Sky. They were blinded as the face of a mirror is breathed upon. Their vision flickered. Now it was only from close up that they could see what was there with any clarity.

And such was the loss of the means of understanding, along with the means of knowing everything, by the four humans. The root was implanted.

And such was the making, modeling of our first grandfather, our father, by the Heart of Sky, Heart of Earth.

A<small>ND THEN THEIR WIVES AND WOMEN CAME INTO BEING.</small> Again, the same gods thought of it. It was as if they were asleep when they received them, truly beautiful women were there with Jaguar Quitze, Jaguar Night, Not Right Now, and Dark Jaguar. With their women there they really came alive. Right away they were happy at heart again, because of their wives.

Red Sea Turtle is the name of the wife of Jaguar Quitze.

Prawn House is the name of the wife of Jaguar Night.

Water Hummingbird is the name of the wife of Not Right Now.

Macaw House is the name of the wife of Dark Jaguar.

So these are the names of their wives, who became ladies of rank, giving birth to the people of the tribes, small and great.

AND THIS IS OUR ROOT, WE WHO ARE THE QUICHÉ PEOPLE. And there came to be a crowd of penitents and sacrificers. It wasn't only four who came into being then, but there were four mothers for us, the Quiché people. There were different names for each of the peoples when they multiplied, there in the east. Their names became numerous: Sovereign Oloman, Cohah, Quenech Ahau, as the names of the people who were there in the east are spoken. They multiplied, and it is known that the Tams and Ilocs began then. They came from the same place, there in the east.

Jaguar Quitze was the grandfather and father of the nine great houses of the Cauecs.

Jaguar Night was the grandfather and father of the nine great houses of the Greathouses.

Not Right Now was the grandfather and father of the four great houses of the Lord Quichés.

There were three separate lineages. The names of the grandfathers and fathers are not forgotten. These multiplied and flowered there in the east, but the Tams and Ilocs also came forth, along with thirteen allied tribes, thirteen principalities, including:

The Rabinals, Cakchiquels, those of Bird House.

And the White Cornmeals.

And also the Lamacs, Serpents, Sweatbath House, Talk House, those of Star House.

And those of Quiba House, those of Yokes House, Acul people, Jaguar House, Guardians of the Spoils, Jaguar Ropes.

It is sufficient that we speak only of the largest tribes from among the allied tribes; we have only noted the largest. Many more came out afterward, each one a division of that citadel. We haven't written their names, but they multiplied there, from out of the east. There came to be many peoples in the blackness; they began to abound even before the birth of the sun and the light. When they began to abound they were all there together; they stood and walked in crowds, there in the east.

There was nothing they could offer for sustenance, but even so they lifted their faces to the sky. They didn't know where they were going. They did this for a long time, when they were there in the grasslands:

149

black people, white people, people of many faces, people of many languages, uncertain, there at the edge of the sky.

And there were mountain people. They didn't show their faces, they had no homes. They just traveled the mountains, small and great. "It's as if they were crazy," they used to say. They derided the mountain people, it was said. There they watched for the sunrise, and for all the mountain people there was just one language. They did not yet pray to the tree-stone.

These are the words with which they remembered the Maker, Modeler, Heart of Sky, Heart of Earth. It was said that these were enough to keep them mindful of what was in shadow and what was dawning. All they did was ask; they had reverent words. They were reverent, they were givers of praise, givers of respect, lifting their faces to the sky when they made requests for their daughters and sons:

> "Wait!
> thou Maker, thou Modeler,
> look at us, listen to us,
> don't let us fall, don't leave us aside,
> thou god in the sky, on the earth,
> Heart of Sky, Heart of Earth,
> give us our sign, our word,
> as long as there is day, as long as there is light.
> When it comes to the sowing, the dawning,
> will it be a greening road, a greening path?
> Give us a steady light, a level place,
> a good light, a good place,
> a good life and beginning.
> Give us all of this, thou Hurricane,
> Newborn Thunderbolt, Sudden Thunderbolt,
> Newborn Nanahuac, Sudden Nanahuac,
> Falcon, Hunahpu,
> Sovereign Plumed Serpent,
> Bearer, Begetter,
> Xpiyacoc, Xmucane,
> Grandmother of Day, Grandmother of Light,
> when it comes to the sowing, the dawning,"

they said when they made their fasts and prayers, just watching intently for the dawn. There, too, they looked toward the east, watching closely for the sun carrier, the great star at the birth of the sun, of the heat for

THEY DID NOT YET PRAY TO THE
TREE-STONE: *A wooden stele
commemorating a new year. The
cluster of branches and leaves at the
top is the glyph for te' or "tree," while
the glyph at the foot of the stele is for
tun or "stone." The snake (kan) near
the top is a pun on "sky" (kan); the
inscription on the strip of paper
hanging from the stele is represented
only by footprints that signify the
passage of time, following the reading
order of a column of glyphs. From the
Dresden Codex.*

DRAWING BY KARL TAUBE

what is under the sky, on the earth, the guide for the human work, the human design.

They spoke, those who are Jaguar Quitze, Jaguar Night, Not Right Now, and Dark Jaguar:

"We're still waiting for the dawning," they said, these great knowers, great thinkers, penitents, praisers, as they are called. And there was no tree-stone in the keeping of our first mother-fathers, and they were weary at heart there, waiting for the sun. Already there were many of them, all the tribes, including the Mexican people, all penitents and sacrificers.

"Let's just go. We'll look and see whether there is something to keep as our sign. We'll find out what we should burn in front of it. The way we are right now, we have nothing to keep as our own," said Jaguar Quitze, Jaguar Night, Not Right Now, and Dark Jaguar. They got word of a citadel. They went there.

AND THIS IS THE NAME OF THE MOUNTAIN WHERE THEY WENT, Jaguar Quitze, Jaguar Night, Not Right Now, Dark Jaguar, and the Tams and Ilocs: Tulan Zuyua, Seven Caves, Seven Canyons is the name of the citadel. Those who were to receive the gods arrived there.

151

And they arrived there at Tulan, all of them, countless people arrived, walking in crowds, and their gods were given out in order, the first being those of Jaguar Quitze, Jaguar Night, Not Right Now, and Dark Jaguar. They were happy:

"We have found what we were looking for," they said. And this one was the first to come out:

Tohil is the name of the god loaded in the backpack borne by Jaguar Quitze. And the others came out in turn:

Auilix is the name of the god that Jaguar Night carried.

Hacauitz, in turn, is the name of the god received by Not Right Now.

Middle of the Plain is the name of the god received by Dark Jaguar.

And there were still other Quiché people, since the Tams also received theirs, but it was the same Tohil for the Tams, that's the name received by the grandfather and father of the Tam lords, as they are known today.

And third were the Ilocs: again, Tohil is the name of the god received by the grandfather and father of those lords, the same ones known today.

And such was the naming of the three Quichés. They have never let go of one another because the god has just one name: Tohil for the Quiché proper, and Tohil for the Tams and Ilocs. There is just one name for their god, and so the Quiché threesome has not come apart, those three. Tohil, Auilix, and Hacauitz are truly great in their very being.

And then all the tribes came in: Rabinals, Cakchiquels, those of Bird House, along with the Mexican people, as the names are today. And the languages of the tribes changed there; their languages became differentiated. They could no longer understand one another clearly when they came away from Tulan.

And there they broke apart. There were those who went eastward and many who came here, but they were all alike in dressing with hides. There were no clothes of the better kinds. They were in patches, they were adorned with mere animal hides. They were poor. They had nothing of their own. But they were people of genius in their very being when they came away from Tulan Zuyua, Seven Caves, Seven Canyons, so says the ancient text.

THEY WALKED IN CROWDS WHEN THEY ARRIVED AT TULAN, AND THERE WAS NO FIRE. Only those with Tohil had it: this was the tribe whose god was first to generate fire. How it was generated is not clear. Their fire was already burning when Jaguar Quitze and Jaguar Night first saw it:

Tohil . . . was first to generate fire: *Here he sits amid swirls of smoke and fire (or clouds and lightning), some of which originate from his own forehead and tongue. One of his legs, turned to the right, can be seen turning into a snake (lightning) below his knee. From an incised potsherd found at Rotten Cane (Utatlán), now in the Peabody Museum, Harvard University.*

REPRODUCED BY PERMISSION OF DOVER PUBLICATIONS

"Alas! Fire has not yet become ours. We'll die from the cold," they said. And then Tohil spoke:

"Do not grieve. You will have your own even when the fire you're talking about has been lost," Tohil told them.

> "Aren't you a true god!
> Our sustenance and our support!
> Our god!"

they said when they gave thanks for what Tohil had said.

> "Very well, in truth,
> I am your god: so be it.
> I am your lord: so be it,"

the penitents and sacrificers were told by Tohil.

And this was the warming of the tribes. They were pleased by their fire.

After that a great downpour began, which cut short the fire of the

153

tribes. And hail fell thickly on all the tribes, and their fires were put out by the hail. Their fires didn't start up again. So then Jaguar Quitze and Jaguar Night asked for their fire again:

"Tohil, we'll be finished off by the cold," they told Tohil.

"Well, do not grieve," said Tohil. Then he started a fire. He pivoted inside his sandal.

After that, Jaguar Quitze, Jaguar Night, Not Right Now, and Dark Jaguar were pleased.

After they had been warmed, the fires of the other tribes were still out. Now they were being finished off by the cold, so they came back to ask for their fire from Jaguar Quitze, Jaguar Night, Not Right Now, and Dark Jaguar. They could bear the cold and hail no longer. By now they were chattering and shivering. There was no life left in them. Their legs and arms kept shaking. Their hands were stiff when they arrived.

"Perhaps we wouldn't make ourselves ashamed in front of you if we asked to remove a little something from your fire?" they said when they arrived, but they got no response. And then the tribes cursed in their thoughts. Already their language had become different from that of Jaguar Quitze, Jaguar Night, Not Right Now, and Dark Jaguar.

"Alas! We left our language behind. How did we do it? We're lost! Where were we deceived? We had only one language when we came to Tulan, and we had only one place of emergence and origin. We haven't done well," said all the tribes beneath the trees and bushes.

And then a person showed himself before Jaguar Quitze, Jaguar Night, Not Right Now, and Dark Jaguar, and he spoke as a messenger of Xibalba:

"Truly, since you have your god, your nurturer, and he is the representation, the commemoration of your Maker and your Modeler, don't give the tribes their fire until they give something to Tohil. You don't want them to give anything to *you*. You must ask for what belongs to Tohil; to *him* must come what they give in order to get fire," said the Xibalban. He had wings like the wings of a bat.

"I am a messenger of those who made you and modeled you," said the Xibalban. So now they were happy; now they thought all the more of Tohil, Auilix, and Hacauitz. When the Xibalban had spoken he made himself vanish right in front of them, without delay.

And so again the tribes arrived, again done in by the cold. Thick were the white hail, the blackening storm, and the white crystals. The cold was incalculable. They were simply overwhelmed. Because of the cold all the tribes were going along doubled over, groping along when they arrived in the presence of Jaguar Quitze, Jaguar Night, Not Right Now, and

Dark Jaguar. There was great pain in their hearts; they had covetous mouths and covetous faces.

And now they were coming as thieves before Jaguar Quitze, Jaguar Night, Not Right Now, and Dark Jaguar:

"Wouldn't you take pity on us if we asked to remove a little something from your fire? Wasn't it found and wasn't it revealed that we had just one home and just one mountain when you were made, when you were modeled? So please take pity on us," they said.

"And what would you give us for taking pity on you?" they were asked.

"Well, we'd give you metal," said the tribes.

"We don't want metal," said Jaguar Quitze and Jaguar Night.

"Whatever might you want, if we may ask?" the tribes said then.

"Very well. First we must ask Tohil, and then we'll tell you," they were told next. And then they asked Tohil:

"What should the tribes give you, Tohil? They've come to ask for your fire," said Jaguar Quitze, Jaguar Night, Not Right Now, and Dark Jaguar.

"Very well. You will tell them:

" 'Don't they want to be suckled on their sides and under their arms?

THEY'VE COME TO ASK FOR YOUR FIRE: *This is a scepter held by a ruler, one of the forms taken by* K'awil, *the lowland Maya counterpart of Tohil, or Hurricane. On his forehead he wears an obsidian mirror with a burning torch emerging from it. His body and his one normal leg are omitted here, leaving only the leg that becomes a serpent (or lightning). This is a reconstruction from several Late Classic stucco reliefs at Palenque.*

DRAWING BY THE AUTHOR

Isn't it their heart's desire to embrace me? I, who am Tohil? But if there is no desire, then I'll not give them their fire," says Tohil. "When the time comes, not right now, they'll be suckled on their sides, under their arms," he says to you,' you will say," they were told, Jaguar Quitze, Jaguar Night, Not Right Now, and Dark Jaguar, and then they spoke the word of Tohil.

"Very well. Let him suckle. And very well, we shall embrace him," said the tribes, when they answered and agreed to the word of Tohil. They made no delay but said "very well" right away, and then they received their fire.

After that they got warm, but there was one group that simply stole the fire, there in the smoke. This was the Bat House. Snake Tooth is the name of the god of the Cakchiquels, but it looks like a bat. They went right past in the smoke then, they sneaked past when they came to get fire. Those fiery Cakchiquels didn't ask for their fire. They didn't give themselves up in defeat, but all the other tribes were defeated when they gave themselves up to being suckled on their sides, under their arms.

And this is what Tohil meant by being "suckled": that all the tribes be cut open before him, and that their hearts be removed "through their sides, under their arms." This deed had not yet been attempted when Tohil saw into the middle of it, nor had Jaguar Quitze, Jaguar Night, Not Right Now, and Dark Jaguar received fiery splendor and majesty.

WHEN THEY CAME AWAY FROM TULAN ZUYUA, they weren't eating. They observed a continuous fast. It was enough that they watch intently for the dawning, that they watch closely for the rising of the sun, taking turns at watching for the great star named sun carrier. This one came first before the sun when the sun was born, the newly risen sun carrier.

And there, always, they were facing the east, when they were there in the place named Tulan Zuyua. Their gods came from there. It wasn't really here that they received their fiery splendor and their dominion, but rather there that the tribes, great and small, were subjugated and humiliated. When they were cut open before Tohil, all the peoples gave their blood, their gore, their sides, their underarms. Fiery splendor came to them all at once at Tulan, along with great knowledge, and they achieved this in the darkness, in the night.

And now they came away, they tore themselves away from there. Now they left the east:

"Our home is not here. Let's go on until we see where we belong," said Tohil. He actually spoke to them, to Jaguar Quitze, Jaguar Night, Not Right Now, and Dark Jaguar.

"It remains for you to give thanks, since you have yet to take care of bleeding your ears, yet to take stitches in your elbows. You must worship. This is your way of giving thanks before your god."

"Very well," they replied, then they bled their ears. They cried in their song about coming from Tulan. They cried in their hearts when they came away, when they made their departure from Tulan:

> "Alas!
> We won't be here when we see the dawn,
> when the sun is born,
> when the face of the earth is lit,"

they said.

AND THEN THEY CAME AWAY, JUST CAMPING ON THE ROAD. People were just camping there, each tribe slept and then got up again. And they were always watching for the star, the sign of the day. They kept this sign of the dawn in their hearts when they came away from the east. In unity they passed beyond the place named Great Hollow today.

And then they arrived on top of a mountain there. All the Quiché people got together there, along with the other tribes, and all of them held council there. The name the mountain has today is from when they took counsel together; Place of Advice is the name of the mountain. They got together and identified themselves there:

"Here am I: I am a Quiché person, and you there, you are Tams, this will be your name," the Tams were told. And then the Ilocs were told:

"You are the Ilocs, this will be your name. The three Quichés must not be lost. We are united in our word," they said when they fixed their names.

And then the Cakchiquels were named; their name became Cakchiquels. So, too, with the Rabinals; this became their name. It hasn't been lost today.

And then there are those of Bird House, as they are named today.

These are the names they named for one another. When they held council there, they were still waiting for the dawning, watching for the appearance of the rising star, the one that came before the sun when it was born.

157

"When we came away from Tulan, we broke ourselves apart," they told each other.

This is what kept weighing on their hearts, the great pain they went through: there was nothing to eat, nothing to feed on. They were just smelling the tips of their staffs as if they were thinking of eating them, but they weren't eating at all as they came.

And it isn't clear how they crossed over the sea. They crossed over as if there were no sea. They just crossed over on some stones, stones piled up in the sand. And they gave it a name: Stone Courses, Sand Banks was their name for the place where they crossed through the midst of the sea. Where the waters were divided, they crossed over.

And this is what weighed on their hearts when they took counsel: that they had nothing to eat. They had one beverage to drink, just one atole, which they brought up on the mountain named Place of Advice. And they also brought Tohil, Auilix, and Hacauitz.

Observing a great fast was Jaguar Quitze, with his wife; Red Sea Turtle is his wife's name.

Likewise doing it was Jaguar Night, with his wife, named Prawn House.

And Not Right Now was also there at the great fast, with his wife, named Water Hummingbird, along with Dark Jaguar, whose wife's name is Macaw House.

So these were the ones who fasted, there in the blackness, in the early dawn. Their sadness was great when they were there on the mountain named Place of Advice today. And their gods spoke there.

A ND THEN TOHIL, ALONG WITH AUILIX AND HACAUITZ, SPOKE TO THEM, to Jaguar Quitze, Jaguar Night, Not Right Now, and Dark Jaguar:

"Let's just go, let's just get up, let's not stay here. Please give us places to hide. It's nearly dawn. Wouldn't you look pitiful if we became plunder for warriors? Construct places where we can remain yours, you penitents and sacrificers, and give one place to each of us," they said when they spoke.

"Very well. Let's get out and search the forests," they all replied.

After that they packed each one of the gods on their backs.

And then Auilix went into the canyon named Concealment Canyon, as they called it, into the great canyon in the forest. Auilix's Place is the name today. He was left there, placed in the canyon by Jaguar Night, coming first in the sequence of placements.

158

And then Hacauitz was placed at the top of a great pyramid. Hacauitz is the name of the mountain today, and it became their citadel. So the god Hacauitz remained there, and Not Right Now stayed with his god. This was the second god to be hidden by them. Hacauitz didn't stay in the forest. It was on a bare mountain that Hacauitz was hidden.

And then came Jaguar Quitze. He arrived in the great forest there. Tohil was put into hiding by Jaguar Quitze; the mountain is called Tohil's Place today. Then they gave Concealment Canyon an epithet: Tohil Medicine. Masses of serpents and masses of jaguars, rattlesnakes, fer-de-lances were there in the forest where he was hidden by the penitents and sacrificers.

So they were there in unity: Jaguar Quitze, Jaguar Night, Not Right Now, and Dark Jaguar. In unity they waited for the dawn, there on top of the mountain named Hacauitz.

Also, a short distance away, was the god of the Tams, together with the Ilocs. Tam Tribe is the name of the place where the god of the Tams was, there at the dawn. Net Weave Tribe is the name of the place where dawn came for the Ilocs. The god of the Ilocs was just a short distance away.

Also there were all the Rabinals, Cakchiquels, those of Bird House, all the tribes, small and great. In unity they stopped there, and in unity they had their dawning there. In unity they waited there for the rising of the great star named sun carrier.

"It will rise before the sun when the dawn comes," they said, and they were in unity there: Jaguar Quitze, Jaguar Night, Not Right Now, and Dark Jaguar. There was no sleep, no rest for them. They cried their hearts and their guts out, there at the dawning and clearing, and so they looked terrible. Great sorrow, great anguish came over them; they were marked by their pain. They just stayed that way.

"Coming here hasn't been sweet for us. Alas! If we could only see the birth of the sun! What have we done? We all had one identity, one mountain, but we sent ourselves into exile," they said when they talked among themselves. They talked about sorrow, about anguish, about crying and wailing, since their hearts had not yet been set to rest by the dawn.

And these are the ones who did feel settled there: the gods who were in the canyons, in the forests, just out in the bromeliads, in the hanging mosses, not yet set on pedestals. At first, Tohil, Auilix, and Hacauitz actually spoke. The greatness of their day and the greatness of their breath of spirit set them above all the other tribal gods. Their genius was manifold and their ways were manifold, their strategies. They were chilling, they were frightening in their very being and in the hearts of the tribes, whose thoughts were calmed by Jaguar Quitze, Jaguar Night, Not

Right Now, and Dark Jaguar. Their hearts did not yet harbor ill will toward the gods who had been taken up and carried away when they all came from Tulan Zuyua, there in the east, and who were now in the forest.

These were the dawning places: Tohil's Place, Auilix's Place, and Hacauitz, as they are called today. And this is where our grandfathers, our fathers had their sowing, their dawning.

This is what we shall explain next: the dawning and showing of the sun, moon, and stars.

Aᴺᴰ ʜᴇʀᴇ ɪs ᴛʜᴇ ᴅᴀᴡɴɪɴɢ ᴀɴᴅ sʜᴏᴡɪɴɢ ᴏꜰ ᴛʜᴇ sᴜɴ, ᴍᴏᴏɴ, ᴀɴᴅ sᴛᴀʀs. And Jaguar Quitze, Jaguar Night, Not Right Now, and Dark Jaguar were overjoyed when they saw the sun carrier. It came up first. It looked brilliant when it came up, since it was ahead of the sun.

After that they unwrapped their copal incense, which came from the east, and there was triumph in their hearts when they unwrapped it. They gave their heartfelt thanks with three kinds at once:

Mixtam Copal is the name of the copal brought by Jaguar Quitze.

Cauiztan Copal, next, is the name of the copal brought by Jaguar Night.

Godly Copal, as the next one is called, was brought by Not Right Now.

The three of them had their copal, and this is what they burned as they incensed the direction of the rising sun. They were crying sweetly as they shook their burning copal, the precious copal.

ɪᴛ ᴡᴀs ᴀʜᴇᴀᴅ ᴏꜰ ᴛʜᴇ sᴜɴ: *The band across the top is sky, with the glyph for Venus in the middle. Below Venus, lying on the earth, is the profile of the sun god. From a Late Classic Maya relief on a bench at Copán.*

DRAWING BY KARL TAUBE

160

After that they cried because they had yet to see and yet to witness the birth of the sun.

And then, when the sun came up, the animals, small and great, were happy. They all came up from the rivers and canyons; they waited on all the mountain peaks. Together they looked toward the place where the sun came out.

So then the puma and jaguar cried out, but the first to cry out was a bird, the parrot by name. All the animals were truly happy. The eagle, the white vulture, small birds, great birds spread their wings, and the penitents and sacrificers knelt down. They were overjoyed, together with the penitents and sacrificers of the Tams, the Ilocs.

And the Rabinals, Cakchiquels, those of Bird House.

And the Sweatbath House, Talk House, Quiba House, those of Yokes House.

And the Mexican Sovereigns—however many tribes there may be today. There were countless peoples, but there was just one dawn for all tribes.

And then the face of the earth was dried out by the sun. The sun was like a person when he revealed himself. His face was hot, so he dried out the face of the earth. Before the sun came up it was soggy, and the face of the earth was muddy before the sun came up. And when the sun had risen just a short distance he was like a person, and his heat was unbearable. Since he revealed himself only when he was born, it is only his reflection that now remains. As they put it in the ancient text,

"The visible sun is not the real one."

And then, all at once, Tohil, Auilix, and Hacauitz were turned to stone, along with the icons of the puma, jaguar, rattlesnake, fer-de-lance, which the White Sparkstriker took with him into the trees. Everywhere, all of them became stone when the sun, moon, and stars appeared. Perhaps we would have no relief from the voracious animals today—the puma, jaguar, rattlesnake, fer-de-lance—and perhaps it wouldn't even be our day today, if the original animals hadn't been turned to stone by the sun when he came up.

There was great happiness in the hearts of Jaguar Quitze, Jaguar Night, Not Right Now, and Dark Jaguar. They were overjoyed when it dawned. The people on the mountain of Hacauitz were not yet numerous; just a few were there. Their dawning was there and they burned copal there, incensing the direction of the rising sun. They came from there: it is their own mountain, their own plain. Those named Jaguar Quitze, Jaguar Night, Not Right Now, and Dark Jaguar came from there, and they began their increase on that mountain.

And that became their citadel, since they were there when the sun, moon, and stars appeared, when it dawned and cleared on the face of the earth, over everything under the sky.

And there began their song named "Camacu." They sang out the lament of their very hearts and guts. In their song they stated:

> "Alas!
> We were lost at Tulan!
> We shattered ourselves!
> We left our elder brothers behind!
> Our younger brothers!
> Where did they see the sun?
> Where must they be staying,
> now that the dawn has come?"

They were speaking of the penitents and sacrificers who were the Mexican people.

"Even though Tohil is his name, he is the same as the god of the Mexican people, who is named Yolcuat and Quitzalcuat. When we divided, there at Tulan, at Zuyua, they left with us, and they shared our identity when we came away," they said among themselves when they remembered their faraway brothers, elder and younger, the Mexican people whose dawn was there in the place named Mexico today.

And again, some of the people stayed there in the east; Sovereign Oloman is their name.

"We left them behind," they said. It was a great weight on their hearts, up there on Hacauitz. The Tams and Ilocs did likewise, except that they were in the forest. Tam Tribe is the name of the place where it dawned for the penitents and sacrificers of the Tams, with their god, the same Tohil. There was just one name for the god of all three divisions of the Quiché people.

And again, the name of the god of the Rabinals was the same. His name was only slightly changed; "One Toh" is the way the name of the god of the Rabinals is spoken. They say it that way, but it is meant to be in agreement with the Quichés and with their language.

And the language has differentiated in the case of the Cakchiquels, since their god had a different name when they came away from Tulan Zuyua. Snake Tooth is the name of the god of the Bat House, and they

162

speak a different language today. Along with their god, the lineages took their names; they are called Keeper of the Bat Mat and Keeper of the Dance Mat. Like their god, their language was differentiated on account of a stone, when they came from Tulan in the darkness. All the tribes were sown and came to light in unity, and each division was allocated a name for its god.

And now we shall tell about their stay and their sojourn there on the mountain. The four were there together, the ones named Jaguar Quitze, Jaguar Night, Not Right Now, and Dark Jaguar. Their hearts cried out to Tohil, Auilix, and Hacauitz, who were now amid the bromeliads and hanging mosses.

AND HERE THEY BURN THEIR COPAL, and here also is the origin of the masking of Tohil.

And when they went before Tohil and Auilix, they went to visit them and keep their day. Now they gave thanks before them for the dawning, and now they bowed low before their stones, there in the forest. Now it was only a manifestation of his genius that spoke when the penitents and sacrificers came before Tohil, and what they brought and burned was not great. All they burned before their gods was resin, just bits of pitchy bark, along with marigolds.

And when Tohil spoke now it was only his genius. When the gods taught procedures to the penitents and sacrificers, they said this when they spoke:

"This very place has become our mountain, our plain. Now that we are yours, our day and our birth have become great, because all the peoples are yours, all the tribes. And since we are still your companions, even in your citadel, we shall give you procedures:

"Do not reveal us to the tribes when they burn with envy over us. They are truly numerous now, so don't you let us be hunted down, but rather give the creatures of the grasses and grains to us, such as the female deer and female birds. Please come give us a little of their blood, take pity on us. And set the pelts of the deer aside, save them. These are for disguises, for deception. They will become deerskin bundles, and they will also serve as our surrogates before the tribes. When you are asked:

'Where is Tohil?' then you will show them the deerskin bundle, yet you won't be giving yourselves away. And there is still more for you to do. You will become great in your very being. Defeat all the tribes. They must bring blood and lymph before us, they must come to embrace us. They belong to us already," said Tohil, Auilix, and Hacauitz. They had a youthful appearance when they saw them, when they came to burn offerings before them.

So then began the hunting of the young of all the birds and deer; they were taken in the hunt by the penitents and sacrificers.

And when they got hold of the birds and fawns, they would then go to anoint the mouth of the stone of Tohil or Auilix with the blood of the deer or bird. And the bloody drink was drunk by the gods. The stone would speak at once when the penitents and sacrificers arrived, when they went to make their burnt offerings.

They did the very same thing before the deerskin bundles: they burned resin, and they also burned marigolds and stevia. There was a deerskin bundle for each of the gods, which was displayed there on the mountain.

They didn't occupy their houses during the day, but just walked in the mountains. And this was their food: just the larva of the yellow jacket, the larva of the wasp, and the larva of the bee, which they hunted. As yet there wasn't anything good to eat or good to drink. Also, it wasn't obvious how to get to their houses, nor was it obvious where their wives stayed.

And the tribes were already densely packed, settling down one by one, with each division of a tribe gathering itself together. Now they were crowding the roads; already their roadways were obvious.

As for Jaguar Quitze, Jaguar Night, Not Right Now, and Dark Jaguar, it wasn't obvious where they were. When they saw the people of the tribes passing by on the roads, that was when they would get up on the mountain peaks, just crying out with the cry of the coyote and the cry of the fox. And they would make the cries of the puma and jaguar, whenever they saw the tribes out walking in numbers. The tribes were saying:

"It's just a coyote crying out," and "Just a fox."

"Just a puma. Just a jaguar."

In the minds of all the tribes, it was as if humans weren't involved. They did it just as a way of decoying the tribes; that was what their hearts desired. They did it so that the tribes wouldn't get really frightened just yet; that was what they intended when they cried out with the cry of the puma and the cry of the jaguar. And then, when they saw just one or two people out walking, they intended to overwhelm them.

Each day, when they came back to their houses and wives, they brought just the same things—yellow jacket larvae, wasp larvae, and bee larvae—and gave them to their wives, each day. And when they went before Tohil, Auilix, and Hacauitz, they thought to themselves:

"They are Tohil, Auilix, and Hacauitz, yet we only give them the blood

164

of deer and birds, we only take stitches in our ears and our elbows when we ask for our strength and our manhood from Tohil, Auilix, and Hacauitz. Who will take care of the death of the tribes? Should we just kill them one by one?" they said among themselves.

And when they went before Tohil, Auilix, and Hacauitz, they took stitches in their ears and their elbows in front of the gods. They spilled their blood, they poured gourdfuls into the mouths of the stones. But these weren't really stones: each one became like a boy when they arrived, happy once again over the blood.

And then came a further sign as to what the penitents and sacrificers should do:

"You must win a great many victories. Your right to do this came from over there at Tulan, when you brought us here," they were told. Then the matter of the suckling was set forth, at the place called Stagger, and the blood that would result from it, the rainstorm of blood, also became a gift for Tohil, along with Auilix and Hacauitz.

Now here begins the abduction of the people of the tribes by Jaguar Quitze, Jaguar Night, Not Right Now, and Dark Jaguar.

A ND THEN COMES THE KILLING OF THE TRIBES. This is how they died: when there was just one person out walking, or just two were out walking, it wasn't obvious when they took them away.

After that they went to cut them open before Tohil and Auilix.

After that, when they had offered the blood, the skull would be placed in the road. They would roll it onto the road. So the tribes were talking:

"A jaguar has been eating," was all that was said, because their tracks were like a jaguar's tracks when they did their deed. They did not reveal themselves. Many people were abducted.

It was actually a long time before the tribes came to their senses:

"If it's Tohil and Auilix who are after us, we have only to search for the penitents and sacrificers. We'll follow their tracks to wherever their houses are," said all those of the tribes, when they shared their thoughts among themselves.

After that, they began following the tracks of the penitents and sacrificers, but they weren't clear. They only saw the tracks of the deer, the tracks of the jaguar. The tracks weren't clear, nothing was clear. Where they began the tracks were merely those of animals. It was as if the tracks were there for the sole purpose of leading them astray. The way was not clear:

It would get cloudy.

It would get dark and rainy.

It would get muddy, too.

It would get misty and drizzly.

That was all the tribes could see in front of them, and their search would simply make them weary at heart. Then they would give up.

Because Tohil, Auilix, and Hacauitz were great in their very being, they did this for a long time, there on the mountain. They did their killing on the frontiers of the tribes when the abductions began; they singled them out and cut them down. They would seize the people of the tribes in the roads, cutting them open before Tohil, Auilix, and Hacauitz.

And the boys hid there on the mountain. Tohil, Auilix, and Hacauitz had the appearance of three boys when they went out walking; these were simply the spirit familiars of the stones. There was a river. They would bathe there on the bank, just as a way of revealing themselves, and this gave the place its name. The name of the river came to be Tohil's Bath, and the tribes saw them there many times. They would vanish the moment they were seen by the tribes.

Then the news spread as to the whereabouts of Jaguar Quitze, Jaguar Night, Not Right Now, and Dark Jaguar, and this is when the tribes realized how they were being killed.

FIRST THE TRIBES TRIED TO PLAN THE DEFEAT OF TOHIL, AUILIX, AND HACAUITZ. All the penitents and sacrificers of the tribes spoke to the others. They roused and summoned one another, all of them. Not even one or two divisions were left out. All of them converged and presented themselves, then they shared their thoughts. And they said, as they questioned one another:

"What would assure the defeat of the Cauecs, the Quiché people? Our vassals have met their ends because of them. Isn't it clear that our people have been lost because of them? What if they finish us off with these abductions?"

"Let it be this way: if the fiery splendor of Tohil, Auilix, and Hacauitz is so great, then let this Tohil become our god! Let him be captured! Don't let them defeat us completely! Don't we constitute a multitude of people? And as for the Cauecs, there aren't as many of them," they said, when all of them had assembled. Some among the tribes also said this when they spoke:

"Who could be bathing every day at the riverbank? If it's Tohil, Auilix, and Hacauitz, then we can defeat them ahead of time. Let the defeat of the penitents and sacrificers begin right there!" some of them said, and then they spoke further:

"How shall we defeat them?" And then they said:

"Let this be our means for defeating them: since they present the appearance of adolescent boys at the river, let two maidens go there. Let them be choice maidens who radiate preciousness, so that when they go they'll be desirable," they said.

"Very well. So we'll just search for two perfect maidens," the others replied. And then they searched among their daughters for those who were truly radiant maidens. Then they gave the maidens instructions:

"You must go, our dear daughters. Go wash clothes at the river, and if you should see three boys, undress yourselves in front of them. And if their hearts should desire you, you will titillate them. When they say to you:

'We're coming after you,' then you are to say:

'Yes.' And then you will be asked:

'Where do you come from? Whose daughters are you?' When they say that, you are to answer them:

'We are the daughters of lords, so let a sign be forthcoming from you.' Then they should give you something. If they like your faces you must really give yourselves up to them. And if you do not give yourselves up, then we shall kill you. We'll feel satisfied when you bring back a sign, since we'll think of it as proof that they came after you," said the lords, instructing the two maidens.

Here are their names: Lust Woman is the name of the one maiden, and Wailing Woman is the name of the other.

Aɴᴅ ᴛʜᴇʏ ꜱᴇɴᴛ ᴛʜᴇ ᴛᴡᴏ ᴏꜰ ᴛʜᴇᴍ, ɴᴀᴍᴇᴅ Lᴜꜱᴛ Wᴏᴍᴀɴ ᴀɴᴅ Wᴀɪʟɪɴɢ Wᴏᴍᴀɴ, over to the place where Tohil, Auilix, and Hacauitz bathed. All the tribes knew about this.

And then they went off. They were dressed up, looking truly beautiful, when they went to the place where Tohil bathed. They were carrying what looked like their wash when they went off. Now the lords were pleased over having sent their two daughters there.

And when they arrived at the river, they began to wash. They un-dressed themselves, both of them. They were on the rocks, on their hands and knees, when Tohil, Auilix, and Hacauitz came along. They got to the bank of the river and just barely glanced at the two maidens washing there, and the maidens got a sudden scare when Tohil and the others arrived. They did not go lusting after the two maidens. Then came the questioning:

"Where do you come from?" the two maidens were asked. "What do you intend by coming here, to the bank of our river?" they were also asked.

"We were sent here by the lords, so we came. The lords told us:

'Go see the faces of Tohil and the others, and speak to them,' the lords told us, 'and also, there must come a sign as to whether you really saw their faces. Go!' is what we were told," said the two maidens, explaining their errand.

But this is what the tribes had intended: that the maidens should be violated by the spirit familiars of Tohil and the others. Then Tohil, Auilix, and Hacauitz spoke, answering the two maidens named Lust Woman and Wailing Woman:

"Good. Let a sign of our word go with you. But you must wait for it, then give it directly to the lords," they were told.

And then Tohil and the others plotted with the penitents and sacrificers. Jaguar Quitze, Jaguar Night, and Not Right Now were told:

"You must inscribe three cloaks, inscribe the signs of your being. They're for the tribes; they'll go back with the maidens who are washing. Give them to the maidens," Jaguar Quitze, Jaguar Night, and Not Right Now were told.

After that, they inscribed all three of them. Jaguar Quitze wrote first: the jaguar became his image, he inscribed it on the face of his cloak.

Then there was Jaguar Night: the eagle was now his image, he inscribed it on the face of his cloak.

The next to write was Not Right Now: swarms of yellow jackets, swarms of wasps were his images, his figures; he inscribed them on the face of his cloak. Then their figures were complete, all three of them; they had done the threefold inscription.

After that, when Jaguar Quitze, Jaguar Night, and Not Right Now went to give the cloaks to those who were named Lust Woman and Wailing Woman, they spoke to them:

"Here is the proof of your word. When you come before the lords you will say:

'Tohil really spoke to us, and here is the sign we've brought back,' you'll tell them, and give them the cloaks to try on," the maidens were told when they were given their instructions.

So then they went back, taking the inscribed cloaks.

And when they arrived, the lords were happy the moment they spotted what they had asked for, hanging from the arms of the maidens.

"Didn't you see the face of Tohil?" they were asked.

"See it we did," said Lust Woman and Wailing Woman.

"Very good. You've brought back some sort of sign. Isn't that so?" said the lords, since there seemed to be signs of their sin—or so thought the lords. So then they were shown the inscribed cloaks by the maidens: one with a jaguar, one with an eagle, and one with yellow jackets and wasps figured on the inside, on a smooth surface.

And they loved the way the cloaks looked. They costumed themselves. The one with the jaguar figured on it didn't do anything; it was the first to be tried on by a lord.

And when another lord costumed himself with the second inscribed cloak, with the eagle figured on it, he just felt good inside it. He turned around in front of them, unfurling it in front of all of them.

And then came the third inscribed cloak to be tried on by a lord, he costumed himself with the one that had yellow jackets and wasps inside it.

And then he started getting stung by the yellow jackets and wasps. He couldn't endure it, he couldn't stand the stings of the insects. That lord yelled his mouth off over the insects, mere written images, the figures of Not Right Now. It was the third inscription that defeated them.

And then the maidens named Lust Woman and Wailing Woman were reprimanded by the lords:

"How did you get these things you brought back? Where did you go to get them, you tricksters!" the maidens were told when they were reprimanded.

Again, all the tribes were defeated because of Tohil. This is what they had intended: that Tohil would be tempted to go after the maidens. It then became the profession of Lust Woman and Wailing Woman to bark shins; the tribes continued to think of them as temptresses.

So the defeat of Jaguar Quitze, Jaguar Night, and Not Right Now was not brought about, since they were people of genius.

And then all the tribes plotted again:

"How are we going to beat them? They are truly great in their very being," they said when they shared their thoughts.

"Even so, we'll invade them and kill them. Let's fit ourselves out with weapons and shields. Aren't we a multitude? There won't even be one or two of them left," they said when they shared their thoughts. All the tribes fitted themselves out. There were masses of killers, once the killers of all the tribes had joined together.

And as for Jaguar Quitze, Jaguar Night, Not Right Now, and Dark Jaguar, they were there on the mountain. Hacauitz is the name of the mountain where they were, and those spirit boys of theirs were hidden there on the mountain. They were not a numerous people then; their numbers were not equal to the numbers of the tribes. There were just a few of them on the mountain, their fortress, so when it was said that the tribes had planned death for them, all of them gathered together. They held a council; they all sent for one another.

AND HERE IS THE JOINING TOGETHER OF ALL THE TRIBES, all decked out now with weapons and shields. Their metal ornaments were countless, they looked beautiful, all the lords, the men. In truth, they were just making talk, all of them. In truth, they would become our captives.

"Since there is a Tohil, and since he is a god, let's celebrate his day—or let's make him our prize!" they said among themselves. But Tohil already knew about it, and Jaguar Quitze, Jaguar Night, and Not Right Now also knew about it. They had heard about it while it was being plotted, since they were neither asleep nor at rest.

So then all the lance-bearing warriors of the tribes were armed.

After that, all the warriors got up during the night, in order to enter

---

THEY WOULD BECOME OUR CAPTIVES: *This warrior has bound his prisoner's arms behind his back and stripped him of nearly all his paraphernalia. From the Dresden Codex.*

DRAWING BY CARLOS A. VILLACORTA

our very midst. They set off, but they never arrived. They just fell asleep on the way, all those warriors.

And then they were defeated again by Jaguar Quitze, Jaguar Night, and Not Right Now, since every last one of them fell asleep in the road. Now they couldn't feel a thing. A multitude slept, all of them, and that's when things got started. Their eyebrows were plucked out, along with their beards.

And then the metal was undone from their cloaks, along with their headdresses.

And their necklaces came off too, and then the necks of their staffs. Their metal was taken just to cause them a loss of face, and the plucking was done just to signify the greatness of the Quiché.

After that, they woke up. Right away they reached for their headdresses, along with the necks of their staffs. There was no metal on their cloaks and headdresses.

"How could it have been taken from us? Who could have plucked us? Where did they come from? Our metal has been stolen!" said all the warriors.

"Perhaps it's those tricksters who've been abducting people! But it's not over with. Let's not get frightened by them. Let's enter their very citadel! That's the only way we'll ever see our metal and make it ours again!" said all the tribes, but even so, they were just making talk, all of them.

The hearts of the penitents and sacrificers were content, there on the mountain, but even so, Jaguar Quitze, Jaguar Night, Not Right Now, and Dark Jaguar were making great plans.

AND THEN JAGUAR QUITZE, JAGUAR NIGHT, NOT RIGHT NOW, AND DARK JAGUAR HAD A PLAN. They made a fence at the edge of their citadel. They just made a palisade of planks and stakes around their citadel.

Next they made manikins; it was as if they had made people. Next they lined them up on the parapet. They were even equipped with weapons and shields. Headdresses were included, with metal on top, and cloaks were included. But they were mere manikins, mere woodcarvings. They used the metal that belonged to the tribes, which they had gone to get in the road. This is what they used to decorate the manikins. They surrounded the citadel.

And then they asked Tohil about their plan:

"What if we die, and what if we're defeated?" They spoke straight from their hearts before Tohil.

"Do not grieve. I am here. And here is what you will use on them. Do not be afraid," Jaguar Quitze, Jaguar Night, Not Right Now, and Dark Jaguar were told, and then the matter of the yellow jackets and wasps was set out.

And when they had gone to get these insects and come back with them, they put them inside four large gourds, which were placed all around the citadel. The yellow jackets and wasps were shut inside the gourds. These were their weapons against the tribes.

And they were spied upon and watched from hiding; their citadel was studied by the messengers of the tribes.

"There aren't many of them," they said, but when they came to look it was only the manikins, the woodcarvings, that were moving, with weapons and shields in their hands. They looked like real people, they looked like real killers when the tribes saw them.

And all the tribes were happy when they saw there weren't many of them. The tribes themselves were in crowds; there were countless people, warriors and killers, the assassins of Jaguar Quitze, Jaguar Night, and Not Right Now, who were there on the mountain called Hacauitz. This is where they were when they were invaded. Here we shall tell about it.

AND THESE ARE THE ONES WHO WERE THERE: JAGUAR QUITZE, JAGUAR NIGHT, NOT RIGHT NOW, AND DARK JAGUAR. They were in unity on the mountain with their wives and children.

And then all the warriors came, the killers, and it was nothing less than eight hundred score, or even thirty times eight hundred people who surrounded the citadel. They were bellowing, bristling with weapons and shields, rending their mouths with howling and growling, bellowing, yelling, whistling through their hands when they came up below the citadel. But the penitents and sacrificers had no fear; they just enjoyed the spectacle from the parapet of the stockade. They were lined up with their wives and children. Their hearts were content, since the tribes were merely making talk.

And then they climbed up the mountainside, and now they were just a little short of the edge of the citadel.

And then the gourds were opened up—there were four of them around the citadel—and the yellow jackets and wasps were like a cloud of smoke when they poured out of each of the gourds. And the warriors were done in, with the insects landing on their eyes and landing on their noses, on their mouths, their legs, their arms. The insects went after them wherever they were, they overtook them wherever they were. There were yellow jackets and wasps everywhere, landing to sting their eyes. They had to watch out for whole swarms of them, there were insects going after every single person. They were dazed by the yellow jackets and wasps. No longer able to hold on to their weapons and shields, they were doubling over and falling to the ground, stumbling. They fell down the mountainside.

And now they couldn't feel a thing when they were hit with arrows and cut with axes. Now Jaguar Quitze and Jaguar Night could even use sticks; even their wives became killers.

Now some of them turned away, then all the tribes just took off running. The first to be overtaken were finished off, killed, and it wasn't just a few people who died. For those who didn't die the chase was carried into their very midst when the insects caught up with them. There were no manly deeds for them to do, since they no longer carried weapons and shields.

Then all the tribes were conquered. Now the tribes humbled themselves before Jaguar Quitze, Jaguar Night, and Not Right Now:

"Take pity on us! Don't kill us!" they said.

"Very well. Although you were destined to join the dead, you will be payers of tribute for as long as there are days and as long as there is light," they were told.

Such was the defeat of all the tribes by our first mother-fathers. It was done there on the mountain named Hacauitz today. This is where they first began. They grew, they multiplied, they had daughters, they had sons on Hacauitz. They were happy, once they had beaten all the tribes, who were defeated there on the mountain.

In this way they accomplished the defeat of the tribes, all the tribes.

After that, their hearts were content. They informed their sons that their death was approaching. They very much intended to be taken by death.

NOW THIS IS WHERE WE SHALL TELL ABOUT THE DEATH OF JAGUAR QUITZE, JAGUAR NIGHT, NOT RIGHT NOW, AND DARK JAGUAR, as they are named. Since they knew about their death and disappearance, they left instructions with their sons. They weren't sickly yet, they weren't gasping for breath when they left their word with their sons.

These are the names of their sons:

Jaguar Quitze begot these two: Noble Two was the name of the first-born and Noble Raiment was the name of the second of the sons of Jaguar Quitze, the grandfather and father of the Cauecs.

And again, Jaguar Night begot two. These are their names: Noble Acul was the name of his first son, and the other was called Noble Acutec, the second son of Jaguar Night, of the Greathouses.

And Not Right Now begot just one son, named Noble Lord.

These three had sons, but Dark Jaguar had no son. They were all true penitents and sacrificers, and these are the names of their sons, with whom they left instructions. They were united, the four of them together. They sang of the pain in their hearts, they cried their hearts out in their singing. "Camacu" is the name of the song they sang.

And then they advised their sons:

"Our dear sons: we are leaving. We are going back. We have enlightened words, enlightened advice to leave with you—and with you who have come from faraway mountains, our dear wives," they told their wives. They advised each one of them:

"We are going back to our own tribal place. Again it is the time of our Lord Deer, as is reflected in the sky. We have only to make our return. Our work has been done, our day has been completed. Since you know this, neither forget us nor put us aside. You have yet to see your own home and mountain, the place of your beginning.

"Let it be this way: you must go. Go see the place where we came from," were the words they spoke when they gave their advice.

And then Jaguar Quitze left a sign of his being:

"This is for making requests of me. I shall leave it with you. Here is your fiery splendor. I have completed my instructions, my counsel," he said when he left the sign of his being, the Bundle of Flames, as it is called. It wasn't clear just what it was; it was wound about with coverings. It was never unwrapped. Its sewing wasn't clear because no one looked on while it was being wrapped.

In this way they left instructions, and then they disappeared from there on the mountain of Hacauitz. Their wives and children never saw them again. The nature of their disappearance was not clear. But whatever the case with their disappearance, their instructions were clear, and the bundle became precious to those who remained. It was a memorial to their fathers. Immediately they burned offerings before this memorial to their fathers.

When the lords began their generation of the people, the Cauecs took

IT WAS WOUND ABOUT WITH COVERINGS: *The rounded shape and large knot on top are characteristic of lowland Maya sacred bundles. From a Late Classic vase.*

DRAWING REPRODUCED BY PERMISSION OF MICHAEL D. COE AND THE GROLIER CLUB

their start from Jaguar Quitze, the grandfather and father; his sons, named Noble Two and Noble Raiment, were not lost.

Such was the death of all four of our first grandfathers and fathers. When they disappeared their sons remained there on the mountain of Hacauitz; their sons stayed there for a while. As for all the tribes, it was now their day to be broken and downtrodden. They no longer had any splendor to them, though they were still numerous.

All those on Hacauitz gathered on each day that was for the remembrance of their fathers. For them, the day of the bundle was a great one. They could not unwrap it; for them it stayed bundled—the Bundle of Flames, as they called it. It was given this epithet, this name when it was left in their keeping by their fathers, who made it just as a sign of their being.

Such was the disappearance and loss of Jaguar Quitze, Jaguar Night, Not Right Now, and Dark Jaguar, the first people to come from beside the sea, from the east. They came here in ancient times. When they died they were already old. They had a reputation for penitence and sacrifice.

PART
FIVE

ND THEN THEY REMEMBERED WHAT HAD BEEN SAID ABOUT THE EAST. This is when they remembered the instructions of their fathers. The ancient things received from their fathers were not lost. The tribes gave them their wives, becoming their fathers-in-law as they took wives. And there were three of them who said, as they were about to go away:

"We are going to the east, where our fathers came from," they said, then they followed their road. The three of them were representative sons:

Noble Two was the name of the son of Jaguar Quitze who represented all the Cauecs.

Noble Acutec was the name of the son of Jaguar Night who served as the sole representative of the Greathouses.

Noble Lord was the name of the only son of Not Right Now, representing the Lord Quichés.

So these are the names of those who went there beside the sea. There were only three who went, but they had skill and knowledge. Their being was not quite that of mere humans. They advised all their brothers, elder and younger, who were left behind. They were glad to go:

"We're not dying. We're coming back," they said when they went, yet it was these same three who passed over the sea.

And then they arrived in the east; they went there to receive lordship. Next comes the name of the lord with dominion over those of the east, where they arrived.

ND THEN THEY CAME BEFORE THE LORD NAMED NACXIT, the great lord and sole judge over a populous domain.

And he was the one who gave out the signs of lordship, all the emblems; the signs of the Keeper of the Mat and the Keeper of the Reception House Mat were set forth.

And when the signs of the splendor and lordship of the Keeper of the Mat and Keeper of the Reception House Mat were set forth, Nacxit gave a complete set of the emblems of lordship. Here are their names:

Canopy, throne.

Bone flute, bird whistle.

Sparkling powder, yellow ocher.

Puma's paw, jaguar's paw.

Head and hoof of deer.

Leather armband, snail-shell rattle.

Tobacco gourd, food bowl.

Parrot feathers, egret feathers.

So they came away bringing all of these. Then, from beside the sea, they brought back the writing of Tulan, the writing of Zuyua. They spoke of their investiture in their signs, in their words.

Also, after they had reached their citadel, named Hacauitz, all the Tams and Ilocs gathered there. All the tribes gathered themselves together; they were happy. When Noble Two, Noble Acutec, and Noble Lord came back, they resumed their lordship over the tribes. The Rabinals, the Cakchiquels, and those of Bird House were happy. Only the signs of the greatness of lordship were revealed before them. Now the lords became great in their very being; when they had displayed their lordship previously, it was incomplete.

This was when they were at Hacauitz. The only ones with them were all those who had originally come from the east. And they spent a long time there on that mountain. Now they were all numerous.

And the wives of Jaguar Quitze, Jaguar Night, and Not Right Now died there. Then they came away, they left their mountain place behind. They sought another mountain where they could settle. They settled countless mountains, giving them epithets and names. Our first mothers and our first fathers multiplied and gained strength at those places, according to what the people of ancient times said when they told about the abandonment of their first citadel, named Hacauitz.

A<small>ND THEN THEY CAME TO A PLACE WHERE THEY FOUNDED A CITADEL NAMED</small> T<small>HORNY</small> P<small>LACE.</small> They spent a long time there in that one citadel. They had daughters and sons while they were there. There were actually four mountains, but there came to be a single name for the whole town. Their daughters and sons got married. They just gave them away. They accepted mere favors and gifts as sufficient payment for their daughters. They did only what was good.

Then they examined each division of the citadel. Here are the names of the divisions of Thorny Place: Dry Place, Bark House, Boundary Marker, and Stronghold are the names of the mountains where they stayed.

And this is when they looked out over the mountains of their citadel. They were seeking a further mountain, since all the divisions had become more numerous. But those who had brought lordship from the east had died by now; they had become old in the process of going from one citadel to another. But their faces did not die; they passed them on.

They went through a great deal of pain and affliction; it was a long time before the grandfathers and fathers found their citadel. Here is the name of the citadel where they arrived.

Aₙd Bₑₐᵣdₑd Pₗₐcₑ ᵢₛ ₜₕₑ ₙₐₘₑ ₒf ₜₕₑ ₘₒᵤₙₜₐᵢₙ ₒf ₜₕₑᵢᵣ ᴄɪᴛᴀᴅᴇʟ. They stayed there and they settled down there.

And they tested their fiery splendor there. They ground their gypsum, their plaster, in the fourth generation of lords. It was said that Noble Rooftree ruled when Nine Deer was the Lord Minister, and then the lords named Noble Sweatbath and Iztayul reigned as Keeper of the Mat and Keeper of the Reception House Mat. They reigned there at Bearded Place. It was through their works that it became an excellent citadel.

The number of great houses only reached three, there at Bearded Place. There were not yet a score and four great houses, but only three of them:

Just one Cauec great house.

And just one great house for the Greathouses.

And finally, just one for the Lord Quichés.

But the three were housed in just two buildings, one in each of the two divisions of the citadel.

This is the way it was when they were at Bearded Place:

They were of just one mind: there was no evil for them, nor were there difficulties.

Their reign was all in calm: there were no quarrels for them, and no disturbances.

Their hearts were filled with a steady light: there was nothing of stupidity and nothing of envy in what they did.

Their splendor was modest: they caused no amazement, nor had they grown great.

And then they tested themselves. They excelled in the Shield Dance, there at Bearded Place. They did it as a sign of their sovereignty. It was a sign of their fiery splendor and a sign of their greatness.

When it was seen by the Ilocs, the Ilocs began to foment war. It was their desire that the Lord Noble Sweatbath be murdered, and that the other lord be allied with them. It was the Lord Iztayul they wanted to persuade; the Ilocs wanted him as their disciple in committing murder. But their jealous plotting behind the back of the Lord Noble Sweatbath

THEY WERE CAPTURED AND
THEY WERE MADE PRISONERS: *A*
Late Classic Maya drawing from
Tikal, depicting a captive warrior
from Calakmul.

DRAWING REPRODUCED BY PERMISSION OF UNIVERSITY OF PENNSYLVANIA MUSEUM

failed to work out. They just wanted it over with, but the lord wasn't killed by the Ilocs on the first try.

Such were the roots of disturbances, of tumult and war. First they invaded the citadel, the killers were on the move. What they wanted was to obliterate the very identity of the Quichés. Only then, they thought, could they alone have sovereignty, and it was for this alone that they came to kill. They were captured and they were made prisoners. Not many of them ever got their freedom again.

And then began the cutting of flesh. They cut the Ilocs open before the gods. This was in payment for their wrongs against Lord Noble Sweatbath. And many others went into bondage; they were made into slaves and serfs. They had simply given themselves up in defeat by fomenting war against the lord and against the canyon and the citadel. What their hearts had desired was the destruction and disintegration of the very identity of the Quiché lord, but it did not come to pass.

182

In this way it came about that people were cut open before the gods. The shields of war were made then; it was the very beginning of the fortification of the citadel at Bearded Place. The root of fiery splendor was implanted there, and because of it the reign of the Quiché lords was truly great. They were lords of singular genius. There was nothing to humble them; nothing happened to make fools of them or to ruin the greatness of their reign, which took root there at Bearded Place.

The penance done for the gods increased there, striking terror again, and all the tribes were terrified, small tribes and great tribes. They witnessed the arrival of people captured in war, who were cut open and killed for the splendor and majesty of Lord Noble Sweatbath and Lord Iztayul, along with the Greathouses and the Lord Quichés. There were only three branches of kin there at the citadel named Bearded Place.

And it was also there that they began feasting and drinking over the blossoming of their daughters. This was the way the ones they named the "Three Great Houses" stayed together. They drank their drinks there and ate their corn there, the payment for their sisters, payment for their daughters. There was only happiness in their hearts when they did it. They ate, they feasted inside their palaces.

"This is just our way of being thankful and grateful that we have good news and good tidings. It is the sign of our agreements about the daughters and sons born to our women," they said.

Epithets were bestowed there, and the lineages, the allied tribes, the principalities gave themselves names there.

"We are intermarried: we Cauecs, we Greathouses, and we Lord Quichés," said those of the three lineages and the three great houses. They spent a long time there at Bearded Place, and then they sought again and saw another citadel. They left Bearded Place behind.

ND THEN THEY GOT UP AND CAME TO THE CITADEL OF ROTTEN CANE, as the name is spoken by the Quichés. The Lords Noble Sweatbath and Plumed Serpent came along, together with all the other lords. There had been five changes and five generations of people since the origin of light, the origin of continuity, the origin of life and of humankind.

And they built many houses there.

And they also built houses for the gods, putting these in the center of the highest part of the citadel. They came and they stayed.

After that their domain grew larger; they were more numerous and more crowded. Again they planned their great houses, which had to be regrouped and sorted out because of their growing quarrels. They were jealous of one another over the prices of their sisters and daughters, which were no longer a matter of mere food and drink.

So this was the origin of their separation, when they quarreled among themselves, disturbing the bones and skulls of the dead. Then they broke apart into nine lineages, putting an end to quarrels over sisters and daughters. When the planning of the lordships was done, the result was a score and four great houses.

It was a long time ago when they all came up onto their citadel, building a score and four palaces there in the citadel of Rotten Cane. That was the citadel blessed by the lord bishop after it had been abandoned.

They achieved glory there. Their marvelous seats and cushions were arranged; the varieties of splendor were sorted out for each one of the lords of the nine lineages. One by one they took their places:

The nine lords of the Cauecs.

The nine lords of the Greathouses.

The four lords of the Lord Quichés.

The two lords of the Zaquics.

They became numerous. Those who were in the following of a given lord were also numerous, but the lord came first, at the head of his vassals. There were masses, masses of lineages for each of the lords. We shall name the titles of the lords one by one, for each of the great houses.

AND HERE ARE THE TITLES OF THE LORDS WHO LED THE CAUECS, beginning with the first in rank:

Keeper of the Mat.

Keeper of the Reception House Mat.

Keeper of Tohil.

Keeper of the Plumed Serpent.

Master of Ceremonies for the Cauecs.

Councilor of the Stores.

Quehnay Emissary.

Councilor in the Ball Court.

Mother of the Reception House.

So these are the lords who led the Cauecs, nine lords with their palaces ranged around, one for each of them. And now to show their faces . . .

184

AND NOW THESE ARE THE LORDS WHO LED THE GREATHOUSES, beginning with the first lord:

Lord Minister.

Lord Herald.

Minister of the Reception House.

Chief of the Reception House.

Mother of the Reception House.

Master of Ceremonies for the Greathouses.

Lord Auilix.

Yacolatam, meaning the "corner of the mat" or the zaclatol.

Chief Yeoltux Emissary.

So there were nine lords who led the Greathouses.

AND NOW THESE ARE THE LORD QUICHÉS. Here are the titles of the lords:

Herald.

Lord Emissary.

Lord Master of Ceremonies for the Lord Quichés.

Lord Hacauitz.

Four lords led the Lord Quichés, with their palaces ranged around.

AND THERE WERE ALSO TWO LINEAGES OF ZAQUIC LORDS:

Lord Corntassel House.

Minister for the Zaquics.

There was just one palace for these two lords.

Such was the arrangement of the score and four lords, and there came to be a score and four great houses as well.

THEN SPLENDOR AND MAJESTY GREW AMONG THE QUICHÉ. The greatness and weight of the Quiché reached its full splendor and majesty with the surfacing and plastering of the canyon and citadel. The tribes came, whether small or great and whatever the titles of their lords, adding to the greatness of the Quiché. As splendor and majesty grew, so grew the houses of gods and the houses of lords.

But the lords could not have accomplished it, they could not have done the work of building their houses or the houses of the gods, were it not for the fact that their vassals had become numerous. They neither had to lure them nor did they kidnap them or take them away by force, because each one of them rightfully belonged to the lords. And the elder and younger brothers of the lords also became populous.

Each lord led a crowded life, crowded with petitions. The lords were truly valued and had truly great respect. The birthdays of the lords were made great and held high by their vassals. Those who lived in the canyons and those who lived in the citadels multiplied then. Even so they would not have been numerous, had not all the tribes arrived to give themselves up.

And when war befell their canyons and citadels, it was by means of their genius that the Lord Plumed Serpent and the Lord Noble Sweatbath blazed with power. Plumed Serpent became a true lord of genius:

On one occasion he would climb up to the sky; on another he would go down the road to Xibalba.

On another occasion he would be serpentine, becoming an actual serpent.

On yet another occasion he would make himself aquiline, and on another feline; he would become like an actual eagle or a jaguar in his appearance.

On another occasion it would be a pool of blood; he would become nothing but a pool of blood.

Truly his being was that of a lord of genius. All the other lords were fearful before him. The news spread; all the tribal lords heard about the existence of this lord of genius.

And this was the beginning and growth of the Quiché, when the Lord Plumed Serpent made the signs of greatness. His face was not forgotten by his grandsons and sons. He didn't do these things just so there would be one single lord, a being of genius, but they had the effect of humbling all the tribes when he did them. It was just his way of revealing himself, but because of it he became the sole head of the tribes.

This lord of genius named Plumed Serpent was in the fourth generation of lords; he was both Keeper of the Mat and Keeper of the Reception House Mat.

And so he left signs and sayings for the next generation. They achieved splendor and majesty, and they, too, begot sons, making the sons still

HE WOULD MAKE HIMSELF . . .
FELINE: *A dancing shaman transforms himself into a jaguar. From a Late Classic Maya vase from Altar de Sacrificios.*

DRAWING BY KARL TAUBE

more populous. Tepepul and Iztayul were begotten; they merely served out their reign, becoming the fifth generation of lords. They begot another generation of lords.

AND HERE ARE THE NAMES OF THE SIXTH GENERATION OF LORDS. There were two great lords; they were fiery. Quicab was the name of one lord; Cauizimah was the name of the other.

And Quicab and Cauizimah did a great deal in their turn. They added to the greatness of the Quiché because they truly had genius. They crushed and they shattered the canyons and citadels of the tribes, small and great—the ones that had citadels among them in ancient times, nearby:

There was a mountain place of the Cakchiquels, called Nettles Heights today.

And also a mountain place of the Rabinals, Place of Spilt Water.

And a mountain of the Caoques, Plaster House.

And then a citadel of the White Earths, Hot Springs Heights.

Under Ten, Front of the Monument, and Willow Tree.

They all hated Quicab. They made war, but in fact they were brought down, they were shattered, these canyons, these citadels of the Rabinals, Cakchiquels, White Earths. All the tribes went down on their faces or flat on their backs. The warriors of Quicab kept up the killing for a long time, until there were only one or two groups, from among all the enemies, who hadn't brought tribute. Their citadels fell and they brought tribute to Quicab and Cauizimah. Their lineages came to be bled, shot full of arrows at the stake. Their day came to nothing, their heritage came to nothing.

Projectiles alone were the means for breaking the citadels. All at once the earth itself would crack open; it was as if a lightning bolt had shattered the stones. In fear, the members of one tribe after another went before the gum tree, carrying in their hands the signs of the citadels, with the result that a mountain of stones is there today. Only a few of these aren't cut stones; the rest look as though they had been split with an axe. The result is there on the plain named Petatayub; it is obvious to this day. Everyone who passes by can see it as a sign of the manhood of Quicab. He could not be killed, nor could he be conquered. He was truly a man, and all the tribes brought tribute.

And then all the lords made plans; they moved to cordon off the canyons and citadels, the fallen citadels of all the tribes.

AFTER THAT CAME THE SENTRIES, to watch for the makers of war. Now lookout lineages were established to occupy the conquered mountains:

"Otherwise the tribes would return to inhabit their citadels," all the lords said when they had all shared their thoughts. Then the assignments were given out:

"Let them be like a palisade to us, and like doubles for our own lineages, and like a stockade, a fortress to us. Let them now become our anger, our manliness," said all the lords. The assignments were given to each of the lineages that were to provide opposition to the makers of war.

And then they were notified, and then they went to their posts, occupying the mountain places of the tribes:

"Go, because these are now our mountains. Do not be afraid. The moment there are makers of war again, coming back among you as your

PROJECTILES ALONE WERE THE
MEANS FOR BREAKING THE
CITADELS: *In Mixtec books,
conquest is signified by darts
thrust into a place name, which in
this example consists of the sign
for a mountain. From the Codex
Nuttall.*

DRAWING BY THE AUTHOR

murderers, send for us to come and kill them," Quicab and the Minister
and the Herald told them, notifying all of them.

Then they went off, those who are called the Point of the Arrow, Angle
of the Bowstring. Their grandfathers and fathers split up then; they were
on each of the mountains. They went just as guards of the mountains,
and as arrowhead and bowstring guards, and as guards against the makers
of war as well. None of them had been there at the dawning nor did any
of them have his own god; they just blocked the way to the citadel. They
all went out:

The keepers of Nettles Heights, keepers of Mirror Side, White River,
Deer Dance Plaza, Plank Place, Eighteen.

Also, the keepers of Earthquake, Meteor, Hunahpu Place.

And the keepers of Spilt Water, keepers of Among the Rocks, keepers
of Plaster House, keepers of Ziya House, keepers of Hot Springs, keepers
of Under Ten, of the plains, of the mountains.

The war sentries, the guardians of the land, went out, they went on
behalf of Quicab and Cauizimah, Keeper of the Mat and Keeper of the
Reception House Mat, and on behalf of the Minister and the Herald.
There were four lords who posted messengers and sentries against the
makers of war:

Quicab and Cauizimah are the names of the two lords who led the
Cauecs.

Woven is the name of the lord who led the Greathouses.

And Armadillo Dung is the name of the lord who led the Lord
Quichés.

So these are the names of the lords who posted messengers and couri-
ers. Their own vassals went to the mountains, to each one of the moun-

189

tains, and as soon as they had gone, spoils kept coming back, and prisoners of war kept coming back to Quicab and Cauizimah, to the Minister and the Herald. The Points of the Arrows and Angles of the Bowstrings made war. They took spoils and prisoners again. There came to be heroes again, among those who were sentries. They were given seats and honored; they were generously remembered by the lords when they came to turn over all their spoils and their prisoners.

After that, when the Lords Keeper of the Mat, Keeper of the Reception House Mat, Minister, and Herald had shared their thoughts, their decision came out:

"When it comes to the ennobling of the lookout lineages, we'll induct only those who are first in rank. I am Keeper of the Mat."

"And I am Keeper of the Reception House Mat."

"The nobility of Keeper of the Mat, which is mine—and that which is yours, Lord Minister—should enter into this. Ministers will be ennobled." And all the lords spoke as they gathered their thoughts. The Tams and Ilocs did just the same; the three divisions of the Quiché were in concord when they carried out the investiture. They titled those of the first rank among their vassals.

In this way the decision was reached. But they weren't inducted at Quiché. The mountain where the first-ranking vassals were inducted has a name; all of them were summoned, from each of the mountains where they were, and they gathered in just one place. Under the Twine, Under the Cord is the name of the mountain where they were inducted, where they entered into nobility. It was done at the boundary of Mirror Side.

And here are their titles, their honors, and their marks: a score of Ministers and a score of Keepers of the Mat were created by the Keeper of the Mat and the Keeper of the Reception House Mat, and by the Minister and the Herald.

All of these entered the nobility: Ministers, Keepers of the Mat, eleven Masters of Ceremonies, Minister for the Lords, Minister for the Zaquics, Military Minister, Military Keeper of the Mat, Military Walls, and Military Corners are the titles that came in when the soldiers were titled and named to their seats, their cushions.

These were the first-ranking vassals, watchers and listeners for the Quiché people, Points of the Arrows, Angles of the Bowstrings, a palisade, an enclosure, a wall, a fortress around Quiché.

And the Tams and Ilocs did the same thing; they inducted and titled the first-ranking vassals for each mountain.

So this was the origin of the noble Ministers and Keepers of the Mat that exist for each of the mountains today. The sequence was such that they came out later than the Keeper of the Mat proper and the Keeper of the Reception House Mat, and later than the Minister and the Herald.

ND NOW WE SHALL NAME THE NAMES OF THE HOUSES OF THE GODS, although the houses have the same names as the gods:

Great Monument of Tohil is the name of the building that housed Tohil of the Cauecs.

Auilix, next, is the name of the building that housed Auilix of the Greathouses.

Hacauitz is the name, then, of the building that housed the god of the Lord Quichés.

Corntassel, whose house of sacrifice can still be seen, is the name of another great monument.

These were the locations of the stones whose days were kept by the Quiché lords. Their days were also kept by all the tribes. When the tribes burned offerings, they came before Tohil first.

After that, they greeted the Keeper of the Mat and Keeper of the Reception House Mat next, then they handed over their quetzal feathers and their tribute to the lords, these same lords.

And so they nurtured and provided for the Keeper of the Mat and Keeper of the Reception House Mat, who had been victorious over their citadels.

THEY CAME BEFORE TOHIL FIRST: *Seated in his temple (shown in cross section behind him), K'awil (the lowland Maya counterpart of Tohil) receives offerings in bowls and (at extreme left) a censer full of flaming copal. From the Dresden Codex.*

DRAWING BY CARLOS A. VILLACORTA

They were great lords, they were people of genius. Plumed Serpent and Noble Sweatbath were lords of genius, and Quicab and Cauizimah were lords of genius. They knew whether war would occur; everything they saw was clear to them. Whether there would be death, or whether there would be famine, or whether quarrels would occur, they knew it for certain, since there was a place to see it, there was a book. Council Book was their name for it.

But it wasn't only in this way that they were lords. They were great in their own being and observed great fasts. As a way of cherishing their buildings and cherishing their lordship, they fasted for long periods, they did penance before their gods.

And here is their way of fasting:

For nine score days they would fast, and for nine they would do penance and burn offerings.

Thirteen score was another of their fasts, and for thirteen they would do penance and burn offerings before Tohil and their other gods. They would only eat zapotes, matasanos, jocotes; there was nothing made of corn for their meals.

Even if they did penance for seventeen score, then for seventeen they fasted, they did not eat. They achieved truly great abstinence.

This was a sign that they had the being of true lords. And there weren't any women with them when they slept; they kept themselves apart when they fasted. They just stayed in the houses of the gods, each day. All they did was keep the days, burn offerings, and do penance. They were there whether it was dark or dawn; they just cried their hearts and their guts out when they asked for light and life for their vassals and their domain. They lifted their faces to the sky, and here is their prayer before their gods, when they made their requests.

AND THIS IS THE CRY OF THEIR HEARTS, here it is:

> "Wait! On this blessed day,
> thou Hurricane, thou Heart of the Sky-Earth,
> thou giver of ripeness and freshness,
> and thou giver of daughters and sons,
> spread thy stain, spill thy drops
> of green and yellow;
> give life and beginning
> to those I bear and beget,

that they might multiply and grow,
nurturing and providing for thee,
calling to thee along the roads and paths,
on rivers, in canyons,
beneath the trees and bushes;
give them their daughters and sons.

"May there be no blame, obstacle, want, or misery;
let no deceiver come behind or before them,
may they neither be snared nor wounded,
nor seduced, nor burned,
nor diverted below the road nor above it;
may they neither fall over backward nor stumble;
keep them on the Green Road, the Green Path.

"May there be no blame or barrier for them
through any secrets or sorcery of thine;
may thy nurturers and providers be good
before thy mouth and thy face,
thou, Heart of Sky; thou, Heart of Earth;
thou, Bundle of Flames;
and thou, Tohil, Auilix, Hacauitz,
under the sky, on the earth,
the four sides, the four corners;
may there be only light, only continuity within,
before thy mouth and thy face, thou god."

So it was with the lords when they fasted during nine score, thirteen score, or seventeen score days; their days of fasting were many. They cried their hearts out over their vassals and over all their wives and children. Each and every lord did service, as a way of cherishing the light of life and of cherishing lordship.

Such were the lordships of the Keeper of the Mat, Keeper of the Reception House Mat, Minister, and Herald. They went into fasting two by two, taking turns at carrying the tribes and all the Quiché people on their shoulders.

At its root the word came from just one place, and the root of nurturing and providing was the same as the root of the word. The Tams and Ilocs did likewise, along with the Rabinals, Cakchiquels, those of Bird House, Sweatbath House, Talk House. They came away in unity, having heard, there at Quiché, what all of them should do.

It wasn't merely that they became lords; it wasn't just that they received occasional gifts from nurturers and providers who merely made food and drink for them. Nor did they wantonly falsify or steal their lordship, their splendor, their majesty. And it wasn't merely that they crushed the canyons and citadels of the tribes, whether small or great, but that the tribes paid a great price:

There came turquoise, there came metal.

And there came drops of jade and other gems that measured the width of four fingers or a full fist across.

And there came green, yellow, and red feather work, the tribute of all the tribes. It came to the lords of genius Plumed Serpent and Noble Sweatbath, and to Quicab and Cauizimah as well, to the Keeper of the Mat, Keeper of the Reception House Mat, Minister, and Herald.

What they did was no small feat, and the tribes they conquered were not few in number. The tribute of Quiché came from many tribal divisions.

And the lords had undergone pain and withstood it; their rise to splendor had not been sudden. Actually it was Plumed Serpent who was the root of the greatness of the lordship.

Such was the beginning of the rise and growth of Quiché.

And now we shall list the generations of lords, and we shall also name the names of all these lords.

AND HERE ARE THE GENERATIONS, THE SEQUENCES OF LORDSHIPS, so that all of them will be clear.

Jaguar Quitze, Jaguar Night, Not Right Now, and Dark Jaguar were our first grandfathers, our first fathers when the sun appeared, when the moon and stars appeared.

And here are the generations, the sequences, of lordships. We shall begin from here, at their very root. The lords will come up two by two, as each generation of lords enters and succeeds the previous grandfathers and lords of the citadel, going on through each and every one of the lords.

And here shall appear the faces of each one of the lords.

AND HERE SHALL APPEAR THE FACES, ONE BY ONE, OF EACH OF THE QUICHÉ LORDS . . .

Jaguar Quitze, origin of the Cauecs.

Noble Raiment, in the second generation after Jaguar Quitze.

Jaguar Noble Rooftree, who began the office of Keeper of the Mat, was in the third generation.

Noble Sweatbath and Iztayul, in the fourth generation.

Plumed Serpent and Noble Sweatbath, at the root of the lords of genius, were in the fifth generation.

Tepepul and Iztayul next, sixth in the sequence.

Quicab and Cauizimah, in the seventh change of lordship, were the culmination of genius.

Tepepul and Xtayub, in the eighth generation.

Black Butterfly and Tepepul, in the ninth generation.

Eight Cord, with Quicab, in the tenth generation of lords.

Seven Thought and Cauatepech next, eleventh in the sequence of lords.

Three Deer and Nine Dog, in the twelfth generation of lords. And they were ruling when Tonatiuh arrived. They were tortured by the Castilian people.

Black Butterfly and Tepepul were tributary to the Castilian people. They had already been begotten as the thirteenth generation of lords.

Don Juan de Rojas and Don Juan Cortés, in the fourteenth generation of lords. They are the sons of Black Butterfly and Tepepul.

So these are the generations, the sequences of lordships for the Keeper of the Mat and Keeper of the Reception House Mat, the lords who have led the Cauecs of Quiché. Next we shall name the lineages.

And here are the great houses of each one of the lords in the following of the Keeper of the Mat and Keeper of the Reception House Mat. These are the names of the nine lineages of the Cauecs, nine great houses. Here are the titles of the rulers of each one of the great houses:

Lord Keeper of the Mat, with one great house. Granary is the name of the palace.

WHEN TONATIUH ARRIVED: *A Quiché sketch of the coat of arms of the Hapsburgs, rulers of Austria and Spain when Pedro de Alvarado (Tonatiuh) invaded the Quiché kingdom. From the sixteenth-century Título de los Señores de Coyoy.*

Lord Keeper of the Reception House Mat. Bird House is the name of his palace.

Master of Ceremonies for the Cauecs, with one great house.

Lord Keeper of Tohil, with one great house.

Lord Keeper of the Plumed Serpent, with one great house.

Councilor of the Stores, with one great house.

Quehnay Emissary, with one great house.

Councilor in the Ball Court, Xcuxeba, with one great house.

Sovereign Mexican, with one great house.

So these are the nine lineages of the Cauecs. Many vassals are counted in the following of these nine great houses.

AND HERE ARE THOSE OF THE GREATHOUSES, with nine more great houses. First we shall name the genealogy of the lordship. It began, from just one root, at the origin of the root of the day and the light:

Jaguar Night, first grandfather and father.

Noble Acul and Noble Acutec, in the second generation.

Noble Chahuh and Noble Inscription House, in the third generation.

Nine Deer next, in the fourth generation.

Noble Sweatbath, in the fifth generation of lords.

And Monkey House next, in the sixth generation.

And Iztayul, in the seventh generation of lords.

Noble Sweatbath then, eighth in the sequence of lordships.

Nine Deer, ninth in the sequence.

Woven, as the next one was called, in the tenth generation.

Lord Noble Sweatbath, in the eleventh generation.

Don Cristóbal, as he was called, became lord in the presence of the Castilian people.

Don Pedro de Robles is Lord Minister today.

And these are all the lords who come in the following of the Lord Minister. Now we shall give the title of the ruler of each one of the great houses:

Lord Minister, the first-ranking lord at the head of the Greathouses, with one great house.

Lord Herald, with one great house.

Lord Minister of the Reception House, with one great house.

Chief of the Reception House, with one great house.

Mother of the Reception House, with one great house.

Master of Ceremonies for the Greathouses, with one great house.

Lord Auilix, with one great house.

Yacolatam, with one great house.

So these are the great houses at the head of the Greathouses; these are the names of the nine lineages of the Greathouses, as they are called. There are many branch lineages in the following of each one of these lords; we have named only the first-ranking titles.

A ND NOW THESE ARE FOR THE LORD QUICHÉS. Here are their grandfathers and fathers:

Not Right Now, the first person.

Noble Lord is the name of the lord of the second generation.

Red Banner.

Noble Short One.

Noble Doctor.

Seven Cane.

Noble Mortal.

Noble Caller.

Person of Bam.

So these are the lords at the head of the Lord Quichés; these are their generations and sequences.

And here are the lords within the palaces, with just four great houses:

Herald for the Lords is the title of the first lord, with one great house.

Emissary for the Lords, the second lord, with one great house.

Master of Ceremonies for the Lords, the third lord, with one great house.

And Hacauitz, the fourth lord, with one great house.

And so these are the four great houses at the head of the Lord Quichés.

A ND THERE ARE THREE MASTERS OF CEREMONIES IN ALL. They are like fathers to all the Quiché lords. They come together in unity, these three Masters of Ceremonies. They are givers of birth, they are Mothers of the Word, they are Fathers of the Word, great in being few, these three Masters of Ceremonies:

Master of Ceremonies for the Cauecs, first.

And Master of Ceremonies for the Greathouses, second.

Lord Master of Ceremonies for the Lord Quichés, third of the Masters of Ceremonies.

And so there are three Masters of Ceremonies, one representing each of these lineages.

THIS IS ENOUGH ABOUT THE BEING OF QUICHÉ, given that there is no longer a place to see it. There is the original book and ancient writing owned by the lords, now lost, but even so, everything has been completed here concerning Quiché, which is now named Santa Cruz.

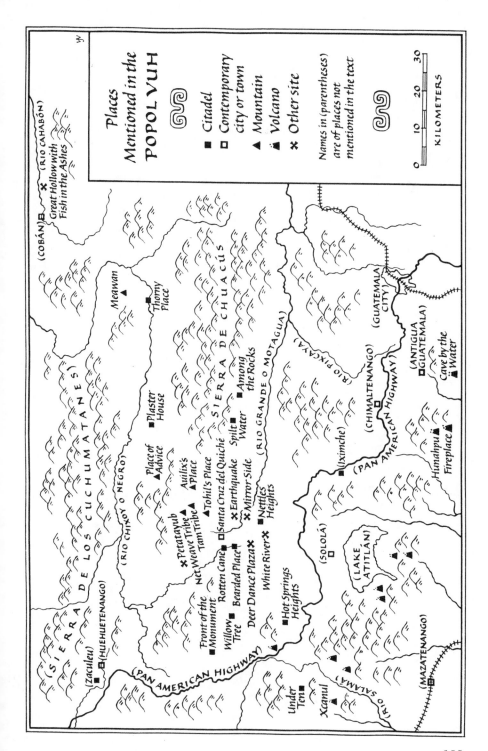

Places
Mentioned in the
POPOL VUH

■ Citadel
□ Contemporary city or town
▲ Mountain
♠ Volcano
✗ Other site

Names in (parentheses) are of places not mentioned in the text

0   10   20   30
KILOMETERS

✗ Great Hollow with Fish in the Ashes
(RIO CAHABÓN)
(COBÁN) ■

▲ Meawan
■ Thorny Place

SIERRA DE LOS CUCHUMATANES

(RIO CHIXOY O NEGRO)

■ Plaster House

▲ Place of Advice

SIERRA DE CHUACÚS

■ Among the Rocks
■ Spilt Water

▲ Avilix's Place
✗ Tohil's Place
□ Santa Cruz del Quiché
✗ Earthquake
✗ Mirror-Side

(RIO GRANDE O MOTAGUA)

✗ Patatayub
✗ Net Weave Tribe ▲
Tam Tribe ▲
Rotten Cane □
■ Bearded Place ✗
Deer Dance Plaza ✗
✗ White River

■ Nettles Heights

(Uxamche) ■

(PAN AMERICAN HIGHWAY)

(CHIMALTENANGO) □

(RIO PIXCAYÁ)

(GUATEMALA CITY)

(ANTIGUA GUATEMALA) □
Cave by the ▲ Water

■ Front of the Monument
■ Willow Tree

▲ Hunahpú
▲ Fireplace

■ Hot Springs Heights

(SOLOLÁ) □

(LAKE ATITLÁN)

(HUEHUETENANGO) □

(Zaculeu) ■

(PAN AMERICAN HIGHWAY)

▲ Under Ten

Xcanul ▲

(RIO SALAMÁ)

(MAZATENANGO) □

199

NOTES
AND COMMENTS

ORTHOGRAPHY

Words from the Mayan languages of Guatemala, when they appear in italics, are written in the new alphabets of the Academia de las Lenguas Mayas de Guatemala (1988), except that vowels have been reduced to the five found in both hieroglyphic texts and early alphabetic documents. With the following exceptions, consonants may be pronounced as in English: *j* is like Spanish *j*, with the tongue farther back than for English *h; l* is like Welsh *ll*, with the tongue farther forward than for English; and *q* is like Hebrew qoph, with the tongue farther back than for English *k*. Two other Mayan sounds are found in English but are spelled differently: *tz* is like *ts* in English "bats," and *x* is like English *sh*. The glottal stop, equivalent to *tt* in the Scottish pronunciation of "bottle," is indicated by *'*; when it follows a consonant, it is pronounced simultaneously with that consonant. Vowels are approximately like those of Spanish or Italian. Stress is nearly always on the final syllable of a word. In most cases words in italics from Mayan languages outside of Guatemala or from Nahuatl, the language of the Aztecs, retain the orthographies of the sources consulted.

In the Popol Vuh and other early alphabetic documents in Quiché and other Quichean languages, vowels followed by glottal stops were written *aa, ee, ii, oo, uu*; in the new spellings these become *a', e', i', o', u'*. Among the glottalized consonants, *b* becomes *b', tt* becomes *t', 4h* becomes *ch'*, and *4,* becomes *tz'*. Among k sounds, the plain front variety formerly written *c* or *qu* is now *k*, while the plain back variety formerly written *k* is now *q*. The glottalized forms once written *4* and *3* are now *k'* and *q'*, respectively. And finally, *h* becomes *j*, while *z* and *ç* become *s*. Where untranslated proper names appear in roman type, they follow the original spellings of the documents. Otherwise, original spellings (in roman type enclosed in brackets) are given only where the new spellings of the same words (in italics) include corrections of phonetic or scribal errors.

The names of the Guatemalan Mayan peoples and languages mentioned in this work, as written in the new official alphabets, are *K'iche', Kaqchikel, Tz'utujil, Poqomchi, Q'eqchi', Ixil, Mam*, and *Jakalteko*. The spellings used in the present work are the ones most commonly followed in Spanish and English publications: Quiché, Cakchiquel, Tzutuhil, Pokomchí, Kekchí, Ixil, Mam, and Jacaltec. It is true that most of these spellings are imperfect reflections of the way speakers of Mayan languages pronounce the names, but they do reflect the way the names are commonly pronounced in the context of Spanish or English discourse. In the same way, *inglés* is a Spanish rendition of *English, Jakalteko* is a Mayan rendition of Nahuatl *uacaltica,* and *Castilian* and *kaxlan* are English and Mayan renditions of *castellano.*

ABBREVIATIONS

Citations of vocabulary sources are given by a letter code, as with DB for Domingo de Basseta; see the first page of the Bibliography for the key to this code. PV abbreviates Popol Vuh and MS refers to the Popol Vuh manuscript.

MAYAN POETICS

When the gods of the PV first try to make humans and come up with animals instead (see p. 67), they nevertheless attempt to teach their creations to speak. The lesson they offer is not only an exercise in pronunciation and grammar, but an exercise in basic Mayan poetics as well. It consists of a few lines of prayer, limited to a list of divine names, but its forms would be appropriate for any other kind of formal oratory. First comes an item that stands alone, but what follows is parallel verse, constructed by pairing words or phrases that are partly the same and partly different:

Juraqan,	Hurricane,
ch'ipi kaqulja,	Newborn Thunderbolt,
raxa kaqulja,	Sudden Thunderbolt,
uk'ux kaj,	Heart of Sky,
uk'ux ulew,	Heart of Earth,
tz'aqol,	Maker,
b'itol,	Modeler,
alom,	Bearer,
k'ajolom.	Begetter.

The count of syllables shifts from one couplet to the next, and in two cases it even shifts from one half of a couplet to the other. There are rhythms here, but they are not rhythms constructed for the sake of sound alone. Rather, they are built from whole words and phrases, as when *ch'ipi* and *raxa*, "newborn" and "sudden," trade places as adjectives modifying *kaqulja*, "thunderbolt." At a smaller scale, they are built from stems such as *tzaq-* and *b'it-*, "make" and "model," and affixes such as *-ol*, something like English "-er." In other words, these rhythms work at the level of syntax, where sounds have already been organized to make meanings.

If the animals had mastered their first lesson they might have been taught some additional tricks. Skilled Quiché orators do not deliver verse mechanically, but rather ring changes on it through the timing of their pauses. Recast in lines separated from one another by pauses rather than by verse structure alone, the passage quoted above might go like this:

> Hurricane,
> Newborn Thunderbolt,
> Sudden Thunderbolt,
> Heart of Sky, Heart of Earth,
> Maker, Modeler, Bearer, Begetter.

A skilled performance also requires changes in the verse structure itself. The parallelism of couplets can and should be varied, from time to time, with triplets. The list of animals made by the gods provides a simple example:

kej,	deer,
tz'ikin,	birds,
koj,	pumas,
b'alam,	jaguars,
kumatz,	serpents,
sochoch,	rattlesnakes,
k'anti	fer-de-lances

But whatever the groupings according to meaning, a list of this kind would be delivered today without any more marking of the transition between jaguars and serpents than that between pumas and jaguars. There would be no pause until the run of parallel nouns came to a halt or the breath of the speaker ran out. On this basis I have chosen not to break such lists into lines of verse in the present translation, but have run them on as prose.

Another variation on the couplet takes the form of a quatrain in which the first two parts establish a pattern, the third departs from it (often by means of simplification), and the fourth returns to it. Here is an example from the narration of how the earth was made (p. 63):

203

ukaj tz'ukuxik,	fourfold siding,
ukaj xukutaxik	fourfold cornering,
retaxik,	measuring,
ukaj che'xik	fourfold staking

There do come moments in Quiché poetry when sounds seem to come to the foreground against syntax, but even then they are put in the direct service of meaning, this time by way of onomatopoeia. The following passage is dense with alliteration and assonance, both inside its words and between them, but it opens language toward the direct imitation of what is outside it, evoking the sounds of a primordial world that consists only of a flat sea and an empty sky:

K'a katz'ininoq,	Now it still ripples,
k'a kachamamoq,	now it still murmurs,
katz'inonik,	ripples,
k'a kasilanik,	it still sighs,
k'a kalolinik,	it still hums,
katolona puch.	and it is empty.

For ears attuned to patterns that run below the level of syntax, this seems to be one of the most densely poetic passages in the PV. For Quiché ears it is rather the sound of chaos—not the maelstrom of Old World mythology, but a chaos of vibrations and pulsations.

In narrative the vertical movement of verse, which dwells on the moment, must be modified by the horizontal movement of prose, which carries the action forward. When the two forces alternate, the result is a diagonal trajectory:

xchaw ruk' ri tepew q'ukumatz
xech'a k'ut, ta xenaojinik
  ta xeb'isonik,
    xeriqo kib'
    xkikuch kitzij
      kinaoj

He spoke with the Sovereign Plumed Serpent,
and they talked, then they thought,
    then they worried.
      They agreed with each other,
      they joined their words,
        their thoughts.

Sometimes the balance may swing more toward the verticality of verse than in this example and sometimes more toward the horizontality of prose. When action moves fast during the telling of a story, parallel verse may be reduced to an occasional couplet or triplet, afloat on a river of prose. As a rule, I have chosen to cast my translation in a verse format only where parallelism is sustained for more than one or two couplets, and only where parallel meanings are expressed in parallel syntax. For more on Mayan verse, see D. Tedlock (1983a; 1983b: chap. 8; 1987), Hanks (1989), and Sam Colop (1994).

The division of the translation into paragraphs is largely based on two considerations. The first is the occurrence of what Dell Hymes calls "initial particles" (Hymes 1981:318–20). Examples in Quiché are *k'ut*, "And here" or "And this is"; *k'ate k'ut*, "And next"; and *keje k'ut*, "And so." The second consideration is the occurrence of quotations. In contemporary Quiché speech there are deliberate pauses both before and after phrases consisting of initial particles, and immediately before quotations (see D. Tedlock 1983b: chap. 4; 1987).

THE MAYAN CALENDAR

The foundation of Mayan timekeeping, and that of Mesoamerican timekeeping in general, is a divinatory calendar of 260 days. It is made up of two shorter cycles, one consisting of an endlessly repeating sequence of thirteen day numbers and the other of an endlessly repeating sequence of twenty day names. Since 13 and 20 have no common factor, the interaction of 13 numbers with 20 names produces a larger repeating sequence of 260 combinations ($13 \times 20 = 260$). If we begin with the day that combines the number 1 with the name *Kej*, the list of successive days proceeds as follows:

QUICHÉ DAY NAMES WITH NUMBERS
(Yucatec names in parentheses)

1 Kej	(Manik')	11 No'j	(Kaban)
2 Q'anil	(Lamat)	12 Tijax	(Ets'nab)
3 Toj	(Muluk)	13 Kawuq	(Kawak)
4 Tz'i'	(Ok)	1 Junajpu	(Ahaw)
5 B'atz'	(Chuen)	2 Imox	(Imix)
6 E	(Eb)	3 Iq'	(Ik')
7 Aj	(Ben)	4 Aq'ab'al	(Ak'bal)
8 Ix	(Ix)	5 K'at	(K'an)
9 Tz'ikin	(Men)	6 Kan	(Chikchan)
10 Ajmak	(Kib)	7 Kame	(Kimi)

From *7 Kame* the count goes on to *8 Kej*, *9 Q'anil*, and so forth, returning to *1 Kej* after 260 days.

Contemporary daykeepers often call this sequence of days "the calendar of the earth," thus setting it apart from astronomical intervals such as the solar year. Andrés Xiloj, among others, insists that the period of human pregnancy is the basis for its length, and 260 days is indeed close to an average figure for the interval between first missed menses (the earliest definitive sign of pregnancy) and birth. It should also be noted that the growth cycle of one of the varieties of corn planted in highland Guatemala is such that it is ideally harvested 260 days after planting (see B. Tedlock 1985; 1992: chap. 8).

Ancient Mayan astronomers measured the rhythms of lunar, planetary, and solar cycles against those of the divinatory calendar. In the eclipse table of the Dresden Codex, a series of 405 lunations is reckoned as beginning on the Yucatec day *13 Muluk* and ending on *12 Lamat* (Lounsbury 1978:796). The equivalent Quiché day names, *Toj* and *Q'anil*, are the same ones Blood Moon invokes (in that order) when she prays before the single cornstalk in Xmucane's field (translated as Thunder and Yellow on p. 103). The lunations of the eclipse table are divided into groups that most often consist of six moons, and that is the number of moons that go by before Blood Moon's father discovers her pregnancy (p. 99).

The Mayan Venus calendar is best known from a table in the Dresden Codex (Thompson 1972:62–71), but the presence of Venus reckoning in the Guatemalan highlands is attested by the PV and by a Quiché almanac dating from 1722 (Berendt n.d.). A given Venus synodic period (lasting 584 days) is divided into four stages, with Venus appearing as the morning star at the beginning of the first stage and remaining visible throughout it (236 days or 8 synodic moons). During the second stage (90 days), Venus goes through its last 27 days (one sidereal moon) as the morning star, disappears for 50 days, and runs through its first 13 days as the evening star. It remains visible as the evening star throughout the third period (250 days) and stays out of sight throughout the fourth period (8 days), after which it returns to the first stage.

During a given 584-day period the 20 day names repeat 29 times, giving 580 days with a remainder of 4; this means that a new Venus cycle will always begin 4 days later in the sequence of 20 day names than the previous cycle. And since 20 is evenly divisible by 4 ($20 \div 4 = 5$), only 5 of the day names can ever begin a Venus cycle. In the Dresden Codex the chosen days (here given their Quiché names) were *Junajpu, K'at, Q'anil, E,* and *Ajmak,* followed by *Junajpu* again. Starting from *1 Junajpu* (as the Dresden Codex does) and running through five complete periods so as to show all of the possible day names, the beginning dates for the four stages within each Venus period work out as follows:

Dates for Five Successive Venus Periods

	First	Second	Third	Fourth	Fifth
Appears as morning star:	1 Junajpu	13 K'at	12 Q'anil	11 E	10 Ajmak
Becomes invisible:	3 Ajmak	2 Junajpu	1 K'at	13 Q'anil	12 E
Appears as evening star:	2 Kame	1 Tz'i'	13 Ix	12 Tijax	11 Iq'
Becomes invisible:	5 Ajmak	4 Junajpu	3 K'at	2 Q'anil	1 E

After five complete cycles totaling 2,920 days, the movements of Venus fill eight idealized years of 365 days each and come within hours of spanning 99 lunations. At this point Venus begins repeating the same series of period-beginning day names but with different numbers, while at the same time coming very close to repeating its relationship to the fixed stars and the seasons of the solar year. To get back to a morning appearance on *1 Junajpu*, Venus must repeat the full set of five periods a total of thirteen times.

In the PV, the divine names One and Seven Hunahpu (*Junajpu*) and One and Seven Death (*Kame*) point directly to the Venus calendar, and specifically to the first of the five periods charted above. Andrés Xiloj pointed out that combining the numbers 1 and 7 with a given day name is a conventional way of indicating all 13 days bearing that name. The reason is that when one traces a single day name through all of its occurrences in a given 260-day cycle, the accompanying numbers fall out in the sequence 1, 8, 2, 9, 3, 10, 4, 11, 5, 12, 6, 13, and 7. This means that if the divine names in question here refer to astronomical events, these should be events whose day names remain constant but whose day numbers are variable, which is indeed the case. The ball game One and Seven Hunahpu play on their own court corresponds to the appearance of Venus as the morning star on a day that bears their name, their death by sacrifice at the court of One and Seven Death corresponds to the appearance of the evening star on a day named *Kame,* and the eventual resurrection of Seven Hunahpu by Hunahpu and Xbalanque corresponds to the return of the morning star to its original day name. Just as there are five kinds of Venus period, so there are fivefold recurrences in their story, the most obvious of these being the five test houses where Hunahpu and Xbalanque spend the night in the underworld (see the notes to p. 97). Also five in number are the severed heads (corresponding to the evening star) of the underworld episodes: One Hunahpu's head is placed in a tree, the underworld lords use an artificial skull as a ball, Hunahpu's head is put into play as a ball, a carved squash is substituted for his head, and finally Xbalanque cuts off Hunahpu's head in a mock sacrifice.

Two characters in the PV, One Monkey (*1 B'atz'*) and One Artisan (*1 Chuen*), respectively bear the Quiché and Yucatec names of the same day on the divinatory calendar. This suggests that they might correspond to an astronomical phenomenon whose canonical divinatory date is constant in both number and name, which would require a periodicity of 260 days or an even multiple thereof. The only planetary possibility is Mars, whose average synodic period of 780 (3 × 260) days is reflected in the fact that the Mars table in the Dresden Codex is organized around a single day number and name. The table also reflects the extreme variability of Mars from one period to the next, using this one day as a focal point at the near end of a 63-day range of possibilities for the heliacal rise of the planet (Bricker and Bricker 1986:66–68). The day in question is *3 Lamat* (*3 Q'anil* in Quiché), which happens to be followed, 63 days later, by *1 Chuen* (*1 B'atz'*). It would appear, then, that the Mars table used by the Quiché must have had the latter date as its anchor. If so, we may imagine that the animals illustrated in this table were not the "Mars beasts" of the Dresden Codex, which have the snouts of reptiles and the legs of peccaries, but rather the monkeys of the PV narrative. This interpretation is supported by a Kekchí myth recorded among the contemporary Mopán Maya, in which the brother of the gods of the sun and Venus, having been transformed into a monkey, becomes an unspecified planet that is probably Mars (Thompson 1970:355). For more on planetary astronomy in the PV, see D. Tedlock (1992a; 1992b) and D. and B. Tedlock (1993).

Among all the astronomical periods to fall into place in the PV, the invariable Mayan solar year of 365 days is the last. In a given year all 20 day names are repeated 18 times, giving 360 days with a remainder of 5; this means that the next solar year will always begin with a day name that comes 5 days later in the cycle of 20 than the name that began the previous year. And since 20 is evenly divisible by 5 (20 ÷ 5 = 4), only 4 of the 20 day names, evenly spaced within the name cycle, can ever begin a solar year. For the Quiché, these new year's day names were and are the same as in the Dresden Codex; their Quiché names are *Kej, E, No'j,* and *Iq',* followed by *Kej* again. As for the new year's day number, the 13 numbers are repeated 28 times in a given year, giving 364 days and a remainder of 1, which means that a given solar year will always begin with a day number that comes a single place later in the cycle of 13 than the number that began the previous year. The year as a whole is designated by the number and name of its beginning day; starting with a year bearing the name *1 Kej*, the reckoning of successive years proceeds as follows:

QUICHÉ YEAR DESIGNATIONS

1 Kej	6 E	11 No'j
2 E	7 No'j	12 Iq'
3 No'j	8 Iq'	13 Kej
4 Iq'	9 Kej	1 E
5 Kej	10 E	etc.

Two of these day names, *E* and *Iq'*, also have a potential for events pertaining to Venus (see the Venus calendar above). They occur in the fourth and (more markedly) in the fifth and final Venus period, just as the solar dimension of the story of Hunahpu and Xbalanque waits for two scenes that come late. In the first, one of the four old possums or vagabond actors whose job it is to bring the new year makes a personal appearance (pp. 127–28). In the second, after a five-day period corresponding to the end of an old year, Hunahpu and Xbalanque disguise themselves as the bearers of a new year (p. 132).

INTRODUCTION

22–33

My account of Mayan archaeology is based largely on M. Coe (1987; 1994), Hammond (1982), Fash (1991), and various essays in Chase and Rice (1985) and Sabloff and Andrews (1986). David Stuart (n.d.) is my source of information on the relationship between Copán and Teotihuacan. The Postclassic Mexican impact on the highlands is notably weaker than in Yucatán. The PV and other highland documents from the sixteenth century contain many fewer Nahua words than the Chilam Balam books of Yucatán. The notion that elite highland lineages came from the Gulf coast, which has been repeated uncritically by many scholars, originated with Recinos (see Recinos et al. 1950:62–68). Ignoring the fact that the PV and other highland documents have these lineages moving westward to reach their present homes, and that the Quiché kingdom subsequently expanded westward, he gave them a common origin with the Tutul Xiu, who moved eastward along the Gulf to reach Yucatán. Brown (1985) points to the absence of archaeological evidence for the Gulf connection.

23

For a general discussion of what is known about Mayan books from early Spanish sources, see Thompson (1972: chap. 1). The story of the surviving books (or codices) and their rediscovery by modern scholars is told by M. Coe (1992: chaps. 3–6). The Dresden Codex is fully reproduced in Thompson (1972), the Paris Codex in Love (1994), and the fragment found in Chiapas (the Grolier Codex) in Coe (1973). On similarities between the illustrations in such books and wall paintings along the east coast of Yucatán, see Miller (1982:54–59) and Paxton (1986:202–11). For general introductions to the Mayan writing system, see Lounsbury (1989) and Houston (1989). Whittaker (1986) has found Nahua words in the Dresden Codex.

27

For a comparison of the towns of Quiché and Chichicastenango during the colonial period, see Carmack (1981:76, 106, 304, 328).

27

For a longer account of the odyssey of the MS of the PV (Ximénez c.1701), see Recinos et al. (1950:32–45); on Ximénez and his works, see Carmack (1973:189–92).

27

For the Vienna volume see Ximénez (1857); for the Paris volume see Brasseur de Bourbourg (1861). The title chosen by Scherzer for the Vienna volume is the one used by Ximénez; Brasseur was the first to call the alphabetic version of the ancient book by the name of its hieroglyphic predecessor. His version of the Quiché text leaves much to be desired; by far the best version ever published is that of Schultze Jena (1944). For a highly legible facsimile see Ximénez (1973). For evidence that the manuscript Ximénez worked from contained at least a few hieroglyphs, see the notes to pp. 184 and 194 of the present translation. The monkey patrons of writing and painting and the close relationship between these arts are discussed in M. Coe (1977). My discussion of the influence of ancient Mayan syllabic spelling conventions on the alphabetic spellings in the PV was inspired by Bricker (1989), who explored similar influences in Yucatec alphabetic texts. Another indication that the authors of the PV were familiar with hieroglyphic writing is their failure to consistently differentiate the k sounds of Quiché, which come in plain front (*k*) and back (*q*) forms as well as glottalized front (*k'*) and back (*q'*) forms. If ancient Quiché scribes used the same inventory of syllabic signs as their Yucatec counterparts, then the front/back contrast would not have been provided for, leaving only the plain/glottalized contrast.

29

For discussions of the four sides and corners and their differences from European cardinal directions, see Hunt (1977:207–208) and B. Tedlock (1992:173–78). The directional language used in the PV has no exact ethnographic parallel, but it seems likely that on the earthly plane, the four corners were marked by the horizon positions of the rising and setting sun at the solstices. Only for the night sky is it likely that the corners partially corresponded to cardinal directions, with "north" located somewhat above the horizon, at Polaris, and "south" located below the horizon, opposite Polaris; "east" and "west" would have been marked by the rising and setting points of major stars located very near the celestial equator, such as those in Orion's belt.

29–30

See Tozzer (1941:153–54) for a description of the reading of a hieroglyphic book in Yucatán. At present there are public readings of alphabetic manuscripts in the Yucatec ceremonial center of Xcacal, in Quintana Roo; see Burns (1977; 1983:22–23, 71–72).

30

For a further discussion of the Ancient Word and its relation to the preaching of God, see D. Tedlock (1983b: chap. 12).

30

In holding open the possibility that the authors of the alphabetic PV had access to the hieroglyphic version I am in agreement with Edmonson (1971:6–7). For a discussion of the role of dialogue in the Quiché story of the origin of the world and the contrasting monologue of Genesis, see D. Tedlock (1983b: chap. 11).

33

For more on the Mesoamerican ball game, see Leyenaar and Parsons (1988:94–149), which includes an account of present-day versions, and Scarborough and Wilcox (1991).

35

The sexual symbolism of the Zipacna story was pointed out by Andrés Xiloj, whose full comments will be found in the notes to p. 84 of the translation.

35

Together, Zipacna and Earthquake probably correspond to the two-headed celestial monster of Classic Maya iconography, whose features include those of a caiman (Taube 1989).

39

It was Andrés Xiloj who pointed out that the ritual performed with the ears of corn in the PV is the same as a contemporary ritual; his detailed comments on this and other connections between the PV and contemporary practices may be found throughout the notes to the PV translation itself. For an account of contemporary sound plays on day names, see B. Tedlock (1982).

44

Contemporary Quiché mother-fathers are discussed in B. Tedlock (1992:74–85).

45

For detailed arguments as to the identity of Tulan Zuyua, see D. Tedlock (1993a:12–15, 236–37) and the notes to p. 151; Brown (1980) has argued that it was Kaminaljuyú. For a general discussion of the widespread use of the name Tollan (or Tula) and its Mixtec equivalent, see Smith (1973:70–75). David Stuart (n.d.) has recently found that the royal dynasty of Copán traced its origins to Teotihuacan, naming that city with a glyph in the form of a bundle of cattails.

The main cave at Teotihuacan and its relationship to a Mexica tradition concerning seven caves are discussed by Doris Heyden (1975).

48

In Quiché theory, at least, the reckoning of the 260-day cycle should have been in synchrony everywhere in Mesoamerica. We do know that Cuauhtémoc, the successor of Moctezuma, surrendered the city of Tenochtitlán to Hernán Cortés on an Aztec day whose name means "One Snake," falling on August 13, 1521, on the Julian calendar (Thompson 1960:303). Tracing the contemporary Quiché calendar back to that same Julian date, we come to a day whose Quiché name, *Jun Kan,* also means "One Snake." In other words, when it was One Snake in Tenochtitlán, it was One Snake a thousand road miles away in the town of Quiché. For Classic Mayan dates, epigraphers and archaeologists have recently favored a correlation that runs the corresponding Yucatec dates two days later (Lounsbury 1983), but ethnohistorians and ethnographers favor a correlation that brings all these calendars into synchrony (Bricker and Bricker 1986:54; D. Tedlock 1992a:267–69).

48

It was Linda Schele who found the name Hacauitz in an inscription at Seibal and kindly passed the information along.

50

It took 52 years of 365 days each for all four year-beginning day names to occur in combination with all thirteen day numbers (4 × 13 = 52). The seniority given by the Quiché to *Kej* or "Deer" among the year-beginning day names is noted in B. Tedlock (1992:99).

50

According to the Title of the Lords of Totonicapán (Chonay and Goetz 1953:176), both Noble Two and his brother Noble Raiment set off to get the emblems of lordship from Nacxit. The former went east and succeeded in his mission, while the latter went west, getting as far as the Gulf coast, and returned empty-handed. Here is further confirmation of the strong eastern ties of the Quiché elite, in contradiction to the Gulf coast theory of Recinos.

50

Alternative accounts of the names and generational positions of the Quichés who went on the pilgrimage, and of the titles that were given to them, may be found in the Title of the Lords of Totonicapán (Chonay and Goetz 1953:176–79). On the east coast of Yucatán as a pilgrimage center, see Miller (1982:96).

50

The reference to the body of water crossed by the Quiché forefathers as a "sea" is a hyperbole; it is called both a "lake" and a "sea" in other Quiché accounts (see the notes to p. 158). On causeways at Cobá, one of which runs to the south southwest across a lake, see Thompson (1966:185–86).

51

A long list of the citadels settled by the Quichés between Hacauitz and Thorny Place is given in the Title of the Lords of Totonicapán (Chonay and Goetz 1953:180–83).

53

For a full discussion of the buildings of *Q'umaraq aj* (Rotten Cane) or Utatlán (the Nahuatl name for the same place), see Carmack (1981: chap. 9).

53–54

The military exploits of Quicab are discussed in Carmack (1981:134–37). The citadels that made up the town of Quiché, in addition to Rotten Cane, were *Chi ismachi* or Bearded Place to the south, which now belonged to the Tams; *Piloqab'* or Iloc Place to the north, belonging to the Ilocs; and Resguardo, or Atalaya, to the east, whose Quiché name and lineage affiliation are unknown (Carmack 1981: chap. 8).

55–56

For the full story of Alvarado's conquest of the Quiché kingdom, which was resisted by a large military force, see Bricker (1981:39–41) and D. Tedlock (1993a:102–108, 245–46; 1993b).

56

On the dating of the writing of the alphabetic PV, see Recinos et al. (1950:22–23). For more on the Spanish journey of Juan Cortés and the warning sent to Philip II, see Pedro Carrasco (1967).

56

The lineal descendants of Juan de Rojas and Juan Cortés continued to litigate well into the eighteenth century. The Cortés line died out by 1788; the de Rojas line still lives, but its members lost all remaining vestiges of their lordly privileges with the coming of liberal reforms in 1801 (Carmack 1981:321, 362).

57

For more on contemporary matchmakers (or "road guides"), see B. Tedlock (1992:74, 110, 117, 156); on the eloquence of their speeches, see Sam Colop (1994:116–43).

57

The name Cristóbal Velasco may be found in Carmack and Mondloch (1983a:164–65, 200). He is not to be confused with the Don Cristóbal mentioned in the PV, who is a member of the Greathouse rather than the Cauec lineage.

58

The Dresden Codex page that begins an otherwise torn-off section is discussed in Thompson (1972:78–80).

58

On the character of the Palenque inscriptions, see Schele (1984).

59–60

For more on the dialectical nature of Quiché thought see B. Tedlock (1992:145–46, 176–77). The role of myth in Mayan thinking about history is explored by Bricker (1981: chaps. 1 and 14).

Popol Vuh

PART ONE

63

the beginning: This is *uxe,* literally "its base" or "root"; it is as if the writers were starting at the bottom of something vertical and working their way up.

63

this place called Quiché: That "Quiché" is meant as a place name here is confirmed at the very end of the PV (p. 198): "everything has been completed here concerning Quiché, which is now named Santa Cruz" (see Santa Cruz in the Glossary). The same name, appearing as [quiche] or [queche] in the MS and as [4iche] in TK and TT, can serve to designate a people or a language; in the new orthography it is *k'iche'.* The general assumption is that *k'iche'* comes from a combination of *k'i,* "many," and *che',* "trees," thus carrying approximately the same meaning as Cuautemallan, the Nahuatl name for what is now called Guatemala.

63

citadel: This is *tinamit,* from a Nahua source; *tenamitl* is "enclosure, or wall of a city" in Nahuatl proper (AM). In the PV the term refers to a town in a defensible position, whether on top of a hill or mountain or between two canyons, with walls or stockades at points of easy access. Under Spanish rule most such towns were relocated to weaker sites as a matter of colonial military policy; today *tinamit* (or *tinimit*) is the general Quiché term for "town," regardless of location.

how things were put in shadow and brought to light: This is *ewaxib'al saqirib'al* [zaquiribal], "being-hidden-instrument becoming-light-instrument." The first word is built on a passive (*-x*) form of *ewaj,* which FV glosses as "to hide" but then explains that it has to do with shadows or dark places. The second word is built on an inchoative (*-ir*) form of *saq,* "be light," which is also found in *saqirik,* "to dawn." As will be seen, the gods not only bring things to light but can also darken what was once in the light. The two words could also be translated as "the hiding place, the dawning place," since *-b'al* can either be instrumental or indicate place. The "hiding place" would be *ewab'al siwan* or "Concealment Canyon" (see Glossary), where the gods were hidden away before the dawn (p. 158); the "dawning place" would be the place (or places) where the founding ancestors of the ruling Quiché lineages were keeping vigil when the morning star and then the sun rose for the first time (p. 160), places which are referred to as *saqirib'al* [zaquiribal].

Maker, Modeler: These names are *tz'aqol* [tzacol] and *b'itol,* consisting of an agentive suffix, *-ol,* added to two different verb stems. In both ancient and modern Quiché, *tz'aq-* has to do with making things out of clay, plaster, cement, or stone; the objects made range through bricks and walls to monuments, mounds of earth, and buildings of all sizes. *B'it-,* on the other hand, has to do with making definite shapes out of a pliable and otherwise formless material; the gloss in FX is "to make jars, to fabricate things from clay." Andrés Xiloj said of *tz'aq-* (which today is agentivized as *tz'aqal*), "This is to make or construct, like a building, a wall." Of *b'it-* he said, "This *b'itik* is to form, as when we were small and played with mud; we made forms. *Qab'itik,* 'we form it.'" He saw *tz'aqol* and *b'itol* as referring, respectively, to the amassing of clay and then its shaping into forms such as vessels or figures.

Hunahpu Possum, Hunahpu Coyote: The next time these names are used they seem to be epithets for Xpiyacoc and Xmucane (p. 69), but they may be epithets for Hunahpu and Xbalanque in their roles as vagabond dancers and magicians (see p. 232).

Great White Peccary, Coati: These names are given here as *saqi* [zaqui] *nim aq* [ac] and *tzi's;* the latter appears elsewhere as *saqi nima tzi's.* That the peccary is both white (*saqi*) and great (*nim*) points to the white-lipped peccary (*Tayasu pecari*), which has white jowls and is markedly larger than the collared peccary (*Tayasu tajacu*). The *tzi's* or coati mundi (*Nasua narica*) is a raccoon-like animal that resembles a peccary in having a long, flexible snout. In Classic Maya art both members of this pair are shown as peccaries.

63

Sovereign Plumed Serpent: Here and elsewhere, the title *tepew* or "Sovereign" serves to distinguish the god named Plumed Serpent, who bears it nearly every time he is mentioned, from the Quiché king named Plumed Serpent, who never bears it. *Tepew* is from a Nahua source; *tepeuani* is "conqueror or victor in battle" in Nahuatl proper (AM). Quiché *tepewal,* an adjectival form (marked by -*al*), is glossed by DB as "majesty, dignity." The name rendered as Plumed Serpent is *q'ukumatz* [4ucumatz], in which *q'u-* is from *q'uq',* which refers to the resplendent quetzal (*Pharomachrus mocinno*) when used as a bird name but extends to precious feathers in general when it modifies other words, and *kumatz,* a generic term for snakes. The Yucatec name *k'uk'ulkan* is constructed in the same way: *k'uk'* (used here in the adjectival form *k'uk'ul*) carries the same range of meanings as Quiché *q'u-* or *q'uq',* and *kan* is generic for "snake" (AB). The Nahuatl name *quetzalcoatl* fits the same pattern, combining *quetzal-,* which refers to precious feathers in general but is taken from the species name *quetzalli,* with *coatl,* "snake" (RS). It is the sense of value and splendor adhering to the quetzal and its feathers that has led to the standard English translation followed here, using "plumed" instead of the more ordinary "feathered" and then, as if that were not quite strong enough, using "serpent" instead of "snake."

63

plate shaper, bowl shaper: This is *ajraxa laq* [la3], *ajraxa tzel,* in which *aj-* is occupational and *raxa,* which in some contexts is "green," means "wet" in the context of earth (in this case earthenware). In other words, the pottery in question is as yet unfired, which places the focus on the stage at which it is shaped. The plate and bowl may refer ultimately to the earth and sky. Andrés Xiloj pointed out that when the head of a contemporary patrilineage (who is always a diviner) dies, his successor must be installed in office by the head of a neighboring lineage, who is hired as an *ajch'ajb'al laq, ajch'ajb'al tasa,* "washer of the plate, washer of the cup." Before the new lineage head can take office, the "washer" must go to all of that lineage's shrines and clean out the ashes of all the offerings burned by the deceased lineage head. Such shrines are lined and covered with slabs of stone and pieces of pottery, spoken of as "plates" and "cups." In the PV, "plate shaper, bowl shaper" could refer to Xpiyacoc and Xmucane in their general roles as those who look after (and even create) shrines, or it might refer to pottery vessels used for burning incense rather than to shrines as such.

63

midwife, matchmaker: These roles, *iyom* and *mamom,* are mentioned in the predominant female/male order of Quiché discourse but refer, respectively, to the divine daykeepers Xmucane and Xpiyacoc, who are always named with Xpiyacoc (the male) first. *Iyom* means "midwife" in both ancient (FX) and modern (AG) Quiché. Xmucane's midwife role suggests that she could be the Quiché counterpart of lowland Maya Goddess O (as iconographers label her), an elderly goddess of medicine, childbirth, and weaving whose name is *chak chel* in the codices and *ix chel* or *chakal ix chel* in alphabetic documents (Roys 1965:146, 153; Taube 1992:99–105; 1994a:657–58, 663–64). Andrés Xiloj recognized *mamom* only as a term addressed to a matchmaker in the ceremonial language of a bride-asking ceremony. Ordinarily such a person (always a male) would be referred to as *k'amal b'e*, "road guide."

63

Xpiyacoc, Xmucane: It is difficult to discover the meaning of these names, except that the initial *x*- means "she of" or "small." The male member of the pair, Xpiyacoc, has a feminine aspect that is indicated not only by the *x*-, but also by the fact that he is later subsumed under the double epithet "Grandmother of Day, Grandmother of Light." This recalls the fact that contemporary diviners (of either sex) are symbolically androgynous, female on the left side of the body and male on the right. Andrés Xiloj suggested that the *-pi-* in Xpiyacoc might be *-pe-*, "to come," and he derived *-yak-* from *yekik* (*yakik* in some dialects), "to be put in order, to be lifted up," a verb diviners use with reference to the problems of clients. In ancient Quiché *yako* is a numeral classifier for counting tribute (DB); the *yako* in Xpiyacoc could refer to the counting (and manipulation) of the divining seeds (described on p. 70) rather than to the "lifting up" of the client. In the case of Xmucane, Xiloj derived *mukane* from *mokonik*, "to do something requested" or "to do a favor"; he pointed out that a diviner who has ascertained the cause of a problem may then be hired to make prayers and offerings on behalf of the client. Another possibility is that her name refers to her preparation of maize for the making of the first humans, suggested by the Pokomchí verb *muqunem*, "to make a tortilla" (OS).

63

defender, protector: This translates *matzanel, ch'uqenel* [chuquenel]. DB glosses *matzo* as "shelter after the manner of a hen" and (under the same heading) *matzanel* as "defender," while *ch'uqu* [chu3u] is "cover over" and (under the same heading) *ch'uqonal* [chukonal] is "protector." Andrés Xiloj pointed out that a daykeeper, when he or she states the case of a client in a prayer, may be called an "abogado," Spanish for "lawyer" or (more literally) "advocate."

63

as enlightened beings, in enlightened words: "Enlightened" is my translation, for the present context, of *zaqil* [zaquil], "lightness" or "whiteness." This insistence that the aforementioned Quiché deities and their words have the properties of light is directly juxtaposed to a mention of God and Christendom in the sentence

217

that follows; it can thus be read as a direct and deliberate contradiction of the missionary teaching that all indigenous gods were devils.

63

amid the preaching of God, in Christendom now: This couplet contains the first Spanish or Spanish-derived words to appear in the MS, *Dios* and *christianoil;* no more such words are used until p. 184 (see the note for *the lord bishop* on p. 321). The "preaching" is *ch'ab'al,* literally "manner of speaking" or just plain "talk"; the phrase *uch'ab'al Dios,* "talk of God," came to be the standard Quiché way of referring to Christian doctrine and is still used in that sense by both Quichés and missionaries, but the original choice of these words to translate "la palabra de Dios" must have been made by a Quiché rather than a missionary. The proper Quiché term for an authoritative and abiding "word" was and still is *tzij* rather than *ch'ab'al;* the writers of the PV refer to their own work as containing *ojer tzij,* "the Ancient Word," but neither they nor contemporary Quichés use *tzij* as a way of referring to "la palabra de Dios." In choosing to translate *uch'ab'al Dios* as "the preaching of God" in the present context, I have tried to combine the "Christian doctrine" sense of this phrase with the more general sense of *ch'ab'al* as an act of speaking.

63

a place to see it: The original pre-Columbian PV is referred to here and much later (p. 192) as an *ilb'al re* (miswritten [ibal re] in the latter place), "an instrument (or place) for the seeing of something." What was "seen" there included "how things were put in shadow and brought to light" by the gods, together with future events such as war, death, famine, and quarrels (pp. 63, 192). DB has an entry for *ilb'al re* (under *ilo*) glossed as "figure, picture." Today *ilb'al* or *ilob'al* (without the *re*) refers to crystals used for gazing by diviners and to eyeglasses, binoculars, and telescopes.

63

Council Book: The MS has *popo wuj* here and *popol wuj* the second time the book is mentioned (p. 152); *pop wuj,* the spelling preferred by Chávez (1979), occurs in TY but not in the PV itself. *Pop* is "mat," *-ol* is adjectival, and *wuj* is "paper" or "book." In ancient Quiché, *popol* occurred in many phrases in which it had the effect of "public" or "in common," such as *popol ja,* "council house" (DB); *popoj,* a verb built on the same root, was "to hold a council" (FX, FV), and the pronouncements of a council were *popol tzij,* in which *tzij* is "word." *Popol,* literally "partaking of a mat," is a metonym for a council, referring to the mat on which its members sat; at the same time it might have been a metaphor for the way councils were structured, weaving diverse interests together. Alternative translations of *popol wuj* would be "Common Book" or "Council Paper."

"The Light That Came from Beside the Sea": This epithet for the PV is *saq petenaq ch'aqa palo* [zac petenac chaca palo], "light come-from-perfect beside sea." Some translators have rendered *ch'aqa palo* as "from the other side of the sea," as I did in the previous edition of the present work, but the Quiché scholar Enrique Sam Colop (1994:237–38) makes a conclusive linguistic argument for the revised translation offered here. In the present context, the phrase alludes to the fact that the sons of the first Quiché lords, on their return from a pilgrimage to a great lord named Nacxit, "brought back the writing of Tulan, the writing of Zuyua" from beside the sea (see p. 180).

There is the original book and ancient writing, but the one who reads and assesses it has a hidden identity: "There is" is my translation of *k'o;* some translators have used the past tense here, but there is nothing in the text that calls for it. "The one who reads" translates *ilol,* literally "one who sees"; DB gives *ilol* as "seer" or "prophet," and *ilol wuj* (literally "book seer") as "reader." The full range of *ilol* is covered by an English translation built on "read," which still retains divinatory usages that go all the way back to its Germanic root. The one who "assesses" is *b'isol,* in which the stem *b'iso-* refers to deliberation or care in Quiché and Cakchiquel but retains a clear reference to the making of measurements in Kekchí (EH). In the present context the very next sentence describes a process of measurement (see two notes below). The known hieroglyphic books are filled with astronomical measurements; these same books (or others) may have included detailed descriptions of territorial boundaries as well, as does the script of the Rabinal Achi (a drama contemporary with the alphabetic text of the PV). "Hidden identity" translates *ewal uwach,* literally "hidden his/her-face," in which the meanings of face extend to a person's social identity. Edmonson (1971:7) is correct in interpreting this phrase as referring to the reader of the PV rather than to the book itself.

It takes a long performance and account to complete the lighting of all the sky-earth: "Performance" translates *peyoxik* [peoxic], which I read as a passive and nominalized form of *peyoj,* "to hire" (TC, FV), probably meaning something like "service rendered." "Lighting" is *tzuk'* [tzuk], translated on the basis of the verb stem *tzuk'u-,* referring in both ancient and modern Quiché to the placing of a light (such as a candle or torch) in a high place (FX, FV, MX, AG). The only alternative readings of [tzuk] would be *tzuq,* referring to the giving of sustenance, and *tz'uk,* referring to sides, but both of these are written [tzuc] everywhere else in the MS, and the placement of lights does fit the present passage. The next sentence (see the following note) refers to the placement of stakes at the four corners of the world, corresponding to the solstitial rising and setting points of the sun. Moreover, the full account of the origins of the sun, moon, and stars, or "the lighting of all the sky-earth," will indeed be "long" (as stated here), taking up better than half the book.

63–64

the fourfold siding, fourfold cornering, / measuring, fourfold staking, / halving the cord, stretching the cord / in the sky, on the earth, / the four sides, the four corners: "Siding" and "side" are *tz'ukuxik* [tzucuxic] and *tz'uk* [tzuc]; TC cites a prior dictionary as giving "side" for *tz'uk*, which is also the translation suggested by Andrés Xiloj. "Cornering" and "corner" translate *xukutaxik* and *xukut;* Xiloj uses the latter word in his prayers, saying *kaj xukut kaj, kaj xukut ulew,* "four corners of sky, four corners of earth." The "fourfold staking" is *ukaj che'xik,* which he understood to be four sticks or poles driven into the ground at the four corners. The "measuring" is *retaxik,* literally "its-being-measured," translated on the basis of *etaj,* "to measure, to mark out" (DB), and the reading offered by Xiloj. The unit of measurement in question, still used by Quichés, is the *k'a'm* or "cord," a length of rope about twenty yards (or paces) long. Xiloj was familiar with the phrasing used here, *umej k'a'maxik* [camaxic], "its-folded cording," and *uyuq k'a'maxik* [uyuc camaxic], "its-stretched cording." He explained that the "folded" measurement is done with the cord doubled back on itself to halve its length, while the "stretched" measurement is done with the cord pulled out to its full length. His reading of *k'a'maxik* (which has a passive ending) is confirmed by an entry in DB, *k'a'maj* [caamaah] (with an active ending), "to measure lands." He observed that the PV describes the measurement of sky and earth as if a cornfield were being laid out for cultivation; house and loom construction are also suggested by this passage (B. Tedlock and D. Tedlock 1985). In the Book of Chilam Balam of Chumayel, the measurement of the world is described in terms of twenty footsteps (equal to a cord) that span the twenty day names of the divinatory calendar (Roys 1967:116–18). The same source refers to a celestial cord (Ibid.:155); according to Yucatec Mayas living near Valladolid, a cord suspended in the sky once linked Tulum and Cobá with Chichén Itzá and Uxmal (Tozzer 1907:153).

64

giver of heart, . . . upbringer: These are respectively *k'uxlanel* and *k'uxla'y,* both built on the stem *k'ux,* "heart," which in its *k'uxla-* forms has to do with thought in the sense of "memory" and "will." Andrés Xiloj defined *k'uxlanel* as follows: "One who raises us and has a good reputation for doing this." In the translation I have tried to preserve the full range of *k'uxla-* by staying literal for its first occurrence ("giver of heart") and translating for sense the second time around ("upbringer").

64

in the light that lasts: Here I have tried to preserve in English the relationship that exists between the corresponding words of the text, *saqil amaq'el* [zaquil amaquil]. These two words are linked by assonance and alliteration, giving them a parallel sound, but they are not properly parallel in their syntax—in fact, the latter word *modifies* the former. *Saqil* is composed of *saq,* an adjective meaning "light" or "white," and *-il,* which makes it into an abstract noun; *amaq'el,* on the other hand, whether in ancient or modern Quiché, is a unitary, unanalyzable form (at least where proper morphology is concerned). It means "always," "all the time," "continuous," or "eternal." In rendering *saqil amaq'el* as "the light that lasts," I change parts of speech as the original phrase does (though not in precisely the same way), while at the same time linking the two halves of the phrase through alliteration.

64

Now it still ripples, now it still murmurs, ripples, it still sighs, still hums, and it is empty: This is *k'a katz'ininoq, k'a kachamamoq, katz'inonik, k'a kasilanik, k'a kalolinik, katolona puch,* with [ca] corrected to *k'a,* [-oc] to *-oq,* and [tzini-] and [tzino-] to *tz'ini-* and *tz'ino-. K'a* is "still, yet"; *ka-* is the incomplete aspect; and *-oq* has the effect of "now." What we are hearing here is the performer's effort to make the primordial state of the world *present* for his listeners, setting a scene rather than recounting a past event, but translators have generally put this passage in the past tense. They have also transformed its activity into a static state, not only changing the first five verbs into adjectives, but choosing such adjectives as "quiet" or "silent." In fact the verb stems *tz'inin-, chamam-, tz'i-non-,* and *lolin-,* each of which contains reduplicative alliteration and/or assonance, are onomatopoeic. Colonial and modern dictionary entries for these stems do indeed include some of the glosses translators have chosen, but DB gives "ring" for *tz'ino-,* and FV, under the entry for [silee], explains that *silan-* refers to the (audible) process through which windy weather is calmed. Further, Andrés Xiloj identifies *lolin-* as the standard Quiché way of rendering the sound of a cricket. In translating this passage I have chosen quiet sounds that can be expressed as verbs; my ripples are derived from the fact that there is nothing but sky and water in this opening scene, as will be seen further on; for the same reason I have avoided obvious animal sounds. The quiet in question here is not so much a complete silence as it is white noise, the kind of sounds one hears when there are no other sounds—in this case, the white noise of the primordial world itself. For a further discussion of the system of ideophonic words in the PV, see D. Tedlock (1988).

64

the first eloquence: Ximénez translates *uchan* as "eloquence," the same gloss offered by DB (under the entry for *chan*).

64

It is at rest; not a single thing stirs: Some translators have made the first half of this sentence negative by joining it to the negative clause that precedes it, but in fact it is the last in a series of three sentences with the same positive-negative clause structure. The negativity of the second clause of the present sentence is marked by *junta*, "not one thing" (DB), which is not to be confused with *jutaq*, "each one." My reading follows the one offered by Andrés Xiloj, who found this passage perfectly clear.

64

It is held back: This is *kamal kab'antaj*, which is difficult to translate. I find my clue in the entry for [camalo] in DB, which is glossed "late, not quick"; the entire phrase might be read as, "it is made to be late (or slow)."

64

a glittering light: This is *saqtetoj* [za3tetoh], which DB glosses as "the brightness that enters through cracks." The light in question here might be escaping between the feathers with which the Bearers and Begetters are covered (see the next two sentences), but it could also be a twinkling star. In any case it is down at the level of the water, perhaps on the horizon. Its "glittering" corresponds, in the sensory domain of sight, to the soft and repetitive nature of the primordial sounds described earlier.

64

in quetzal feathers, in blue-green: This is *pa q'uq'* [cuc], *pa raxon*, in which *q'uq'* is the primary term for the quetzal or its feathers and *raxon* is identified by PG as an alternative term for the same thing. *Raxon* is a nominal form of *rax*, a color adjective covering the blue to green range.

64

in their very being: This is *chikik'ojeik*, "at-their-being-there." I have translated it as "in their *very* being" because the writers of the PV, wherever they add a form based on *k'ojeik* to a statement in which the verb "to be" is already present or understood, are making a *pointedly* ontological statement. Some translators have softened the ontological abstractness of these statements by using such phrases as "by their nature," but *k'ojeik* has no aura of the natal or the biological hanging about it the way "nature" does, and in fact I know of no Quiché concept that corresponds to "nature." If I were translating *k'ojeik* into German, I would choose "Dasein."

65

the name of the god: Through most of the PV, *k'ab'awil* or "god" refers to the patron deities of the ruling Quiché lineages and to the sacred stones that were the material embodiments of these deities (see the notes to p. 161). But the present passage—given that the term is linked specifically to the Heart of Sky, and given that the Heart of Sky will shortly hereafter be described as a trinity— must be read as an allusion to Christian teachings. Note carefully that when the passage is read literally rather than as an allusion, it contains nothing that directly contradicts indigenous Quiché theology; Heart of Sky is among the names uttered before gods whose bodies have turned to stone in a prayer given much later (pp. 192–93). For a general discussion of biblical allusions in the PV see D. Tedlock (1983b: chap. 11).

65

in the early dawn: In this phrase the authors make their first allusion to the 260-day divinatory calendar. Instead of the ordinary word for "early dawn," *aq'ab'il,* the text has *aq'ab'al,* an archaic form that is also the proper name of a day. Like other day names, *Aq'ab'al* is often given a divinatory interpretation by means of sound play, and one of the words used to play on it today is in fact *aq'ab'il,* an allusion to the fact that *Aq'ab'al* is a day whose rituals are best performed during the very early dawn. The rituals in question, appropriately enough, involve the first steps toward the negotiation of new social relationships that will last a lifetime (B. Tedlock 1992:77–81). When a daykeeper who holds the office of mother-father needs to schedule a visit to the shrines of his patrilineage in order to ask his ancestors to approve a forthcoming marriage negotiation, *1 Aq'ab'al* is a particularly auspicious date, and a day with the same name (but some other number) may be chosen for the actual marriage proposal at the house of the prospective bride. On *1, 8,* and *9 Aq'ab'al,* a mother-father who has agreed to train and install the successor of his deceased counterpart in a neighboring lineage goes to the ancestral shrines of that lineage to ask for the approval of the novice. In both the marriage and the installation the negotiation has two levels: it is not only the living who must give their approval to the bond between husband and wife or the spiritual marriage between the new mother-father and the shrines, but the ancestors. In the PV, when Heart of Sky goes before Sovereign Plumed Serpent in the early dawn (*aq'ab'al*), they originate both kinds of ritual, eventually creating the first four human mother-fathers and the first four married couples who ever existed.

65

the generation: This is *winaqirik* [uinaquiric]. Others have translated it as "creation," but it has to do with such processes as the seasonal rising of springs in places that would otherwise be dry, and the growth or formation of algae or larvae in still water (FV). The word "creation" is too heavily laden with an implied ontological priority of the spiritual over the material to be imported into the present account of origins, which contains no word quite like it.

65

Hurricane: This god, who causes a cataclysmic rainstorm later on in Part One, is designated here by the epithet *juraqan* [huracan], shortened from *jun raqan,* "one-legged." In Part Four he will take the form of Tohil, the patron deity of Quiché rulers, standing on one leg to make fire and shrouding himself in clouds and rain. His lowland Maya counterpart, variously labeled God K, GII, or "the manikin scepter" by iconographers, sometimes takes the form of a fire-striking or lightning-striking axe, with the head of the axe sticking out of an obsidian mirror on his forehead and the handle taking the place of one of his legs or serving as his only leg (see p. 298). In some cases artists represented this god's fire-making capacity by means of a pun on the term for obsidian (*tah*), substituting a burning torch (*tah*) for the axe blade (Schele and Miller 1986:49). No such pun is possible in Nahuatl, which suggests that the Nahuatl name Tezcatlipoca, meaning "smoking mirror," might have a Mayan image behind it. As a god, Tezcatlipoca is both one-legged and a causer of hurricanes (Hunt 1977:241–42). In a story told among the Sierra Popoluca (speakers of a Mixe-Zoquean language in eastern Veracruz), a god whose name Foster reports only as "Hurricane" (1945:194) fractures one leg after falling from a great height. Throughout the West Indies and along the north coast of South America, among Carib and Arawakan peoples, there is a god of the hurricane whose names are cognate with *juraqan* and who is one-legged in the Guianas (Lehmann-Nitsche 1924–25). As for the word "hurricane," which came into English via Spanish or French, dictionary compilers favor a Taino (Arawakan) rather than a Mayan origin, but the Taino word could have come from a Mayan source (for evidence of Mayan contact with Caribbean peoples see Roys 1967:142).

65

Thunderbolt Hurricane comes first, the second is Newborn Thunderbolt, and the third is Sudden Thunderbolt: The term for thunderbolt is *kaqulja* [caculha], referring to a shaft of lightning (with the accompanying thunder), as contrasted with *koyopa,* referring to sheet lightning seen in the distance (without visible shafts or audible thunder). Thunderbolt is a fitting addition to the name Hurricane (or "one-legged") not only because hurricanes bring violent thunderstorms, but because lightning that strikes the ground is typically concentrated in one main shaft. Another of Hurricane's names, Tohil, originally meant "thunderer" (see p. 296). Carib and Arawakan hurricane gods (see the previous note) are also thunderbolt gods, whereas the Sierra Popoluca Hurricane has a companion named Thunderbolt. In the names of the Quiché Hurricane's thunderbolt companions, "Newborn" translates *ch'ipi,* written [chipa] here but [chipi] nearly everywhere else, meaning "youngest (or smallest) child," while "Sudden" translates *raxa,* "green, raw, fresh, sudden." These two names refer not only to shafts of lightning but to fulgurites, glassy stones formed by lightning in sandy soil. This is apparent from the "rayo" and "relámpago" entries in TC, where *ru ch'ipil kaqolajay* is "the tiny child of the thunderbolt," *ru naq' ru pub' kaqolajay* is "the shot (pellet) of the blowgun of the thunderbolt," and both of these expressions refer to "a small stone that congeals where lightning hits the ground." Newborn and Sudden Thunderbolt are the Quiché counterparts of the lowland Mayan deities labeled God B or GI by iconographers and named *chak* or "thunderbolt" in hieroglyphic and alphabetic texts; indeed, the name *raxa kaqulja* has exactly the same meaning as Yucatec *yaxal chak* (Roys 1965:160). In Classic and Postclassic images the *chak* gods wield lightning-striking axes that sometimes take the form of God K (Taube 1992:73).

65

So there were three of them: This appears to be an allusion to the Christian trinity, but there is no lack of trinities among pre-Columbian Mayan gods. There is, for example, the so-called Palenque triad (Schele and Miller 1986:48–51), which resembles the Quiché Thunderbolt triad in that two of its members are God B and God K (see the previous two notes). Another Quiché triad, which may be the same as the Thunderbolt triad, consists of the patron deities of the three ruling Quiché lineages, who are repeatedly named together (beginning in Part Four) as Tohil, Auilix, and Hacauitz.

65

"How should the sowing be, and the dawning?": "Sowing" (*awax-*) and "dawning" (*saqir-*) are frequently paired throughout the portion of the PV that deals with the predawn world. The meanings of these two words, which run through them several different threads when they are paired, have something of the structure of a Möbius strip. If we start with the literal meaning of sowing in the present context, the reference is to the beginning of plants; but if we trace that idea over to the other side of our strip, the sprouting of those same plants is expressed metaphorically as "dawning." If, on the other hand, we start from the literal meaning of "dawning," the present reference is to the first of all dawns; but if we trace that idea back over to the other side of the strip, the origin of that dawn is expressed metaphorically as a "sowing," referring to the fact that the Quiché gods who eventually become Venus and the sun and moon must first descend into the underworld. The head of one of these gods becomes the fruit of a calabash tree (p. 97), while another has his head replaced by a squash (p. 127)—that is, at least two of them acquire plant characteristics in the underworld before the coming of the first literal dawning.

The pairing of sowing and dawning receives a further meaning when it is taken to refer to human beings whose perfection is the principal goal of the world-making gods of the present passage. To trace out this meaning, we must have recourse to ethnography. In Momostenango a mother-father or patrilineage head "sows" and "plants" an unborn child in certain shrines of his lineage by announcing its mother's pregnancy there (B. Tedlock 1992:80). On the "dawning" side of this process, the woman who gives birth to the child *kuya ri saq*, "gives it light" (Ibid.: 211). This particular tracing remains metaphorical on both sides of the "sowing" and "dawning," but it retains a twist in that it is specifically built on the model of the literal sowing and metaphorical "dawning" of vegetation. A second human tracing, also metaphorical on both sides but twisted in that it seems to be built on the model of the metaphorical "sowing" and literal dawning of heavenly bodies, is followed out in death and its aftermath. Here the body is put in the earth, but the deceased "becomes light" or "dawns" (both *saqirik*) in two different senses: the body itself is reduced to plain white (light-colored) bones, but the spirit becomes a spark of light, something like a star.

65

provider, nurturer: This is *tzuqul q'o'l* [tzucul cool]; both words broadly refer to sustenance, but the latter seems to refer more overtly to actual food than the former (at least in DB), and the only word that resembles it today is *q'ob'ik*, "to get fat" (MX). The providers or nurturers ultimately intended here are human beings, who will one day sustain the gods through prayer and sacrifice, but for the time being the gods will succeed only in making animals. Eventually deer and birds will indeed be among those who nurture the gods with their blood, but only when there are humans to sacrifice them (p. 163); these same sacrificers will also provide their own blood to the gods (p. 165) and will ultimately offer the blood and hearts of human captives (foretold on p. 156 and first carried out on p. 165).

65

But there will be no high days and no bright praise: The paired words here are *uq'ijilab'al* [uquihilabal] and *uq'alaib'al* [ucalaibal]. The first is literally "its-day-ness-instrument," referring to the keeping or setting aside of a specific day on the calendar for ritual purposes; I chose "high days" because the notion of "holidays" has become secularized in English (despite the etymology of that word). The second is "its-brightness (or manifestness)-instrument" and carries a sense of proclamation.

65–66

just like a cloud, like a mist, now forming, unfolding. Then the mountains were separated from the water: The "unfolding" here is *upupujeik*, which for both Andrés Xiloj and DB describes the way in which clouds form around mountains. "Separated" translates *xtape;* DB has *tapo*, "to pick out." On reading this passage Xiloj immediately commented, "It's just the way it is right now, there are clouds, then the clouds part, piece by piece, and now the sky is clear." It is as if the mountains were there in the primordial world all along and were revealed, little by little, as the clouds parted. But Xiloj complicated this interpretation by saying, "Haven't you seen that when the water passes—a rainstorm—and then it clears, a vapor comes out from among the trees? The clouds come out from among the mountains, among the trees." This lends a cyclical movement to the picture: the clouds come from the mountains, then conceal the mountains, then part to reveal the mountains, and so on.

By their genius alone, by their cutting edge alone: The paired terms here are *nawal* and *pus*. The former term is from a Nahua source but is not limited to the concept of an animal alter ego, as it is in central Mexico. In Quiché it can refer to the spiritual essence or character of a person, animal, plant, stone, or geographical place, thus corresponding to English "genius" in its older sense as "spirit familiar." The latter term, *pus,* carries one central literal meaning from its Mixe-Zoque (and possibly Olmec) origins (Campbell 1983:83) right down to its use in modern Quiché: it refers to the cutting of flesh with a knife (see D. Tedlock 1983b:265). At the time of the European invasion it was the primary term for sacrifice. In the present context, it implies that "the mountains were separated from the water" through an act resembling the extraction of the heart (or other organs) from a sacrifice. As if to confirm this allusion, the text goes on to refer to the earth as the "mountain-plain," or *juyub' taq'aj* [tacah], which is today the principal Quiché metaphor for the human body. When used together, *pus* and *nawal* serve as metonyms for shamanic power, referring to the ability to make genius or spiritual essence visible or audible by means of ritual.

When Andrés Xiloj read these lines, he shifted away from the idea that the preceding lines about cloud formation and dispersal referred to something happening in the atmosphere around the mountains, moving toward the idea that this process was a simile for the formation and differentiation of the mountains themselves. That the mountains under discussion were made by means of *nawal* rather than physical labor suggested a certain insubstantiality to him, and he commented, "Then these mountains are for no other reason than *representing* that there are hills or volcanoes." That is to say, he interpreted the mountains not as hard realities but as mere "signs" (*retal*), unfolding themselves "just like a cloud, like a mist."

66

it was brought forth by the Heart of Sky, Heart of Earth, as they are called, since they were the first to think of it: Andrés Xiloj took this to mean that the formation of the earth was an act of self-revelation on the part of the Heart of Sky and Heart of Earth. He compared them to the present-day *uk'ux pwaq* or "Heart of Metal (or silver or money)," which reveals itself to the fortunate. As he explained it, "When one has luck, one picks up some kind of rock, but in the form of an animal; this is the Heart of Metal. When the moment comes, suddenly it appears." Such rocks may be volcanic concretions that happen to resemble animals, or they may be ancient stone artifacts. They are properly kept in the indoor half of a pair of patrilineage shrines called the *meb'il,* which consists of a wooden box placed on a family altar (B. Tedlock 1992:81). "This is where one prays, this is where the fortune, the money, abounds. Here in the PV, the Heart of Sky and the Heart of Earth appeared, and this is where the earth was propagated." The objects in a *meb'il* should multiply of their own accord, and that, as Xiloj would have it, is what happened to the object or objects from which the earth began.

The notion that the "Heart of Sky" is a hard object is supported by a much later passage in which the names Heart of Sky and Heart of Earth are both addressed to gods whose bodies have been petrified. The connection between these gods and the sky lies in the fact that they were petrified when the sun first rose and burned them. Among the objects called "Heart of Metal" today, volcanic concretions are said to have been formed in the same way, while ancient stone artifacts are said to have been formed where thunderbolts struck the ground. Here we may note that Newborn Thunderbolt, one of the epithets or aspects of Heart of Sky, is also a term for fulgurites, formed where lightning strikes the ground (see p. 224). The Book of Chilam Balam of Chumayel takes the question of celestial stoniness home to the sky itself, declaring that the "Heart of Heaven" is a bead of precious stone (Roys 1967:91).

66

all the guardians of the forests: Andrés Xiloj commented, "The animals are the caretakers of the woods. They [the gods] thought, 'There is a need for animals, so that people won't be able to enter the woods. The animals will frighten them.'" For the contemporary Quiché, wild animals are the domestic animals of the Mundo, or earth deity. One cannot hunt deer without first asking permission of the Mundo. When a family is in arrears in its offerings, the Mundo may send a predator from out of the woods to raid its flocks or herds.

66

fer-de-lances: In Quichean languages the name of this snake species (*Bothrops atrox*) is *k'anti* [canti], borrowed from Cholan, in which *k'an* is "yellow," as contrasted with *q'an* in Quichean, and *ti'* means "lips" (JH), as contrasted with "bite" in Quichean. In Cholan the name refers to a yellow zone around the mouth of the fer-de-lance.

66

"Why this pointless humming?": The "humming" and "rustling" referred to in this passage are the *lolin-* and *tzinin-* sounds discussed earlier (see the notes to p. 64). What the gods are ultimately looking for here is the sound of articulate human speech, but they will not succeed in hearing it until p. 147. In the present scene, all they can hear on the earth are sounds that are indefinitely repetitive or vibratory and therefore without meaning, just as sounds lacked meaning when there was only the sea.

67

"You, precious birds": This is *ix ix tz'ikin*, in which the second *ix*, though it might appear to be a scribal error, is essential to the full understanding of the phrase. The first *ix* is plainly enough "you," in the familiar and plural, but

228

the second one has a double meaning. At one level it is diminutive, making the whole phrase translatable as "You, precious (or little) birds," but at another level it is the day name *Ix*, which immediately precedes *Tz'ikin* or "Bird" in the sequence of twenty day names. Today, 7 *Ix* and 8 *Tz'ikin* are the days devoted to the rites of the contemporary patrilineage shrine called the *meb'il*, which is often referred to simply by naming these two days.

67

a place to sleep: This is *warab'al,* and it alludes to patrilineage shrines, which are called *warab'alja,* "foundation of the house" or, literally, "sleeping (or resting) place of the house." The animals that are given places to sleep in this passage, *kej* or "deer" and *tz'ikin* or "birds," give their names to two of the days used for *warab'alja* rites today. The human mother-father or patrilineage head uses a low-numbered day bearing the name *Kej* to go to the parts of the *warab'alja* dedicated to human beings in order to announce that a woman

SLEEPING PLACE OF THE HOUSE: *A foundation shrine belonging to a patrilineage in Momostenango. The stone slab that covers the shrine marks it as a place of worship that is private rather than open to the public; only the head of the patrilineage that owns this particular shrine may pray and burn copal here.*

PHOTO BY THE AUTHOR

married into his lineage is pregnant, and to pray for the child she bears. This ritual is called a "sowing," and so is the long process in which the divine mother-fathers of the PV speak of making humans and prepare for their coming long before they actually succeed in their project. Deer result from one of their four attempts to make humans; these animals are, in effect, an approximation of real humans, their fault being that they walk on all fours and lack articulate speech. The implication here is that in visiting his shrines to announce a child on the day named Deer, the human mother-father commemorates the process whereby properly walking and talking humans were spoken of and approximated by the divine mother-fathers (Maker and Modeler) before they were realized.

The most startling link between shrines and deer—deer as animals rather than days named Deer—manifests itself in dreams. On this point I can give firsthand testimony. During the period of my formal apprenticeship as a day-keeper in Momostenango, I told Andrés Xiloj of dreaming that I was followed along a path by a series of large deer. After a laugh of immediate recognition he told me that I had been followed by shrines! He explained that outdoor shrines have spirit familiars that frequently take the form of deer—and, these days, of horses and cattle. The path, of course, was that of the days of the calendar, along which each shrine had its proper place in a sequence (see D. Tedlock 1993a:67–69 for more detail).

67

"Talk, speak out. Don't moan, don't cry out": Here again (as on p. 66) the gods express their desire for articulate human speech, this time contrasted with moans and cries rather than humming and rustling. Not only that, but they want to hear their own names and praises, and they ask the animals to "keep our days." This last idea is expressed by *kojiq'ijila'* [cohiquihila], literally, "to-us-you (plural familiar) day (transitive imperative)," analogous to the form rendered as "high days" on p. 65. If English permitted "day" to be a verb, one could translate *kojiq'ijila'* as "dayify us," with the pun on "deify" being appropriate enough. A less direct translation would be "calendrify us."

67

They just squawked, they just chattered, they just howled: New sounds have been added to the world here. They are not yet the sounds of speech, but neither are they like the rippling, murmuring, and humming of the world that had only a sea (see p. 64). Those sounds tended toward vowel harmony and repeated consonants, as with *tz'inin-* and *chamam-*, whereas the new sounds retain vowel harmony without repeating their consonants: *wachela-*, *karala-*, and *wojo-*.

67

It wasn't apparent what language they spoke: The text has *mawi xwachinik uwach kich'ab'al*, literally, "not faced-out its face their-talk-instrument." The active verb *wachinik*, built on *wach*, "face," is used primarily with reference to

230

the bearing of fruit by plants. The implication is that the sounds made by the animals contained a potential for articulate speech, but that this potential was never realized.

69

It talked at first, but senselessly: The person of mud is unique among all the creatures made by the gods in that it not only lacks sensible speech, but is not even quoted by means of onomatopoeia. Note also the correlate lack of articulation of its body. But the subtlest point here is that the only creature made of mud is also the only one made in the singular, which makes this episode an allusion to the Adamic myth. What the writers of the PV have to say about Adam, in their indirect way, is that a singular creature of mud could neither have made sense, nor walked nor multiplied. If there ever was such a creature, there is no way it could have left a trace of itself; it must have dissolved.

69

"a counting of days, a counting of lots": This is *uq'ijixik* [uquihixic] *ub'itaxik,* "its-being-dayed (or timed) its-being-modeled (or shaped)." As daykeepers, Xpiyacoc and Xmucane will divine by counting the day numbers and names of the 260-day divinatory cycle, dividing or "shaping" a fistful of seeds from the coral tree (see Glossary) into lots.

69

midmost seers: This is *nik' wachinel* [nicuachinel], composed of *nik',* "middle"; *wachin,* "see with one's own eyes" (FV); *-el,* agentive. In TC, where the words *pa ya'* or "into water" are added, the term refers to diviners who look into water. From this it would seem that the unmodified term must refer to any diviners who use gazing techniques.

69

Grandmother of Day, Grandmother of Light: This is *ratit q'ij* [quih], *ratit saq* [zac], "its-grandmother day (or sun), its-grandmother light," referring to both Xpiyacoc and Xmucane despite the fact that the former is described in other contexts as a grandfather (*mama*). Andrés Xiloj commented that a grandmother (or grandfather) of "day" and "light" would be a grandmother "until the end of the world," that is, for as long as light lasts, and would go back to the beginning of light. In this context, then, "day" and "light" are a dyadic and less direct way of referring to what Indo-European languages reduce to the unitary concept of "time."

69

"the human form": "Form" translates *anom;* DB has *anomal,* "mold."

69

"fulfill your names": Some of the names or terms in this list refer to Xpiyacoc and Xmucane, but others refer to their grandsons. One Monkey and One Artisan account for the various occupational terms, while Hunahpu and Xbalanque, in their roles as vagabond actors, may account for the names Hunahpu Possum and Hunahpu Coyote. Great Peccary and Great Coati resemble Xpiyacoc and Xmucane in being an elderly couple, but they are later treated as distinct from them (p. 79).

69

"lapidary, jeweler": This is *ajk'wal* [ahcuual], *ajyamanik,* in which *aj-* is occupational, *k'wal* is "medicinal or precious stones" (FV), and *yamanik* is "ancient jewels" (FV).

69

"sawyer, carpenter": This is *ajch'ut* [ahchut], *ajtz'alam* [ahtzalam], in which *aj-* is occupational, *ch'ut* is "sawyer of canes and boards" (FV), and *tz'alam* is "board" (TC, AG).

69

"incense maker, master craftsman": This is *ajq'ol, ajtoltekat,* in which *aj-* is occupational; *q'ol* is copal incense. *Toltekat* is from a Nahua source; *toltecatl* is "master of mechanical arts" in Nahuatl proper (AM).

70

"Run your hands over the kernels of corn, over the seeds of the coral tree": The verb stem here is *mala-,* "to run the hand over something" (FV). The contemporary Quiché daykeeper first pours the seeds out of a small bundle into a pile on a table and mixes them, moving the right hand over them with palm down flat and fingers spread, and then grabs a fistful. The remaining seeds are then set aside; those from the fistful are sorted into lots of four seeds each, arranged in parallel rows so that the days can easily be counted on them, one day for each lot. When seeds are left over from the division into fours, a remainder of three seeds is made into two additional lots (with two seeds in one and one seed in the other), while a remainder of one or two seeds counts as one additional lot. Once the clusters are complete the diviner begins counting the days of the 260-day cycle, starting in the present (the day of the divination itself), the past (the day the client's problem began), or the future (the day of an action contemplated by the client). The augury is reckoned from the portent of the day that is reached by counting through to the final lot of seeds.

70

the borrowing: This is *uqajik,* a term that Andrés Xiloj, as a daykeeper, recognized immediately. When today's daykeeper speaks the opening prayer for a

RUN YOUR HANDS . . . OVER THE
SEEDS OF THE CORAL TREE: *A
divination in progress in front of
burning offerings at Tohil's Place.
Coral seeds and crystals from a
random handful are being sorted
out in lots of four each; once the
arrangement is complete the
daykeeper will count the days of
the 260-day calendar (one day for
each lot), starting from the
current day or the day the client's
problem began. At left is the
bundle in which the seeds and
crystals are carried; the coin on
top is the fee paid by the client.
The hands are those of the
translator, who is a trained and
initiated daykeeper.*

PHOTO BY BARBARA TEDLOCK

divination, invoking the sheet lightning, clouds, mists, and damp breezes of the
world, he or she is said to be "borrowing" these forces from the days themselves,
each of which is ruled by a lord, and from the mountains of the world, each of
which has a spirit familiar (B. Tedlock 1992:155, 157, 162). Xpiyacoc and Xmucane are not as modest as this human daykeeper in their own borrowing of
lightning, moisture, and air currents: they name the Heart of Sky, whose electri-
cal aspect ultimately manifests not as far-off and silently flickering sheet lightning but as close-up thunderbolts, and who is also known as Hurricane, the
bringer of rains and winds of world-destroying proportions. Meteorological
forces, large or small, serve to connect the cosmos, both temporally and spatially,
with the microcosmic scene of the divination, transmitting information about

233

distant places or times through the counting of days and through lightning-like sensations that occur in various parts of the diviner's own body.

70

the lots: This is *b'it,* apparently the same as the stem in the name *b'itol,* "Modeler" (see Maker, Modeler in the Glossary). It is my guess that it refers to the clusters of seeds that are made up from the random fistful taken up by the diviner (as described above); in effect, the diviner is giving shape to a chaotic mass. I translate *b'it* as "lots" because that word both fits the groups of seeds, which are arranged in lots of four, and figures in English-language divination terminology. "Diviner" (on p. 70) is a translation of *ajb'it,* in which *b'it* has the occupational prefix.

70

who stands behind others: This is [chiracan], which Andrés Xiloj identified as part of a phrase used today by daykeepers: *chiraqan uq'ab',* "at-his/her-legs his/her-arms" (in which legs and arms include feet and hands). To be at someone's feet and hands means to give assistance, as a daykeeper does when praying and giving offerings on behalf of a client, or a midwife does when assisting a birth.

70

"may you succeed, may you be accurate": Like Xpiyacoc and Xmucane, the contemporary daykeeper speaks to the seeds while arranging them, asking for a clear outcome.

70

"Have shame, you up there, . . . attempt no deception": Andrés Xiloj was not surprised to hear the Heart of Sky addressed in this manner. He pointed out that today's daykeepers (including himself) also ask that the gods not deceive their divinatory clients. The praying diviner may say, for example, *Ma b'an la ri mentira,* "Do not make a lie." In the PV the client in question is none other than the god Sovereign Plumed Serpent.

70

manikins, woodcarvings: Andrés Xiloj remarked, "Then these will only be *representations* of humans."

70

They just went and walked wherever they wanted: Andrés Xiloj commented, "Then they're like animals." In Quiché thinking one of the major differences between animals and humans is that humans must ask permission of the gods to go abroad in the world. To pray that nothing bad happen to one in the road is to ask permission to pass; the need for such permission is more acute in the case of visits to powerful shrines or distant towns. In prayers that prepare the way for a long trip, one asks not only that there be no robbers in the road, but that policemen, soldiers, and customs officials should be inattentive.

71

The man's body was carved from the wood of the coral tree: The body of the icon presently called Maximón in the Tzutuhil town of Santiago Atitlán is made of this wood (Mendelson 1959:57).

71

hearts of bulrushes: This is *sib'aq* [zibac], referring to the "heart" (FV, FX) or "pith or insides" (DB) of rushes of the kinds whose leaves are woven into mats (FV). This would be the white and fleshy (as opposed to green and fibrous) parts of rushes (including cattails), which can be found inside the lower parts of stalks.

71

a rain of resin: Andrés Xiloj commented, "This was turpentine that fell, and it was burning as it fell."

71

Gouger of Faces: This is *k'otk'owach* [cotcouach], composed of *k'otk'o,* a reduplicated form of *k'oto,* "to carve out," and *wach,* "face." Andrés Xiloj gave the modern name as *k'ot kiwach,* "gouges out their faces," and identified it as a kind of animal, commenting that "they still exist, but I don't know whether in the sky or the forest. They stay in the darkness, and when the sun doesn't shine they come out."

71

Sudden Bloodletter: This is *kamalotz,* in which *lotz* is "puncture, let blood" (FX); *kama-* is probably related to *kajmaj,* "fright, surprise attack" (FV).

71

Crunching Jaguar: This is *kotz'b'alam* [cotzbalam], in which *kotz'* is from *kotz'ij,* "grind" (FV).

71

Tearing Jaguar: This is *tukumb'alam;* TC has *tukum,* "scratch."

72

black rainstorm: This is *q'eqal jab'* [quecal hab]. As Andrés Xiloj explained, the phrase does not mean that the rain itself was black, but refers to the darkness created by an intense rainstorm.

72

Into their houses came: This is *xok ula'* [xoc ula], "entered as visitors." Today any invasion of the house (including its patio) by a wild animal is viewed as a sign sent by the earth deity, whether it is a fox or possum that attacks domestic animals or, say, a bird that happens to fly indoors. Andrés Xiloj pointed out that such animals do not speak (ch'awik) but rather give signs (retal) by their cries or movements. Note that even under the cataclysmic conditions of the present episode the speaking is done by domestic animals and by artifacts; it is not attributed to wild animals.

72

turkeys: This is *ak'* [ac], which became the term for the Old World chicken during colonial times. A number of colonial dictionaries give the term for turkey as *qitzij ak'* (FT, FV), meaning "true *ak',*" or *masewal ak'* (PG), "Indian *ak',*" so named to contrast it with the European chicken. This makes it clear that the pre-Hispanic term for turkey was simply *ak'.* Today the turkey is called *no's* (AG), a term that had already appeared by the seventeenth century (DB has [noz]).

72

r-r-rip, r-r-rip, / r-r-rub, r-r-rub: This is *joli, joli, juqi, juqi* [juqui], onomatopoeic for the sound of a handstone (mano) rubbing against a grinding stone (metate); the verb stem for "rub together" is *juqu-* (AG). If the performance of the present Quiché story was anything like that of North American Indian tales, these lines were probably sung. It must be kept in mind that *j* in Quiché is rough, like Spanish *j* or German *x*, and that *q* (as contrasted with *k*) is rough as well. This harshness would probably be exaggerated in a dramatic oral rendering, hence my suggestion that the *r* in the translation be trilled. Andrés Xiloj immediately heard a sound play in these lines, which he rendered as follows:

> *Jo' ali, jo' ali,*
> *juquwik, juquwik.*
>
> Let's go girl, let's go girl,
> rubbing together, rubbing together.

72

their hearthstones were shooting out: Andrés Xiloj compared this incident with stones shooting out of a volcano. It appears to be an origin story for the stars Alnitak, Saiph, and Rigel in Orion, which are said by Quichés to be the three hearthstones of the typical Mayan kitchen fireplace, arranged to form a triangle. The stars enclose the Orion nebula (M-42), which is said to be a smoky fire (B. Tedlock 1985:86). Inscriptions on Stele C at Quiriguá and in the Temple of the Cross at Palenque reveal that the Classic Maya reckoned the age preceding the present one as ending with a similar event. The interpretation of these inscriptions by Freidel et al. (1993:64–70) obscures the similarity, placing the event at the beginning of a new age and raising the entire sky rather than just the hearthstones. In fact the inscriptions give the date as a period-ending one, 4 Ahaw 8 Kumk'u 13.0.0.0.0 (falling in 3114 B.C. by Western reckoning). The Palenque text reads, *Hal k'ohba, ox tun tzukah, . . . ch'a chan yax ox tunal* (Schele 1992:122–25), or, in my translation, "The image is lifted up, the stones are arranged in their three places, . . . the place with three stones is taken into the sky for the first time" (D. Tedlock 1995). For a further discussion of hearthstones in lowland Mayan iconography, see Taube 1994b.

73

wood alone was used for their flesh: Andrés Xiloj remarked, "They lacked blood, or quickening, which is what corn gives." As it turns out later, real human beings are indeed made of corn.

73

Seven Macaw: In this name the term for macaw is *kaqix* [caquix], combining *kaq,* "red," and *qi'x,* "feather" (MX) and thus fitting the scarlet macaw (*Ara macao*), which has more red feathers than any other macaw. This identification is confirmed by the statement that Seven Macaw's nose "shines white," the scarlet macaw being the only one with a white beak. The Yucatec counterpart of Seven Macaw is *k'inich k'ak'mo,* "Sun-eyed Fire-macaw," who is like him in having solar pretensions and in being given to self-aggrandizement in general (Roys 1954:42). In the art of Izapa and the Protoclassic and Classic Maya, Seven Macaw has an ancestor in the winged monster iconographers call the Principal Bird Deity (Taube 1987), whose attributes sometimes include those of the king vulture (*Sarcoramphus papa*) and who is often shown with a snake in his beak. Just as the scarlet macaw is the showiest of all macaws and parrots, so the king vulture stands out among vultures, with complex red, orange, black, and white markings on the head, neck, beak, and wattles, and with parallel rows of black and white wing and tail feathers. Macaw, vulture, and snake all meet in the Cakchiquel *xib'alb'ay kaqix* or "underworld macaw," which is "a bird like a vulture that eats snakes" (PG).

73

"I am their sun . . . their months": "Sun" is *q'ij* [quih] here, which could either be "sun" or "day," but "months" is *ik'il* [iquil], as contrasted with *ik',* "moon." The PV only mentions this exaggerated claim to an astronomical role, but Seven Macaw's actual (and lesser) role is indicated by the fact that some present-day speakers of Quiché use his name as a term for the seven stars of the Big Dipper (DL, MA). In West Indian Carib myths the Big Dipper has a feathered headdress that shows by day as the rainbow, which suggests that Seven Macaw might also have a rainbow aspect. What the Big Dipper has in common with the rainbow is that

its appearance marks the end of storms, only it does so seasonally, fully returning to the night sky at the end of the hurricane season (see the notes to p. 74).

73

"I am the walkway and I am the foothold of the people": "Walkway" is *b'inib'al* and "foothold" is *chakab'al; -b'al* is an instrumental suffix. Andrés Xiloj explicated Seven Macaw's statement as follows: *"B'inib'al* is to give light for walking, or to go out on a somewhat clear road; and *chakab'al*—now we say *chakanib'al* —is the same. These words are in the prayers we say at the *warab'alja* [patrilineage shrines], to ask permission for anyone who goes out of the house to whatever place. They can walk, they can crawl—*chakanib'al* is to crawl on all fours. Seven Macaw is saying that he is a person's feet, since he knows that he has light [to show a person where to step], but in fact the person sees darkly, it isn't very clear."

73

"they stand out": This is *kawakoj;* MX has *kawakik,* "to have big teeth (and thus to be unable to close the mouth)."

74

the scope of his face lies right around his own perch: Seven Macaw, as the Big Dipper, swings around the pole star in the northern part of the sky rather than traveling the longer paths of the true sun and moon.

74

This was when the flood was worked upon the manikins, woodcarvings: In timing the demise of Seven Macaw to coincide with the great disaster that befalls the wooden people, the PV follows a mythological pattern that is widespread in Mesoamerica and the Caribbean. In these latitudes, the movement of the Big Dipper is associated with the hurricane season (Lehmann-Nitsche 1924–25). The season begins when the Big Dipper is already in steep descent at dusk (in mid-July) and continues through a period when it disappears completely for as much as half the night, ending only when all seven stars make it above the eastern horizon before dawn (in mid-October).

PART TWO

77

Hunahpu: This name is composed of *jun,* "one"; *aj-,* agentive or occupational; and possibly *pub',* "blowgun," giving "One Blowgunner." In Yucatec, *p'uh* is a verb for "hunt" (but not a term for "blowgun"), while *ahp'uh* means "hunter" (AB). *Junajpu* (Hunahpu) is one of the twenty day names of the Quiché version

HUNAHPU: *The glyph for his Yucatec counterpart, which reads* Hun Ahaw.

DRAWING BY KARL TAUBE

of the 260-day divinatory calendar. Since Quiché speakers take no more notice of the blowgunner contained in this name than English speakers take notice of Thor in Thursday, it has been left untranslated in the body of the present work. The *jun* is so embedded in the name that in both ancient and modern Quiché the particular *Junajpu* day that bears the number one is called *Jun Junajpu*. The corresponding Yucatec day name is *Ahaw* or "Lord," without the embedded number, but the name of the cognate deity (designated God S by iconographers) was written by prefixing the head variant of the day name glyph with the number one (see illustration above), yielding *Hun Ahaw* (M. Coe 1989:167–68; Taube 1992:115–16). In Classic Maya art this god, like Hunahpu, hunts with a blowgun and plays ball (M. Coe 1989:169–73).

77

Xbalanque: The final syllable of this name is ambiguously spelled in the MS, where there is a tendency to use [qu] for any one of four distinct k sounds. The correct sound is revealed by the name contemporary speakers of Kekchí give to the sun when it passes beneath the earth at night, which is *b'alamq'e* (EH). At present they have no term for the sun in general, but the original solar meaning of *-q'e* is made clear by *saq'e,* their term for the daytime sun, which combines *saq* ("white" or "light") with *-q'e. B'alam* means both "hidden" and "jaguar" in Kekchí, while *xb'alam* (with a third-person singular possessive prefix) means "its hidden part (or aspect)." *Xb'alamq'e* would thus mean "sun's hidden aspect," and the correct form of the PV version of the name would be *Xb'alanq'e.* The existence of a prefixed version of Kekchí *b'alamq'e* is confirmed by Las Casas (1967:330, 619), who reports a tradition that a god named Exbalanquen entered the underworld through a cave near Cobán (which is in Kekchí territory). In the PV, the specifically underworld character of Xbalanque is revealed by scenes in which he and his brother Hunahpu depart from their habit of acting in unison. Hun-

XBALANQUE: *The glyph for his Yucatec counterpart, which reads* Yax Balam.

DRAWING BY KARL TAUBE

239

ahpu takes the lead only when they are on the surface of the earth, whereas Xbalanque does so only when they are in Xibalba. The name of the Yucatec deity (God CH) corresponding to Xbalanque was written by prefixing the head variant of the glyph for the number nine with *yax*, "first" (see illustration on p. 239), yielding *yax bolon* as a literal reading (M. Coe 1989:168; Taube 1992:60–63). The profiled head is always shown with a patch of spotted jaguar fur on the jaw, indicating that the intended reading is *balam*, which puns on *bolon* and means "jaguar."

77

We could shoot him while he's at his meal: The timing of this event is limited by three factors: (1) the seven stars of the Big Dipper (corresponding to Seven Macaw) must be high in the sky, (2) Venus (corresponding to Hunahpu) must be on the horizon, and (3) the nance tree must provide fruit for Seven Macaw's meal. The two astronomical possibilities, both of which find the Big Dipper high over Polaris, are a June evening, with Venus visible on the western horizon, or a December morning, with Venus rising on the eastern horizon. As for nances, their ripening begins in June and continues (depending on local conditions) for several months, but they are unavailable in December (Breedlove and Laughlin 1993:151–52). In the Dresden Codex, confrontations between a god of Venus and Seven Macaw occur on the last page of the Venus table, where the lowland Maya equivalent of Junajpu is shown sitting on a sky band (corresponding to the ecliptic) in the top picture and Seven Macaw is named on the same page (in the third column of text) as *7 k'ak'mo'* or "7 Fire Macaw." The confrontation occurs when Venus makes one last appearance as the evening star on a day named *Eb* (*E* in Quiché), eight days before reappearing as the morning star on a day named *Ahaw* (*Junajpu*). During the era for which the table is set up, such occurrences fell in early June—for example, on the Gregorian date June 10, 1235, or 11.0.11.2.12 1 Eb 5 Mak on the Mayan calendar.

77

Zipacna: This character and his brother, Earthquake (see below), constitute the Quiché version of a pair of Mesoamerican dragons, often represented as a two-headed dragon by the Classic Maya, whose features variously combine those of reptiles or (less often) fish or birds. Zipacna has the habits of a caiman, bathing beside a river and hunting in its waters. His name (*sipakna* in modern orthography) resembles a number of other Mayan god names in ending with *na*, meaning "house" in Yucatec. The rest of the name could well have its source in the Yucatec verb stem *sip-*, referring to a sliding or slipping motion (like that of a caiman) and nominalized by *-ak* (AB). Zipacna has an obvious Yucatec counterpart in the patron deity of the month named *sip*, whose glyph consists of the profiled head and snout of a caiman. Together, *sipakna* and *sip* are cognate, in both their caiman features and their names, with the Mexican dragon whose Nahuatl name is *cipactli*.

240

77

Earthquake: The name of the second son of Seven Macaw, *kab'raqan,* is the common term for "earthquake" in both ancient and modern Quiché. It has been read as combining *kab'-,* "two," with *raqan,* "his legs," but the Cakchiquel version of the name, *kab'araqan,* instead suggests *kab'a,* "pile up a quantity of earth" (FV); the sense of the name as a whole could be something like "earthen (are) his legs." The Yucatec dragon named *itzam kab ayin* (AB), meaning something like "monster earth caiman," seems akin to both Earthquake and his brother, Zipacna.

77

Chimalmat: This name is from a Nahua source; *chimalli* is "round shield" and *matlatl* is "net" in Nahuatl proper (AM). A netted shield was the emblem of Chimalli, the central Mexican warrior goddess who served as the patron deity of midwives (Klein 1993:46–47). Chimalmat has her Yucatec counterpart in *chimal k'inich k'ak'mo,* "Shield of Sun-eyed Fire Macaw" (Roys 1967:22, 82). In that same language, *chimal ek'* or "Shield Stars" is a term for "the guards of the north (Ursa Minor)" (AB), a constellation that probably combines the stars in the arc of the Little Dipper with other nearby stars to make a circle. Chimalmat should have a similar celestial identity, given that her husband, Seven Macaw, corresponds to the neighboring stars of the Big Dipper.

77

Fireplace, Hunahpu, Cave by the Water, Xcanul, Macamob, Huliznab: These are all volcanoes lying along the Pacific Rim. Fireplace or *chiq'aq'* [chicac] is generally thought to be the Volcán de Fuego (southwest of Antigua). Hunahpu is described in the Annals of the Cakchiquels as being separated from Fireplace by a *kojol* or "notch" (Brinton 1885:86), which points to the Volcán Acatenango, located just a few kilometers north of Fuego. Cave by the Water, which may well be the Volcán de Agua (south of Antigua), is *pekul ya'* [ya]; TC gives *ru pekul ya'* [ya] as "cave on the bank of a river or lake." Xcanul or *xk'anul,* with a feminine prefix (*x-*), is the Volcán Santa María (south of Quetzaltenango). The name Macamob may be from *makamo,* "to do something suddenly" (FV), while the *jul* in Huliznab is probably "hole." The locations of these last two volcanoes are uncertain.

77

the mountains . . . are softened by him: "Softened" translates *neb'onik;* Andrés Xiloj read it as "soaked," while MX glosses *neb'enik* as "overcooked." Xiloj commented, "When the earth is completely soaked it can be destroyed by the water. When there are rains of forty-eight or sixty hours, there may be destruction. Landslides are the work of such rains."

241

he goes up the tree every day: Scarlet macaws typically feed in the tops of fruit and nut trees from dawn to dusk (Forshaw 1973:365). Their habitat, like that of the nance tree whose fruit is eaten by Seven Macaw, consists of rain forest margins, savannas, and the lower slopes of mountains.

78–79

Then he went up over the tree and fell flat on the ground: When birds are shot they fly upward in a spasm before falling from a tree. But Seven Macaw's movement also suggests that of the Big Dipper; assuming that his head and body correspond to the bowl of the Big Dipper and his tail to its handle, his climbing of the tree to eat his nances, his going up over the tree when shot, and his fall to the ground all follow the pattern of the Big Dipper, which rises with its handle down, goes up over Polaris (counterclockwise) in a momentarily horizontal position, and then sets with its bowl end down.

79

the arm of Hunahpu . . . was seized by Seven Macaw: At this point Seven Macaw's behavior departs from that of an actual macaw and suggests his identity with the Principal Bird Deity of Izapa and the lowland Maya, a monstrous creature partly modeled on the king vulture (see the notes to p. 73). As Karl Taube has pointed out to me, a newly discovered Classic Maya relief at Toniná, in Chiapas, shows this monster perched above Hun Ahaw (the lowland equivalent of Hunahpu), whose lower arm has been amputated (see Yadeun 1993:108, 111, 114). A similar scene is depicted on a Protoclassic stele at Izapa (Norman 1976: fig. 3.26). See also the note headed "All my teeth are just loose," below.

79

tricksters: Here and elsewhere, the term translated as "trickster" or "tricksters" is *k'axtok'*, which occurs in the PV only in quoted dialogues. It is addressed to characters who have pulled a trick or are suspected of having done so, including Hunahpu and Xbalanque, Zipacna, Blood Moon, Tamazul, and Lust Woman and Wailing Woman, along with Quiché warriors who play a joke on sleeping enemies. It is glossed as "devil" in dictionaries compiled by missionaries (DB and FV).

79

"they've dislocated my jaw": This is the origin of the way a macaw's beak looks, with a huge upper mandible and a small, retreating lower one.

79

"All my teeth are just loose": "Loose" is *chu;* DB glosses a reduplicated form, *chuyucha,* as "to rattle." Today, the bark of the nance (the kind of tree in which

Seven Macaw was perched when he was shot) is chewed by the Tzotzil Maya as a cure for loose teeth (Breedlove and Laughlin 1993:151).

79

" 'Do forgive us' ": The addition of "Do" to this phrase is my way of translating *qi* [qui], which carries a sense of exaggerated politeness (FV).

80

with great effort: This is *nimaq wa' ch'ij* [nimac ua chih], literally "great this effort," in which *ch'ij* is translated on the basis of *ch'ijinik*, "the strength to do something" (MX).

80

"What sweets can you make, what poisons can you cure?": The "sweets" and "poisons" are both *ki'* [qui], a word that carries both these meanings to this day; see the notes to p. 83.

80

"We just pull the worms out of teeth": There is a contemporary Mopán Maya myth in which Lord K'in ("Sun" or "Day") causes the chief of the vultures to have a toothache and then is begged to come and cure it (Thompson 1930:129–32). The motive of this trickery is the protagonist's desire to get his wife back from the vultures.

80

"we just cure eyes": As a medical specialty, the curing of eyes fits under the same heading as bones and teeth because the Quiché language classifies the eyes as bones. In the PV eyes are *ubaq* [ubac] *uwach*, literally "its-bones (or pits) his/her-eyes"; today they are *ub'aq'och*. Andrés Xiloj himself covers a medical territory similar to that of Hunahpu and Xbalanque: in addition to being a bonesetter and healer of sprains, he knows how to make eyedrops.

80

"It's a worm, gnawing at the bone": The present-day Quiché retain the notion that a toothache is caused by a worm gnawing at the bone. According to T. J. Knab (personal communication), there is a Mesoamerican parasite that takes up residence in the gums.

80

a coating: This is *q'u* [cu], "covering" (MX).

80

he was plucked around the eyes: The verb stem here is *ch'olik* [cholic], "to cut or pull out hair or feathers" (MX), or "flay, skin, take off crust" (FV). This is clearly meant to be the origin of the large, white, and completely featherless eye patches of the scarlet macaw (see Forshaw 1973:364–67). I take it that Seven Macaw sported two large metal disks where the patches of the scarlet macaw are now. As Charles Bigelow (a keeper of macaws) has shown me, excitement or anger brings a distinct blush to these patches. Perhaps the Quiché once took this blush to be a reminder of the bird's former solar pretensions.

81

What they did was simply the word of the Heart of Sky: In a similar fashion the Zunis sometimes portray the Ahayuuta warrior heroes—who, like Hunahpu and Xbalanque, are tricksters—as simply carrying out the word of the Sun Father, though they may appear to be acting on their own (see D. Tedlock 1972:234–48).

81

a post for their hut . . . the lintel of their hut: This passage is indeterminate as to what use the Four Hundred Boys intend for their log. The "post" is *aqan* [acan], literally "leg"; Andrés Xiloj explained that this would be a vertical post with a fork at the top. The "lintel" is *wapalil* (*apalil* today), which he specified as a term for a horizontal beam over a door or window.

82

"We'd like some help": This is *kaqachaq'imaj* [cacachaquimah] *tana,* in which *kaqa-* is "incomplete-we" and *tana* indicates supplication; the verb stem, *chaq'imaj,* is given by FV as "ask to borrow."

82

"we'll throw him down": The verb stem here is *tzaq* [tzac], "fling, cast" (MX). This is mere bravado; it is not what the Four Hundred Boys actually end up doing.

82

" 'Why are you spilling dirt in the hole?' ": The verb stem here is written [macaha], but with the stem of the *h* crossed off to make it into an *n;* MX has *mak'inik,* "to spill." Here the Four Hundred Boys are proposing to make a sarcastic statement to Zipacna, but once again, as when they talked about throwing him into the hole, they are indulging in bravado.

82

"wedged": This is [pachal]; MX has *pach'alik,* "be between two walls or in a crack."

82

"we'll wham a big log": The verb stem here is *tar-;* in MX, the entries dealing with *tar* and *t'ar-* have a sense of giving a blow that makes a sound. In effect the

Four Hundred Boys are planning to drop a major vertical post for their hut into place, resting its butt end on a sacrifice victim.

82

he dug a separate hole to one side: Edmonson notes here that in digging a hole for the present-day Flying Pole Dance, Quichés place offerings in a hole dug to one side from the post hole proper (Edmonson 1971:45). There is a story in the Achí dialect of Quiché in which a character now known as Zipac carries a log the narrator compares with the pole used in the Monkey Dance (Shaw 1971:48).

82–83

"on another level, or two levels away": "Level" translates *eleb'al;* literally this would be "place of egress," but I take my cue from Burgess and Xec (1955:42), who decided on "elevation," which fits with the general Mesoamerican notion of a stratified underworld.

83

sweet drink: This is *ki'* [qui], "sweet," "poison," "maguey," and (according to PG) "wine or chicha." In contemporary Quiché "maguey," is *ki* and "sweet" is *ki'* (AG), but PG (a reliable colonial source) has *ki'* for both. The "wine" in question would be some variety of the maguey drink known as pulque (from Nahuatl) in Mexico, which is no longer made in Guatemala. In the PV, it requires cooking at some stage, takes three days to ferment, and sends the Four Hundred Boys "out of their senses" (p. 83). At least one kind of Mexican pulque requires cooking, a variety in which maguey cuttings are boiled together with honey prior to fermentation. Pulque (with or without honey) is sweet to the taste before fermentation and bitter afterward; perhaps the seemingly contradictory meanings of *ki'* reflect the paradox of a drink that starts out sweet and harmless and ends up bitter and (in sufficient quantities) sickening.

83

to dedicate: This is [lacabebal], with an instrumental suffix (*-b'al*); DB has *laq'ab'ej,* "to inhabit some place, occupying it."

83

Having taken their pickings: The verb stem here is [culun]; MX has *q'ulunik,* "to pluck, devastate, strip."

84

Hundrath and *play on words:* In this passage the authors are wondering whether the term for the Pleiades, which is *motz,* might actually come from *omuch'* in *omuch' k'ajolab',* "Four Hundred Boys," or whether the connection is merely a *sakb'al tzij,* literally "play-instrument words"; FX gives *saki* as "play cards or dice." *Omuch'* is composed of *o-,* "five," and *much',* "eighty," yielding

245

$5 \times 80 = 400$. Verbs with the stem *much'-*, which takes the form *moch'-* in Kekchí (EH), have such meanings as "take hold of a fistful" or "make a pile" (FX). *Motz,* in addition to being a term for the Pleiades, means "heap" or "pile," while verbs with the stem *motz-* can be used to refer to the crowding together of numerous people (FX). From all of this it seems clear that *motz,* as a term for the Pleiades, might well have its origin in an archaic form of the Quichean name for the Four Hundred Boys. For this reason I have chosen to translate *motz* as Hundrath, an archaic (Old Norse) form of English "hundred." In today's Quiché thought the Pleiades symbolize a fistful of seeds. The planting season for high-altitude maize, in March, is marked by evening settings of the Pleiades, which leave them invisible for most of the night; by May, when low-altitude maize is planted, the Pleiades enter a period of complete invisibility.

84

counterfeiting: This is *jalwachixik;* FV has *jalwachir,* "change one thing for another."

84

the forearms: This is *xul,* translated on the basis of an entry in FV that is missing its heading but falls between *xulb'aq* and *xulu;* the gloss is "the little arms of crabs or shrimps."

84

where they opened: This is [pa hac]; *pa* is "in" and [hac] is translated on the basis of the entry for *jaq* in FV, "to open things" (such as curtains or eyelids).

84

the claws: This is *uko'k* [ucoc] *q'ab,* "its-carrying-device arm," in which *ko'k* is translated on the basis of an entry in MX.

84

They used a flagstone for the back of the crab, which clattered: Andrés Xiloj commented, "A crab is just like a wristwatch: it has the meat inside and it's pure bone outside."

84

they put the shell beneath an overhang: Andrés Xiloj pictured this as a spot beneath a waterfall.

84

"By now I can't stand the hunger": "Hunger" is a Quiché metaphor for sexual appetite; that this metaphor is intended here becomes more obvious as the story unfolds.

84

"please come point her out, boys": Andrés Xiloj chuckled as he read this and said, "This Zipacna is abusing the boys here, he's saying they shouldn't be afraid. It says here, *kib'e ta iwab'a,* which could be *kib'e ta iwab'a',* 'If only you would come along to *iwab'a'*—to point it out,' but it could also be, *keb'e ta iwab'aj,* 'If only *iwab'aj*—your stones, your balls—would come along.' Today, when someone runs from a fight, the saying is *ke'me ta iwab'aj,* 'Don't hide your balls.' So Zipacna is saying, 'Don't you have any balls, boys?' They're still young." The puns in this passage cannot be preserved in English, but I have tried to make its sexual dimension more obvious by using feminine pronouns for the crab (though Quiché pronouns do not have gender), since the crab is the object of Zipacna's "hunger."

85

"But won't you please": This sentence begins with *la qi* [qui]; *la* makes it a yes/no question and *qi* (according to FV) indicates exaggerated politeness.

85

"I'll show you a place where there are plenty of birds": Continuing along the lines of his comment above, Andrés Xiloj said, "There it is again, only now it's *nuwab'a',* 'I show you something,' or else *nuab'aj,* 'my balls'—he's got balls." As for the "birds" (*tz'ikin*), the primary metaphor for penis is "bird" in Quichean languages. Edmonson takes this metaphor to be a recent borrowing from Spanish (1965:130), but it is already present in colonial dictionaries (TC, PM, FV). *Pich',* the Quichean term for a redheaded woodpecker (probably *Dryocopus lineatus*), provides a more specific metaphor, not only for penis but for penetration (PG, FT, FV, FX). This word is the obvious source of one of the Guatemalan Spanish slang terms for penis, "picha" (Rubio 1982).

85

"We were entering": The verb stem here is *ok-,* glossed (literally) as "enter" throughout this passage, a simple solution that keeps the same double meaning going in English that is present in the original.

85

"face down . . . on our back": These two opposite body positions are given throughout the present episode as *jupulik* and *pakalik,* respectively. Although they have caused difficulties for some translators, they are spelled correctly in the MS, are glossed in DB in the same way I have translated them, and were perfectly transparent to Andrés Xiloj.

85

her shell is gleaming red there: Some translators have complained about the color of this crab, but there are species of crab that are red before they are cooked.

"perhaps I'd better enter on my back": By this time Andrés Xiloj had already begun snickering as he read, but now he burst into laughter. Explaining himself, he said, "Clearly, the crab is a woman. As you already know, a woman does it on her back, but here it's in reverse: the man is on the bottom and the crab will go on top. These are trial runs. In ancient times, I think, they didn't know what sin was. They were looking for a way to understand everything." Speakers of Mopán Maya use their term for crab, *yux,* as a metaphor for "vulva" (see the entry for *is* in UU).

only his kneecaps were showing now! At this point Xiloj sat back and said, "My God! All the way to the knees!"

He gave a last sigh and was calm: The "sigh" here is [biquitahic], translated as suggested by Xiloj; MX gives *b'iq'b'itik,* "sigh." Xiloj translated *xlilob'* as "was calm"; FV gives *lilot* as "tranquil." On Zipacna's state Xiloj commented, "Nothing will bother him now." The story of Zipacna and the crab prompted him to tell a story that has been published elsewhere (D. Tedlock 1983b:317–20). In the Achí dialect of Quiché there is a contemporary story about a character named Zipac that makes the sexual dimension more overt than it is in the PV (Shaw 1971:48–51).

"Lure this Earthquake into sitting down": "Lure" is *b'ochi'j,* following DB; "sitting down" is *ku'b'ik* [cu ubic], following MX. I have supplied "this Earthquake" in order to clarify the sense of the sentence, setting it apart from the plural reference of the previous sentence.

"in the course of the days, in the course of the light": This is *chi b'e q'ij* [quih], *chi b'e saq* [zac], "in-road day (or sun), in-road light." According to Andrés Xiloj, it means "for all time. Just the way we in my family are weavers. All the time, and for all time, we are weavers." For an alternative translation of this line and a further comment by Xiloj, see the note headed "as long as there is day" on p. 294.

"Lead the way": This is *chik'ama qab'e* [chicama cabe], literally "imperative-you-take our-road," a common Quiché idiom that I have translated into the equivalent English idiom.

86

they just blow at the birds when they shoot: Andrés Xiloj remarked, "When people go out hunting today with guns, and when they see that an animal is coming, they do this: [blows a quick puff of air]. It is like magnetism, they pull it, the animal stops—it feels, it thinks there is a person hidden. When the animal has stopped for a moment, the person shoots, and there it is. The animal stopped to see what this noise was."

86

made fire with a drill: This is *xkib'aq k'u kiq'aq'* [xquibac cu quicac], "they-drilled then their-fire." An example of the same idiom is given by DB as *kanub'aq q'aq'* [ca3], "I start a fire"; FV gives *b'aq* as "to drill."

87

"the one to be made and modeled": The reference is to humankind, and the problem is the same one the twins discuss on pp. 77–78. Like so many other American Indian hero twins, they are monster slayers, making the earth habitable for humans.

87

"the human heart": I have supplied "human" here, assuming that the subject of the discussion has not changed since the previous sentence.

87

"a bite of meat, a meal of flesh": The parallel items here are *ti'k* and [chacuxic], which have been translated in many different ways; my version is based on *ti'nik,* "to eat meat" (MX), and *ch'akuj,* "to eat meat" (FV).

87

his ankles were bound to his wrists: The "ankles" and "wrists" are *ukul raqan uq'ab* [racan ucab], literally "its-necks his-legs his-arms"; as Andrés Xiloj explained, the "neck" of a leg or arm is its "ankle" or "wrist" in Quiché. In effect he is being prepared for a bundle-style burial, with his knees drawn up under his chin; perhaps this is what Hurricane was referring to when he told the twins to lure him "into sitting down."

PART THREE

91

let's just drink to the telling: The verb for "drink" here is [camuh]; I follow Edmonson in reading it as *qumuj,* "to drink" (Edmonson 1971:58), and find confirmation of the corrected spelling in FT and TC. If the authors of the PV are holders of the title of Master of Ceremonies (see the Introduction and the notes to pp. 184, 197), then the drink in question is a cacao beverage and the readers are being asked to imagine themselves at a wedding banquet. The traditional vessel for drinking cacao, from Mexico to Panama, was a calabash (McBryde 1947:57), and the story the authors are about to tell will account for the origin of the calabash.

91

One Hunahpu and Seven Hunahpu, as they are called: These names are *jun junajpu* and *wuqub'* [uucub] *junajpu,* in which *junajpu* is one of the twenty day names of the divinatory calendar. The MS leaves out Seven Hunahpu here, but everything else in the sentence is in the plural and the two brothers are named together two sentences later. As their numbers show, One and Seven Hunahpu represent all thirteen possible days bearing the name *Junajpu* (see p. 207).

91

One Monkey and One Artisan: These names are *jun b'atz'* [batz] and *jun chuen* [chouen]. *B'atz'* is a day name in Quiché and in Chol (JH), meaning "howler monkey" in both languages. *Chuen* is the Kekchí (EH) and Yucatec (AB) name for the same day, referring to craftsmanship in Yucatec. The name of the Yucatec counterpart of the monkey twins is *yaxal chuen,* "first artisan" (CB).

91

Egret Woman: This name is *xb'aqiyalo* [xbaquiyalo], in which the *x-* is "she of"; *b'aqiya-* seems equivalent to Yucatec *bak' ja',* in which *bak'* (like Quiché *baq*) means "bone" and *ja'* (like Quiché *ya'*) means "water." *Bak' ja'* is the Yucatec term for a white heron or egret, while *-lo'* may be a Yucatec demonstrative suffix meaning "that" (AB). The crested head of a snowy egret (*Egretta thula*) is featured in the name glyph for Egret Woman's Classic Maya counterpart at Palenque, where the tablet in the Temple of the Cross describes her as the mother of twins and possibly triplets (D. Tedlock 1990; 1992a:254, 263–66).

91

a partner: This is *laq'el* [laquel]. FV gives an example of the use of this term in which a woman may refer to another woman who shares the same man with her as *nulaq'el* (*nu-* is "my").

91

flautists, singers, and writers; carvers, jadeworkers, metalworkers: In these two sets of three skills each, writing is grouped with the performing arts rather than with handicrafts. This points to its close association with oral recitation (see also the notes to p. 63). A writer is *ajtz'ib',* in which *tz'ib'* refers to writing, painting, and designs produced by brocading; a carver is *ajk'ot,* in which *k'ot* means "thing worked in wood" (FX) and (as a verb stem) "to sculpt" (TC). The term for a jadeworker is *ajxit,* in which *xit* is "the very green stone like turquoise" (PG).

91

falcon: The term for this bird is *wok,* probably synonymous with *wak,* the laughing falcon that comes to the ball court in a later passage. The laughing falcon begins its song with a syllable that can be heard as either *wok* or *wak* (see the notes to p. 114). It flies quickly and directly from one place to another rather than gliding in circles (Álvarez del Toro 1971:46), which matches the movements described in the present passage.

91

Xibalba: This name, *xib'alb'a* in the new orthography, comes from the same root as *xib'ij,* "frighten"; the final *-b'a* could be from *-b'al,* "place of," or it could be reduplicative. In the terms of terrestrial reckoning it designates the underworld, as contrasted with the face of the earth (*uwach ulew*), but in celestial terms it may designate a world beyond the visible sky. In Yucatec the name survives as that of a "devil" (AB); in Quiché it is still the name of the underworld, to be uttered with caution.

91

One Death and Seven Death: These names are *jun kame* and *wuqub'* [uucub] *kame,* in which *kame* is one of the twenty day names of the divinatory calendar; it shares the same root with such forms as *kamel,* "dead person," but it is not the ordinary term for "death" (that would be *kamik* or *kamikal*). One and Seven Death are treated in the narrative as two persons, as are One and Seven Hunahpu, but their numbers show that they represent all thirteen possible days bearing the name Death (see p. 207).

91

"They're really determined to run right over us!": This is *xax kejikik uloq* [uloc] *paqawi* [pacaui], literally "certainly they-cut-straight hither above-us."

92

Scab Stripper and Blood Gatherer: These names are *xik'iri* [xiquiri] *pat* and *kuchuma kik'* [quic], translated so as to fit with each other and with the explanatory remark made by the authors. In Kekchí, *xik'i-* has to do with slipping and sliding, while *pat* is "scab" (EH); *kuchu-* is "gather, join together" in Quiche (FX, AG) and Cakchiquel (TC), while *kik'* "is blood." But these could be Quichean versions of the names of the lowland Maya personage labeled God L by iconographers, who is marked as a god of the underworld by the owl that sometimes sits on his hat and as a merchant by the trader's pack he sometimes carries on his back (Taube 1992:79–88). In Chol, *pat* is "back," while *kuch* is "load" and *kuchu-* is "carry" (JH).

251

92

to draw blood from people: Andrés Xiloj commented, "When there is strife, when people begin to fight, they strike one another. The blood comes out, and Xibalba receives this blood. We see that it fell, but it fell into the flasks of the evil ones. It is like their food."

92

Demon: This translates *ajal,* a term that occurs in Quiché only in compound names of "demons" (FX). In Chol it is a general term for "evil spirit" (AA).

92

to make pus come out of their legs, to make their faces yellow, to cause jaundice: This passage could refer not only to hepatitis but to yellow fever (if yellow fever was present in pre-Columbian times), whose symptoms include jaundice. The pus in the legs would be sores spread out along the lymphatic system. "Jaundice" translates *q'anil,* literally "yellowness."

92

to reduce people to bones . . . until they die from emaciation and edema: The first of these ailments is *siyaj b'aq* [bac], in which the first word may be a form of *siy,* "stretched" (FX), and the second is "bone"; DB gives *siyaj b'aq* as "skeleton" and *siyaj b'aqil* as the name of an unspecified illness; MX gives *baqil,* literally "bony," as "thin, weak." The second ailment is *xupan,* "dropsy" (FV and PG), better known today as edema, swelling caused by excess fluid in the tissues or cavities of the body. According to Andrés Xiloj, the contemporary shamans called *ajmesa,* "keeper of the table," sometimes go bad and practice a ritual called *chaqij mesa,* "dry table," in which they ask Xibalba to cause emaciation: "They put bones into the body of a person by means of prayers, in order to dry him up. They put a skull into the body of a person. They dry up the whole body." He told of a recent case in Momostenango in which a man was brought to court because "there were skulls, and bones of the arms and legs, in the place where this man burned his offerings. It was by means of these things that he screwed people up." Edema is caused by a separate ritual, called *rax mesa,* "fresh (or sudden, strong) table." Xiloj continued, "This, too, is done with bones. They put the bone in water, or whatever they put it in, and this same bone comes to be left in the body of the person, who then swells up. It's like an injection, but the evil is contained by this bone. The moment it is put in the body, the evil befalls one."

92

to give people a sudden fright: The verb here is *k'ulwachij,* which FV translates as "to run into someone." For Andrés Xiloj, it expresses what happens in a certain type of dream: "When one is in bed, not yet really sleeping . . . then

252

comes the apparition; it is represented. A person comes right up to touch one, one feels they are coming to touch one directly, but one can neither move nor cry out." This is what dream researchers call a "hypnagogic hallucination" (see B. Tedlock 1987:116).

92

whenever they have filth or grime in the . . . house: According to Andrés Xiloj, the best way to keep the agents of Xibalba out of one's house is to keep the place swept out and not allow trash to accumulate. See the story in the first note to p. 93 (below) for a case in which a house is cleaned out as a way of ending the deeds of a Xibalban.

92

in the doorway of the house, the patio of the house: This is *chirij ja,* "at the back of the house," and *chuwa ja,* "at the face of the house." In Quiché, as Andrés Xiloj explained, the "back" of a house is the side that has a door or entranceway giving access to a public road or path, while the "face" is the side that gives onto a patio (whether enclosed on all four sides or not).

92

that people should die in the road, just "sudden death": This affliction is *rax kamikal,* "fresh (or unripe, sudden, strong) death." According to Andrés Xiloj, it is like edema (see the above note headed "to reduce people to bones") in being caused by practices that come under the heading of *rax mesa:* "They come to frighten one in the road, and now one doesn't arrive home. Suddenly one may fall in the ditch, *rax kamikal.* As it says here in the Popol Vuh, 'Blood comes to the mouth,' it is as if one had pneumonia, suddenly one begins to vomit blood, and one dies in a moment. It is a matter of the *rax mesa.* They put a bone in the lung, and it is damaged instantly. One begins to vomit pure blood. They carry their materials on their shoulders, as it says here: 'the load on his shoulders.' When they are encountered in the road, they can kill one. But it isn't the *ajmesa* directly, but rather his genius [spirit familiar] or *win* [were animal]." Wing and Packstrap, the Xibalban lords responsible for this form of death, have a lowland Maya counterpart known to iconographers as God Q (Taube 1992:105–107), who attacks God M (a merchant) on a road in the Madrid Codex (50a, 54c).

93

Such are those who shared their thoughts: At this point Andrés Xiloj was reminded of a story, which he told on the spot. It is about a young man who gets aggravated with his wife almost to the point of taking a machete to her, all because an emissary of Xibalba keeps sneaking hairs or bits of rag or even bugs into the food she prepares. Moving in for the kill, the Xibalban tells the young man he has just seen his wife serving lunch to another man. Sure enough, when he gets home for lunch and asks his wife to give him the breast of the chicken she has prepared, she cannot find it in the pot. Later the young man is seized with the idea of climbing a tree; the earth rumbles and he suddenly finds himself looking down on the spot where the lords of Xibalba regularly assemble to banquet on blood that has been spilled by violence. He sees Blood Gatherer (the head lord) come out, and the last one to arrive, named Jodido (a Spanish word roughly translatable as "screwed-up"), turns out to be the very Xibalban who has been plotting against him. Jodido brags about how he sneaked the chicken breast out of the pot and tells the others they will soon enjoy the blood of the poor woman who was cooking it. After the Xibalbans leave the young man returns home and throws boiling water in each corner of his house. Returning to the banquet spot in time to see the Xibalbans reassemble, he sees Jodido come in late, barely able to move because of the scalding he has received. After this no more foreign objects appear in the young man's food.

93

they were piqued and driven: This is *xetzayixik* [xetzaixic] "they were salted (spiced)" (MX), and *xekotob'ax,* "they were pursued" (DB).

93

gaming equipment: This is *etz'ab'al* [etzabal], "play-instrument." The kilt is *tz'u'm,* "hide"; it is clearly shown to be hide in lowland Classic Maya art. The yoke, made of wood or hide and worn on one side at hip level (Leyenaar and Parsons 1988:107), is *b'ate,* a possible combination of *bat,* which is attested in Yucatec (AB) and Mopán (UU) as a term for "axe," with Cholan *te',* "wood, tree"; it is used as a term for the game itself over wide areas of Mesoamerica and in the Caribbean as well. Hunahpu and Xbalanque will later receive and return the ball with their yokes when they play against Xibalba. The arm guard or *pach'q'ab'* provided protection when a player hitting the ball from a squatting position braced himself with one arm on the ground (Leyenaar and Parsons 1988:114). The panache, shown as a long bunch of feathers attached to the crowns of the heads of the players in the ball court reliefs of Chichén Itzá, is *yachwach;* DB gives *yachwachib'ej* as "to crown." The headband, probably corresponding to the wreaths or turbans worn at forehead level by the Chichén Itzá players, is *wach sot,* in which *wach* is "face" and *sot* is "to make circular, like a crown or ring" (FV). The rubber ball is *kik',* literally "blood" but also referring to tree resins in general and rubber in particular. It was in the Caribbean and Mesoamerica that Europeans saw rubber balls for the first time.

93

"Military Keepers of the Mat": This title is *rajpop achij,* "its-keeper-mat soldier."

94

And these messengers of theirs are owls: Andrés Xiloj remarked, "At times an owl suddenly arrives near the house and begins to sing. This is a warning. Yes, it is a warning from Xibalba." Shooting Owl is *ch'ab'i tukur,* in which *tukur* is "owl"; *ch'ab'ij* is "shoot with an arrow" (FV) or "swoop down like a bird of prey" (DB, FX).

94

Great Hollow with Fish in the Ashes: This place is called *nim xob' karchaj* here and *nim xol* (Great Hollow) later (p. 157); in other documents it appears as *nim xol karchaj* (TV) and *xol karchaj* [chakaj] (RA). The location in question is that of the town near Cobán whose official name is San Pedro Carchá but whose spoken name in Kekchí (the local Mayan language) is *nim karcha. Nim* is "great" in both Kekchí and Quiché; among contemporary Kekchí speakers, *karcha* is said to be composed of *kar,* "fish," and *cha,* "ashes" (see the notes to p. 132). The writers of the PV could have given this name the same interpretation, since *kar* has the same meaning in Quiché while "ashes" is *chaj,* accounting for the final *j* in their spelling. As for the difference between *xob'* and *xol,* the former is Kekchí and refers to a geological depression or hollow (EH), while the latter is Quiché and refers to a space between things (FX). There are numerous karstic depressions in the area in question, but the Title of the Lords of Totonicapán narrows the possible locations by stating that the Great Hollow is the location of a *ch'uti cho* or "small lake" (Carmack and Mondloch 1983a:74–75). This points to Las Islas, a park located on the edge of the town of San Pedro Carchá. Here the Río Cahabón (the only local source of fish) forms a large pool where it traverses the bottom of a large, round-sided depression, just before entering a long and deepening canyon (see "to the mouth where the canyons change," below).

94

repeated their words, reciting the exact words: This is *ta xkitzaq* [xquizac] *k'ut* [cut] *kitzij xawi xere ucholik utzij.* DB gives *tzaqonisaj ri tzij* as "to fulfill words," and FV gives *tzaqantik* as "deliver up, render, regurgitate"; *xawi xere* is "yet the same," and *ucholik* is a nominalized form of *chol,* "to say in an ordered way" (FV).

94

"Don't the lords . . . speak truly?": That this line is part of the dialogue rather than the narrative is made obvious by the next line, which is clearly a reply.

94

"We're going, . . . even though we've just arrived": "Even though" translates *xaet,* which DB glosses as "in vain, uselessly." Antitheses are frequent in the speech of Hunahpu and Xbalanque.

94

"just play and just sing": The playing here (*tzuan-*) is specifically on the flute. In staying behind while One and Seven Hunahpu go down to Xibalba, One

Monkey and One Artisan reflect the fact that Mars would stay behind if it were near Venus when the latter dropped out of sight as the morning star.

94

to the mouth where the canyons change: This is *chuchi'* [chuchi] *jalja siwanub'*, in which the first word is "to-its-mouth"; the second is shortened from *jalaja*, "change, differentiate" (TC); and the third is the plural of *siwan*, "canyon." The place where the twins start their journey, Great Hollow with Fish in the Ashes (see p. 255), is located at the head of a deepening canyon through which the Río Cahabón flows eastward. The whole region is full of karstic depressions and caves, and about forty kilometers from Carchá the river disappears inside a cave called Semuc, emerging 350 meters later to continue on its way through what would be, were it not for the cave, a separate drainage. "The mouth where the canyons change" could be the mouth of this cave (see also following note).

94

Rustling Canyon, Gurgling Canyon: This passage reads *nu'* [nu] *siwan, k'ulk'u* [cul, cu] *siwan,* in which *siwan* is canyon; TC gives *nu'* as "shake" and FX specifies the trembling of leaves; *k'ulk'uch* (listed under *culcutc* in EH) is Kekchí for the "sound of intestines." This may be the place where the Río Cahabón disappears into a system of caves and then emerges again (see above).

95

Scorpion Rapids: This is *jaljal ja'* [ha] *sinaj* [simah]; DB has *jalja ja'* [ha], "waters that join and revolve." In reading [simah] as *sinaj*, "scorpion," I agree with Edmonson (1971:68). At the terrestrial level of interpretation this would be a place in or beyond Rustling Canyon, Gurgling Canyon (see above). At the astronomical level it would be on the road of the ecliptic, a short distance west of the place where it crosses the Great Rift in the Milky Way (see following note). That would put it in Scorpius, the location of the *sina'n ek'* or "scorpion stars" of the Yucatec zodiac (AB).

95

Crossroads: This is *kajib'* [caib] *xalkat b'e,* in which *xalkat* refers to any branching of roads but *kajib'* or "four" specifies a four-way intersection. The authors go on to list the four Mayan roads that link the very cosmos together. On the terrestrial plane, red and black correspond to east and west, while white and yellow correspond to north and south. At the celestial level, Black Road and Road of Xibalba, or *q'eqa* [queca] *b'e* and *ri b'e xib'alb'a,* are present-day Quiché terms for the Great Rift that splits a portion of the Milky Way lengthwise. White Road or *saqi* [saqui] *b'e* designates the rest of the Milky Way. From the identity of One and Seven Hunahpu (or their rubber ball) as Venus, and from the fact that they go down to Xibalba from a ball court located far in the east, it may be deduced that they descended at a time when Venus was ending its period of visibility as the morning star in a sidereal position near the Great Rift, having begun its crossing of the Milky Way in Scorpius and continuing into Sagittarius.

95

"Morning": This is *q'alaj* [calah], literally "clear, bright, plainly visible," used as a morning greeting in the PV. Today the preferred greeting for the morning is *saqirik,* "it is getting light (or dawning)."

96

they got no relief: This is *mawi xeyakamarik,* in which *mawi* is negative; DB gives *yakamarik* as "be relieved, alleviated."

96

the laughter rose up like a serpent in their very cores: Kumatz or "serpent" is a term for various kinds of disabling cramps (see B. Tedlock 1992:54, 56). Concerning the present case of *kumatz,* Andrés Xiloj said, "There are people who begin to make an uproar when one passes by, they die laughing. This is because those of Xibalba are among them; it is as if they had been ordered to do this. This is a work of Xibalba, and this is what the Popol Vuh is talking about. People get a serpent here in the breast [indicates a diagonal through his trunk, from one shoulder to the opposite hip] for having laughed so hard. Now one can't bear laughing because of the pain of the serpent; now it doesn't let one breathe. We could go out in the street right now. There could be a group of people there. They could begin to make an uproar, killing themselves laughing, and we couldn't hear what they were laughing about. But Xibalba would know what they were saying."

96

down to their blood and bones: This is *chi kikik'* [quiqui] *kib', chi kib'aq* [quiba] *kib',* literally, "that they-blooded themselves, that they-boned themselves." That is, they became nothing but blood and bones, having laughed their flesh away; in idiomatic English, "they laughed themselves sick."

96

This ball of theirs: The term for "ball" here is *cha'j,* spelled [chah] at this point but [chaah] later on in the same passage. This term often means "ball game" in the PV, but wherever it is used for the ball itself, as here, it refers to the ball of Xibalba, whereas the ball used by One and Seven Hunahpu (and later by Hunahpu and Xbalanque) is always called *kik'* [quic], literally "blood" but meaning "rubber (ball)" in the context of the game. I suspect that *cha'j* was a generic term and therefore translate it (wherever it refers to the ball) as just plain "ball," as contrasted with "rubber ball."

White Dagger: This is *saqi toq'* [zaqui toc], in which *toq'* is "knife" or "stab" (FV) or "flint" (PG).

their torch was brought: The torch is *chaj*, literally "pine"; in the present context it is the Quiché term for what is more widely known in Mesoamerica as ocote (a Nahuatl-derived term), a split-off stick of extremely resinous pine wood, still widely used for torches and kindling.

they were cowering: The verb here is *chokochoj*, a reduplicated (and therefore emphasized) form of *chokol-*, "to crouch" (DB).

Xibalba is packed with tests: In a later episode (pp. 119–26), the sons of One and Seven Hunahpu go through all five of the test houses listed here. Rattling House is called Cold House in that passage, and Razor House moves from the fifth to the second position in the sequence, which otherwise remains the same. The test houses may correspond to constellations entered by Venus when it disappears after a term as the morning star or else as the evening star. Either kind of disappearance falls at five different times of year and therefore corresponds to five different parts of the sky. An alternative interpretation is that all five houses belong to a single transfer of Venus from the morning to the evening role at one particular time of year. In the Dresden Codex this kind of transition is reckoned as lasting 90 days, a period sufficient to move Venus through five of the thirteen divisions of the Mayan zodiac as charted in the Paris Codex.

whistling with drafts, clattering with hail: This is *saq* [zac] *xuruxuj, saq k'arakoj* [caracoh], in which *saq* may be shortened from *saqb'ach*, "hail." The first verb is similar to *xururik*, "the penetration of cold" (into a house) or "a sharp whistling" (MX); the second is similar to *k'ararem*, "the sound of hail falling" (MX). My translation retains the drafts and the hail while at the same time preserving the onomatopoeia. In translating the name of this house, *xuxulim ja*, as "Rattling House," I have considered both the falling hail and a dictionary entry that glosses *xuxulim* as a continuous buzzing or humming (DB).

The blades are moving back and forth: "Back and forth" is *sakleloj*, which DB gives as "in alternation." In translating the name of this house, *ch'ayim* [chaim] *ja*, as "Razor House," I have considered that *ch'ay*, as a noun, refers to cutting instruments made of stone (PG), among them a "razor" that was probably an obsidian blade (FX). As a verb stem (here nominalized by *-im*) it refers to the act of beating or pressing on something (FV, FX), which in the present context would be the percussion and pressure techniques used in making stone tools.

97

Place of Ball Game Sacrifice: This is *pusb'al cha'j*; in the [pucbal] of the MS, [c] is an error for [ç]. *Pusb'al* is "place of sacrifice" (DB), while *cha'j* is "ball game" (DB, FX). The reference is probably to a feature of ball courts in general rather than to a specific geographical location. That this feature was near or even within the playing area itself is indicated by the fact that *jom,* once the Quiché term for a ball court, had become a term for "cemetery" by the early eighteenth century (FX) and remains so today. Hunahpu and Xbalanque, who later address the remains of Seven Hunahpu at the place where he was sacrificed and buried, tell him, "You will be prayed to here" (p. 141). Today, as Andrés Xiloj pointed out, people visit graveyards on days bearing the name *Junajpu.*

97

"Put his head in the fork of the tree that stands by the road": As Wendy Ashmore has pointed out to me, a cache of skulls was discovered on the west side of the temple known as Structure 38 at Tikal, not far from the ball court in the East Plaza (see W. Coe 1967:72). This temple stands beside the Méndez Causeway, just as the tree at the Place of Ball Game Sacrifice stands beside a road. Andrés Xiloj (like Ximénez long before him) offered "fork of the tree" as a reading for *xol che'* [che]. At the astronomical level of interpretation the head of One Hunahpu would be Venus as evening star, which is represented as a skull in Mayan iconography (Carlson 1983; D. Tedlock 1992b:234), and the form of the tree has two possible interpretations. On the one hand, it could represent the forked or crossed sticks Mesoamerican astronomers used for sighting heavenly bodies (see Aveni 1980:18–21); on the other hand, it could be part of a tree constellation lying somewhere along the zodiac. Once the calabash tree of the story bears fruit, the head of One Hunahpu cannot be told apart from the fruit, which suggests the presence of Venus (as evening star) among a number of closely grouped stars.

97

This is the calabash, as we call it today, or "the skull of One Hunahpu": The term for calabash (see the Glossary) is given as [zima] in the PV but otherwise occurs only as *tzima* in Quiché. It is *tzima* in contemporary Chol (AA) and *tzima'* in Tzotzil (RL), and in both of these languages it is extended to a bald-headed person—bald, we might say, like the skull of One Hunahpu in the calabash tree. In an earlier passage the authors proposed that we drink to One Hunahpu, implicitly offering us a cacao beverage in a calabash; here they tell us, in effect, that we have been drinking from his very skull. An allusion to the origin of the calabash occurs in the Quiché play known as the Rabinal Achi, when a war captive facing sacrifice comments on the vessel in which his host serves him his last drink:

> Is this what you drink from, sir?
> Perhaps it's the skull of my grandfather,
> perhaps it's the skull of my father.
> Is that what I'm looking at, what I see before me?
> Then won't this also become a work of some kind, an artifact,
> this bone of my crown, bone of my head,
> carved in back and carved in front?
> (Brasseur 1862:102, translation mine)

Explaining these lines to me, José León Coloch of Rabinal said, "He's comparing himself to a calabash." Since colonial times and probably before, Rabinal has been the principal Guatemalan site for the production of carved calabash vessels.

Classic Maya vases often bear an inscription that identifies them as cacao-drinking vessels (Houston et al. 1989:722). Most such vessels are cylindrical (unlike a calabash), but at least one carries the evidence of calabash use in its inscription, which reads *utsimal, hay yuch'ab k'ak tsih kakaw,* "his calabash, his thin-walled drinking vessel for hot fresh cocoa" (Reents-Budet 1994:256). In contrast with gourds, calabashes are watertight and have thin walls (*hay*); even on pottery vessels that carry no direct reference to a calabash there is frequent reference to thin walls. A number of vessels are actually shaped like a calabash, and Reents-Budet has pointed out to me that many potters, whether they used the calabash shape or not, went to great lengths to produce remarkably thin walls. Many vessels are painted with scenes from stories like those of the PV (M. Coe 1973, 1989), while others depict receptions of royal visitors that take place with containers of food and drink on display (Reents-Budet 1994: chap. 3). Among the Quiché today, the principal occasions for banqueting on a scale that brings members of different lineages together are *tz'onoj* or "asking" cere-monies, in which the family of a young man comes to the house of a young woman to negotiate a marriage, and the *k'ulanem* or "marriage" itself.

98

Blood Moon is the name of the maiden: In her name, *xkik',* the prefix *x-* makes her feminine, while *kik'* means "blood" and plays on *ik',* "moon."

98

' *"Its fruit is truly sweet!" they say':* The last two words translate *kacha'* [cacha], the only occurrence in the entire PV of the Quiché word that is used to mark general hearsay. A more literal translation would be "it says" or "it is said," but I have rendered it as "they say" because that is what a speaker of English would be likely to use when citing hearsay. As Andrés Xiloj pointed out, the hearsay in question here is misinformation, since the fruit referred to is not only not sweet, but is not even edible. For a general discussion of how the writers of the PV address the epistemological questions raised by their text, see D. Tedlock (1983b: chap. 12).

99

"Stretch out your right hand here": Andrés Xiloj explained that the right side of the body (whether that of a male or female) is symbolically male, while the left is female. Further, the hands unite the fingers, which symbolize the living members of a family, graded from babies (the little finger of each hand) on up to the elderly (thumbs). The fact that Blood Moon receives the sign from the skull in her right hand already points toward the bearing of a male child; in fact she will bear male twins.

99

"It is just a sign I have given you, my saliva, my spittle": Because of the mention of "sign" (*retal*) here, Andrés Xiloj remarked, "Then this is a dream." Asked what would be augured by being spit on in a dream, he said, "This is two matters. It depends on whether the saliva is good or bad. When it is good it has a lot of foam; when it is just clear water it is bad. But here in the Popol Vuh, one isn't told which kind of saliva it is."

99

"Keep the word": The stem of the verb here is *ok-*, "follow where someone else is going" (FV).

99

they were of one mind: This is *xawi kinaoj*, "same their-thoughts"; it is the narrators' way of explaining how they could attribute the actions of the head in the tree to both brothers, even though Seven Hunahpu's *physical* head was buried with his body. In this way the twins in Blood Moon's belly are given a dual fatherhood; in a later passage, Seven Hunahpu will be described not as *kikan*, "their uncle," but as *kiqajaw*, "their father" (p. 141).

99

"It's just a bastard": "Bastard" is *joxb'al*, literally "fornication-instrument," glossed as "bastard" by DB.

99

"Get her to open her mouth": This is *chakoto uchi'*, literally "Dig it out of her mouth," an idiom for close questioning. In terms of the somatic mapping of actual or potential speech, as conceived by Quichés, this implies that Blood Moon knows perfectly well what her father wants her to say; if her word were

"in her belly," on the other hand, it would mean that she could not readily articulate a response even if she wanted to. See also the notes to pp. 111, 115.

100

"there is no man whose face I've known": This statement is not only true in its figurative reference to Blood Moon's sexual innocence, but in its literal sense: she never knew the fleshly face of the skull in the tree. For the importance of a man's "face" (and personal identity) in sexual encounters, see pp. 168–69.

100

"take it in their hands": This is *kik'ololej* [quicololeh], a reduplicative form of *k'olej*, "take something round in the hand" (FV); DB gives *kolola* as "turn, revolve."

100

"So please stop": The verb here is *keke;* DB gives *kekeb'a* as "stop, detain."

100

" 'they will make themselves familiar with its composition' ": This is *xchikijunam wachij utz'akic* [utzaquic], "will-they-compare appearance its-being-made (or constructed)"; MX gives *junamanik* as "compare" and DB gives *junamaj wach* as "reconcile."

100

"nor will your homes be here": This means that future owls will be free to move around the surface of the earth.

101

"only blood": "Blood" is a literal translation of *kik'* [quic], which also refers to gums and resins from trees (including latex), in this case the blood-red resin of the cochineal croton (see croton in Glossary).

101

"use the fruit of a tree": This is a figurative reference to nodules of sap from the cochineal croton.

101

it formed a surface like blood: This is *keje k'u* [cu] *ri kik'* [quic] *rij xuxik,* "like then the blood its back (or upper or outer surface) became."

101

"nodules of blood": This is *kik'* [quic] *jolomax.* For a discussion of "blood" in this context, see the notes above. *Jolomax* would seem to be composed of a

verbal form of *jolom,* "head," with a passive suffix (-*x*); in the present context it would mean something like "headed-up," hence "nodules."

101

and when he lifted it up with his fingers: This is *ta xuchuyej k'u* [cu] *aq'anoq* [acanoc], "when he-lifted-with-fingers and upward"; DB gives *chuyej* as "to lift with the fingers."

101

they leaned over it intently: This is *xechiqe* [xechique] *chuwi,* in which *xe-* is "complete-they" and *chuwi* is "over (or on top of)"; FV gives *chiqe* as "to bend the head over" and FX has "to be pensive."

102

the mother of One Monkey and One Artisan: In fact the mother (in the literal sense) of One Monkey and One Artisan has already died by this time (see p. 93); either the present reference to her (which occurs twice) is an error for "grandmother," or "mother" is being used in its role-designating sense rather than in its genealogical sense. One Monkey and One Artisan are living alone with Xmucane, their father's mother, at this point; she is the only person they have who could fill the role of a mother.

102

"my lady": This approximates the effect of Blood Moon's combination of *lal,* marking polite address, with *chichu'* [chichu], "lady" (AG).

102

"I'm your daughter-in-law and I'm your child": The use of "child" here is metaphorical. A Quiché daughter-in-law takes up residence with her husband's family; in offering herself not only as a daughter-in-law but as a "child," Blood Moon both seeks the kind of acceptance a daughter would have and makes an offer of loyalty.

102

"my little babies": Xmucane uses the term *ch'ipa* [chipa] here, which is normally reserved for a youngest child. She seems to be using it endearingly, given that she is never mentioned as having had children other than One and Seven Hunahpu, and given that they were adults when they left home.

102

"They have merely made a way for the light to show itself": "A way . . . to show itself" is *uk'utb'al* [ucutbal] *rib',* literally "its-showing-instrument." The immediate reference, as the rest of the sentence makes clear, is to the symbolic survival of the dead through their offspring (see also p. 99), "light" being a

metaphor for birth. But "light" may also be taken literally here: Blood Moon's twin sons will account for Venus (in some of its cycles) and, in time, the sun and moon (or at least the full moon).

102

"Truly, what I say to you is so!": I take it that this sentence belongs to Blood Moon rather than Xmucane, given that it is followed with *utz b'ala,* "Very well," which signals the beginning of a reply and definitely belongs to Xmucane.

102

"ripe corn ears": Throughout this passage the corn in question is *jal,* hardened or ripened ears, as contrasted with *aj,* green corn or roasting ears.

102

"since you are already my daughter-in-law": The grandmother isn't so much accepting Blood Moon's claim to kinship here as she is saying (with sarcasm) something like, "If you *say* you're my daughter-in-law, then *act* like one." Quiché daughters-in-law, who live with the families of their husbands, are subject to the commands of their mothers-in-law, who give them heavy household tasks to do.

102

she went to the garden: "Garden" is *ab'ix,* often translated "milpa." Maize is the principal plant in the highland Mayan milpa, but it is interplanted with beans and squash. Each of these crops has different characteristics in its response to wet or dry conditions at various points in its growth cycle; interplanting assures that when one crop suffers during a given season, another will prosper.

103

but there was only one clump: In Mesoamerica corn is properly grown in thick clumps, not stalk by stalk in single file; clumps survive high winds better.

103

"Come on out, rise up now, come on out, stand up now": This is *ta tul waloq, ta tul tak'aloq* [tacaloc], in which *ta tul* is perfectly good Cakchiquel (but not possible in Quiché), while *waloq* and *tak'aloq* are perfectly good Quiché (but not possible in Cakchiquel). In *ta tul, ta* marks the phrase as a plea, *t-* marks the second-person singular familiar, and *-ul* is a verb stem meaning "to come out" (TC). In the verbs *waloq* and *tak'aloq, -oq* is imperative. The rest of Blood Moon's prayer is entirely in Quiché.

103

"Thunder Woman, Yellow Woman": This reads *xtoj, xq'anil* [xcanil], in which *x-* is "she of" and *Toj* and *Q'anil* are the names of two adjacent days on the 260-day

264

calendar, invoked in reverse order here. This is not a matter of a momentary lapse on the part of a scribe, since the order of cacao and cornmeal in the following line fits the order of the day names in the present line. *Toj* is a day of payment on the Quiché calendar, and cacao pods once served as currency; *Q'anil* is a day for the harvest of maize, and from that harvest comes cornmeal (B. Tedlock 1992:114–15). The explanation for the apparent reversal of the two days may lie in Blood Moon's lunar character, since by Lounsbury's reckoning (1978:796) the Dresden eclipse table begins on the day *13 Muluk* (*Toj* in Quiché) and then, at the end of an interval of 11,959 days, arrives at *12 Lamat* (*Q'anil* in Quiché). In effect, then, Blood Moon might be invoking, by means of metonymy, the calendrical patrons of all possible moons or groups of moons, from the beginning to the end of an eclipse table. Among the intervening dates specified in the Dresden table are *Muluk* and *Lamat* days with numbers other than 13 and 12, which helps explain why she invokes *Toj* and *Q'anil* in general rather than by specific numbers.

104

they were rowdy and flushed with jealousy: For these two qualities the MS has *kichakimal* and *kikaq* [qui3a3] *wachib'al,* in which *ki-* is "their." DB gives *chaki-mal* as "tumult, clatter, fuss, disturbance; clamor of boys." MX gives *kaq* [quiak] *wachinik,* which would literally be "red in appearance," as "zeal, jealousy."

104

the successors: This is *k'exel* [quexel], "substitute." It may be a reference to the fact that Mars, the planet of One Monkey and One Artisan, sometimes serves as morning star in the absence of Venus, which in at least one of its five cycles is the planet of One and Seven Hunahpu (see the notes on p. 207). When Venus and Mars appear in the east together Mars remains long after Venus has descended into the underworld, just as One Monkey and One Artisan remained on the face of the earth when One and Seven Hunahpu went down to Xibalba.

105

The anger in their hearts came down on their own heads: Andrés Xiloj remarked, "We see a person; we speak behind his back and he doesn't hear what we are murmuring. Then this murmur doesn't fall upon that person, but we are the ones who pay for it." A daykeeper, taking on the task of defending a person who has been the victim of witchcraft, asks in prayer that "the one who did this work should be the one to receive it."

105

They were decoyed: The verb here is *poisaxik;* if English "doll" were a verb, this could be translated literally as "to be dolled"—that is, to be misled by a doll. Today *poisaxik* is most commonly employed with reference to the use of scarecrows in fields.

"but our birds just got hung up in a tree": When birds are shot they sometimes close their feet around the branch where they were sitting and then hang there, dead.

"We'll just turn their very being around": The verb here is [catzolcomih], which Andrés Xiloj read as *katzolq'omij,* "to turn around."

"Just as they wished us to be slaves here": This is *keje ri ala xojpe wi uloq* [uloc] *chi kik'ux,* "like the slaves we-came location here in-their-hearts," in which I take *xojpe chi kik'ux* to be an idiom analogous to the one given in DB as *chi nuk'ux* [cux] *petinaq* [petinac], literally "in-my-heart come-from-perfect" but glossed as "of my own will." *Ala* ("slaves") is shortened here from *alab'il,* which is the form given in a later and similar passage (translated "slaves" on p. 108).

yellow tree: This is *k'ante'* [cante], given as *q'ante* in MA and *k'ante'* in EH, composed of *q'an* (Quiché and Kekchí) or *k'an* (Chol), both meaning "yellow," together with *te'* (Kekchí and Chol), "tree." It is the madre cacao (MA and EH) or *Gliricidia sepium,* a large tree planted to provide shade in cacao plantations. In Chol this same species is called *chante'* (AA), a name meaning "tall tree" or "sky tree."

"How can we grab hold?": The verb stem here is *chanik;* DB has *chanij,* "keep in the fist."

"simply shameless": This is *rax kiwach,* "fresh (or raw or green) their-faces"; DB glosses *rax wach* as "shameless."

"Will you please not laugh": Among the contemporary Jacaltec Maya there are myths in which the hero tricks his elder brother or his mother's brothers into going up a tree that grows taller and maroons them, after which they turn into monkeys. The hero's mother then tries to reverse this transformation but fails (Siegel 1943:122–24; La Farge 1947:53–56), in one case because she disobeys an admonition not to laugh (La Farge 1947:51–53).

One Monkey and One Artisan came back: This episode suggests a scene in which Mars (corresponding to the monkey twins) goes into retrograde motion, turning back toward Venus (corresponding to Hunahpu and Xbalanque) for a time but then resuming forward motion and drawing away again.

107

the patio of the house: See the notes to p. 92 for a discussion of the parts of a house.

107

the skinny little things below their bellies: This is *chi xiririk xe kipam;* Ximénez translated *xiririk* as "that which is thin," and Andrés Xiloj read it as "round little thing," chuckling as he did so. This refers not to the "bellies" of the monkeys (*kipam*) but to what is "below" or "at the bottom of" (*xe*) their bellies.

107

and their tails wiggling in front of their breasts: This is *chi chilita je pu chuchi kik'ux,* "that wag tails and at-edge-of their-breasts." Andrés Xiloj read *chuchi* as "up against" in this context. Spider monkeys and howler monkeys both have very long prehensile tails; howlers are seldom observed, but spider monkeys are given to winding their tails around to the front of their bodies and all the way up to their chins.

107

with thin red lips, with faces blank, puckering their lips, wiping their mouths and faces, suddenly scratching themselves: "Thin red lips" are *kaq* [ca3] *ruxruj uchi',* "red thin his-mouth (or lips)"; *ruxruj* seems to be a reduplicated form of *ruxa',* "thin" (MX). "Blank" translates *tak,* which FT glosses as "deaf," MX as "fool," and various other sources as "flat." "Puckering" translates *mutzumaq* [mutzumac], which Andrés Xiloj glossed as "to make small, like a trumpet." "Wiping" translates *mal,* which Xiloj glossed as "to clean"; DB (under [malo]) has *mala,* "to touch lightly." "Scratching" translates [hoquih], which Xiloj read as *joq'oj,* "to scratch." This passage reminded him of the contemporary Monkey Dance in Momostenango: "These monkeys, when they come out here in the fiesta, they scratch themselves, and do their mouths this way [touches himself all around the mouth], as if they had fleas and lice." Two monkeys with stars on their costumes cross the plaza from east to west on a high tightrope, interrupting their progress with midair acrobatics that could be (or might once have been) a dramatization of Martian retrograde motion.

109

their mattock, their hoe: These tools are *mixkina* and *xokem,* respectively; I have rendered the former word as "mattock" because DB glosses it as a "large" hoe.

267

109

leveling . . . the trees: "Leveling" translates [3a3chacachoh]; FV has *kaqchachoj,* "thrown down by the wind."

109

stalks and brambles: "Stalks" translates *tum;* FV has *tun,* "shoot (of a plant)." "Brambles" translates [quixic]; AG has *k'ix,* "spine (or thorn)."

109

dumps wood chips on his head: The verb here is [puquij]; MX has *puk'inik,* "dunk" or "throw." The "wood chips" are *uweb'alche',* glossed as such by DB.

110

they massage, they stretch their legs, their arms: Andrés Xiloj, who is a *wiqol b'aq* or "bonesetter" in addition to being a daykeeper, remarked here that he uses a combination of massage and stretching to treat sprains.

110

fox, coyote: Fox is *yak* in Quiché; the only fox in the region is the gray fox, *Urocyon cinereo-argenteus.* Ximénez translated *yak* as "gato de monte" or "mountain cat," which is what the fox is still called in Guatemalan Spanish (Janson 1981:48–49); some translators of the PV have been led astray by this.

110

"Arise, conjoin, you trees! / Arise, conjoin, you bushes!": This is *yak lin che'* [che] *yak lin k'a'm* [caam], in which *yak* is "for inciting someone" (FV) and is probably related to *yakalik,* "be up high" (MX); *lin* is "to squeeze, press together" and is used for tamping the weft in weaving (DB).

111

"My word is in my belly": Here and in a later passage (p. 115) the animal who makes this statement is assigned its characteristic food in exchange for a message. For the contemporary Quiché diviner, words that are "in the belly" of a person are words that person is unable to bring to consciousness and articulate; words that are higher up, in the chest or the head, are more likely to be spoken, and those that are in the throat or mouth or on the tongue are at the very point of actually being said. As for animals, their utterances are regarded as clear to other members of the same species but very difficult for a human to understand. The fact that the animals in the PV have their word in their bellies is not only an indication of their interest in being given food but an indication of the difficulties of understanding what animals have to say. They may be able to make sounds, but the meaning of these sounds is as hidden as are the crucial

facts a human client may find it difficult to articulate when a diviner asks probing questions. See also the notes to pp. 99, 115.

111

"up under the roof of the house": This is *chuwi ja,* "at-its-top house," which, as Andrés Xiloj explained, means the attic. He pointed out that this is the part of the house where tools are kept today, along with the stored harvest.

111

"But what will your grandmother say if she sees me?": Andrés Xiloj commented, "When the rat speaks it isn't understood what he says, *'witz', witz', witz'.'* When a boy is born, then the rat doesn't cry, they say. He is content, because the boy is the one who sows the garden. Now, if a woman is born, then the rat cries, they say, because when the rat comes near a woman in the kitchen she grabs a stick to kill him."

112

they were just fooling: "Fooling" is *mich'b'al* [michbal], literally "means of plucking," an idiom for deception. Note that in a later story the victims of deception are literally plucked (p. 171).

112

loosening the ball: The verb here is *kolon;* DB has *kolo,* "to free."

112

These were taken away: The verb stem here is *majix,* "be taken"; MX has *majanik,* "to take away from."

113

where it could be seen: This is *chuka'yik* [chucayac], in which *ka'y-* is "to look at, to notice" (PG, AG) and *-ik* is transitive passive. The louse has come down from the grandmother's hair.

113

Tamazul: This is from a Nahua source; in Nahuatl proper, *tamazulin* is "toad" (RS). The Quiché term for toad is *xpeq.*

113

"My word is contained": "Contained" is [4oba]; DB has *kob'a,* "to contain" or "keep to oneself."

113

"bent over": This is *pe;* AG has *pek'i'k,* "to warp."

when he had been united with the toad: The verb here is *xriktaxik,* a complete and passive form of the verb given by DB as *rikitajik,* "to join."

Zaquicaz: This name appears as *saqiq'as* in FV and PG; the former source glosses it as "a very thick snake that flees when it sees people, making a noise with its belly," while the latter says only that it is a black snake.

laughing falcon: This is *Herpetotheres cachinnans,* a snake-hunting bird called *wak* in Quiché and *vakos* in Tzotzil (RL), probably the same as the *wok* (translated simply as "falcon") in an earlier passage. The laughing falcon makes two different sounds: a long call consisting of a single, rapidly repeated syllable that resembles laughter, and a short song that makes use of two different phrases or syllables. Davis (1972:25) describes the repeated element of the song as *woo-oo ka-woo,* while Álvarez del Toro (1971:46) renders it as *guaco* (pronounced *wako*). The PV rendition, *wak ko,* is closer to the former version in using a two-part phrase, but closer to the latter in its vowel sequence. The song is heard in the early morning or in the evening, which supports the notion that the ball games of the PV correspond to times when Venus is close to the horizon. The Aztecs, who called this bird *oactli,* were like Hunahpu and Xbalanque in taking its sounds to be portentous. The call, which they heard as uncontrolled laughter, was a bad omen, but the song was good (Sahagún 1950–69, book 5:153–55). Hunahpu and Xbalanque, in a comical move, take the matter of the omen into their own hands, bringing the bird down and demanding that it restate its message in words. The song would seem to be a good omen for them, given that they are like twin tricksters elsewhere in the Americas in jumping at the opportunity for an adventure.

on the rim of the ball court: "Rim" is [zutzil] (in which *-il* is adjectival), translated on the basis of *tzutz,* "to finish weaving" (FX) or "to finish weaving by filling out the space at the edge" (FV). I take it that the falcon alighted at the top of the wall enclosing the ball court.

their blowgun shot: The "shot" of the blowgun is *ubaq* [ubac], literally "its bone" or "its pit" (in the sense of the pit of a fruit).

"My word is contained in my belly": See the notes to p. 111 for a discussion of the meaning of words in bellies. What is notable in the present context, where

the hawk contains the snake that contains the toad that contains the louse who has the message, is a symbolic acting out of the structure of the speech of messengers. Again and again the messengers of the PV deliver their news in the form of multiply embedded quotes; in the present episode each animal corresponds, as it were, to a pair of quotation marks, one pair inside the next.

115

"Blood of sacrifice": This is *lotz kik'* [quic], in which *lotz* is "to puncture, let blood" (FV and FX), and *kik'* covers both "blood" and "resin"; PG specifies *las kik'* as "rubber." The black eye patches of the laughing falcon remain as signs of the incident in which Hunahpu and Xbalanque doctored him with a bit of rubber from their ball.

115

he just sort of drooled: The verb stem here is [caxh]; DB has *kaxajinik,* "to drool."

115

they kicked him: The verb stem here is *yik;* DB has *yikb'al,* "kick with the foot." I have spared the reader the redundancy of the original phrasing, which goes on to specify that the kicking was indeed done with the foot.

115

they crushed the bones: The verb stem here is [cah]; MX has *k'ajinik,* "to crush, crumble."

115

it was right there in his mouth: In terms of the somatic mapping of speech, as conceived by Quichés, this implies that the toad knew perfectly well what the message was; it was not in his belly, a realm of the unconscious or the dimly perceived, but right up front in his mouth (see the notes to pp. 99, 111).

116

"Each of us will plant an ear of green corn": These are not kernels (*ixim*) but ears of corn that are planted (*tik*), and they are roasting (or green) ears (*aj*) rather than ripened ones (*jal*). As will be made clear on p. 40, they are "planted" not in the earth but above it, in the attic of the house, where harvested corn is stored. See p. 285 for a discussion of contemporary rites of the patrilineage shrine called *winel* that answer to this description.

116

"When the corn dries up": "Corn" has been supplied here; the original sentence does not specify what is drying (*chaqijik*). It might be the ears of corn Hunahpu and Xbalanque left in the center of their house, but Andrés Xiloj took it to be

the ripening of a corn crop in their field, which would coincide with the arrival of the dry season.

116

" 'when the sprouting comes' ": This is *ta chipe utux,* "when there-comes its-shoot." It would not be the sprouting of the ears of corn left in the center of the house by Hunahpu and Xbalanque, but of a new crop in the field (see the above note).

116

Hunahpu planted one and Xbalanque planted another: This makes it sound as though there were two ears of corn, but today it would be four: one yellow, one white, one spotted, and one blue. Note that the ears planted by Hunahpu and Xbalanque, however many of them there may have been, are later given four different names (pp. 139–40).

116

where the earth is damp: This is *rax ulew,* literally "green (or raw) earth," in contrast with the *chakij* [chaquih] *ulew* or "dry earth" mentioned in this same sentence; my translation follows the reading offered by Andrés Xiloj.

116

in the middle of the inside of their house: This is *chunik'ajal* [chunicahal] *upa kochoch,* "at-its-middle its-inside their-house." Andrés Xiloj was quite definite that this could only mean indoors, not on the patio.

116

throng birds: These are *tz'ikin molay,* in which *molay* may be from *mol-,* referring to the joining together of what was dispersed (FV); PG gives *mo* as a "large black hawk." These birds have been identified as an autumn migrating flock of Swainson's hawks (*Buteo swainsonii*) by B. Tedlock (1985:80–83). Their plumage is in its dark phase when they funnel through Guatemala in October or early November, and they form spectacular masses before spreading out into South America. At that time, ears of green corn (*aj*) like those picked by Hunahpu and Xbalanque are available in the area where the PV was written, but ripe corn (*jal*) is not. The spring migration of these birds announces the approach of the season's first thunderstorms.

116

the roads of Xibalba: This passage makes it sound as though all four roads eventually lead to or through Xibalba, but in an earlier episode "the" Road of Xibalba, and specifically of its lords, is the Black Road (see the notes to p. 95). In the list of roads given there the colors are paired by opposite directions: red/ black (east/west) and white/yellow (north/south). The present passage drops yellow, adds green, and pairs the colors by their own complementarity: black/

white, red/green. One and Seven Hunahpu took the Black Road, whereas Hunahpu and Xbalanque send a spy in that direction and later travel a road whose color is not specified. Perhaps it is the Green Road, which was not available to their fathers. In the five-part Mesoamerican directional scheme this would be the middle road, the axis mundi. In the PV, the Green Road is the only one a living human being wants to travel (see the prayer on pp. 192–93).

118

each one named by the one ranking above him, and naming in turn the name of the one seated next to him: This is *jujun chijoloman ub'ixik kumal are chib'i'n ub'i jun ri kub'ul chuxukut*, "each-one from-ahead being-named by-them this-one naming his-name one that seated at-his-side." I interpret *chijoloman* as referring to differences in rank, with *chi-* as prepositional and *jolom* as "head" in the sense of leadership (a sense given by FV under the entry for *wi*). In the dialogue that follows each lord is indeed named by the one ranking immediately above him and in turn names the next one down the line; the only exception is One Death, who has no one above him and must therefore be named by Seven Death.

118

"These aren't lords! These are manikins, woodcarvings!": Strictly speaking, this remark refers to the two manikins seated first in the sequence, but it may also be taken as slyly referring to the entire group of lords. They are waiting for a good laugh, like the one they had earlier at the expense of One Hunahpu and Seven Hunahpu (p. 95), but instead the joke is on them.

120

"here's our rubber ball," said the Xibalbans: This is one of the few points at which *kik'*, "rubber ball," is used with reference to the ball belonging to Xibalba, which is otherwise called *cha'j*, a generic term for "ball" (see the notes to p. 96), or else by its proper name, White Dagger (see the Glossary). Given the general air of duplicity in the present passage, we may assume that the Xibalbans are falsely using the term *kik'*.

120

"just a decorated one": This is *xa juch'il* [huchil], in which I take *juch'il* to be an adjectival form of *juch'unik*, "to stripe, put on a design" (MX). The ball of Xibalba is fundamentally different from the rubber ball used by Hunahpu and Xbalanque, but the Xibalbans are claiming that it is merely decorated.

120

"just a skull": The ball of Xibalba is surfaced with crushed bone, as has already been seen. In one of the relief panels in the great ball court at Chichén Itzá, the ball bears the image of a skull (illustrated on pp. 120–21).

120

"we say in return": This is *kojch'a chik,* literally "we-say again." Others have treated *koj* as a separate word here, in which case it would mean "puma," but that leaves *ch'a chik* hanging.

121

"Death is the only thing you want for us! Wasn't it you who sent a summons to us?": This is an ironic reference to the names of One and Seven Death. To put it in other words, "Given that you are named *kame* (Death), no wonder you want our *kamik* (death)!" Hunahpu and Xbalanque play on the name *kame* again in a later episode (p. 137). See the note headed "One Death and Seven Death" for a discussion of their name (p. 251).

121

"One bowl of red petals": "One bowl of" translates *jutikab',* in which *ju-* is one; I take *-tikab'* to be a numeral classifier for counting by the bowlful, similar to *-tuk* in *jutuk,* "one jarful" (FT). The bowls in question here (*sel*) are mentioned just before this. "Petals" translates a word given as *muchij* the first time and *muchit* thereafter, which Andrés Xiloj read as *muchik,* referring to the "undoing" of flowers to get their petals off, rather than as *much',* which is an herb (known as "chipilín" in Spanish) whose leaves are used as a seasoning in beans. Today flower petals are sprinkled on tombs and are used to adorn shrines before offerings are burned.

123

"cutting ants, conquering ants": These are *chay sanik, ch'eken* [chequen] *sanik,* possibly two names for the same species. *Chay* refers to cutting instruments made of stone; FV lists *je chay* as ants that go in swarms. Andrés Xiloj identified *ch'eken sanik* as leaf-cutting ants seen only in the lowlands, called "zompopo" in Guatemalan Spanish.

123

"Whip-poor-will!" and *"Poor-willow!"*: These bird calls are *xpurpuwek* and *pujuyu,* respectively. Andrés Xiloj recognized *xpurpuwek* as the call of the *perpuwaq,* which he described as a ground-dwelling bird that calls out at night. This is obviously a whippoorwill; phonetically the Quiché rendition of its call is not that different from the English version, except for the final consonant. I interpret *pujuyu* as a similar but somewhat simpler call, belonging to a related species, and translate it as "poorwill" when it is used (on this same page) as a species name rather than as a call.

123

the nibbling at their own tails, . . . their own wings: This may be a reference to the fact that the tails and wings of whippoorwills and poorwills are marked with bands, bars, and spots that give them a mottled appearance.

123

an acrobatic performance: This is *tikitoj;* DB has *tikita,* "dance audaciously in front of others."

124

all the Xibalbans looked sick, they paled: The key forms here are *saqkaje* [zaccahe], "be discolored in sickness" (FV), and *saqb'u* [zacbu], "pallid" (DB).

124

their mouths were split wide: Whippoorwills and poorwills are nightjars (*Caprimulgidae*), all of which have small bills but mouths that gape very wide.

124

countless drafts, thick-falling hail: For more about the drafts (*tew*), see the notes to p. 97. The hail is *saqb'oqom* [zacbocom], based on glosses offered by DB and Andrés Xiloj.

125

a house of fire: This is *jun ja chi q'aq',* a descriptive phrase not constructed in the same way as the proper names given the other houses—*b'alami ja,* "Jaguar House," for example. It is omitted from the earlier list of five test houses (p. 97) and is the most briefly described of the houses in the present sequence; it may be a secondary elaboration, based on the immolation undergone by Hunahpu and Xbalanque in a later episode (p. 132). That would leave five proper test houses in both passages. On the astronomical importance of the number five, see p. 207.

125

snatch-bats: These are *kamasotz'* [camazotz], in which *sotz'* is "bat" and *kama*- is probably from *kajmaj,* "fright, surprise attack" (FV). Andrés Xiloj commented, "These are not animal bats, but the bats of Xibalba." DB lists *kamotzoj* as "an animal that eats the moon." Today, in the town of Rabinal, the dance-drama of San Jorge includes a character named *kaman xoch,* costumed as a bat (Teletor 1955:165–66).

125

"Can you see how long it is till dawn?": "How long" translates *janik,* "How much?" (DB).

"What's going on?": This is my reading of *juchalik,* based on *jucha,* "How?" or "What's this?" (DB).

Xbalanque despaired: The verb stem here is [quixbih], translated on the basis of *k'ixb'ej,* "to have shame" (FV) and considerations of context.

"Alas!": This is [acaroc], probably *aqaroq,* which Ximénez translates as "Ay! Ay!" Elsewhere *aqaroq* begins a song of lament (p. 162), where I again translate it as "Alas!" But when it begins prayers (pp. 150, 192) I render it as "Wait!" on the basis of *aqar,* "wait" (FV) and the apparent imperative suffix (*-oq*). A person at prayer is said to "cry" (*oq'ik*) and "call out" (*sik'ij*); to translate *aqaroq* as "Alas!" emphasizes the emotional tone, while "Wait!" emphasizes the attempt to get attention.

He brought a squash: What the coati brings is written as [coc], which must be *q'oq',* "squash," rather than *ko'k,* "turtle." As Edmonson has pointed out (1971:124), turtles do not have seeds (see p. 129), and I would add that a turtle would not burst open when hitting the floor of a ball court. The notion of a squash as a head shows up in the contemporary traditions of Chichicastenango, where an excess of large squashes in a field means that the senior male of a family may die, the squashes being a sign that his head is rotting (Bunzel 1959:54). The vine shown growing out of the head of a ballplayer in one of the ball-court relief panels at Chichén Itzá (see pp. 120–21) may well be a squash vine.

then brains came from the thinker, from the sky: "Brains" translates *tzatz,* glossed as such in FX. According to the riddling "language of Zuyua" in the Book of Chilam Balam of Chumayel, the "brains" of the sky consist of copal (Roys 1967:90, 96). That raises the possibility that "thinker," which is *ajno'j* [ahnaoh] in the present passage, puns on *noj,* "a certain gum" (FX). For a discussion of punning in the language of Zuyua, see Stross (1983).

His strength was just the same: "Strength" is [chuuc], which is the gloss FV gives *chuq'a* and TC and AG give *chuq'ab'.*

old man: This is *mama,* "old man (or grandfather)," which identifies this possum as one of the bearers of new years (see the Introduction). They announce the coming of a new solar year, just as the black streaks (see the next note) announce the coming of a new day.

128

"Possum is making streaks": This is *kaxaqin wuch'* [caxaquin uuch], "he-is-making-black-streaks possum." TC and FV have entries for *xaqin wuch',* "a darkness before dawn," which confirms that [uuch] should be *wuch',* "possum." Ximénez translated "vulture," as if the text had read [4uch]. Andrés Xiloj read the verb stem as *xaqin,* "make black stripes"; FV has "stripe with carbon" as a gloss for *xaqij.* Xiloj commented, "At 4:30 in the morning it is as if black clouds were placed there at the end of the sky [the horizon], they are like a sea, they are in grades or levels, alternating yellow and black. Then, according to the hour, as it clears up, the black becomes blacker, blacker, blacker, and what was yellow becomes redder, as the sun comes nearer. Then it changes, these black clouds are no longer there, now there is only the light of the sun. These black clouds appear to be over the earth, they go far [to the left and right], all the way to wherever. The stripes signal that the sun is already shining; they are a reflection. When one gets up at 4:00 or 4:30 in the morning, *kaq chuwi xekaj,* 'it is red over the end of the sky.' At first only one black band is there, then it divides up. One can see all this in the dry season, but not at this time of year" (as he said this his voice was almost drowned out by the sound of rain).

128

"You should just make lots of threats": The verb stem here is *yekuj,* "be in a threatening attitude" (under the entry for [yecoh] in DB).

128

"ball bags": The term here is *pixk,* changing to *pix* when it is mentioned twice again in this same passage. What is required by the plot is objects of about the same size and shape as a huddled rabbit, a ball, and a squash, so that the rabbit can wait among these objects without being noticed, the ball can land among them and appear to belong there while the running rabbit appears to be the still-bouncing ball, and, finally, so that a squash can be switched for the ball. The problem is that in Quichean languages, *pixk* is normally "acorns" and *pix* is "tomatoes" (FV, FX), both of which are too small to serve the purpose. The solution adopted here is based on the fact that *pix* has to do with wrappings or coverings (and bundles) in Kekchí (EH) and Chol (JH, AA), suggesting that the objects might be bags or wrappers used to carry balls.

129

having recovered the ball from among the bags: I picture Hunahpu and Xbalanque standing among the ball bags, pretending they have found the ball when in fact they have traded it for a squash.

129

The squash was wearing out: The verb stem here is *puq'ab'in* [pucabin]; FV has *puq'*, "wear down."

129

bringing to light its light-colored seeds, as plain as day: This is *saqiram k'u ri usaqilal* [zaquiram cu ri uzaquilal], literally "becoming-light (or white) then the its-lightness-own." *Saqir-* is also "to dawn," and *saqil* is the term for squash seeds; in the translation I have added the word "seeds" and the phrase "as plain as day" in order to make these dimensions more obvious to the reader. Further, *saqir-* is a metaphor for the sprouting of plants, but the phrase "bringing to light its light-colored seeds" turns that metaphor inside out. When the squash bursts and causes a "dawning" of seeds, it is a "dawning" that comes from the harvested fruit of a plant rather than from the planted seeds. To put it another way, the seeds burst forth rather than being sown.

This passage probably has an astronomical dimension as well. Keeping in mind that Hunahpu and Xbalanque, in their Venus or ballplayer aspect, cannot stray from the zodiac, we may speculate that the splattered squash seeds correspond to a constellation, and that this constellation is closer to being "in bounds" with respect to the zodiac than the ball bags discussed in the notes for p. 128. The Pleiades are within the zodiac, though they would seem to be accounted for by the Four Hundred Boys. But the seeds of the burst squash could be somewhere near the Pleiades (perhaps they are the Hyades), since the Four Hundred Boys may be rabbits (see under their name in the Glossary) and since it is a rabbit who leads the Xibalbans away from the ball court.

130

Xulu and *Pacam:* FV describes *xulu* as "(spirit) familiars appearing alongside rivers"; an *ajxulu,* or "keeper of Xulu," is a curer (FV) or diviner (DB). Given that the advice Xulu and Pacam give to the lords of Xibalba results in the reincarnation of Hunahpu and Xbalanque as catfish, there would seem to be a link between *xulu* and the Chol term for "big-bellied catfish," which is *xlu'* or *ajlu'* (AA). As "midmost seers," Xulu and Pacam would presumably be of the particular kind known as *nik' wachinel pa ya'* or "midmost seers into water," whom TC describes as diviners who gaze into water. That the reincarnation of the twins is the result of sinking their bones in water suggests that the name Pacam (which could be *pak'am*) might have its source in something like Chol *pak'*, "to sow" (JH). Many fishing cultures—on the northwest coast of North America, for example—have rituals in which fish are reincarnated by casting their bones into water. In the present case the idea for such an act originates with Hunahpu and Xbalanque, the same gods who establish a ritual for the death and revival of corn. This brings to mind the raised-field complex among the lowland Classic Maya, who harvested fish from the same ditches that drained their cornfields (see Hammond 1982:160–63) and might well have developed a ritual for "replanting" the fish.

130

" 'if we dumped their bones in the canyon' ": T. J. Knab informs me that in the lore of contemporary Nahuatl speakers in the Sierra de Puebla, this is precisely the procedure that would be used to put a permanent and complete end to a person. On the other hand, grinding the bones and putting them directly into water (which is what is finally done with Hunahpu and Xbalanque) would ensure continued life in some form.

130

" 'since you would see their faces' ": This is an allusion to what happened when the head of One Hunahpu was put in a tree.

130

" 'sprinkle them' ": The verb stem here is *ikaj,* "sprinkle" (DB).

130

little Hunahpu: Here and elsewhere, the addition of "little" in front of Hunahpu reflects instances where his name is written [xhunahpu], with the diminutive prefix *x-,* making it like the name of his brother [xbalanque]. The prefix has not been translated in the latter case because it is an inseparable part of the name itself, whereas it seldom appears when Hunahpu is named. The name of the Yucatec equivalent of Hunahpu, Hun Ahaw, is sometimes written [ix hun ahau] (Roys 1965:9).

131

"You'll never put that one over on us": The verb stem here is *mich'* [mich], "pluck," but in the present context a literal translation would not make sense in English (see the notes to p. 171 for a case in which deception involves *literal* plucking of the victim).

131

They grabbed each other by the hands and went head first into the oven: Hunahpu and Xbalanque do not ascend as the sun and moon until p. 141, but their self-immolation here opens the way to that event. In Aztec myth the sun and moon are again a pair of males, Nanahuatzin and Tecuciztecatl, but not brothers. They do not jump into the flames together; instead, the former jumps in because the latter is afraid to, and then the latter follows out of shame. At first they are both like suns, but then Tecuciztecatl is dimmed and becomes the moon (Sahagún 1950–69, book 7:2–7).

131

raising their shouts, raising their cheers: Andrés Xiloj remarked, "It's like they held a fiesta, complete with a marimba."

132

The two of them looked like catfish: The term used here is *winaq* [uinac] *kar*, literally "person fish," identified by PG and TC as "catfish." It should be noted that among speakers of Pokomchí (a Quichean language), *xb'alamq'e* [xba-lamque] was the term for a species of fish belonging to the family that includes perch and bass (DZ), whose members lack the barbels that characterize catfish and (unlike catfish) have spiny fins. Perhaps there was once a version of the story in which only Hunahpu became a catfish, while Xbalanque became a bass. The location for this episode may be Great Hollow with Fish in the Ashes (*nim xob' karchaj*), in or near the present-day Kekchí town of San Pedro Carchá and named elsewhere in the PV as the location of the court where One and Seven Hunahpu and their sons played ball. According to the people who live there today, Carchá (*karcha*) derives its name from an incident that occurred during a heavy rain, when wriggling fish (*kar*) appeared in wet ashes (*cha*); I learned this from Marcello Cho of San Pedro Columbia (a Kekchí village in Belize), who heard it on a visit to Carchá. These fish would seem equivalent to the catfish of the PV, which appear when the burned (and ground) remains of Hunahpu and Xbalanque get wet. Taking our cue from the fact that other PV episodes involve the establishment of customs by Hunahpu and Xbalanque, we may guess that this one established a fishing ritual.

132

vagabonds: This translates *meb'a*, glossed by DB and MX as "poor person" and by FX as "orphan"; I have chosen "vagabonds" because Hunahpu and Xba-lanque later disclaim any attachment to a particular place (p. 133). At this point in their career they probably correspond to the possum actors of the lowland Maya, strolling players who appeared at the transition point between two solar years (Thompson 1970:277).

132

They seemed unrefined: This is *mana chib'ananta kiwach*, literally "not-yet be-come-done their-faces"; *b'an wach* is an idiom meaning "polished, adorned," as indicated by the entries under [bano] in DB.

132

Swallowing Swords: This dance is *xtz'ul* [xtzul], which is also the term for the centipede; the corrected form appears in FV and TC. *Tz'ul* may be from *tz'ulej*, "be together in an embrace and with the legs intertwined" (FV). DB describes the dance as one in which masked performers with tortoiseshell rattles put sticks or daggers in their mouths. FV describes the masks as small and says that the dancers are two in number (as they are in the PV), wear the tails of macaws down their backs, put sticks down their throats and bones into their noses, and give themselves hard blows on their chests with a large stone. The swallowing of sticks cut to a shape like that of swords is also known among the Pueblo peoples of the Southwest United States.

132

Now Xibalba was full of admiration: The "admiration" is [cayic]; DB has *kaiq'*, "watch admiringly."

132

Next they would sacrifice themselves, one of them dying for the other: This implies that either of the twins could assume either role when they did their sacrifice act. When the narrators describe an example of this act they happen to have Xbalanque sacrificing Hunahpu (p. 136), but the Classic Maya painter of the so-called Metropolitan Vase shows the equivalent characters the other way around, with Hun Ahaw about to chop off the head of Yax Balam (see p. 136). Hun Ahaw appears in the guise of Chac (God B or GI), wielding an axe; the catfish barbel coming out of his cheek, itself a Chac attribute (Taube 1992:24–27), recalls the PV scene in which Hunahpu and Xbalanque make an appearance in the guise of catfish just before taking up their formal acting careers. Yax Balam, who usually looks human except for patches of jaguar skin on his face and body, appears on the vase as a caricature of himself, all jaguar except for his head. As different as the two brothers may appear in other respects, both wear their hair pulled forward and tied, as they do in some other depictions (see p. 77). This hairdo is compatible with Hun Ahaw's Chac role, but the point here is that both brothers wear it; further, Yax Balam cooperates with his brother by offering himself for decapitation rather than having to be held down. If this interpretation is correct, then Lounsbury (1985) is correct in identifying the figure wielding the axe as Hun Ahaw but wrong to think Hun Ahaw and GI are the same god, while M. Coe (1989:165–66) is correct in distinguishing Hun Ahaw from GI or Chac but wrong to think the axe-wielder on the vase is Chac in person. Neither of them took the play-acting aspect of the scene into consideration.

133

had to keep coming back: The verb stem here is [machcay]; DB has *machkaiq'*, "to come and go repeatedly."

133

Feigning great humility: This is *kemochochik;* DB gives *mochochik* as "to humble oneself hypocritically."

133

they bowed their heads all the way to the ground: This is *chikixulela kiwach*, in which the second word is "their faces"; DB gives *xulela* as "throwing the face on the ground."

133

down to the rags, to the tatters: The "rags" are *mayokij*, translated on the basis of *makij*, "to throw away"; the "tatters" are *atz'iak* [atziac], which carries this meaning in both ancient and modern Quiché.

133

their mountain: This is *kijuyub'al*, "their-mountain-place." *Juyub'al* is a metonym for almost any settlement, but especially a fortified town or "citadel" (*tinamit*), located on a defensible elevation.

136

And they showed its roundness: This is *xkik'olob'a k'ut* [xquicoloba cut] *chikiwach*, "they-positioned-round-thing then to-their-faces."

136

his legs, his arms were spread wide: The verb here is *xperepoxik*, apparently a complete (*x-*), passive (*-xik*), and reduplicated form of *pere-*, "to put a wide thing somewhere" (FV); DB glosses *perepik* as "wide." The limbs of Mesoamerican sacrifice victims were indeed spread wide.

136

was smothered in a leaf: This is *xch'eqe* [xcheque] *chuwach tz'alik* [tzalic], "stanched in-face-of leaf-wrapping." MX gives *ch'eqelik* as "stop the flow of" and *tz'alik* as "leaves for wrapping." This line has caused much confusion, but Andrés Xiloj found it crystal clear. He commented that *tz'alik* refers to any leaves used to wrap tamales, of which there are several different kinds.

137

"Do it to us! Sacrifice us!": Here Andrés Xiloj remarked, "It didn't please them that they were perfectly well; what pleased them was to be butchered."

137

"What is death to you?": The original question puns on the name of its address-ees and is phrased negatively: *ma pa ix k'o kam*, "Aren't you *kam*?" Lacking any suffixes, *kam* is open to various interpretations: *kaminaq*, "dead person"; *kamikal*, the ordinary term for "death"; or *Kame*, the proper name of a day on the calendar and of the two highest lords of Xibalba, One and Seven Death. In recasting the question in English, I have sought to preserve both the biting tone

of the question and the play on words between Death as a name and death as an event. Hunahpu and Xbalanque also played on the name in an earlier passage (see the notes to p. 121).

137

vassals: Here and elsewhere, this translates *alk'ajol,* a composite term made up of *al,* "child (of a woman)," and *k'ajol,* "son (of a man)." The reference is to members of commoner lineages owing fealty to a lordly lineage. Vassalage was thus conceived as kinship by adoption, but note that *alk'ajol* clouds or averts the issue of lineality by including the term for a woman's children.

138

heart sacrifice: The stem here is *xaraxo-;* DB gives *xaraxoj* as "cut or open the chest and take out the heart."

138

countless ants: This may or may not be metaphorical; if not, it could be that the fate of the vassals of the lords of Xibalba was to become the ants of today. In any case it is very unusual for vassals to come downward to get to where their lords are; it would seem that the domain of Xibalba is the reverse of earthly domains, where lords are situated in citadels rather than at the bottoms of canyons.

138

no cleanly blotted blood for you: This is *ch'ajom k'ik* [chahom quic], literally "washed blood." I take this to be a reference to autosacrifice, in which the blood that flowed from self-inflicted pricks and wounds was blotted up with paper or leaves. During colonial times this practice was modified rather than suppressed, owing to the role of bloodletting in European medicine, but it is no longer done today. Andrés Xiloj pointed out that it is still said of the Xibalbans that they collect blood spilled on the ground—that is, dirty blood.

138

just griddles, just gourds, just brittle things broken to pieces: The "griddles" are *xot,* for toasting tortillas. The "gourds" are [acam]; FV has *aqem,* "gourd." The "brittle things" are *chuch;* DB has *chuchuj,* "delicate, thin." Finally, "broken to pieces" is *xjeraxik;* FV has *jera-,* "crumble." This list suggests the contemporary ritual of the days 7 *Tz'i'* and 8 *B'atz'* (7 Dog and 8 Monkey) at Momostenango, in which novice daykeepers are initiated. On the eve of 8 Monkey, the novice is visited at home by his or her teacher, who breaks a large and previously unused jar and burns copal incense in the shards; the ashes of the copal are put in a small gourd. The next day the shards and the gourd are taken to a shrine called Ch'uti Sab'al or "Little Place of Declaration" and deposited there (see B. Tedlock 1992:65–66 for more details). But this ritual is dedicated primarily to the Mundo (earth deity) and the ancestors; there is no mention of Xibalba in its liturgy. Perhaps members of the Quiché elite of pre-Columbian times were given to defaming the indigenous highland Guatemalan religion as Xibalban, in the same way that Christian missionaries have since defamed it as Satanic.

138

born in the light, begotten in the light: Andrés Xiloj pointed out that only human beings can be referred to in this way; note the contrast with "creatures of the meadows and clearings" in the previous sentence. The point is that the lords of Xibalba will henceforth be denied proper human sacrifices.

139

the blame is clear: The idiom here is *chak umak,* "his sin is clear" (DB).

139

And you will hear petitions over headed-up sap: This is *kixtaon puch chuwi ri kik'* [quic] *jolomax,* "you-listen and over the blood (sap) headed-up." Earlier I translated *kik' jolomax* as "nodules of sap." What this sentence means is that henceforth, when people pray to Xibalbans, they will burn nodules of croton tree sap (see croton in the Glossary) as offerings.

139

they are inciters to wrongs and violence: Andrés Xiloj commented, "They are the ones who send one to do evil. It is as if, in spirit, they enter us, into the head. I think, 'I'm going to do such-and-such a thing,' but I don't know who put this bad idea into me."

139

masters of perplexity: This is *ajlatzab',* consisting of *aj-,* "person or owner of"; *latz,* "embarrassed, perplexed" (DB); and *-ab',* plural.

139

crying and calling out: What the grandmother of Hunahpu and Xbalanque does is *koq'ik kasik'in* [coquic caziquin], translated literally here, but in both ancient and modern Quiché the combination of the verb stems *oq'-* ("cry") and *sik'-* ("call out"), used in that order, refers to the act of praying. This is generally done in a mildly insistent tone rather than a sorrowful one, but the petitioner is nevertheless thought of as seeking pity; the amplitude of the voice is generally low to moderate, but those who are addressed by a prayer are thought of as being summoned from a distance.

139

the ears of green corn they left planted: These are the corn ears Hunahpu and Xbalanque dedicated when they left for Xibalba (p. 116). "They left planted" is *xkitik kanoq* [canoc], "they-plant left," an idiom referring to the establishment of a ritual obligation. Andrés Xiloj recognized one of the obligations of the contemporary mother-father (patrilineage head) in this passage: "What was 'left planted' was a custom. . . . Because of the corn, they would never be forgotten. Now, this is the custom of the *winel* [a pair of shrines located near a cornfield, one above it and the other below]. When the corn is ripe one has to give thanks, to burn copal in the *winel*. One gives thanks so that the seeds will have to sprout again; one carries the corn there to have it at the burning place, and when one is finished praying one passes the ears through the smoke of the copal, saying *are k'u wa ruk'ux* [this here is that which is its heart]. This is what their grand-mother must have done in the Popol Vuh. And after the ears are passed through the smoke they are placed in the center of the house, in the middle of our crop. They are not eaten until another crop is ripe." Although these dedicated ears are not used as seed corn, they are thought of as alive, and it is because "the heart of the corn has not died" that the seed corn is able to sprout and that even the stored corn is able to continue multiplying.

It would seem that Hunahpu and Xbalanque, in addition to their aspects as Venus, year-bearing vagabond actors, and (eventually) the sun and moon, are also maize deities. The rites of the *winel* are performed on two successive days bearing the names *Kej* and *Q'anil* (Deer and Yellowness), with the latter being the principal day (B. Tedlock 1992:77, 80). There are fixed rites each 260 days on 7 Deer and 8 Yellowness; planting rites are carried out on the Deer and Yellowness days nearest the actual planting time, and harvest rites are carried out on the days nearest the actual harvest. The day corresponding to Yellowness (named *Lamat* in Yucatec) also figures prominently in the Venus table of the Dresden Codex, where it is the first day of the morning star that begins the third of five full Venus cycles and the first day of disappearance for both morning and evening stars during the fourth Venus cycle. It may be that at least portions of these Venus cycles symbolize the life cycle of the maize plant; indeed, the lowland Maya maize god is actually depicted at the bottom of the page dealing with the third cycle.

139

And this was when their grandmother burned something: That is, when the corn dried up (ripened), coinciding with the burning of Hunahpu and Xbalanque in the oven.

139

the ears were deified by their grandmother: "Were deified" is *xk'ab'awilax* [xca-bauilax], "complete-deify-passive."

139

Middle of the House, Middle of the Harvest, Living Ears of Green Corn, Bed of Earth: The first two names are *nik'aj ja, nik'aj b'ichok* [nicah ha, nicah bichok], "middle house, middle shucked-corn"; *b'ich-* is "to shell ripened ears of corn" (FV, FX) and Kekchí *b'ich'ok jal* is "remove the husk of a ripened ear of corn" (EH). The other two names are *k'azam* [cazam] *aj, ch'atam* [chatam] *ulew,* "living green-corn-ears, bed (or slab) earth." As Andrés Xiloj pointed out (see the notes to p. 139), Xmucane's act resembles the present-day customs of the patrilineage shrine called the *winel.*

140

the ears had been placed up above an earthen floor: This is *chuwi ch'ata* [chata] *ulew kitik wi aj,* "above bed (or slab or table) earth they-plant to corn-ear," which makes it quite clear that the corn was not "planted" in any ordinary sense of the word—not that one would plant corn *ears* in the first place.

140

their father: Note that the term for father (*qajaw*) is here extended to Seven Hunahpu. See the notes to p. 99 for a discussion of how One and Seven Hunahpu share the fathering of the twins Hunahpu and Xbalanque.

141

he was asked to name everything: The notion here is that articulate speech, with clearly enunciated words, is analogous to a clearly recognizable human face. Seven Hunahpu is not able to articulate the names of all the parts of his face because he has very few parts beyond the ones he does name, having been reduced to bones. The "meat" of his face is irreversibly lost, just as One Hunahpu had said the meat of a dead man's face would be lost (p. 99).

141

each of his former parts: This is *ri ujunal puil,* "the its-each former-ness"; DB has *pujil,* "antiquity."

141

"You will be prayed to here": Andrés Xiloj saw this as the beginning of the veneration of the dead. He explained that when there is a death in the patrilineage, the funeral rites are not complete until the mother-father goes to the lineage shrines on a *Junajpu* day that falls after the actual death. There he prays that the lingering soul of the deceased, which is a spark of light, might pass on into the cool, dark room of the underworld, from which it may later have the good fortune to rise into the sky. The number of the *Junajpu* day is chosen according to the age and importance of the deceased, with a very low number for a small child and a high one for a very old person who occupied important offices. With or without a recent death *Junajpu* days are appropriate for visiting the graves of relatives, where prayers are said and offerings are burned in much the same way as at lineage shrines, except that the entire family can go along and make a day of it, taking along a picnic lunch and strong drink.

141

"you will be the first to have your day kept": This may refer specifically to the day 7 *Junajpu,* but it probably means *Junajpu* days in general, regardless of their number prefix.

141

"Your name will not be lost": Andrés Xiloj, who is the mother-father for his own patrilineage, remarked, "This is just the way it is with our family. The first man who lived in this place was named Gaspar Xiloj, but we are still remembering him right now. Gaspar is the first generation, the second is Juan, the third is Sabino, the fourth is Antonio, the fifth is ourselves, but we are still remembering all of them. That's what it's talking about here in the Popol Vuh." He added that ideally a mother-father would be able to call upon nine or even thirteen generations of predecessors, all of them having lived on the same lands (see the Introduction for a discussion of the naming of predecessors within the PV itself). The list of people invoked in prayers should also include the spouses of all these men (with their maiden names). The names of wives are given only for the first generation in the PV (pp. 148–49), but wives receive more frequent mention in the Annals of the Cakchiquels.

141

the sun belongs to one and the moon to the other: This is *jun k'u* [cu] *q'ij* [quih] *jun nay pu ik'* [ic] *chike,* "one then sun one also and moon to-them." It is not stated that they literally became the sun and moon. From the general order of mention of Hunahpu and Xbalanque and the order of mention of the sun and moon in the present passage, it would appear that the sun pertains to Hunahpu and the moon to Xbalanque, at least on the present occasion. That the occasion is unique is indicated by a later passage, where it is stated that although Sun appeared in person on the first dawn, "it is only his reflection that now remains" (p. 161). As for Xbalanque, Mayan peoples (including the contemporary Quiché) usually put the moon in the keeping of a goddess, but there are examples of male lunar deities in Classic Maya art (Schele and Miller 1986:306, 309; Taube 1992:65–68). The nature of Xbalanque's lunar role is foretold by the fact that he is face-to-face with Hunahpu when they burn together, this being the position of the moon when it is full. The contemporary Quiché use *q'ij,* "sun," as a figure of speech for the full moon, thus saluting its brightness and roundness, and this may help account for the sun (-*q'e*) in Xbalanque's Kekchí name (*xb'alamq'e*). The whole picture fits the Aztec description of the first appearance of the present sun and moon, in which the moon rises when the sun sets and they appear similar to each other (Sahagún 1950–69, book 7:8).

142

they became the sky's own stars: Earlier we were told that the Four Hundred Boys correspond specifically to the Pleiades (p. 84).

PART FOUR

145

They sought and discovered: The root of the latter verb is *kanaisaj;* DB has *kaneisaj,* "discover, find."

145

Split Place, Bitter Water Place: This is *pan paxil, pan k'ayala'* [cayala], in which *pan* is "at" or "in"; today *pan paxil* is known as *paxal* in Mam (JM). *Paxil* is nominalized *paxi-,* "break into pieces," in Quiché (AG), while *paxal* is nominalized *pax-,* "split," in Mam (JM). *K'ayala'* combines Mam *k'ayal,* "bitterness" (JM), which would be *k'ayil* in Quiché (AG), with *a',* which is "water" in both languages. The place in question is a high mountain just south of the Pan American Highway and near the Guatemalan border with Mexico, with a cave and a large spring on its north side. Today the people of the surrounding region, who speak Mam, reckon it as the origin place of corn (Miles 1981). Teosinte, a wild grain that crossbreeds with corn, is abundant in the area.

145

the animals who brought the food: Andrés Xiloj pointed out that all four of these animals eat corn. Of the birds he said, "There are birds that take the kernels from the crop and carry them off to hide them. When the time comes they still know where they are and go to eat them. When they don't find where they left them, a garden is created there."

145

ears of yellow corn and white corn: This is ripe corn (*jal*).

146

Xmucane did the grinding nine times: Andrés Xiloj commented, "The first time corn is ground it is broken open. The second time, it is somewhat fine. The third time is finer." He indicated that ordinarily corn would not be ground nine times; that would be very fine indeed.

146

the water she rinsed her hands with: This is [ha ropenal], which Andrés Xiloj read as the *ja'* (water) a woman uses to wash off *rupenal,* the corn meal that sticks to the hands during grinding.

146

with yellow corn, white corn alone for the flesh: This reminded Andrés Xiloj of a saying used today: *ujral q'anwach, xolob'*, "We are the children [specifically a woman's children] of yellow-faced corn, spotted corn."

146

Jaguar Quitze: This name is *b'alam k'itze* [quitze]; the corrected form may be found in TK and TT. *B'alam* is "jaguar" and *k'itze* may derive from *k'ische*, "cedar" (TC, PG). Note the resemblance to *k'iche'* (Quiché), meaning "many trees."

146

Jaguar Night: This name is *b'alam aq'ab'* [acab]; the corrected form may be found in TK and TT.

146

Not Right Now: This name is *majukutaj* in the PV, elsewhere taking the form *majukotaj* (TK, TT, TV) or *jukutaj* (RA). Whatever the origin of the name, it has a clear meaning in Quiché, combining *ma*, "not," with *jukotaj*, "right away, in a moment" (DB).

146

Dark Jaguar: This name is *ik'ib'alam* [iquibalam], in which *b'alam* is "jaguar." The prefix makes no sense in Quiché, but one of the Chol terms for "jaguar" is *ik' bolay* (JH), in which *ik'* is "dark, black" and *bolay* is the generic Yucatec (and probably Cholan) term for "fierce animals that kill" (AB). As an explanation for the *i* separating *ik'* from *b'alam*, John Justeson (personal communication) suggests that the original Cholan source could have been *ik'il b'alam*, though this form has not been attested; an alternative explanation would be that the extra *i* is an artifact of the syllabic spelling conventions of Mayan hieroglyphic writing (pp. 28, 210).

147

They walked, they worked: The second verb here is *xechapanik*, literally "they grasped," but Andrés Xiloj suggested "worked," since work is done with the hands. Quichés think of the extremities together; walking and using the hands are the physical counterparts of articulate speech. Note that the link between speech and walking is made explicit in the statement, "Isn't your speech good, and your walk?" (p. 147).

148

It was as if they were asleep: This passage seems to allude to Genesis, but it disagrees with Genesis on four crucial points. First, it was only "as if" (*keje*) the men were asleep when the women were made, and it was only afterward that *ki xek'astajik,* "they really came alive." Second, there were four men and then four women, not one and one. Third, the women were not made from parts of men, but were made separately from men. Fourth, gender differences already existed among the gods.

148

Red Sea Turtle: This is *kaqa paluma* [cahapaluna]; Ximénez misread [caka] as [caha], but the corrected form may be found in TT. The name is composed of *kaq,* "red," with the added vowel *-a* (a possible vestige of hieroglyphic spelling conventions), and *palama,* "sea turtle" (PG, TC).

148

Prawn House: This is *chomija,* composed of *chom,* "shrimp" (DB) or "large shrimp" (FT) with the added vowel *-i* (see the previous note), and *ja,* which is literally "house" but means "lineage" in the context of a name.

148

Water Hummingbird: This is *tz'ununija'* [tzununiha], rendered *tz'ununa'* in the Annals of the Cakchiquels (Brinton 1885:112); *tz'unun* is "hummingbird" (with an added *-i* in the PV spelling) and *ja'* or *a'* is "water." FT lists *tz'ununja'* as a bird with "a long beak, white breast, colored green but with white wing tips, frequenting rivers," which is to say the green kingfisher (*Chloroceryle americana*). Water Hummingbird is the name of the Tzutuhil lineage that gave its name to the ancient town that became present-day San Pedro la Laguna, on the south shore of Lake Atitlán (Orellana 1984:53, 82–83).

149

Macaw House: This is *kaqixaja* [caquixaha], in which *kaqix* (with an added *-a* here) is the term for the scarlet macaw (*Ara macao*). It is the name of a Cakchiquel lineage also known as Bat House (Recinos and Goetz 1953:58) and later mentioned in the PV under the latter name. All four of the first women seem to bear the names of patrilineages. In taking Water Hummingbird and Macaw House as their wives, Not Right Now and Dark Jaguar not only marry outside their own lineages, as anyone must, but outside their own tribe, as befits their royal status. The lineages of Red Sea Turtle and Prawn House were probably foreign as well. The paradox is that the first men married outside their lineages before they had even founded them, while the first women bore the names of patrilineages even though they had no fathers. A similar paradox appears in the Classic inscriptions of Palenque, where a woman is reckoned as the founder of the patrilineage of the king named Chan Bahlum (Schele and Freidel 1990: 252–60).

149

ladies of rank: This is *xoqojawab'* [xoccohauab], literally "women-lords."

149

penitents and sacrificers: Here and elsewhere, these are *ajk'ixb'* [ahquix or ahquixb] and *ajk'ajb'* [ahcahb], in which *aj-* is agentive; FV gives *k'ixb'*, which is clearly a verbal form of *k'ix*, "spine," as "to shame"; FX gives *k'ajb'*, which probably has the same root as *k'ajinik*, "to punish" (MX), as "sacrifice of blood." The reference of the pair of terms is to the penitential autosacrifice of blood.

149

Sovereign Oloman: This tribal name is *tepew oloman* (elsewhere *oliman*), from a Nahua source; on *tepew*, see the notes for p. 63. In Nahuatl proper *ollomani* means "ballplayer" (AM). It is later stated (p. 162) that this tribe remained in the east when the Quiché and their allies left Tulan. They may have been speakers of Pipil (a Nahua language) who once occupied part of the Motagua valley, between Rotten Cane and Copán.

149

Quenech Ahau: This is from Yucatec *k'inich ajaw*, "sun-faced lord" (AB), a title that appears in Classic inscriptions (Stuart and Houston 1994:9) and in Chilam Balam books. If it came into Quiché by way of Kekchí, where terms for the sun include the syllable *q'e* (EH), the correct form was probably *q'enech ajaw*. It would appear to be a Quichean term for a people speaking a Yucatecan language, such as Itzá or Mopán.

149

Cauecs: This is *kawiqib'* [cauiquib], singular *kaweq* [cauec]; the corrected *kaweq* form appears in TK.

149

great houses and *lineages:* Here and elsewhere, "great house" translates *nimja*, which can refer to a palace but serves here as a metonym for an organized and named lineage segment (within a larger patrilineage), one with a person of lordly rank at its head. "Lineage" translates *chinamit*, from a Nahua source; in Nahuatl proper *chinamitl* is "hedge or enclosure of cane plants, district" (RS). In Quiché *chinamit* refers to an organized and named patrilineage or to its lands; in the PV it usually refers to a whole group of named lineage segments, but sometimes it is used synonymously with *nimja*.

149

thirteen allied tribes, thirteen principalities: This is *oxlajuj uk'a* [uca] *amaq'* [amac], *oxlajuj tekpan*, in which *oxlajuj* is "thirteen" and *amaq'* is "tribe." *Tekpan* is from a Nahua source; it means "royal house or palace" or "put the people in order" in Nahuatl proper (AM). In Quiché it seems to be a term for a tribe that is organized under a recognized noble house, but a house that is tributary (at least ideally) to the larger Quiché state. The *tekpan* list in this passage contains fifteen names rather than thirteen; some of the names may be subdivisions of larger entities, or some may be synonyms, or else the number thirteen is simply an ideal figure rather than a literal count. There remains the question of how to translate [uca], which requires appeal to the only other passage in the entire PV that combines *amaq'* and *tekpan* in parallel construction (p. 183): *wuk'* [uuc] *amaq'* [amac] *kib' kitikpan* [quiticpan] *k'ib'*, in which *kib'* is "themselves." It stands to reason that [uca] in the first passage should have the same sense as [uuc] in the second passage. By itself the latter form has often been read as a shortened *wuqub'*, "seven," but that is disconfirmed by the reference to thirteen tribes in the earlier passage. I translate both [uca] and [uuc] as "allied" on the basis of two entries in DB: *wuk'ij* [uuquih], "to make friends," and *wuk'*, "friend"; these forms are probably related to the prepositional root *-uk'*, "with."

149

White Cornmeals: This name is *saq k'ajib'* [zacahib], "white cornmeal-plural." The people in question must have settled in the area of the present town of Salcajá, called *saqk'aja* in Quiché, located about ten kilometers northeast of Quetzaltenango.

149

Lamacs, Serpents, Sweatbath House, Talk House, those of Star House: The Sweatbath House (*tujalja*) people correspond to the place still called *tujal* in Quiché, which is the town center of Sacapulas. The town has long been famous for salt production, and Hill and Monaghan note that the term *tuj*, which normally means "sweatbath" in Quiché, is locally extended to the ovens used in salt production (1987:47). They point out that under Spanish rule, the peoples listed here as Lamacs (*lamakib'*) and Talk House (*uch'ab'aja*) were resettled in districts surrounding the center of Sacapulas, and the same point can be made for the remaining two groups on the list. Clearly, the Serpents (*kumatz*) and Star House (*ajch'umilaja*), both given Quiché names in the PV, correspond to the groups Hill and Monaghan found listed in colonial documents as Coatecas and Sitaltecas (1987:47), names derived from Nahuatl *coatl*, "snake," and *citlali*, "star" (RS).

149

those of Yokes House: This is *ajb'atenaja* [ahbatenaba], in which *aj-* is "those of," *b'ate* is the yoke used in the ball game, *-na* is plural, and *ja* is "house."

149

Guardians of the Spoils: This is *kanchajeleb',* composed of *kan-* from *kanab',* "spoils of war" (DB); *chajel,* "guardian"; and *-eb',* plural.

149

Jaguar Ropes: This is *b'alam kolob',* composed of *b'alam,* "jaguar"; *kolo,* "rope" (DB); and *-b',* plural.

149

each one a division of that citadel: This is probably a reference to Tulan Zuyua, a place that will not be properly discussed until later (p. 151).

150

And there were mountain people: In this passage the PV would appear to follow the lines of Toltec myths of national origin, exemplified by the claim of the powerful Aztecs (or Mexicas) to a humble past as Chichimec hunters and gatherers. But in the present context the reference might rather be to Quichean peoples (the "allied tribes") as they were during the Classic period, which is to say rustic and small in numbers by comparison with lowland Mayans. The ancestors of the Quiché proper and related tribes will later be described as being "adorned with mere animals hides" (p. 152), and the Quiché ancestors in particular will be described as hunters of deer, birds, and larvae who stay apart from more populous tribes (p. 164).

150

for all the mountain people there was just one language: I have supplied "mountain people" here; the intent seems to be to separate the mountain people, which is to say speakers of Quichean languages, from others who were present in the east, where there were "people of many languages" (p. 150).

150

tree-stone: This is a literal translation of *che' ab'aj,* the exact Quiché equivalent of Cholan *te' tun,* the term for a stele in the Classic Maya inscriptions of Copán (Schele and Stuart 1986). This is one of various indications that the great eastern city where Quichean peoples received their patron deities (see the next episode) was a Classic Maya site.

150

lifting their faces to the sky: Andrés Xiloj explained, "When one prays, as here, asking for things, one looks to heaven; afterward, when waiting for the blessing, one looks to earth."

150

"as long as there is day, as long as there is light": This is an alternate translation of the line discussed in the notes to p. 86 ("in the course of the days"). In the present context Andrés Xiloj commented, "Today one says *qab'e q'ij, qab'e saq* [our-road day, our-road light]. This is the time that goes forward; it is the road of time, the number of years one is going to live, or the number of times there will be until the end of the world."

150

"will it be": This line has been translated as a question because it begins with *kita,* which DB glosses as "what" or "how."

150

"a good life and beginning": Andrés Xiloj commented, "These words would be used in prayer when someone was setting up a new household."

150

"Newborn Nanahuac, Sudden Nanahuac": As Schultze Jena pointed out (1944:187), Nanahuac would appear to be the Aztec deity Nanahuatl (or Nanahuatzin), who throws a thunderbolt to open the mountain containing the first maize. *Nanahuatl* means "warts" in Nahuatl (AM), giving us one of several bits of evidence that there might be an allusion to mushrooms in the names of the previous line, "Newborn Thunderbolt, Sudden Thunderbolt." On the basis of fieldwork, Barbara Tedlock and I can confirm Lowy's report that the Quiché word for thunderbolt, *kaqulja,* is also the term for the *Amanita muscaria* mushroom (Lowy 1974:189). We must hasten to add that although Quichés collect and eat wild mushrooms, including *Amanita caesaria,* they regard *muscaria* as a poisonous species best avoided. But it is suggestive that the stipe of a mushroom (like the trunk of a tree) is called *raqan* or "its leg" in Quiché, and that the name *kaqulja juraqan,* earlier rendered as "Thunderbolt Hurricane" (p. 65), could be also translated as "one-legged thunderbolt." The names Newborn and Sudden Thunderbolt suggest the rapidity of mushroom growth. Literal bolts of lightning are sudden as well, and frequently one-legged, but the "warts" of the name Nanahuac do suggest the appearance of *muscaria* when the remnants of its veil still fleck the cap.

150

they made their fasts: The verb stem here is [quilonic]; MX has *q'ilonik,* "avoid, abstain."

150

watching intently: This is *selawachin;* DB has *selawachij,* "to view with close attention."

the sun carrier, the great star: The "sun carrier" is *iqoq'ij* [icoquih], composed of *iqo-* (sometimes *eqo-*), "to carry a burden," and *q'ij,* "sun" or "day." The corrected form is found in FT, TC, and FV. The "great star" or *nima ch'umil* is the planet Venus in general, while "sun carrier" specifies its role as the morning star. This passage is the first of many direct references to Venus that are clustered around and during the visit of Quichean peoples to a great city in the east. Both the focus on Venus and the eastern location are among various indications that the city in question may have been Copán, which is located east of the present-day Quiché homeland. Copán surpasses all Classic Maya sites yet studied in the extent to which its kings timed major ritual events according to the movements of Venus (see Schele and Fash 1991:4; Schele 1991:6).

Tulan Zuyua: Tulan is from a Nahua source; in Nahuatl proper, *tullan* or *tollan* is "place of rushes (or cattails)" (RS). In Postclassic times and possibly earlier, this word served throughout central Mexico and Oaxaca as an honorific title for any town where the investiture of lords could take place. During the sixteenth century, Tullan or Tollan is the name of a lost city of the mythic past in Nahuatl songs, while *tolan* serves as a term for any abandoned building or place in Quiché and Cakchiquel (DB, FX, TC, FV). The often-repeated notion that the name Zuyua [zuiua] is Nahua originates with Brinton (1885:199), who incorrectly stated that it appears in Aztec mythology. It is a Yucatec name, made up of *suy,* which carries the meaning "twisted" in various contexts, and perhaps *wa,* referring to deception (AB); in the Book of Chilam Balam of Chumayel the phrase *suyua t'an,* meaning "twisted, deceptive speech," designates a language game in which pretenders to lordly titles are asked a series of metaphorical riddles in order to test their legitimacy (Roys 1967:88–98). As for the combined Tulan Zuyua of the PV, it fits all the above senses of both names: it is a place where the investiture of lords took place, it belongs to the distant past rather than the time of the authors, and it is the place where those who failed to understand a question containing a deceptive metaphor (see p. 156) became subject to the Quiché lords.

According to the Annals of the Cakchiquels there were four places named Tulan, including one in Xibalba and one in the sky. The other two were on the earthly plane, in the east and west, and the highland tribes traveled eastward (as in the PV) to reach the eastern Tulan (Brinton 1885:68–69). The name Zuyua appears solely as part of the compound name Tulan Zuyua in the PV, but it is used separately in the Annals of the Cakchiquels, where it seems to specify the eastern Tulan (Ibid.:76–77, 82–83). The east-west pairing appears again in the Book of Chilam Balam of Maní, where there is a western place called Tulapan (meaning "on the cattails") and an eastern one called Zuyua (Craine and Reindorp 1979:138). In the Chilam Balam books of Chumayel and Tizimín, Zuyua is treated as a town somewhere in Yucatán (Roys 1967:74, 132; Edmonson

1982:38, 135). In one passage Zuyua is prefixed with Oxlahun, "Thirteen" (Edmonson 1982:135); in other passages it is prefixed with Holtun, referring to a stone with a hole through it, and in one such case Holtun Zuyua is said to be west of Chichén Itzá (Roys 1967:139). There is a place known today as Holtun just two kilometers west of the great ball court at Chichén Itzá; it consists of a cenote (natural well) and an archaeological site important enough to have its own ball court. There were also places called Holtun on both the east and west coasts of Yucatán (Scholes and Roys 1968:81); Thompson (1970:23), in the midst of an argument promoting the importance of the Gulf, proposed that the name Zuyua belonged to the west-coast Holtun.

151

Seven Caves, Seven Canyons: This is *wuqub'* [uucub] *pek, wuqub'* [uucub] *siwan,* an epithet for Tulan Zuyua. Seven Caves would seem to be the Quiché equivalent of Chicomoztoc, the "seven caves" of the mythic Nahua place of origin. Numerous Mayan sites were built directly over natural caves, and at some sites that lack such caves artificial substitutes were dug. There are three artificial caves beneath the ruins of Rotten Cane, the Quiché capital, perhaps belonging to the Cauec, Greathouse, and Lord Quiché lineages. The longest cave, which runs to a point beneath the main plaza, matches the cave beneath the pyramid of the sun at Teotihuacan (which has also turned out to be artificial) in having its entrance at the west end and in having six side chambers that combine with the main tunnel to make the number seven. For more on this cave see Brady (1991) and Brady and Veni (1992).

152

Tohil: This divine name appears to be composed of *Toj,* one of the twenty day names of the 260-day divinatory calendar, and *-il,* "having the quality of." *Toj* is the verb stem for "pay" in Chol (JH) and Quiché, and contemporary Quiché daykeepers give the day named *Toj* its divinatory meaning by saying *tojonik,* "one pays." Another etymology is suggested in the Annals of the Cakchiquels, where the Quiché people (as worshippers of Tohil) are given the epithet *tojojil,* "thunderers" (Brinton 1885:82–83). In Chol, *tojmel* is "to thunder" and *tojokna* is "the way in which clouds come" (AA). All these meanings fit Tohil, a god who is owed a great sacrificial debt and who is able to shroud himself in clouds and rain.

152

the name of the god: This is *ub'i k'ab'awil* [cabauil], in which *ub'i* means "his name" but *k'ab'awil* or "god" also carries a root sense of naming. *K'ab'a'* means "name" or "identity" in Kekchí (EH) and (in the form *k'aba*) in Chol (JH), Mopán (UU), and Yucatec (AB); the *-il* suffix gives the word the sense of "that which has the quality of being named" or "having an identity." In contemporary Kekchí the religious sense of *k'ab'a'* continues in *k'ab'a'tiox* (in which *tiox* is from Spanish "Dios" and marks sacredness), referring not only to sacred names but to religious discourse in general (EH). In the PV the term *k'ab'awil* is used primarily for the patron deities of ruling lineages, acquired in a distant place where the local language was probably a Cholan one. The authors go on to point out a three-way homology in the differentiation of the names of such gods, the identities of the tribes who worship them, and the dialects or languages spoken by those tribes, all of which fits the root sense of *k'ab'awil.* To these differentiations we may add that of place, since some of these gods are destined to be given homes on separate mountains and (later) on separate pyramids that bear their names. In Classic Maya inscriptions the equivalent term is *k'awil,* which is applied to the manikin scepter (God K or GII) held by rulers (Stuart 1987:15–16). *K'awil* is often combined with place names, indicating that it is like *k'ab'awil* in being a general term for the patrons of lineages and/or their places rather than a proper name for one particular god (Grube 1992:210–11).

152

Auilix: In other sources this name appears as *awilis* (TK, TT, TV) or *wilix* (FX). In Kekchí the term for "swallow" (the bird) is *kwilix* (EH) today, but John Justeson (personal communication) points out that the initial *k-* is a recent innovation; in Chol the term for this bird is *wilis chan* (JH). Justeson suggests a Cholan origin for the name *awilix,* combining *aj-,* "lord," with *wilix.* In Cholan languages, he points out, *aj-* becomes plain *a-* in such an environment. *Awilix,* then, would mean "Lord Swallow."

152

Hacauitz: Jak is "to strip off" in Chol (JH); *witz* is "mountain" in Yucatec (AB) and Chol (JH). The writers of the PV seem to be interpreting the name in just this way when they contrast the god Auilix, who was placed in a forest, with Hacauitz, who was placed on what they call a *saqi juyub'; saqi* is literally "white" or "clear" and means "treeless" with respect to terrain (see under *saq* in FV), and *juyub'* is the Quiché equivalent of *witz,* "mountain."

152

because the god has just one name: The logic of this passage lies in the notion that receiving a titular deity (*k'ab'awil*) and receiving a legitimate name (*b'i'*) are two aspects of the same process. The word *k'ab'awil* itself, in its Cholan or Yucatec root sense (see above), means something like "that which has the quality of being named."

152

so says the ancient text: This is *ch'a chupan ojer tzij,* literally "it says within ancient word." Enrique Sam Colop (1994:44–45) points out that the use of *chupan,* which refers to the inside of a physical object, turns "ancient word" into a figure of speech for the contents of an ancient book, which is to say the original version of the PV. The correctness of this interpretation is confirmed by a later passage using *chupan,* in which the reference to writing is made explicit (see the notes to p. 161).

154

He pivoted inside his sandal: The verb phrase here is *xub'aq uloq* [xubac uloc], "he drilled hither"; FV gives *b'aq* as "to drill." Just as he had promised, Tohil gives his followers fire when others have lost it, acting as a fire drill. He pivots on one leg, which serves as the drill, and his sandal serves as the platform. His one-legged pose and the fire identify him with the Classic Maya personage known to iconographers as God K or GII, whose fire is usually shown as a burning torch sticking out of his forehead but sometimes comes out of the mouth of the snake that serves as the longer of his legs or (sometimes) his only leg (Taube 1992:69–79). Tohil is also a manifestation of the god called Hurricane or Thunderbolt Hurricane elsewhere in the PV (see the notes to p. 65).

154

they got no response: The verb stem here is *k'ula-* [cula-]; DB has [culuba], "respond," and TC gives *k'ulub'a* the same meaning.

154

place of emergence: This is *tz'ukib'al* [tzuquibal], in which *-b'al* is "place of"; FV glosses *tz'uk* as "spring forth, sprout."

154

And then a person showed himself: At this point Ximénez, who otherwise confines his own parenthetical remarks to the Spanish translation in the right-hand column of each page of the MS, inserts a remark into the left-hand column, otherwise reserved for the Quiché text. As if avoiding an impropriety he uses Latin, writing "Demonio loquens eis." The writers of the PV probably intended an allusion to Christian demonology in this passage, since they describe the god under discussion as having the wings of a bat and as coming from Xibalba (the underworld), but it should be noted that they make this allusion at the expense of the Cakchiquels, the principal rivals of the Quichés, whose god, they say, "looks like a bat" (p. 156). To this day many Cakchiquel men wear jackets with a bat motif on the back.

154

the representation: This is *k'exwach* [quexuach], literally "substitute-face," which DB glosses as "resemblance" in the entry for [quexel]; Andrés Xiloj offered the same reading.

154

They were simply overwhelmed: The verb stem here is [kulu]; DB and FV have *k'ulum,* "dismay."

154

groping along: The verb stem here is *chakchot;* DB has *chakacha,* "to go like a blind person."

155

they had covetous mouths and covetous faces: This is *chikimaj kichi' chikimaj kiwach.* The combination of *maj* ("rob") with *chi'* ("mouth") and *wach* ("face") is an idiom meaning "to be pained by not having something to trade with or something one has need of" (under [mah] in FV). A more literal translation of the present example would be something like "They had thieving mouths and thieving faces."

155

"Wasn't it found and wasn't it revealed": This is a divinatory phrase, much like the one used by Xpiyacoc and Xmucane at the beginning of their divinatory question concerning the making of humans from wood (p. 70). The verb stems in both cases are *k'ulu* [culu] and *riqo* [rico], "encounter" and "find." In the present context the implication is that those who want fire claim a kinship with those who already have it on the basis of some past divinatory reading rather than on the basis of a clear genealogy. This is what anthropologists call "fictive kinship"; it may have been standard practice in highland Guatemala to include divinatory readings in the negotiation of such relationships.

155

' "Don't they want to be suckled?" ': Throughout this passage I follow Edmonson in translating *tu'nik* [tunic] as having to do with suckling (Edmonson 1971:168), a meaning found in both ancient and modern Quiché. In the present context the suckling is a metaphor for sacrifice by removal of the heart, as is made quite explicit on p. 156. It may be the horror of this metaphor that has caused translators to pass over it heedlessly; even Edmonson's note on the subject suggests that mere sacrifice by self-bleeding is meant. The place where Tohil desires to do his sucking is "on their sides and under their arms," which fits with what is known about Mesoamerican heart sacrifice: the incision was made between the last two ribs on the left side (Robicsek and Hales 1984). The next sentence, "Isn't it their heart's desire to embrace me?" is not only a statement about motivation but a further reference to heart sacrifice. Tohil is no mere sucker of breasts; what he wants from those who embrace him is deep inside the breast, and he wants the whole thing.

156

They made no delay: The verb here is [xquiquiyaluh], which I take to be an error for *xkiyaluj; yaluj* is "to delay oneself" (DB), giving "not complete-they-delay" for the whole phrase.

156

Snake Tooth: This name, *chamalkan,* makes little sense in Quichean languages, but *cha'am* is "molar" in Chol (AA) and Yucatec (AB), while *kan* is "snake" in Yucatec (AB). The comment the authors add here, "but it looks like a bat," suggests that they knew the meaning of *kan.*

156

Those fiery Cakchiquels didn't ask for their fire: The name of these people is usually spelled [ca3chequeleb] or [ca3chiqueleb] in the MS, [3] being an apparent error for [k]; in the new orthography the word would be *kaqchekeleb'* or *kaqchikeleb'. Kaq* means "red" and *che'* means "tree" or "pole," an etymology put forward in the Annals of the Cakchiquels (Recinos and Goetz 1953:55). But in the present PV passage the first syllable of the name is written [3a3] or *q'aq',* meaning "fire," a pun on *kaq* that refers to the Cakchiquel theft of fire. The closest I could come in English was to add the word "fiery."

156

This deed had not yet been attempted: The verb stem here is *tijow;* MX has *tijowik,* "try, practice."

156

newly risen: This translates *raxa,* which could also be "fresh" or "raw"; I assume that the reference is to the first appearance of Venus as morning star after a period of invisibility.

156

they left the east: The verb stem here is *kanaj,* "to leave" (DB).

156

"where we belong": This is *kojtike wi,* "incomplete-we-stop"; FX glosses *tike* as "to stop," and it carries connotations of planting or taking root.

157

"yet to take care of bleeding your ears, yet to take stitches in your elbows": In this passage "bleeding" translates *jutik,* "to let blood" (DB); in contemporary Quiché the verb stem *jut-* means "to run through" (AG). "Take stitches" translates *sisa,* which is similar to *tziso,* "to sew a seam; formerly, to let blood for sacrifice to idols" (DB). The words for "ears" and "elbows" (*xikin and ch'uk*) pun on the words for "birds" and "breechclouts" (*tz'ikin and ch'uq*). The possibilities for a play on *xikin* begin with the fact that it was also used for such appendages as a long handle on a cooking utensil (FV). *Tz'ikin,* the generic term for bird, is the commonest Quiché metaphor for penis, an alternative metaphor

being *pich'*, the term for a red-headed woodpecker (PG, FT, FV, FX). Classic Maya lords did penance by bleeding their penises rather than their ears (Schele and Miller 1986: chap. 4), and bloodletting is precisely what Tohil tells the future Quiché lords to do with their so-called *xikin*. As for what he tells them to take stitches in, that is written as [chuc] in the imprecise spelling of the MS and may be read as either of two words: *ch'uk*, which is indeed "elbow," and *ch'uq*, which refers to covering by means of cloth (FT) and specifically to the covering of a man's genitals (DB). In the present context "elbow" makes a better fit with "ear" if we want a pair of terms for body parts, but if we consider the stitching, a cloth covering works better. The covering serves in turn as a metonym for what it covers, or else as a metaphor for the foreskin, which was the site where blood was drawn. The method was to pass a cord through it (as if sewing). According to a later PV passage (p. 165), the penitents who took these stitches prayed to Tohil for their *achijilal*, which literally means "manhood" but is also a figure of speech for "virile member" (FT).

157

camping on the road: This is *xukanajib'ej ri pa b'e*, literally "it was left in the road."

157

In unity: This is *chikijunam wach*, "in-their-one face," an idiom given in MX as *junam kiwach*, "be in agreement," and in DB as *junamaj wach*, "be in accord."

158

They were just smelling the tips of their staffs: Andrés Xiloj commented, "Perhaps these staffs had some secret. Perhaps they were of a wood like cherry, which has the odor of the fruit."

158

Stone Courses, Sand Banks: These names are *cholochik ab'aj, bokotajinaq* [boco-tahinac] *sanayeb'*, composed of a reduplicated form of *cholo-*, "to order, put in a row"; *ab'aj*, "rocks"; *boko-*, "uproot"; *taji'-*, "cultivate, plow"; *-naq*, perfect; and *sanayeb'*, "sands." In effect, the names describe a causeway like the ones that cross lakes or areas of seasonal flooding in connecting various Mayan sites in the lowlands. The body of water crossed by the present causeway is described as a "sea" (*palo*), but the Historia Quiché de Don Juan de Torres (Recinos 1957:24–25) and the Title of the Lords of Totonicapán (Carmack and Mondloch 1983a:72–73, 175) call it both a lake (*cho*) and a sea, a poetic way of referring to a large body of water. In the latter source, whose authors actively remodeled Quiché traditions along biblical lines, the causeway disappears and Jaguar Quitze becomes Moses, parting the Red Sea with his staff (Chonay and Goetz 1953:170).

158

packed . . . on their backs: The verb stem here is *eqaj* [eca], "to carry on the shoulders or back" (DB).

159

at the top of a great pyramid: This is *chuwi jun nima kaqja* [ca3ha], "on-top one great red-house." Others have followed Ximénez in reading *ja* as *ja'*, thus translating this phrase as "above a great red river." The present reading is supported by at least three dictionary sources for Quiché and Cakchiquel: FV glosses *kaqjay* (in which *jay* is "house") as "rounded mounds of stone and dry earth made by the ancients," DV glosses *kaqay* as "hill made by hand," and FX glosses *kaqjal* [cachal] (in which the *-l* changes "house" into "something pertaining to a house") as "hills made by hand." It is not surprising that the term for pyramid was (literally) "red-house," given that Mayan pyramids (and the temples on top) were painted red, at least up through the Classic period.

159

on a bare mountain: This is *saqi* [zaqui] *juyub'*, in which *saqi* is literally "white" or "clear" and means "treeless" with respect to terrain (see under *saq* in FV); *juyub'* is "mountain." I take it that the writers mean to contrast the situation of Hacauitz with that of Auilix and Tohil, both of whom seem to be "in a great forest" even though the latter, like Hacauitz, is on a mountain.

159

Masses of serpents . . . jaguars, rattlesnakes, fer-de-lances were there in the forest where he was hidden: Today in Momostenango the shrines on the high mountains that bound the community, together with the shrine (atop a very high waterfall) used by those who organize and play parts in the Monkey Dance, are all said to be haunted by dangerous animals. Such animals appear to those whose ritual office does not entitle them to visit a particular shrine; they also appear to those who have a right to visit but have failed to abstain from sexual or violent acts (whether verbal or physical) on the day of their arrival at the shrine.

159

Tam Tribe. . . . Net Weave Tribe: These place names are *amaq'* [amac] *tan* and *amaq'* [amac] *ukin k'at* [cat]. In the first name, *tan* is an archaic or alternative pronunciation of the tribal name otherwise rendered as *tam*. In the second, *u-* is "its," *kin* is "do the warp in weaving" (DB), and *k'at* is "net."

159

they stopped there: The verb stem here is [tacotob]; DB (under *taq'ab'a*) has *taq'atob'ik*, "to stop and not move forward."

159

They cried their hearts and their guts out: Asked why, Andrés Xiloj said, "They were sad in the darkness, there was no light, no day, no night, all the time it was dark." The Quiché do not think of night as simply "dark" as opposed to "light" (see "early dawn" in the notes to p. 65). The conditions before the first dawn in the PV were so bad that one could not even speak properly of night, with its moon and stars and even a faint trace of dawn, to say nothing of the full light of day.

159

in the bromeliads, in the hanging mosses, not yet set on pedestals: Today, *ek'* or bromeliads (*Tillandsia spp.*) and *atz'iyaq* [atziyac] or Spanish moss (*Dendropogon usneoides*) are standard materials in the construction of temporary outdoor arbors or archways for saints. The present passage would seem to mean that the gods were put beneath such arbors, not that they were put up in the trees where these air plants actually grow. Only later were the gods "set on pedestals," presumably in the "houses" at the tops of pyramids (see p. 191).

159

their strategies: This is *kich'akab'al* [quichacabal], "their-win-instrument."

160

Their hearts did not yet harbor ill will: This is *mana chilik cayal ta kik'ux,* in which *mana* is "not yet," *ta* is a further marker of the negative, and *kik'ux* is "their hearts." DB glosses both *chilik* and *kayal* as "become annoyed, have ill will."

160

Mixtam Copal: The name of this copal (*pom*) is from a Nahua source; in Nahuatl proper, *mixtemi* is "be cloudy" (RS). Since this copal and the Cauiztan variety (see below) are said to have come from the east, they might be from the part of the Motagua valley where Pipil (a Nahua language) was spoken.

160

Cauiztan Copal: Again a Nahua name; in Nahuatl proper, *quauitztlan* is "near the thistles" (RS).

160

they incensed: The verb stem here is [zacbiza]; DB has *saqb'isaj* [za3bisah], "to incense" and "to wag his (a dog's) tail." In the next sentence I have translated the same verb as "they shook." A pottery censer of the kind used in Mesoamerica must be shaken or swung back and forth to keep the incense burning.

161

it is only his reflection that now remains: What might lie behind this statement is revealed by a contemporary Mopán Maya tale in which Lord K'in (the sun) goes from his home in the east to the center of the sky and then back to the east again; it appears that he goes clear across the sky because he has placed a mirror at its center (Thompson 1930:132). To interpret the movements of the sun in this manner is to model it on Venus as morning star, which both rises and sets in the east.

161

As they put it in the ancient text: This is *xch'a chupan ki tzij,* literally "it said inside their word." "Ancient" (*ojer*) has been supplied on the basis of a similar phrase occurring earlier, *ch'a chupan ojer tzij* (see the notes to p. 152). In that instance *ojer tzij,* literally "ancient word," was translated as "ancient text" because *chupan,* referring to the inside of a physical object, turns it into a figure of speech for the contents of the original PV.

161

Tohil, Auilix, and Hacauitz were turned to stone, along with the icons of the puma, jaguar, rattlesnake, fer-de-lance, which the White Sparkstriker took with him into the trees: The "icons" here are *uk'ab'awilal* [ucabauilal], "its-godliness," *k'ab'awil* being translated elsewhere as "god." The White Sparkstriker is *saqi k'oxol* [zaqui coxol], composed of *saqi,* "white"; *k'oxo,* a verb stem used for the act of striking stones together "to start a fire" (FV); and -*l,* agentive. This name follows immediately after the fer-de-lance, so that some translators have treated it as part of the list of beings who are turned to stone. However, in terms of what is known about the White Sparkstriker today (see B. Tedlock 1983; 1986), it makes much more sense to treat the name as the subject of the sentence that follows it, *xa xuchap chi uk'aj* [uca] *rib' pa che'* [che], "just he/she took that to-accompany him/herself into trees." Today the White Sparkstriker, who is sexually ambiguous, is the keeper of volcanic concretions and ancient artifacts that resemble animals; these objects, which are said to have been petrified when the sun first rose, are called *meb'il* (the same as the name of the shrine in which they are kept) in Momostenango.

Andrés Xiloj commented on this passage as follows: "When all the birds, animals were converted into stone, they remained as *meb'il.* When the moment comes and one is able to acquire one of these, this is the *meb'il.* Birds, rabbits —in sum, all the different kinds of stones. Now the *k'oxol* [Sparkstriker], this one, yes, he has money, they say. When one has luck, the *k'oxol* presents himself. If he takes off his shoe and leaves it thrown away, then there is the money; or his little bag—because he has a little bag, and if he leaves it thrown away, there is the money. This is the *meb'il* of a person; it is the luck." Lucas Pacheco, a daykeeper from a town near Santa Cruz del Quiché, said that the *k'oxol* lost his/

her shoe when the sun first rose; the *k'oxol* escaped petrifaction by running into the trees, but the shoe did not.

161

Perhaps we would have no relief from the voracious animals today . . . if the original animals hadn't been turned to stone: "Voracious animals" is *tionel chikop,* "biting (or meat-eating) animals." The MS erroneously adds the White Sparkstriker to the list of animals in this sentence; apparently Ximénez (or a copyist) interpreted the previous naming of the White Sparkstriker (see the previous note) as part of a list of animals and then assumed that the name must be missing from the present list. Andrés Xiloj commented, "The *k'oxol* [Sparkstriker] has to take care of the animals; he doesn't allow them to go out, because they are harmful. He keeps them, he has them in a corral." This is the Sparkstriker in his role as gamekeeper (see B. Tedlock 1992:181–87); today the dangerous animals only attack people who have failed in their ritual duties. According to Lucas Pacheco, a daykeeper from a town near Santa Cruz del Quiché, the corral where the Sparkstriker keeps his animals is located deep within a branch of a cave beneath the ruins of Rotten Cane; in that context they take the form of small stones. The fortunate may be allowed to take some of these; the unfortunate fall into a great, wide mouth.

162

their song named "Camacu": This is *k'amaku* [camaku], a Quiché rendition of a Cholan or Yucatec song title. Such titles begin with *k'ay,* the term for "song" in these languages; *k'ay nikte',* for example, means "Song of the Flower" in Yucatec (AB). The song in question here probably resembled the one whose text is given in the Book of Chilam Balam of Chumayel (Roys 1967:38, 114–15). That song is composed of questions and answers, and it opens with questions whose first word is *mak* or "what," for example, *Mak u kobol yutz takil winik?* "What is it that has the best qualities of a man?" (Answer: *In nok, in wex,* "My cloak, my loincloth"). The title of this song is not given, but it could have been *k'ay mak u,* meaning something like "Song of What-is-it." The Chilam Balam and PV songs both have lines beginning with exclamations and interrogatives, and in both cases the singers lament events that took place in a town they have left behind.

162

Yolcuat and Quitzalcuat: These names are from a Nahua source. In the former case the relevant forms in Nahuatl proper are *yollo,* "able, ingenious, intelligent," and *coatl,* "snake" (RS). The latter name has its Nahuatl counterpart in Quetzalcoatl, meaning "quetzal (or plumed) serpent." The equivalent Quiché deity is not Tohil, as the authors claim here, but the god whose Quiché name is *q'ukumatz,* which has exactly the same meaning as Quetzalcoatl and is rendered as "Plumed Serpent" throughout the present translation. Tohil has his closest

Mexican parallel not in Quetzalcoatl but in Tezcatlipoca (see p. 224). Whether or not the authors knew the meaning of the name they wrote as Quitzalcuat, their claim to an equivalence with Tohil makes sense as a political statement, one that aligns the Quiché rulers with the richer and more powerful rulers of Mexico.

162

some of the people: In the earlier edition of this book I followed a number of other translators in treating *chajkar winaq* (in which *winaq* is "people") as a tribal name, which I rendered as "Fishkeeper People," but now, in translating *chajkar* as "some of," I follow the PV translation of Ximénez and the meaning given to this word by DB.

162

And the language has differentiated in the case of the Cakchiquels: In this passage the PV presents a theory that linguistic differentiation correlates with differences in the names originally assigned to tribal gods. The linguistic observations are themselves quite accurate.

163

Keeper of the Bat Mat and Keeper of the Dance Mat: These names are *ajpo sotz'il* [zotzil] and *ajpo xa,* in which *ajpo* is shortened from *ajpop,* "keeper of the mat" and *xa* is shortened from *xajil.* The shortened form *ajpo* does not occur in dictionaries of Quichean languages but is well known from Classic Maya inscriptions. In the Annals of the Cakchiquels (where *xajil* is used instead of *xa*) the two names are used as lordly titles rather than as designations of lineages (Recinos and Goetz 1953:72, 74, 132).

163

their stay: The verb stem here is *yalujik,* "stop, delay" (DB).

163

the masking of Tohil: The "masking" is *kojb'al,* "mask-instrument."

163

they bowed low: The verb here is *wonowoj;* DB has *wonob'a rib',* "contract, as in joining the chin with the knees."

163

Now it was only a manifestation of his genius that spoke: That is to say, the words came not from the stone itself but from an apparition of its spirit familiar, which in this case would be a youth.

306

163

All they burned before their gods was resin, just bits of pitchy bark, along with marigolds: That is to say, they burned things still in their natural forms rather than using proper copal. The resin is *q'ol*, which may be gathered in gummy nodules from the trunks of various trees. The bits of pitchy bark are *rachaq noj*, literally "leavings of pine resin," pieces of bark on which a hard red resin has been formed as a result of the holes bored by worms. The marigold is *iya* [yia], a particular species (*Tagetes lucida*) called "pericón" in Guatemalan Spanish, where it is a common roadside herb with yellow flowers. According to Andrés Xiloj, all of these things are burned as offerings today in Momostenango, but they constitute a poorer offering than copal. Earle (1983) reports the burning of pericón in the eastern Quiché area, and I have seen the unburned remains of bits of bark at a shrine near Chichicastenango.

163

"Do not reveal us to the tribes": Andrés Xiloj compared this hiding of the gods (or the stones that contain their geniuses) to the proper treatment of the valuable objects that are called *meb'il* in Momostenango: "These stones are like *meb'il*. When one finds one, one must not show it to another person, because it's for oneself directly. There are persons who find some little things; they may show them to others, but this *meb'il* won't allow it, now it won't give good fortune to the person who found it. It withdraws. If there is some little thing, an ancient coin found in the woods, or a stone, then one must guard it." See also the notes to p. 66.

163

"they burn with envy over us": This is *kojq'aq'anij rumal*, "us-envied by-them"; FX has *q'aq'aj*, "brand with fire, have envy, burn."

163

"don't you let us be hunted down": This is *mawi kojiralajob'isaj*, "not incom-plete-us-you-hunt (or trap)-cause."

163

"female deer and female birds": "Female" is *xnam* here; FV gives *xnam* as "female deer," but in the present passage *xnam* appears as an adjective with both "deer" and "birds": *xnam kej, xnam tz'ikin.*

163

"deerskin bundles": Here and elsewhere this translates *k'ukej* [cuqueh], com-posed of *k'u-*, which refers to the act of covering or wrapping something when it serves as a verb stem (TC), and *kej*, "deer"; note the reference to "pelts of the deer" (*rismal ri kej*) two sentences earlier. Deerskins served as wrappings for

sacred bundles throughout Mesoamerica, and bundles often corresponded, as they do here, to particular gods.

164

"They belong to us already": This is a reference to the long-standing promise the tribes made in order to get fire, namely, that they would allow themselves to be "suckled"—that is, to have their hearts cut out (see p. 156).

164

they would then go to anoint the mouth of the stone of Tohil or Auilix with the blood of the deer or bird: In the eastern Quiché area today, the mouths of stones (now called *k'amawil* rather than *k'ab'awil* as here) are more commonly given drinks of distilled liquor than of blood, but the blood of sacrificed chickens is sometimes given in the area of Chichicastenango. Drinks of liquor are also put into the mouths of saints. Ideally the liquid offered should quickly disappear, as if actually swallowed by the stone or saint; in the words of the PV, "And the bloody drink was drunk by the gods."

164

stevia: This is *jolom okox,* literally "head of mushroom," but as Ximénez pointed out in his Spanish translation of the PV (1973:205), it is not a mushroom but rather an herb. It is named for the shape of its composite flower head, which consists of numerous tiny, closely spaced white blossoms, and is probably *Stevia serrata,* called "requesón" (after the resemblance of the flower head to a clump of cottage cheese) in Mexico (see Rzedowski and Equihua 1987). In Guatemalan Spanish it is called "pericón blanco" in order to distinguish it from ordinary pericón, a wild marigold whose flowers are yellow (see the notes to p. 163). Today, as in the PV, the burning of marigolds and stevia constitutes a more modest offering than copal incense (see Earle 1983:294, 297). In the present passage the two plants are mentioned in the standard yellow/white order of Quiché ritual discourse.

164

just the larva of the yellow jacket, the larva of the wasp, and the larva of the bee: Andrés Xiloj described these insects, the *wonon, sital,* and *aqaj,* as follows: "The *wonon* is large and striped yellow and black; there is honey in its hive, and it stings. The *sital* is bigger and has red stripes. Its bite is more serious than that of the *wonon;* it causes a large swelling and one could even die. It, too, has honey. The *aqaj* is small, a little bigger than a fly, and stings. It makes a nest, with thousands of *aqaj.* If one can get it down with a stick the *aqaj* stay up there, then one can get whatever pieces of honey there are."

165

"we only take stitches . . . when we ask for . . . our manhood": The interpretation of [chuc] as *ch'uq,* referring at least figuratively to the penis or foreskin (see the

308

notes to p. 157), is reinforced by the fact that *achijilal*, literally "manhood," is given by FT as a figure of speech for "virile member."

165

the mouths of the stones: Whatever the stones may have looked like, mouths are the only anatomical feature ever mentioned for them. Among the contemporary Quiché of the region around Santa Cruz del Quiché, the principal criterion for distinguishing a divine stone from an ordinary rock is the presence of a groove or opening that might serve as a mouth, to be anointed with liquor or (less often) with the blood of sacrificed poultry. It should be noted that the PV term for stones with mouths (and for the beings whose petrified bodies they are), *k'ab'awil* or "god," suggests, by way of sound play, *k'ab'a-* (DB, FT) or *k'ab'e-* (FV), "to be open-mouthed." But the word *k'ab'awil* is no longer used; instead, the terms for stones with mouths are *k'amawil,* "that which receives," and *iq',* which is also one of the twenty day names and an archaic word for "wind."

165

"Your right": This is *ikolb'al iwib',* in which *i-* is "you" and *iwib'* is "yourselves" (both plural familiar); DB gives *kolb'alib'* as "liberty." This is a reference to the agreement the tribes made to allow themselves to be sacrificed (see p. 156 and the next note).

165

the suckling: This is *ri tz'um;* some have taken it to be "pelt," but I translate it on the basis of *tz'umaj* [tzumah], "to suckle" (DB), and take it to be a further reference to the "suckling" (heart sacrifice) pledged by the tribes (see the previous note).

165

the place called Stagger: This name is *silisib';* DB has *silisab',* "sway, swing, stagger." In an earlier passage (p. 156) it was the location (left unnamed) where the tribes other than the Cakchiquels pledged themselves to be "suckled" (or to have their hearts cut out) by Tohil in exchange for fire.

165

the skull would be placed in the road: If the Quichés timed their attacks on their rivals in the same way as the lowland Classic Maya, they may have favored periods when Venus was the evening star (see Lounsbury 1982). The "road" onto which they rolled the head of a sacrifice victim may have been symbolic of the celestial path followed by Venus, and the head may have been thought of on the model of the severed heads that appeared as the evening-star Venus in the story of Hunahpu and Xbalanque and their fathers.

165

the tracks were merely those of animals: This is *kaqan* [cacan] *ri xa kipich,* "their tracks that just their feet," in which "feet" (*pich*) is specifically "the feet of quadrupeds" (FV).

166

dark and rainy: This is *q'eqal* [quecal] *jab',* literally "black rain," but referring (according to Andrés Xiloj) to a storm that is so intense that the sky gets very dark. This supports the notion that Tohil is a manifestation of Hurricane (see the notes to p. 65), who caused a "black rain" when he destroyed the wooden people.

166

misty and drizzly: This is *musmul jab',* "misty rain." Andrés Xiloj explained, "These are days when it doesn't rain strongly; instead the drops are small, little bits of water fall. It is *musmul.*"

166

they singled them out and cut them down: The MS has [echalamicat], in which the only certainty is *e,* "they." My reading is based on *chala,* "to pick out among many" (DB), and (following Edmonson 1971:192) *k'at,* "cut" (in the sense of "reap").

167

"choice": This is *cho'm* [chaom], "select" (FX, AG), and a "metaphor for beauty" (DB).

167

"radiate preciousness": This is *saqloq'oj* [zaclocoh], a combination of "light" (*saq*) and "valuable" or "precious" (*loq'oj*). Andrés Xiloj pictured the maidens as twelve to fifteen years old.

167

Lust Woman and *Wailing Woman:* These names are *xtaj* and *xpuch'* [xpuch], in which *x*- marks them as feminine. *Taj* is "to desire to do something" (FV) and, in the reduplicated form *tajij,* "to sin many times" (FV, FX); AG translates *puch'* with the Spanish term llorón (llorona in its feminine form), which refers to a person who cries a lot. This confirms my argument, made on other grounds (D. Tedlock 1993a:45–58, 242), that these women are the pre-Columbian predecessors of the figure known as La Llorona in the Hispanic folklore of Mesoamerica and the Southwest United States, who haunts rivers and baths and lures men to their deaths. The Title of the Lords of Totonicapán lists a third woman (thus making three women for the three gods), whose full name is *k'ib'atz'un ja*

(TT), in which *ja* is "house" (referring to her lineage), while *k'i* is "many" and *b'atz'un* seems to be a nominalized form of a verb stem for "marry" that appears as *b'atz'o-* in FV, yielding "often married."

167

on their hands and knees: This is *chakachaxinaq* [chacachaxinac], with passive and perfect suffixes (-*xinaq*); DB has *chakachotik*, "go on all fours."

168

Tohil and the others: Here and elsewhere in this episode I have supplied "and the others"; the name Tohil is often used to mean all three gods and may be accompanied by a verb that is marked for a plural subject.

168

" '*there must come a sign as to whether you really saw their faces*' ": Note that when Blood Moon went before the head of One Hunahpu, he gave her a "sign" by spitting in her hand, which made her pregnant (p. 99); in this case the signs will be quite different, intended not for the women but for their fathers.

169

they spotted: This is *xil kiwach*, in which *x-* is complete and *ki-* is "they"; DB has *ilawachij*, "to look with attention."

169

on a smooth surface: This is *chiyulinik wach*, "on-smooth its-face"; DB has *yulunik*, "a smooth thing." The designs were on "the inside" (*upam*) of the cloaks, and it was this side that went next to the body of the lord who was then stung by wasps, despite the "smooth surface."

169

He turned around: The verb stem here is *solowik;* DB has *sololik*, "to give turns."

169

unfurling it: This is *katzonon uq'uxik* [ucuxic], literally "he-undresses his-being-covered"; DB gives *tzonolik* as "undressed." I take it that this lord opened up his cloak so that everyone could see the eagle on the inside of it.

169

It then became the profession of Lust Woman and Wailing Woman to bark shins: "Bark shins" is my translation of *joxol ch'eq* [chec], based on the comments of Andrés Xiloj: "*Ch'eq* is the shin bone. *Joxol* is 'one who wounds.' It is the wound that they [the girls] gave them. A girl or a boy comes to know how the world is [laughs]. Let's suppose we are now old people. We can deceive a girl of fifteen or sixteen years, and there is the wound. The violence. And so a woman can deceive a boy of fifteen or fourteen years, then there it is. The old woman wounded the boy [laughs]. This is *joxol ch'eq,* 'the wounder of shins.' Only now we say *xuporo raqan,* 'she burned his legs.' "

170

those spirit boys: I have supplied "spirit" to make it clearer that the reference is to Tohil, Auilix, and Hacauitz.

170

their fortress: Ximénez translates *katem* as "fortification" here; DB gives *katej* as "to block passage."

171

Their eyebrows were plucked out, along with their beards: The "plucking" here is *mich'* [mich], which is elsewhere a metaphor for deception; this time plucking carries both its literal and metaphorical meanings.

171

made a fence: The "fence" is *k'oxtun* [coxtun]; TC has *k'oxtum,* "fence or wall." In the next paragraph I translate this same word as "parapet" on the basis of context.

171

They just made a palisade of planks and stakes: The materials for this structure are *tz'alam* [tzalam], glossed as "board" by TC and AG, and *ch'ut* [chut], glossed as "sharp point" by AG. The verb for the making of the palisade is *kejb'ej;* DB has *kejom che',* "palisaded." This was definitely not stonework.

171

around their citadel: This is *rij kitinamit,* which is misleading when translated literally as "its-back their-citadel." *Rij,* when applied to a house, means the side or sides that face the outside world, whereas *uwach,* "its-face," means the side or sides that face the patio; I assume that the same scheme was analogously applied to a citadel. That is to say, a citadel turned its "back" to the outside world and its "face" inward. This interpretation is confirmed by the entry for *kotoj chirij tinamit* in DB, literally "surround at-its-back citadel" but glossed (following European reckoning) as the "face of a fortress."

171

They surrounded the citadel: The verb stem here is *kotkomij,* a reduplicated form meaning "surround" (DB).

172

eight hundred score, . . . thirty times eight hundred: This is my attempt to translate Mayan numbers into English without completely converting them from the vigesimal system to the decimal one; "score" in English is of course a remnant of vigesimal reckoning. The numbers in the text are *kachui* and *oxchui,* "2 × 8,000" and "3 × 8,000," 8,000 being the third power of 20 and filling the same place in a vigesimal system that 1,000 fills in a decimal system.

172

they just enjoyed the spectacle: The verb stem here is *kai-,* "to watch admiringly, like watching dances" (listed under [cai3] in DB).

173

their legs, their arms: As Andrés Xiloj pointed out, this is an idiom meaning "all over their bodies."

173

they were doubling over . . . stumbling: The first verb stem here is *won-;* DB has *wonob'a rib',* "to double over as if to join the knees with the beard." The second is *lajajik,* a reduplicated form; DB has *lajab',* "snare."

173

they were hit: The verb stem here is [cac]; DB has *kaq'o,* "hit with stones."

173

Now some of them turned away: "Some of" translates *chajkar;* see the earlier note headed "some of the people" (p. 306).

173

gasping for breath: This is *kejilowik kepolow,* probably an idiom for heavy or laborious breathing; DB has *jilowik,* "sigh of tiredness," and *polow,* "breath."

174

Noble: Many of the names of Quiché lords, beginning with the sons of those who received the emblems of lordship at Tulan Zuyua but becoming rarer in later generations, carry the prefix *k'o-* [co-]; the corrected form is from TT and TY. This appears to be a shortening of expressions described by TC as acknowledgments of great authority, such as *k'o rab', ruxlab',* "it is (or there is) his breath, his spirit" (referring to descent in its sense as a source of life), and *k'o aq'ij, k'o awalaxik,* "it is your day, it is your birth" (referring to destiny and descent). The name Noble Two is *k'okib'* [cocaib], while Noble Raiment is *k'okawib',* in which *kawib'* is "adornment" (FV).

313

174

"our own tribal place": This could be all the way back at the place where they were before arriving at Tulan Zuyua.

174

"Again it is the time of our Lord Deer, as is reflected in the sky": "It is the time" translates *cholan,* "order" (in the sense of sequence). Deer (*kej*) is a day name from the 260-day calendar, connected to recurring events in the sky only in its role as one of the four days that can begin a new year. Any day can be addressed as "Lord" in contemporary ritual language, but only these four are commonly addressed without specifying a day number, as "Lord Deer" is here.

174

"Go see the place where we came from": Given that Jaguar Quitze and the others have already said that they themselves are going to "our own tribal place," it is difficult to interpret their instructions to their sons. Perhaps the answer is that the fathers are going in spirit, whereas their sons will make a pilgrimage in the flesh. Also, the sons will not go until sometime later. In any case, the irreducible difference between the journey of the fathers and that later undertaken by the sons is that the fathers are never seen again.

174

"for making requests": This is *ta'nab'al* [tanabal], "asking-instrument." Andrés Xiloj remarked, "It's like a place to burn offerings. But this word is only used for places that are open to the public, not for shrines that only a mother-father [patrilineage head] can visit."

174

"fiery splendor": This translates *q'aq'al,* "fire-ness" or "hot-ness," a frequent metaphor for the glories and splendors of lordly dominance over others.

175

downtrodden: This is [yocotahinac]; DB has *yoq'o,* "step on."

175

All those on Hacauitz: This phrase has been supplied in order to distinguish the inhabitants of the citadel of Hacauitz from the "broken and downtrodden" tribes.

175

the day of the bundle: This may have been the day named Deer, mentioned by the departing Quiché ancestors on the same occasion as the presentation of the bundle. Today this day is associated, above all others, with mother-fathers, the priest-shamans who perform rites for lineages, cantons, or an entire town (according to their rank). All mother-fathers, as well as the ordinary daykeepers who rank just below them, possess a sacred bundle, but this bundle contains divining paraphernalia and is opened frequently.

PART FIVE

179

who represented all the Cauecs: This is *rech ronojel kawikib'*, literally "of (or belonging to) all the Cauecs." There are similar phrases in the sentences dealing with the Greathouses and Lord Quichés in this same passage.

179

Nacxit: This name is from a Nahua source; its component parts in Nahuatl proper are *naui*, "four," and *icxitl*, "foot" (RS). In Nahuatl texts this is a title held by the king named Quetzalcoatl; in the Book of Chilam Balam of Chumayel, a lord named Nacxit Xuchit is mentioned in connection with events that sound like part of the legend of Quetzalcoatl (Roys 1967:83). Nacxit's "populous domain," as it is called in the PV, was probably a kingdom in Yucatán ruled by a lineage claiming Toltec descent.

179

judge: This is *q'atol* [catol] *tzij*, at present *q'atal tzij* (MX) or *q'atb'al tzij* (AG), "reap-instrument [of] words."

179

Keeper of the Mat and the Keeper of the Reception House Mat: These titles are *ajpop* and *ajpop k'amja* [camha]; the corrected form *k'amja* appears in TV, while PG and FV list the Cakchiquel synonym as *k'amajay*. *Aj-* is occupational and *pop* is mat, a woven mat being a metonym for a council (whose members sat on a mat or mats) and probably, at the same time, a metaphor for a council (whose members might have been thought of as being interwoven like a mat or as serving to interweave those whom they represented). *K'amja* combines *k'am-*, "receive," with *ja*, "house." The Yucatec equivalent, *k'am na*, is still in use today as a term for a guest house or inn (AB). Among the functions of the Keeper of the Reception House Mat was the collection of tribute; Don Juan Cortés, the last known holder of this title, went all the way to Spain in 1557 in an attempt to restore the right of the Quiché lords to collect tribute (Carrasco 1967).

179

emblems of lordship: These are *uwachinel rajawarem*, literally "the means of showing one's having become lord."

Here are their names: The canopy and throne are *muj* and *q'alib'al;* the Keeper of the Mat was entitled to sit beneath four canopies, with three for the Keeper of the Reception House Mat, two for the Lord Minister, and one for the Herald (Carmack 1981:169). The bone flute and bird whistle are *sub'aq* and *ch'amch'am* [chamcham]; the latter word is a reduplicated form related to *ch'anin,* referring to the trilling and warbling of birds (FV), and may refer to a clay ocarina. The sparkling powder is *tatil,* given in DB as *titil,* "bright powder," while the yellow ocher is *q'anab'aj* [canabah], "yellow stone"; *titil* and *q'ana ab'aj* are both listed by TC as cosmetics formerly used by persons who were being installed in lordships. The paws are *tz'ikwil* [tzicuil]; FV gives *tz'ik* as "heel of hand." The leather armband is *makutax,* from a Nahua source; in Nahuatl proper *macuetlax-tli* is "arm band made of leather" (RS). The snail-shell rattle is *t'ot'* [tot] *tatam,* in which *t'ot'* is "snail" (AG) and *tatam* may be related to *tota'nik,* "shake" (MX). The tobacco gourd is *k'us b'us,* from Yucatec *k'us,* "tobacco" (AB, listed as a variant of *k'uts*), and *bux,* "small wild gourd for keeping ground tobacco" (AB). The food bowl is *kaxkon,* from a Nahua source, with *caxcomulli* meaning "bowl (for eating)" in Nahuatl proper (AM). The parrot feathers, following Recinos et al. (1950:209n), are *chiyom,* but in Kekchí *chion* is a "certain small bird" (EH) that may not be a parrot. The egret feathers are *astapulul,* which is Nahua again; *aztatl* is the Nahuatl term for *Egretta thula,* the snowy egret (BS).

Then, from beside the sea, they brought back the writing of Tulan, the writing of Zuyua. They spoke of their investiture in their signs, in their words: In the following version of the text of this passage, routine emendations have been made to change [xquicam] to *xkik'am,* [chaca] to *ch'aqa,* [utzibal] to *utz'ib'al,* and [oquinac] to *okinaq.* The passage is arranged to call attention to two pairs of noun phrases (one pair in each of the indented lines), neither of which makes sense unless we assume a scribal error and supply the missing words marked here by ⟨ ⟩:

> *Ta xkik'am ula ri ch'aqa palo*
> *utz'ib'al tulan, utz'ib'al ⟨suywa⟩.*
> *Xech'a chire ki okinaq*
> *chupan ⟨ketal⟩, chupan kitzij.*

> Then, from beside the sea, they brought back
> the writing of Tulan, the writing of ⟨Zuyua⟩.
> They spoke of their investiture
> in ⟨their signs⟩, in their words.

The first of the supplied words is a place name parallel to Tulan, following the second of two occurrences of *utz'ib'al;* judging from other PV contexts, the name in question could only be Zuyua. This reading is supported by a reference to *utz'ib'al sewan* in the Title of the Lords of Totonicapán (Carmack and Mondloch 1983a:68–69), where *sewan* consistently takes the place of *suywa* in the PV. The second supplied word is a possessed noun parallel to *kitzij,* "their words," following the first of two occurrences of *chupan.* The only possibility offered by other PV contexts is *ketal,* "their signs," which in this context would refer to the characters of the writing of Tulan. "Investiture" translates *okinaq,* literally "that which has already entered"; FV glosses *okenaq jay* (in which *jay* is "house") as "respected house, such as a convent or the house of a mayor or leader." It should be noted that Nacxit, who performed the investiture, was at an unnamed place other than Tulan, which had been abandoned by this time.

180

they examined: This is *xeiko chiri chuwi,* literally "they passed there above," but Andrés Xiloj read it as an idiom meaning "to look over."

180

the divisions of Thorny Place: The ruins of this place, known today as Cauinal, are organized around four separate plazas, each of which was probably the center of one of the four divisions listed here (Ichon 1983:240–41). Two plazas are located on one side of the Río Calá or Blanco and two on the other, a short distance upstream from its confluence with the Río Negro or Chixoy, about twenty kilometers northwest of Rabinal. The name *chik'ix* [chiquix] or "Thorny Place" refers to the thorny scrub vegetation of this area. The division translated as "Boundary Marker" is *k'ulb'a* [culba], from *k'ulb'at,* referring to anything (including a natural feature) that may mark a boundary between properties or towns (FV). The division that gives the site its present-day name, translated here as "Stronghold," is *kawinal,* from *kawij* [kauh], "prepare, arm" (DB); in Kekchí *kawil* is "strong, hard" (EH), equivalent to Quiché *kowil,* whose meanings include "fortress" (DB).

181

But their faces did not die: This is *mana xukam kiwach,* translated almost literally. It alludes to the lecture given to Blood Moon by the skull of One Hunahpu, in which it is stated, "Neither dimmed nor destroyed is the face of a lord" (p. 99).

181

pain and affliction: This is *k'axk'ol* [caxcol] *rail,* translated on the basis of entries in DB, where the two words are treated as synonyms, and on the basis of the entry for *k'axk'ol* in AG.

317

181

They ground their gypsum, their plaster: This seems to be a metonym for major construction. It may not mean that previous Quiché sites lacked gypsum plaster, but in the present context it combines with such phrases as "excellent citadel," "the root of fiery splendor," and "lords of singular genius" to indicate that the building of Bearded Place represented a whole new level in the rise of the Quiché lords.

181

Noble Rooftree: This is *k'onache'*, in which *k'o-* is honorific and the rest suggests *xna' che'*, literally "mother tree," the Kekchí term for a rooftree (EH). In a later passage this lord is called Jaguar Noble Rooftree. According to the Title of the Lords of Totonicapán (Chonay and Goetz 1953:176–77), he was the son of Noble Two's wife and Noble Raiment (Noble Two's brother), conceived while Noble Two was on his pilgrimage to Nacxit. On his return, Noble Two signaled his adoption of this child as his own successor by naming him Jaguar Noble Rooftree, a doubly glorious appellation but one that nevertheless seems to allude (by way of "mother tree") to his unusual origin. After Jaguar Noble Rooftree's death his descendants, beginning with his son Iztayul, were shifted to the second-ranking lordship, supplying Keepers of the Reception House Mat, while the first-ranking title of Keeper of the Mat reverted to the direct descendants of Noble Two.

181

Minister: This is *q'alel*, in which *q'alel* may be from *q'alunel*, "one who holds something in his arms."

181

Iztayul: This name, elsewhere spelled [ztayul] or [xtayub], is from a Nahua source; in Nahuatl proper *iztayo* is "salty" and *iztayotl* is "brine" (RS).

181

one in each: This is my interpolation.

181

Shield Dance: This is simply called *pokob'*, "shield"; it is identified as "an ancient dance" by DB.

181

their desire that the Lord Noble Sweatbath be murdered: According to the Title of the Lords of Totonicapán (Chonay and Goetz 1953:186–87), the plotters first attempted to turn Noble Sweatbath and Iztayul against each other by telling each of them falsehoods about what the other had been saying about him. When this scheme was uncovered they attempted to assassinate Noble Sweatbath in his sweatbath, but he got wind of this and was well guarded when the assassins arrived. Whether he received his name from this incident or his name inspired the sweatbath plot, it is the only name that remains for him. A plot of the same kind is mentioned in the drama known as Rabinal Achi. A warrior named only as Man of Quiché makes the following confession to his captor, a warrior in the service of Lord Five Toh of Rabinal (Quiché text in Brasseur 1862:68; translation mine):

> I myself made the mistake, I came to lure him out,
> your lord, sir, your liege, sir,
> there at Bathing Place, as it is called,
> even though bathing was his only concern.

181

and that the other lord be allied with them: This is *xa k'u* [cu] *jun ajaw xraj ku'* [cu] *kib'*, "just then one (other) lord was-wanted to-keep themselves," in which the translation of *ku'* as "allied" is based on DB. The lord in question here is Iztayul, as the next sentence makes clear; in the present sentence he is being distinguished from Noble Sweatbath.

181

the Ilocs wanted him as their disciple: This is *xraj tijox kumal ilokab'*, "was-wanted disciple by-them Ilocs"; DB glosses *tijoxel* as "disciple."

182

First they invaded the citadel: This is *xkokib'ej nab'e tinamit*, literally "they-entered first citadel"; DB glosses *okib'ej tinamit* as "scale a fortress."

182

This was in payment: The "payment" is *tojb'al*, "pay-instrument," which in this context is a sound play on Tohil, the principal god before whom the Ilocs were sacrificed, and on the day name *Toj*, which was the day of Tohil. This day is still interpreted by diviners as having to do with the payment of debts; in making this interpretation they utilize a sound play on the day name similar to the one used here, moving from *Toj* as a proper name to the verb *tojonik*, "pay" (see B. Tedlock 1992:155).

182

the canyon and the citadel: This is the first of a number of joint appearances of *siwan*, "canyon," and *tinamit*, "citadel"; taken together, they seem to encompass both a citadel proper, in the sense of a high, fortified place with temples and palaces, and what lies around or below that citadel as well. The effect is to extend the sense of settlement or community beyond its fortified core, with temples and palaces, to the surrounding population, creating a compound concept meaning something like "town" or "city." T. J. Knab (personal communication) suggests that this expression might be the Quiché equivalent *altepetl*, the Nahuatl term for town or city, which also involves a juxtaposition of the low with the high; it is compounded of *al* (from *atl*) "water," and *tepetl*, "mountain" (AM). The Quiché also use a water-mountain pairing, but it is applied not to towns but to outdoor shrines, which (ideally) exist in low-high pairs (see B. Tedlock 1992:76, 80).

183

lords of singular genius: "Singular" is *jumaj;* DB has *junaj,* "make oneself unique."

183

nothing happened to make fools of them or to ruin the greatness of their reign: "To make fools" translates *alachinaq;* DB has *alachinik,* "joke." "Or to ruin the greatness" translates *xawi b'anol rech nimal,* in which *xawi* indicates "the same as the aforesaid" and links this clause to the negative one preceding it, while *b'anol* is translated "to ruin" on the basis of *b'anoj,* "disaster" (FV).

183

the blossoming of their daughters: The verb stem here is *si'j,* a form that means "flower" as a noun (MX).

183

ate their corn: The verb here is *wech,* which refers specifically to the eating of foods made of corn, and what I have translated "corn" is *wa,* which refers to these same things, primarily to tamales (which are often made of nothing but corn dough in Guatemala).

183

"our way of being thankful and grateful": The former is *k'amowab'al* [camouabal], "thanks-instrument," and the latter is [pacubal]; DB has *paq'uj,* "be thankful for."

183

allied tribes . . . principalities: See the notes to p. 149 for a discussion of these terms.

183

Rotten Cane: This name is *q'umaraq aj* [cumaracaah], "rotten-plural caneplant."

183

The Lords Noble Sweatbath and Plumed Serpent: The Lord Noble Sweatbath mentioned here is probably not the one who ruled as Keeper of the Mat at Bearded Place, but the one who is mentioned in a number of places as the Keeper of the Reception House Mat who ruled with Plumed Serpent when the latter was Keeper of the Mat (pp. 183, 186, 192). In yet another passage it is stated that Plumed Serpent served as both Keeper of the Mat and Keeper of the Reception House Mat (p. 186); perhaps Noble Sweatbath died during the reign of Plumed Serpent and was not replaced until after the latter's death. However that might be, Plumed Serpent and Noble Sweatbath are jointly credited with founding Rotten Cane, and both of them are treated as lords of genius —that is, as lords with powerful spirit familiars. The Title of the Lords of Totonicapán devotes much attention to Noble Sweatbath but omits any mention of Plumed Serpent.

183

There had been five changes and five generations: This is *xrokexok xrolea puch,* in which *x-* is complete, *ro-* is "five," and *puch* is "and." The rest is translated on the basis of *k'exo* [quexo], "change, return," and *le,* "generation" (DB).

184

their separation, when they quarreled among themselves, disturbing the bones and skulls of the dead: The scribe got into a tangle here, writing as follows (the items in parentheses were written in the margin with their places of insertion marked by daggers): [quihachouic quib ta xqui (tzolbeh quib) tzol (cacbeh) bac uholom caminac xquicacbeh quib]. The only way I can make sense of this is to assume that the scribe meant to cross out the final [xquicacbeh quib] and move it (except for [xqui-]) to a position immediately following the dangling [xqui] he had already written, and to insert a missing [beh] after [tzol]. In the process he unnecessarily repeated [tzol] before [-beh] and then inverted the order of [cac-beh] and [tzolbeh], meanwhile forgetting to cross out the final [xquicacbeh quib]. If I am right, the passage (complete with phonetic emendations) would read, *kijachowik kib' ta xkikaqb'ej kib' tzolb'ej baq ujolom kaminaq,* "their-sorting-out themselves when they-quarreled themselves turning-over bone its-head dead-person."

184

the lord bishop: This is [Sr. obicpo], the first Spanish to appear in the text since p. 63. The person referred to here is Francisco Marroquín, who blessed the ruins of Rotten Cane in 1539, fifteen years after the place had been taken by Pedro de Alvarado.

the Zaquics: This is *saqikib'* [zaquiquib], singular *saqik;* the corrected form is from TT. According to the Title of the Lords of Totonicapán, the founder of this lineage was *ajaw saqik tz'utuja,* who took the place of Dark Jaguar when he died childless and thus kept the number of ruling Quiché lineages at four (Carmack and Mondloch 1983a:189). According to the PV (see p. 185), *ajaw tz'utuja* [tzutuha] or "Lord Corntassel House" was the title of the Zaquic lord who headed one of the two great houses into which the Zaquic lineage was divided. The name *tz'utuja* suggests that this lineage may have had its origin among the Tzutuhil (*tz'utujil*) Maya, who occupy the area around the southern half of Lake Atitlán.

Master of Ceremonies: This title is *nim chokoj,* in which *nim* means "principal"; *chokoj* refers to banquets, weddings, or wedding banquets (FX), while the verb *chokola'* or *chokola'j* refers to doing something in common (TC) or, more specifically, to gathering food and drink that will be shared at a banquet (FX, PG), the most important item being cacao for the making of a drink (FV). Whichever way the borrowing may have gone, there is an obvious relationship between *chokola'* and Nahuatl *chocolatl,* the immediate source of Spanish (and then English) chocolate. Today, cacao remains a key item among the gifts the family of a Quiché groom brings to the banquet at the bride's house.

Councilor of the Stores: This title is *popol winaq* [uinac] *chituy,* "council person at-stack"; in DB, *tuyub'a* is "put one thing on top of another."

Quehnay Emissary: This title is *lolmet kejnay;* PG and TC have *lolmay,* "he who is sent on business, ambassador." Each of the three ruling Quiché lineages had a lord whose title included *lolmet.*

Councilor in the Ball Court: This title combines *popol winaq* [uinac], "council person," with *pa jom tzalatz,* in which *jom* means "ball court" all by itself, and *tzalatz,* which refers to things on a tilt (FX, AG), seems to be added to specify a ball court that has sloping masonry sides.

And now to show their faces: This is *k'ate* [cate] *chik chiwachin uwach,* "next now that-show his-face," singular in Quiché in order to agree with "each of them" in the previous sentence. The notion of "face" is intimately tied up with personal identity in Quiché; a person's day of birth, for example, is called *uwach uq'ij,* "its-face his/her-day," and a number of Quiché lords were named after the days of their birth (see pp. 195–96). A later passage mentioning the "faces" of lords precedes a list of the names of individual lords (p. 194). I have put an ellipsis following both of these mentions of faces to indicate that graphic elements might be missing here, something that was in the manuscript Ximénez discovered but which he did not reproduce. If that manuscript was like the Book of Chilam Balam of Maní, there may have been a graphic device, at least partially based on hieroglyphic writing, corresponding to each lord. In the Maní book the device is a line drawing of a face with a European crown, a latter-day version of the much more stylized face that composes the glyph meaning *ajaw* or "lord," but the individual name of each lord is written in block letters on a scroll beneath the head rather than rendered hieroglyphically (Craine and Reindorp 1979:79–86).

185

Lord Herald: Here and elsewhere, "Herald" translates *ajtzik' winaq* [ahtzic uinac], given as *ajtzij* [atzih] *winaq* in TT. *Aj-* is occupational and *winaq* is "person." One way or another, the rest of this title has to do with the act of speaking: *tzik* is "to count" in Chol (AA); in Quiché and Cakchiquel, *sik'* is "to call out" (including reading aloud), *ajsik'* is "town crier" (PG, FX), and *tzij* is "word" or (as a verb stem) "to put into words."

185

Yacolatam, meaning the "corner of the mat" or the zaclatol: This passage reads *yakolatam, utzam pop saklatol,* but the title proper, given by itself in a later passage (p. 197), is simply Yacolatam, and the rest is offered as an explication. The only Quiché words here, *utzam pop* or "corner of the mat," are offered as a gloss on *yakolatam,* a word from a Nahua source; in Nahuatl proper *yacatl* is "point," while *tam-* or *tan-* figures in various terms for objects made of such materials as corn husks and palm leaves (AM). The word *zaclatol,* offered as a further explanation, looks like a combination of Nahuatl *zacatl* or "straw" with *tollin* or "cattail," the plant whose leaves go into the weaving of the mats called *pop* in Mayan languages.

186

a crowded life, crowded with petitions: "Crowded" translates *molomox,* a passive form of *molomanik,* "many join together" (DB). "Petitions" translates *utab'al tzij,* in which *tab'a* is "supplicate" (DB) and *tzij* is "words."

186

The birthdays: This is *uq'ij* [uquih] *ralaxik,* "its-day his-being-born," the phrase still used for "birthday."

186

On one occasion: This is [hu uuc], a phrase most translators have taken to mean "one seven" (literally) and "seven days" (idiomatically). But "seven" should be *wuqub',* and there is nothing in colonial dictionaries of Quichean languages that would allow for its combination with *ju.* The solution I offer is based on considerations of context and on *wuq'ul,* which refers to pauses or interruptions in the normal course of events (FV); I take the present phrase to be *ju wuq'* and to mean something like "during one interval," or (idiomatically) "one time" or "on one occasion."

186

serpentine. . . . aquiline . . . feline: At some moments the claim is made that Plumed Serpent became an "actual" (*kitzij*) serpent (*kumatz*) or eagle (*kot*) or jaguar (*b'alam*), but at other moments it would seem that he took on the *qualities* of these animals. Wherever I translate with words ending in -ine, the MS has *kumatzil, kotal,* or *b'alamil,* each of which has a suffix meaning "having the quality of."

186

The news spread: This is *xpaxin rib' utaik,* "it-scattered itself its-being-heard."

186

he became the sole head: "Sole" here is [huquizic]; FV has *juk'isik,* "only."

187

Tepepul: This name is from a Nahua source; in Nahuatl proper *tepetl* is "mountain" and *pul* is "big" (RS).

187

Quicab: This name appears in TT as *k'iqab'* and in TY as *k'iq'ab';* it would seem to be composed of *k'i-,* "many," and *q'ab',* "hand" or "arm."

187

Caoques: The correct form of this name, which is [caoqueb] in the MS, may be *kawqeb'* or *kawuqeb',* from the day name *Kawuq* ([cao3] in FX); *-eb'* is a plural suffix. Immediately west of Guatemala City are two towns very close together named Santiago Cauqué and Santa María Cauqué (Palma 1991:107); officially, the name Cauqué has been replaced in both cases with Sacatepéquez, the name of the department in which these towns are located.

188

White Earths: This tribal name, which refers to the Mam Maya, is *saqulewab'* [zaculeuab], "white-earth-plural," formed by adding a plural suffix to *saqulew*

(Zaculeu or Saculeu on maps), the principal Mam citadel. Its ruins are five kilometers west of the present town of Huehuetenango.

188

Under Ten: This is a literal translation of *xelajuj;* the full name of the town, not given in the PV, is *xelajuj kej,* "Under Ten Deer," Ten Deer being a nearby mountain that takes its name from a date on the divinatory calendar. The town is still called Xelajú (or Xela) in everyday Guatemalan speech, whether in Spanish or in Mayan languages, but in government documents and on maps it is known as Quetzaltenango, a Nahuatl name meaning "quetzal citadel." Its former location, when it was truly a citadel, was on one of the hilltops in the vicinity of the present town, but the exact site is not known.

188

went down on their faces or flat on their backs: This is [xuleic, xpacaic]; FV has *xul,* "turn downward," and MX has *pak'alik,* "face up."

188

Their lineages came to be bled, shot full of arrows at the stake: This is *xeok chinamit xelotzik xek'aqik* [xecacquic] *chiche'* [chiche], in which *xeok* is literally "they-entered" but idiomatically "it was their time," and *chiche'* is "at-tree" or "at-pole." In *xelotzik, xe-* is "complete-they"; DB and FV have *lotzo,* "to let blood." The verb stem *k'aq-* has been emended on the basis *k'aqoj,* "shoot with an arrow" (TC). *Xek'aqik* (with a passive suffix) is translated "they were shot with arrows" by Ximénez; DB has *k'aqokej* [cacoqueh] (with an active suffix), "hunt with arrows." This passage confirms that Quiché rituals included arrow sacrifice.

188

Projectiles alone were the means for breaking the citadels: The weapon here is *ch'a* (sometimes *ch'ab'*), "arrow" and (judging from FV) the spear thrown by an atlatl (spear-thrower). *Ch'a* or *ch'ab'* is distinct from *cha* or *cha',* which is the term for any lithic projectile point or cutting instrument and (today) for glass (see *ch'a* and *cha'* in FV, [chab] and *cha* in DB, and *ch'ab'* and *cha* in MX). In Mixtec codices, towns (or citadels) are identified by place signs whose basic element is a mountain; the conquest of a town is signified by showing its place sign pierced with a projectile (Smith 1973:33 and fig. 51). The present passage sounds like a literal reading of a codex of this style, or else such codices represented a ritual practice in which the very earth or native stone of a conquered citadel was actually pierced or broken. Whatever the case with codices, people from the towns conquered by the Quiché came to Petatayub, "carrying in their hands the signs of the citadels," which "look as though they had been split with an axe."

188

one . . . after another: This is *libaj chi,* given by DB as "step by step."

188

the gum tree: I follow Edmonson in reading [col che] as *q'ol che',* "gum tree" (Edmonson 1971:236), rather than as a place named "Colche," partly because the name of the place discussed in this passage is otherwise accounted for.

188

carrying in their hands: This is [chelah]; MX has *ch'elenik,* "to carry with the hands."

188

cut stones: I have supplied "stones" here, assuming that they are still the subject of the discussion; "cut" translates *xq'atatajik* [xcatatahic], "complete-cut-result-passive." Reading the verb stem as *q'ata,* "cut," fits with *xchoy chi ikaj,* "split with an axe," later on in this same sentence, and with the general sense of the paragraph up to this point.

188

Petatayub: This name is from a Nahua source; in Nahuatl proper *petlatl* is "mat" and *ayutl* is "turtle" (AM). The place in question should be in the vicinity of the town of Tecún Umán, formerly known as Ayutla, on the Pacific coastal plain near the Mexican border (Recinos et al. 1950:221–22n). It is known from the Title of the Lords of Totonicapán that the conquests of Quicab reached that far (Carmack and Mondloch 1983a:200, 264).

188

"and like doubles for our own lineages": This is [quehe pu cacachinamit], which I read as *keje pu qakakab' chinamit,* "like and our-pair lineages."

189

"send for us to come and kill them": Here the text has both *nu,* first person singular, and *qa* [ca], first person plural. It reads [chulibiih chibe nu ca camizah], in which [ca] is written somewhat above the line, just after *nu;* for this reason, and because the statement quoted here is attributed to three people, I take *nu* to be an error the scribe forgot to cross out when he added [ca].

189

Point of the Arrow, Angle of the Bowstring: This is *uchi' ch'a, uchi' k'a'm* [uchi 4ha, uchi cam], "its mouth arrow, its mouth cord." Andrés Xiloj pointed out that in Quiché the "mouth" of an arrow is its tip, while the "mouth" of a bowstring is the point at which the butt end of the arrow is pulled back against it.

189

nor did any of them have his own god: That is to say, those who were sent to occupy the conquered citadels did not have stone gods (*k'ab'awil*) of the kind that were brought from Tulan Zuyua. We do not know whether the previous lords of these citadels had such stones or what might have been the fate of their stones. It is interesting to note that the present-day term *k'amawil,* which covers large stones found in outdoor shrines, is used only in the region around the ruins of Rotten Cane. Shrines in the western Quiché area lack such stones, and the small stone objects collected for household altars are called by a different term, *meb'il.*

189

Mirror Side: This name is *chulimal,* in which *chu-* is probably shortened from *chuwa-,* "in front of," signaling that the place in question is named for a separate place that lies nearby; the final *-l* turns the name of that nearby place into an adjective. That leaves *lima,* which in all probability has its origin in *lemowa'* or "Mirror Water," the name of a lake that in fact lies a short distance to the west of *chulimal,* which is itself the northernmost rural district of the present-day town of Chichicastenango.

189

Meteor: This is [cabicac] in the text column of the MS but [chabicac] in the translation column, the latter being an approximation of *ch'ab'iq'aq',* literally "arrow fire." A comet, by contrast, is *uje ch'umil,* "star's tail."

189

Among the Rocks: This is *xoy* (or *xay*) *ab'aj,* a name derived by FX from *xol ab'aj,* "among the rocks."

190

"the ennobling of the lookout lineages": The "ennobling" is *keqalem* [quecalem], in which *k-* is "their"; DB glosses [ecalem] as "dignity" or "nobility." In its literal sense the root *eqa-* has to do with taking a load on the shoulders; it is used today in various expressions having to do with taking on responsibilities, such as those of mother-fathers for people they train as daykeepers, or those of daykeepers for the clients they are currently praying for. Eventually, members of these newly ennobled lineages staged a revolt against Quicab, who survived an assassination attempt but lost much of his power (Carmack 1981:136–37).

190

"we'll induct": This is *qachapa* [cachapa], literally "we-take-hold-of," but FV notes that *chapa* is also an idiom for "putting into lordship."

190

"which is mine . . . which is yours": This translates *we,* "of mine," and *awe,* "of yours (singular familiar)"; others have missed the sense of this sentence, trying to make these two pronouns agree; Edmonson has [ui] for the [ue] of the MS (Edmonson 1971:240).

190

in concord: This is *junam wach* (elsewhere *junamaj wach*), given in DB as "be in concord."

190

Under the Twine, Under the Cord: This is *xeb'alax, xek'a'maq* [xecamac], in which *xe-* is "under"; *b'alax* is a passive form of *b'al,* "to make or twist a cord" (FV); and *k'a'maq* is a perfect form of *k'a'maj,* "to cord (measure land with a cord)." In other words, this mountain is named for the fact that a boundary passes over it. In the next sentence, "at the boundary of Mirror Side" translates *chiri chulimal,* literally, "at the Mirror Side." The reference is to the boundary between the lands that were ruled directly by the Quiché lords at Rotten Cane and the lands of their vassals at Mirror Side. To this day, Mirror Side (*chulimal*) lies just outside the lands of Santa Cruz del Quiché, the colonial town that was founded to replace Rotten Cane. That the heads of vassal lineages should be elevated to lordship in a peripheral location rather than within the citadel itself would seem to befit their collective status as a human "palisade," ultimately guarding the larger boundary that encloses the entire kingdom.

191

Military Walls, and Military Corners: This is *rajtz'alam* [rahtzalam] *achij, utza'm* [utzam] *achij,* "its-keeper-wall soldier, its-corner (or angle) soldier." *Tz'alam* is "wall" in FV, while other sources give "plank"; the "walls" and "corners" here are undoubtedly those of a stockade. These positions seem analogous to the "sides" and "corners" of the sky-earth, suggesting that a fortified town was seen as a microcosm. The statement that the holders of these and the other newly created titles formed "a fortress around Quiché" suggests that the entire kingdom was conceived as a gigantic fortress, an enlargement of the citadel at its center.

191

Great Monument of Tohil: The term translated as monument is *tz'aq* [tzac], which refers to constructions whose major materials are earth, stone, or cement rather than wood. In the PV and other sixteenth-century documents, it refers to platform mounds or pyramids and to the houses or temples they support. It is not clear whether the Great Monument of Tohil housed the original Tohil stone brought from Tulan by Jaguar Quitze or whether that stone was left at Tohil's

Place and was represented by some secondary object in Rotten Cane. In today's ritual practice, one can use a shrine close at hand to summon up a deity whose proper residence is another and quite distant shrine. The diviners of El Palmar, a community whose founders emigrated from Momostenango, have named their local shrines after those of their parent town but address the shrines of Momostenango itself from a distance; they try to make a pilgrimage to the parent shrines once each 260 days (Saler 1976). In a like manner, the priest of Tohil at Rotten Cane might have addressed the mountain named Tohil's Place while he was actually on the pyramid of Tohil, making periodic pilgrimages to the mountain itself.

191

house of sacrifice: This is *kajb'aja,* which I take to be composed of *kajb',* "sacrifice" (see the notes to p. 149), and *ja,* "house." Some have taken *kajb'aja* to be a reference to the place called Sajcabajá today, but that is written [zacabaha] or [zaccabaha] in the MS and combines *ja* with *saqkab'a,* "plaster."

191

they nurtured and provided for the Keeper of the Mat and Keeper of the Reception House Mat: The gods are spoken of at various points as needing nurturers and providers (beginning on p. 65); the present passage means that the relationship between lords and vassals was conceived in the same terms as that between gods and humans. Note here that the text goes right on to emphasize the greatness of the lords under discussion.

192

everything they saw was clear to them: That is to say, they were able to recover the clairvoyance possessed by the first humans before "they were blinded as the face of a mirror is breathed upon" (p. 148).

192

there was a place to see it, there was a book: The "place to see it" is [ibal re], earlier written as [ilbal re]. With the book the lords are able to recover the full vision of the first humans; such vision, as this passage makes clear, reached into future time.

192

a way of cherishing: This is *loq'b'al* [locbal], "love (or desire or value) instrument." Andrés Xiloj suggested "something that shows esteem or expresses a sense of value."

192

For nine score days they would fast: "Nine score" is *belej winaq* [uinac]; Edmonson is correct in reading this as 9 × 20 rather than "nine persons" (Edmonson

329

1971:243). As he has observed, 180 is half a *tun,* the 360-day cycle used by the lowland Maya in reckoning chronologies. The "thirteen score" (or 260) mentioned next is the length of the so-called divinatory cycle, while the "seventeen score" (or 340) is the combined length of the 90- and 250-day segments of the Venus cycle (see p. 206).

192

They would only eat zapotes, matasanos, jocotes: For identifications of the tropical fruits listed here, see the Glossary. Of this kind of diet, Andrés Xiloj said, "This was so that they would have strength. This Tecum Umam [hero of Quiché resistance to the Spanish] didn't eat cooked things, only raw [or green] things. Because of this, the people of that time were muscular. Whatever place they went, whatever kind of fruit they found, they ate in place of tamales."

192

abstinence: This is *awasinik;* DB (under *awatz*) has *awasim,* "forbidden."

192

there weren't any women with them when they slept: This does not mean that women were not present at all. When people "keep the days" at present, the abstinence always includes sexual contact but never avoidance of all interaction with the opposite sex. If the fasts described here were like those of the first four Quiché ancestors, it was not only the lords who fasted but their wives as well (see p. 158).

192

"On this blessed day": This is *ato'b uq'ij* [uquih], in which *uq'ij* is "its-day"; DB gives [atob] as "good."

192

"ripeness and freshness": literally *q'anal,* "yellowness," and *raxal,* "greenness." Andrés Xiloj commented, "When one prays, *q'anal* means to have corn, to have money, to do business. Yes, it is like 'yellow' but it isn't yellow, but rather that it ripens. *Raxal* is like a plant that is green, it is developing to give fruit. *Q'anal* is when it ripens."

192

"spread thy stain, spill thy drops / of green and yellow": This is a fairly literal translation of *chatz'iloj, chamak'ij uloq* [chatziloh, chamaquih uloc] *araxal, aq'anal.* Of the connotations Andrés Xiloj said, *"Tz'iloj* is to use [sexually]; now they are going to have a family. *Mak'ij* is the sin. The man looks for his companion, there it is. And there is that liquid [semen]. And the green [raxal], there it is, it is the son or daughter, and the yellow [q'anal]; and they, in turn, have to produce again. Here it is like a plant, the sowing of a plant, and its ripening."

330

193

"that they might multiply": This is *chipoq taj* [chipo3tah]. Andrés Xiloj commented, *"Poq taj* is that it produces. Like a seed: when we cast it, we say to it, *kapoq la,* 'Come out [sprout], produce more.' " Commenting on the prayer as a whole, he said, "We're using this now; it's just that the language has changed somewhat."

193

"may they neither be snared nor wounded, / nor seduced, nor burned, / nor diverted below the road nor above it": "Burned" is paired with "seduced" here because, as Andrés Xiloj pointed out, the act of seducing an innocent person may be expressed in the phrase *xuporo raqan,* "He (or she) burned her (or his) legs." He suggested that a contemporary prayer for safety in the road might include the following lines:

> Do not let us fall into the hands
> of this person, this neighbor,
> who has a pistol, who has a dagger,
> who has a knife, who has a revolver;
> keep away the legs and arms
> of people at the corners, on the streets.

Contemporary prayers also include numerous passages with lists of negative requests; here is an example from a prayer by Esteban Ajxub of Momostenango, a professional *ajb'ix* or "singer":

> May there be no pain,
> may there be no trouble,
> may there be no jail,
> may there be no prison,
> may there be no weakness,
> may there be no feebleness,
> may there be no stiffness,
> may there be no lies and gossip.

193

"secrets or sorcery of thine": This is [acuil auitzmal], in which *a-* is "your (singular familiar)." Andrés Xiloj read [cuil] as *k'uyil,* "hidden"; *itzmal* is translated on the basis of *itzim,* "witched" (MX). Xiloj commented, "God gives all the good and all the evil."

193

"before thy mouth and thy face": Placement "before" someone's "face" is the commonest Quiché way of saying something like English "in" someone's "pres-

ence"; sometimes this is elaborated, as here, by adding "mouth" to "face," in which, if "face" is a metonym for the whole front of the body, "mouth" is a metonym for the whole face. In the present context "mouth" has an additional connotation, given that it refers in part to Heart of Earth, the deity called "Mundo" today. This is the great Mesoamerican earth deity, the ultimate swallower of all living things, depicted in Classic Maya art (in the Palenque relief panels, for example) as an enormous pair of jaws upon whose lips even the feet of great lords must rest in precarious balance, and into whose throat even great lords must fall. Turning to the contemporary scene, daykeepers who visit the main cave beneath the ruins of Rotten Cane, the last Quiché capital, speak of the danger of falling into "the open mouth of the Mundo" there, which is said to be more than four yards wide.

193

carrying the tribes and all the Quiché people on their shoulders: This is *reqalaxik amaq'* [re3alaxic amac] *ruk' ronojel k'eche winaq* [queche uinac], "its-being-carried (on the shoulders) tribe, with all-of Quiché people."

194

they became lords: The verb stem here is *ajawarik,* "to make oneself a lord" (DB).

194

received occasional gifts: This is *xkikak kochij,* in which *xki-* is "complete-they"; FX and FV have *kaka,* an auxiliary verb that makes an action uneven or hesitant, and *kochij,* "to receive a gift."

194

food and drink: This is [uain ucaha], translated on the basis of the reading offered by Andrés Xiloj, who uses the phrase *wa'im ok'aja,* "food, drink," in his own prayers.

194

falsify: This is *tzub'a;* DB has *tzub'u,* "deceive."

194

drops . . . that measured the width of four fingers or a full fist across: "Drops" is my translation of *raqan* [racan], literally "its leg" but also a term for the large drops of rain that begin or end a thunderstorm (FV). The first of the two measurements is *kajq'ab'* [cahcab]; DB (under [3a]) has *kajq'a* , "measured with the four fingers together." The second is [tuic]; DB has *tuwik,* "the fist closed with the thumb out; it is a measurement."

332

194

green, yellow, and red feather work: This is *raxon k'ub'ul* [cubul] *chaktik,* in which *raxon* is a noun that refers to something green, often paired with *q'uq'* to make it clear that quetzal feathers are meant. *K'ub'ul* is "oriole" in Kekchí (EH), Chol (AA), and Yucatec (AB), probably referring to a number of Icteridae with prominent yellow feathers. *Chaktik,* in which *chak* is Yucatec or Cholan for "red," is glossed by DB (a Quiché source) as "a species of red bird." That "feather work" is meant in the present context (rather than feathers or birds as such) is indicated by [cubulchactic] in PG, glossed as "thing made of feathers."

194

rise and growth: The MS has [unimaric ri unimaric puch], in which the second [unimaric] is probably an error for *uwinaqirik,* giving "its-big-becoming its-growth and."

194

two by two: In the list of Cauec lords that follows, the pairing of lords will not actually begin until the fourth generation.

194

succeeds: This is [camiheic], which Ximénez translates in this same way; his own dictionary (FX) has "to continue imitating" for [camih], but no other colonial source consulted here has a closely corresponding form.

194

the faces . . . of each of the Quiché lords: Again, as on p. 184, it would seem that something is missing here; perhaps the source Ximénez copied had name glyphs for the lords in the list that follows this statement.

195

Black Butterfly: This is *tekum,* "the large, black butterfly that flies with great speed" (FT).

195

Eight Cord: This is *wajxakib' k'a'm* [uahxaqui caam], in which "Cord" is a Quiché translation of the Nahua day name which is *Malinalli* in Nahuatl proper, meaning "twisted cord" (RS). *Malinalli* occupies the same position in the Nahuatl sequence of days as *E* or "Tooth" in the Quiché sequence.

195

Cauatepech: This is a Nahua name; in Nahuatl proper *cauani* is "leave a memory behind" and *tepechtli* is "base, foundation" (RS), yielding something like "founder."

195

Tonatiuh: In the MS this is [Donadiu], from *tonatiuh,* Nahuatl for "sun" (RS) or, more literally, "he who goes along getting hot." This was the name given by the Indians of central Mexico to Pedro de Alvarado before he came to Guatemala.

195

They were tortured by the Castilian people: The verb stem here is *jitz'* [hitz], which literally refers to the act of suspending or hanging something or someone (FX, AG). Numerous historians, assuming that this passage refers to execution by hanging, have rejected it in favor of Alvarado's claim that he burned the Quiché lords. They ignore the fact that Alvarado says he suspected the lords of plotting to kill him, and that he extracted confessions from them before he burned them. In the Spanish jurisprudence of his time, the standard method for obtaining a confession was to hang a prisoner by the wrists and then, if necessary, apply further tortures. That the lords were indeed tortured is confirmed by the Annals of the Cakchiquels, where it is stated that the Quiché rulers were "tortured" before they were "burned" (Recinos and Goetz 1953:120). Apparently the authors of the PV found torture more remarkable than execution, and the same may be said of their contemporaries among the Yucatec Maya. For a more general discussion of the use of torture in obtaining testimony from Mayans, and of the use and misuse of such testimony by scholars, see D. Tedlock (1993b).

196

Chief of the Reception House: The MS repeats this title after Mother of the Reception House and leaves out Chief Yeoltux Emissary, the final name on an earlier list of titles belonging to the Greathouses (p. 185).

197

Red Banner: This is *kaq laq'an* [ca3 lacan], with *kaq,* "red"; DB gives *laq'am* as "banner."

197

Noble Short One: This is *k'ok'osom* [cocozom], in which *k'o-* is honorific and *k'osom* is "shortened" in Kekchí (EH).

197

Noble Mortal: This is *k'okamel,* in which *k'o-* is honorific and *kamel* is literally "dead person" and figuratively "humble person" (FX).

197

Noble Caller: This is *k'oyab'akoj,* translated on the basis of Kekchí *yab'ak,* "call out" (EH).

197

They come together in unity: In this passage the authors make it clear that the lordly title they give as *nim chokoj* [nim chocoh], translated here and elsewhere as "Master of Ceremonies," is not an error for *nim ch'okoj* [nim 4hocoh], the spelling given in the Title of the Lords of Totonicapán. *Chokoj,* which fits the present context, has to do with occasions when people come together to share food and drink (see the notes to p. 91); *ch'okoj,* on the other hand, merely refers to the act of sitting down. The authors of the PV digress in order to exalt the Masters of Ceremonies, whereas the Totonicapán authors, whatever their political motives may have been, go out of their way to belittle the Master of Ceremonies for the Cauecs. For them, he is not a *nim chokoj* but a *nim ch'okoj,* a "Master of Sitting," and they go on to describe him as *xa ch'okojil tem,* "just a sitter on a bench," a minor official who, they insist, was never given the right to his own lordly domain (Carmack and Mondloch 1983a:101, 183).

197

great in being few: This is *nim skakin uk'ojeik,* "great few (or little bit) its-being-there."

198

the original book and ancient writing: This is simply *nab'e ojer,* "original (or first) ancient" in the MS, abbreviated from a phrase near the opening of the PV, *nab'e wujil, ojer tz'ib'am* [tzibam] *puch,* translated as "the original book and ancient writing" on p. 63. I have repeated the full phrase here to make the echo of the opening more obvious. In general the closing paragraph is terse, as if the hand that wrote it were running downhill toward the finish.

GLOSSARY

ACUL PEOPLE *Ak'ul winaq,* one of thirteen allied tribes the Quichés regarded as having come (like themselves) from the east. *Ak'ul* remains today as the name of a major district of the Ixil Maya town of Nebaj, to the west of the town center. See also Noble Acul.

AMONG THE ROCKS *Xoy ab'aj,* the town known today as Joyabaj, occupied by vassals of the Quiché lords during the reign of Quicab.

ANCIENT WORD *Ojer tzij,* also translatable as "Prior Word." A word, whether in the narrow sense of a single word or in the broad sense of an extended discourse, that carries the authority of tradition rather than being mere hearsay.

ANONAS *Q'awex,* a tropical fruit (*Annona spp.*) sometimes called "cherimoya" or "custard apple" in English. Heart-shaped, green outside and creamy inside, segmented, and incredibly sweet.

ARMADILLO *Ib'oy,* name of a dance done by Hunahpu and Xbalanque in their guise as vagabonds.

ARMADILLO DUNG *Achaq ib'oy,* Crier to the People for the Lord Quiché lineage when Quicab was Keeper of the Mat; possibly a nickname for one of the Lord Quiché lords listed on p. 197.

ATOLE *A' ixim,* literally "corn water," a corn-gruel drink widely known in Mesoamerica by the Nahuatl-derived name atole.

AUILIX *Awilix,* patron deity of the Greathouse lineage, received at Tulan by Jaguar Night, who took him to Auilix's Place for the first dawn. The temple dedicated to Auilix at Rotten Cane was itself called Auilix, and the priest of that temple was called Auilix or Lord Auilix. The priest was seventh in rank among the lords of the Greathouses and the head of one of the nine great houses into which their lineage was divided after the founding of Rotten Cane. The name Auilix is of Cholan origin, meaning "Lord Swallow."

AUILIX'S PLACE *Pawilix,* the place where Jaguar Night took the god Auilix and saw the first dawn, in or near Concealment Canyon and not far from Tohil's Place.

BALL COURT *Jom,* the I-shaped courtyard in which the Mesoamerican ball game was played. The playing field was paved with stone and bounded by stone walls; the side walls of the narrow part (connecting the two ends of the I) sloped upward in opposite directions from the playing surface, resembling grandstands in appearance but in fact constituting part of the playing surface. Today *jom* is the Quiché term for "graveyard," which suggests the deadly nature of the game described in the Popol Vuh, at least when it is played in the underworld court of the lords of Xibalba (see Place of Ball Game Sacrifice). The playing fields of the ball courts in Mesoamerican archaeological sites typically lie on a lower plane than that of the nearby plazas or courtyards.

BARK HOUSE *Jumetaja,* one of the four parts into which the citadel of Thorny Place was divided.

BAT HOUSE *Sotz'ija,* one of the tests of Xibalba, possibly corresponding to a position on the Mayan zodiac. Bat House is also the name of a lordly Cakchiquel lineage, otherwise known as Macaw House, whose founders stole fire from the Quichés rather than pledge themselves as sacrifice victims.

BEARDED PLACE *Chi ismachi,* citadel of the Quiché lords after they left Thorny Place and before they built Rotten Cane, founded by Noble Sweatbath. When the Cauec, Greathouse, and Lord Quiché lineages later left for Rotten Cane, Bearded Place was left to the Tam lineage. The ruins are located one kilometer south of Rotten Cane, separated from the latter by a canyon.

BEARER, BEGETTER *Alom, k'ajolom,* sometimes pluralized (*e alom, e k'ajolom*). Names or epithets for the gods who make the earth, plants, animals, and humans. The bearing and begetting is metaphorical, since these gods do their work by means of words, genius, and sacrifice rather than through procreation. The same gods are also called Maker, Modeler, and they include Sovereign Plumed Serpent.

BIRD HOUSE *Tz'ikinaja,* the palace, at Rotten Cane, of the Keeper of the Reception House Mat, second in rank among all the Quiché lords. Not to be confused with *ajtz'ikinaja,* "those of Bird House," a branch of the people known today as the Tzutuhil, who speak a language of the Quichean family and are located south and west of Lake Atitlán. Those of Bird House belong to a group of thirteen allied tribes the Quichés regarded as having come (like themselves) from the east.

BLACK BUTTERFLY *Tekum,* name of the Keeper of the Mat in the ninth generation of Cauec lords. A second Black Butterfly, who held the same position in the thirteenth generation, was taken hostage when Rotten Cane fell to the Spanish in 1524; he was the son of Three Deer, the Keeper of the Mat who was tortured and executed by Pedro de Alvarado. His accession to his father's title was later recognized by Alvarado, but eventually he, too, was executed, having been accused of plotting a rebellion. He is not to be confused with the famous warrior named Tecum Umam Quicab, "Black Butterfly Grandson of Quicab," who died in a battle with Alvarado's forces before the attack on Rotten Cane took place.

BLACK ROAD *Q'eqa b'e,* one of four cosmic roads. Black is the color of the west on the earthly plane, but the Black Road of the sky corresponds to the Great Rift in the Milky Way, which runs northward from the place where the ecliptic crosses the Milky Way in Sagittarius. See also Crossroads and Road of Xibalba.

BLOOD GATHERER *Kuchuma kik'*, fourth-ranking lord of Xibalba. By this same name he plays a role in present-day Quiché stories, sitting at the head of the banquet table where the other lords of Xibalba bring human blood that has been shed in violence or through illness.

BLOOD MOON *Xkik'*, daughter of Blood Gatherer and mother of Hunahpu and Xbalanque. As a moon goddess she may account only for the waxing moon, leaving the waning moon to her mother-in-law, Xmucane, and the full moon to Xbalanque.

BLOOD OF SACRIFICE *Lotz kik'*, a metaphor for rubber, used by Hunahpu and Xbalanque when they take a bit of rubber from their ball to cure the eye of a laughing falcon.

BLOOD RIVER *Kik' ya'*, a river that crosses the road to Xibalba. Blood River and Pus River may have been the names of actual dark (deep) and light (muddy) rivers that flow from the Guatemalan highlands into the northern lowlands. For today's Quiché the region that drops off toward the Atlantic in the vicinity of Cobán is still an abode of evil.

BLOODY TEETH, BLOODY CLAWS *Kik' re', kik' rixk'aq*, two lords of Xibalba. They are omitted from earlier lists of the lords (pp. 92, 94) but appear as the eleventh- and twelfth-ranking lords in later lists (pp. 117–19). The situation is just the opposite for Demon of Filth and Demon of Woe, who appear only in the earlier lists and may be these same two lords under different names.

BONE SCEPTER, SKULL SCEPTER *Ch'amiya b'aq, ch'amiya jolom*, seventh- and eighth-ranking lords of Xibalba.

BOUNDARY MARKER *K'ulb'a*, one of the four parts into which the citadel of Thorny Place was divided.

BROMELIADS *Ek'*, air plants (*Tillandsia spp.*) abounding in the trees of highland Guatemala. In some species the flowers have pointed petals and grow at the ends of stiff stalks that jut out from the rest of the plant; hence their use by Hunahpu and Xbalanque in constructing the arms and claws of an artificial crab.

BUNDLE OF FLAMES *Pisom q'aq'al*, a sacred relic left to the Quiché lords by Jaguar Quitze. Like the sacred bundles of North American peoples, a cloth-wrapped ark with mysterious contents.

CACAO *Kako* or *kakaw*, the seeds or seed pods of *Theobroma cacao*, a tree domesticated by Mesoamerican peoples. They used the seeds as money and continue to use them to make cocoa or chocolate.

CACAO WOMAN, CORNMEAL WOMAN *Xkakaw, ix tziya*, names or epithets for the goddess who guards the crops of One Monkey and One Artisan. She is also called Thunder Woman, Yellow Woman.

CAKCHIQUELS *Kaqchikeleb'* or *kaqchekeleb'*, a people who border the Quiché on the south and east and speak a language of the Quichean family. They belong to a group of thirteen allied tribes the Quichés regarded as having come (like themselves) from the east. One of the Cakchiquel citadels, Nettles Heights, was conquered by the Quiché lords during the reign of Quicab.

CALABASH *Sima* or *tzima*, the fruit of *Crescentia cujete*, a lowland tree, or the tree itself. The fruit is halved and hollowed to make drinking vessels that are especially valued for cacao beverages. The tree did not bear fruit until the head of One Hunahpu was placed in a fork of its branches. See also skull of One Hunahpu.

"CAMACU" *K'amaku*, possibly from Yucatec *k'ay mak u*, "Song of What-is-it," the title of a song full of questions. It is sung by Jaguar Quitze, Jaguar Night, Not Right Now, and Dark Jaguar, who lament being separated from the other peoples who were together at Tulan before the first dawn.

CAOQUES *Kawqeb'*, a tribe whose citadels once included Plaster House, which was among the places conquered by the Quiché lords during the reign of Quicab. In the Guatemalan department of Sacatepéquez, near San Pedro Sacatepéquez, there are Cakchiquel villages named Santa María Cauqué and Santiago Cauqué.

CAUATEPECH Keeper of the Reception House Mat in the eleventh generation of Cauec lords. The name, from a Nahua source, means "founder."

CAUECS *Kawiqib'* (singular *kaweq*), the first-ranking Quiché lineage, founded by Jaguar Quitze and divided into nine segments or great houses after the founding of Rotten Cane.

CAUIZIMAH Keeper of the Reception House Mat in the seventh generation of Cauec lords.

CAUIZTAN COPAL The type of copal used by Jaguar Night to incense the direction of the rising sun. The name is of Nahua origin, meaning "near the thistles."

CAVE BY THE WATER *Pekul ya'*, one of the volcanoes made by Zipacna. It may be the Volcán de Agua, south of Antigua Guatemala, which once had a lake at its summit.

CHIEF OF THE RECEPTION HOUSE *Nima k'amja*, title of the lord who was fourth in rank among the Greathouses and head of one of the nine great houses into which their lineage was divided after the founding of Rotten Cane.

CHIEF YEOLTUX EMISSARY *Nima lolmet ye'oltux*, title of the lord who ranked ninth among the Greathouses and headed one of the nine great houses into which their lineage was divided after the founding of Rotten Cane. This title is omitted in the second of the two lists of Greathouse lords (pp. 196–97).

CHIMALMAT Wife of Seven Macaw and mother of Zipacna and Earthquake. Her husband's stars are those of the Big Dipper, while hers form a circle that includes the arc of the Little Dipper. Her name, from a Nahua source, means "shield net."

COATI *Tzi's*, an omnivorous, tree-dwelling mammal (*Nasua narica*) related to the raccoon, with a long, flexible snout and a long, erect tail; ranges from southern Arizona to South America, confined to the lowlands in Guatemala.

COCHINEAL See croton.

COHAH A people belonging to a group of thirteen allied tribes the Quichés regarded as having come (like themselves) from the east.

COLD HOUSE *Tew ja,* one of the tests of Xibalba, possibly corresponding to a position on the Mayan zodiac. Also called Rattling House.

CONCEALMENT CANYON *Ewab'al siwan,* a great canyon in a forest, located somewhere between Santa Cruz del Quiché and San Andrés Sajcabajá in the Sierra de Chuacús. See also Auilix's Place and Tohil Medicine.

COPAL *Pom,* a type of incense widely used in Mesoamerica to this day, better known as copal (from Nahuatl *copalli*). The basic ingredient is the resin from the bark of the incense tree (*Bursera bipinnata*).

CORAL TREE, CORAL SEEDS *Tz'ite,* a tree known in Spanish as the palo pito (*Erythrina corallodendron*) or the tree's hard, red, bean-like seeds. The seeds are used by Xpiyacoc and Xmucane in performing calendrical divination for the gods who seek the proper materials for the human body; the wood of the tree is then used in making an experimental male figure.

CORNTASSEL HOUSE *Tz'utuja,* temple of the patron deity of the Zaquic lineage at Rotten Cane or perhaps at a site now known as El Resguardo, one kilometer to the east. Lord Corntassel House was the title of the first-ranking lord of the Zaquic lineage, who headed one of the two great houses into which that lineage was divided; he must have been the priest of the Corntassel god.

CORTÉS, DON JUAN Lord Keeper of the Reception House Mat in the four-teenth generation of Cauec lords, alive when the Popol Vuh was written. His title was recognized by the Spanish, but he was unsuccessful in his attempt to restore the full powers of the Cauec lords to Don Juan de Rojas (Keeper of the Mat) and himself, an effort that took him all the way to Spain.

COUNCIL BOOK *Popol wuj* or *popo wuj,* the hieroglyphic book used by the council of Quiché lords to see into the past or future.

COUNCILOR IN THE BALL COURT *Popol winaq pa jom tzalatz,* title of the lord who was eighth in rank among the Cauecs and head of one of the nine great houses into which their lineage was divided after the founding of Rotten Cane. The second time this title is mentioned (p. 196) the untranslatable name Xcuxeba is added. The ball court at Rotten Cane ran east-west and was located immediately south of the Great Monument of Tohil, adjacent to the main plaza.

COUNCILOR OF THE STORES *Popol winaq chituy,* title of the lord who was sixth in rank among the Cauecs and head of one of the nine great houses into which their lineage was divided after the founding of Rotten Cane.

CRISTÓBAL, DON Lord Minister in the twelfth generation of Greathouse lords, still in office by September of 1554.

CROSSROADS *Kajib' xalkat b'e,* a four-way intersection of the roads that link the cosmos together. At the celestial level, this is the place where the ecliptic crosses the Great Rift of the Milky Way near Sagittarius. See also Black Road, Green Road, Red Road, White Road, Yellow Road, and Road of Xibalba.

CROTON *Kaqche'* or *chuj kaqche',* "red tree" or "cochineal red tree," called "sangre de dragón" in Spanish (*Croton sanguifluus*). The shade of red called

340

cochineal is named for a dye made from scale insects that feed on prickly pear cactus. In the case of the croton tree it is the sap that is red, suggesting blood when it flows from a fresh cut and drying in scabrous nodules. A large nodule of this sap is passed off as the heart of Blood Moon by the messengers of Xibalba, and the burning of such nodules is established as an appropriate offering to the lords of Xibalba.

CRUNCHING JAGUAR *Kotz'b'alam,* one of the monsters who ends the era of the wooden people.

DARK HOUSE *Q'equmaja,* one of the tests of Xibalba, possibly corresponding to a position on the Mayan zodiac.

DARK JAGUAR *Ik'ib'alam,* one of the first four human males. He had no son and therefore did not found a lineage. The name is of Cholan origin.

"DAWN OF LIFE, THE" *Saq k'aslem,* an epithet for the Popol Vuh, referring to the first dawning of the present sun and contrasting with another epithet, "Our Place in the Shadows." An alternative reading would be "The Life in the Light."

DAYKEEPER *Ajq'ij,* diviners who count the days of the divinatory calendar using coral seeds. The daykeepers in the Popol Vuh are Xpiyacoc and Xmucane.

DEER DANCE PLAZA *Xajb'a kej,* a place six kilometers northwest of Chichicastenango, occupied by vassals of the Quiché lords during the reign of Quicab.

DEMON OF FILTH, DEMON OF WOE *Ajal mes, ajal toq'ob',* lords of Xibalba who rank ninth and tenth in earlier lists (pp. 92, 94) but are omitted from later ones. See Bloody Teeth, Bloody Claws.

DEMON OF PUS, DEMON OF JAUNDICE *Ajal puj, ajal q'ana,* lords of Xibalba ranking fifth and sixth.

DRY PLACE *Chichaq,* one of the four parts into which the citadel of Thorny Place was divided.

EARTHQUAKE *Kab'raqan,* name of the second son of Seven Macaw and Chimalmat; younger brother of Zipacna. He loses the strength in his limbs when he eats a bird coated with earth and ends up buried in the earth, where his continuing attempts to move cause quakes. Named after him is a place nine kilometers southeast of Rotten Cane, occupied by vassals of the Quiché lords during the reign of Quicab.

EGRET WOMAN *Xb'aqiyalo,* the wife of One Hunahpu and the mother of One Monkey and One Artisan. Her name is partly derived from *bak ha',* the Yucatec term for the snowy egret (*Egretta thula*).

EIGHT CORD *Wajxakib' k'a'm,* Keeper of the Mat in the tenth generation of Cauec lords. *K'a'm,* meaning "cord," is a Quiché translation of the Nahua day name Malinalli.

EIGHTEEN *Waxalajuj,* a place of uncertain location, occupied by vassals of the Quiché lords during the reign of Quicab.

EMISSARY FOR THE LORDS See Lord Emissary.

FALCON *Wok,* a divine name paired with Hunahpu in a prayer and a term for a falcon that serves as a messenger for Heart of Sky. Probably the same as *wak* (see laughing falcon).

FIREPLACE *Chiq'aq',* one of the volcanoes made by Zipacna. Generally thought to be the Volcán de Fuego, southwest of Antigua Guatemala, which forms twin peaks with the Volcán de Acatenango (see Hunahpu).

FOUR HUNDRED BOYS *Omuch' k'ajolab',* the youths who attempt to kill Zipacna but are killed by him instead, eventually becoming the Pleiades (see Hundrath). They die while in a drunken stupor, just as the four hundred rabbits of Nahua mythology do, and like those rabbits they were probably the patron deities of an alcoholic beverage (see sweet drink) and of drunkenness.

FRONT OF THE MONUMENT *Chuwa tz'aq,* the town labeled on maps as Momostenango, a Nahua name meaning "Citadel of Shrines," formerly located five kilometers northwest of its present site. Conquered by the Quiché lords during the reign of Quicab.

GODLY COPAL *K'ab'awil pom,* the kind of copal used by Not Right Now to incense the direction of the rising sun. It came from the east.

GOUGER OF FACES *K'otk'owach,* one of the monsters that ends the era of the wooden people, coming with a great, dark rainstorm.

GRANARY *Kuja,* name of the palace, at Rotten Cane, of the Keeper of the Mat, first in rank among all the Quiché lords.

GRANDMOTHER OF DAY, GRANDMOTHER OF LIGHT *Ratit q'ij, ratit saq,* meaning grandmother for as long as day or light have existed or may yet exist. Epithets for Xpiyacoc and Xmucane, although Xpiyacoc is sometimes described as a grandfather.

GREAT HOLLOW *Nim xol,* the same place as Great Hollow with Fish in the Ashes.

GREAT HOLLOW WITH FISH IN THE ASHES *Nim xob' karchaj,* in or near a present-day town eight kilometers east of Cobán, named San Pedro Carchá in printed sources but called *nim karcha* in Kekchí, the Mayan language spoken there. One and Seven Hunahpu (and later Hunahpu and Xbalanque) play ball there before they make their descent into Xibalba. Later, when the Quiché people migrate westward into the highlands, they pass by the same place on their way from Stagger to Place of Advice. There are numerous hollows (karstic depressions) in the area.

GREAT HOUSE *Nimja,* a term for a named and formally organized lineage segment (within a larger patrilineage) with a person of lordly rank at its head, and for the palace that served as headquarters for that segment.

GREATHOUSES *Nijayib',* second-ranking Quiché lineage, founded by Jaguar Night and divided into nine segments or great houses after the founding of Rotten Cane.

GREAT MONUMENT OF TOHIL *Nima tz'aq tojil,* the temple and supporting pyramid dedicated to the god Tohil in the citadel of Rotten Cane, on the west side of the main plaza and facing east.

GREAT WHITE PECCARY, GREAT WHITE COATI *Saqi nim aq, saqi nima tzi's,* terms referring to the white-lipped peccary (*Tayasu pecari*), a wild pig, and the coati mundi (*Nasua narica*), a relative of the raccoon; names of a pair of curers, an elderly husband and wife who specialize in problems affecting the teeth, eyes, and bones.

GREEN ROAD *Raxa b'e*, a cosmic road, one of four appearing in a list (p. 116) where it replaces the Yellow Road of an earlier list (p. 95). It is the only road the Quiché lords mention when they pray, asking that the gods keep their subjects on it. In the Mayan scheme of directional colors, green normally pertains to the center or axis mundi. See also Crossroads.

GUARDIANS OF THE SPOILS *Kanchajeleb'*, a people belonging to a group of thirteen allied tribes the Quichés regarded as having come (like themselves) from the east.

HACAUITZ *Jakawitz*, patron deity of the Lord Quiché lineage, received at Tulan by Not Right Now, who carried him to the mountain named for him and placed him at the top of a great pyramid. The Lord Quichés were at Hacauitz when the first dawn came, and the same mountain was the site of the first Quiché citadel, built by Jaguar Quitze, Jaguar Night, Not Right Now, and Dark Jaguar. The temple dedicated to Hacauitz at Rotten Cane bore the same name as the god, and the priest of that temple was called Lord Hacauitz. The priest was fourth in rank among the lords of the Lord Quiché lineage and headed one of the four great houses into which their lineage was divided after the founding of Rotten Cane. *Jakawitz* is a Cholan name meaning "bald mountain."

HEART OF SKY, HEART OF EARTH *Uk'ux kaj, uk'ux ulew*, epithets for the gods otherwise named Hurricane, Newborn Thunderbolt, and Sudden Thunderbolt.

HEART OF THE LAKE, HEART OF THE SEA *Uk'ux cho, uk'ux palo*, epithets for the gods who were in or on the sea before the raising of the earth. They are also known as Maker, Modeler and as Bearer, Begetter, and they include Sovereign Plumed Serpent. Their counterparts, with whom they cooperate in making the earth, are covered by a contrasting pair of epithets: Heart of Sky, Heart of Earth.

HERALD *Ajtzik' winaq*, title of the lord who ranked first among the Lord Quichés and headed one of the four great houses into which their lineage was divided after the founding of Rotten Cane; also called Herald for the Lords. He ranked fourth among the four lords who jointly ruled the Quiché state from Rotten Cane, with the Keeper of the Mat, Keeper of the Reception House Mat, and the Lord Minister above him. A slightly different title, Lord Herald, pertained to the lord who ranked second among the Greathouses and headed one of the nine great houses of that lineage.

HOT SPRINGS See Hot Springs Heights.

HOT SPRINGS HEIGHTS *Chuwi miq'ina'*, the town known in Spanish as San Miguel Totonicapán, capital of the Department of Totonicapán, formerly located on one of the hilltops above the present site. Once a citadel of the

343

White Earths (Mam Maya), conquered by the Quiché lords during the reign of Quicab. Today the inhabitants speak Quiché.

HULIZNAB One of the volcanoes made by Zipacna; location uncertain.

HUNAHPU *Junajpu,* sometimes *xjunajpu* or "little Hunahpu," a hunter and ball-player, the elder twin brother of Xbalanque. Their mother is Blood Moon and their fathers, who jointly conceived them, are One and Seven Hunahpu. The astronomical roles of Hunahpu include that of the planet Venus, which still bears his name when it appears as the morning star, and that of the sun that appeared on the first day of the present age. Hunahpu is also the name of one of the volcanoes made by Zipacna, possibly the Volcán de Acatenango, which forms twin peaks with the Volcán de Fuego (see Fireplace).

"HUNAHPU MONKEY" *Junajpu k'oy,* title of a tune played on the flute by Hunahpu and Xbalanque. One Monkey and One Artisan, having been turned into monkeys, danced and did acrobatics to it, climbing up over their grandmother's house instead of using the door. Today in Guatemala there are numerous Mayan towns whose fiestas include a Monkey Dance. The version done in Momostenango seems to confirm the celestial aspect of One Monkey and One Artisan: two monkeys, with stars on their costumes, climb a high pole and do acrobatics on a tightrope.

HUNAHPU PLACE *Chi junajpu,* a place of uncertain location, occupied by vassals of the Quiché lords during the reign of Quicab.

HUNAHPU POSSUM, HUNAHPU COYOTE *Junajpu wuch', junajpu utiw,* epithets that may refer to Hunahpu and Xbalanque in their guise as vagabond dancers and magicians whose arrival signals the transition from one solar year to another.

HUNDRATH *Motz,* the Pleiades, the group of stars formed by the Four Hundred Boys after Zipacna brought their house down on top of them. For today's Quiché the Pleiades symbolize a fistful of seeds. The planting season for maize, running from March to May depending on altitude, is marked by evening settings of the Pleiades that end when they enter a period of complete invisibility.

HURRICANE *Juraqan,* the god who causes the rain and flood that end the era of the wooden people and who periodically gives instructions to Hunahpu and Xbalanque. He is also called Thunderbolt Hurricane and Heart of Sky, Heart of Earth. Tohil, the first-ranking patron deity of the Quiché people, is one of his earthly manifestations.

ILOCS *Ilokab'* (singular *ilok*), one of the allied groups of lineages called "the three Quichés," the other two members being the Quiché proper (comprising the Cauecs, Greathouses, and Lord Quichés) and the Tams.

IZTAYUL Keeper of the Reception House Mat in the fourth generation of Cauec lords, with Noble Sweatbath as Keeper of the Mat. A second Iztayul was Keeper of the Reception House Mat in the fifth (p. 187) or sixth (p. 195) generation of Cauecs, with Tepepul as Keeper of the Mat. A third Iztayul was

344

Lord Minister in the seventh generation of Greathouse lords. The name is of Nahua origin, meaning "brine." See also Xtayub.

JAGUAR HOUSE *B'alamija,* one of the tests of Xibalba, possibly corresponding to a position on the Mayan zodiac. Jaguar House is also the name of a people belonging to a group of thirteen allied tribes the Quichés regarded as having come (like themselves) from the east.

JAGUAR NIGHT *B'alam aq'ab',* one of the first four human males and founder of the Greathouse lineage.

JAGUAR NOBLE ROOFTREE *B'alam k'onache',* the first to rule with the title of Keeper of the Mat, coming in the third generation of Cauec lords; a contemporary of Nine Deer, who was Lord Minister in the fourth generation of Greathouse lords.

JAGUAR QUITZE *B'alam k'itze,* one of the first four human males and founder of the Cauec lineage.

JAGUAR ROPES *B'alam kolob',* a people belonging to a group of thirteen allied tribes the Quichés regarded as having come (like themselves) from the east.

JOCOTES *Q'inom,* a tropical fruit (*Spondias purpurea*), yellow in color and resembling small plums.

KEEPER OF THE BAT MAT *Ajpo sotz'il,* a Cakchiquel lordly title, treated in the Popol Vuh as the name of the Cakchiquel lineage whose god was Snake Tooth.

KEEPER OF THE DANCE MAT *Ajpo xa* or *xajil,* a Cakchiquel lordly title, treated in the Popol Vuh as the name of a Cakchiquel lineage.

KEEPER OF THE MAT *Ajpop,* title of the lord who ranked first among the Cauecs and headed one of the nine great houses into which their lineage was divided after the founding of Rotten Cane. He also ranked first among the four lords who jointly ruled the Quiché state from Rotten Cane, with the Keeper of the Reception House Mat, Lord Minister, and Herald for the Lords coming below him. The signs or emblems that accompanied these titles were given out by Nacxit, the lord of a "populous domain" located in the east. During the reign of Quicab, the title of Keeper of the Mat was conferred upon the heads of twenty vassal lineages, presumably lineages that were specifically vassals of the Cauecs.

KEEPER OF THE PLUMED SERPENT *Ajq'ukumatz,* title of the priest of the god Sovereign Plumed Serpent at Rotten Cane; he was fourth in rank among the lords of the Cauecs and headed one of the nine great houses into which their lineage was divided after the founding of Rotten Cane. The temple of Sovereign Plumed Serpent was located near the center of the main plaza, where the outline of its circular foundation can still be seen.

KEEPER OF THE RECEPTION HOUSE MAT *Ajpop k'amja,* title of the lord who ranked second among the Cauec lords and headed one of the nine great houses into which the Cauecs were divided after the founding of Rotten Cane. He ranked second among the four lords who jointly ruled the Quiché state from Rotten Cane, coming below the Keeper of the Mat and above the Lord Minister and Herald for the Lords. Among his functions was the collection of tribute.

KEEPER OF TOHIL *Ajtojil*, title of the priest of the god Tohil at Rotten Cane; he was third in rank among the lords of the Cauecs and headed one of the nine great houses into which their lineage was divided after the founding of Rotten Cane.

LAKE-SEA *Chopalo*, composed of *cho*, "lake," and *palo*, "sea" (or else a large lake such as Atitlán), but pronounced as a single word. A term for all the pooled water of the world.

LAMACS *Lamakib'*, a people belonging to a group of thirteen allied tribes the Quichés regarded as having come (like themselves) from the east. Under Spanish rule they were resettled near Sacapulas.

LAUGHING FALCON *Wak*, a snake-hunting falcon (*Herpetotheres cachinnans*) that appears over ball courts and received its identifying black eye patch from Hunahpu and Xbalanque. Its cries are interpreted as omens by peoples ranging from Central Mexico to Brazil.

"LIGHT THAT CAME FROM BESIDE THE SEA, THE" *Saq petenaq ch'aqa palo*, an epithet for the Popol Vuh, referring to the splendid emblems of lordship the Quiché lords brought back from a pilgrimage to Yucatán. See also Nacxit.

LIVING EARS OF GREEN CORN, BED OF EARTH *K'azam aj, ch'atam ulew*, names given by Xmucane to the unripe ears of corn she incenses and then puts in the attic of her house, repeating what Hunahpu and Xbalanque did when they left for Xibalba. She calls these ears "living" because corn lives to sprout again after a harvest, and because Hunahpu and Xbalanque rise again after their death in the underworld. "Bed of Earth" refers to the floor beneath the attic and alludes to the field from which planted corn sprouts and the earth from which Hunahpu and Xbalanque ascend to the sky. See also Middle of the House, Middle of the Harvest.

LORD CORNTASSEL HOUSE See Corntassel House.

LORD EMISSARY *Lolmet ajaw* or *ajaw lolmet*, title of the lord who ranked second among the Lord Quichés and headed one of the four great houses into which their lineage was divided after the founding of Rotten Cane.

LORD HACAUITZ See Hacauitz.

LORD HERALD See Herald.

LORD MINISTER See Minister.

LORD QUICHÉS *Ajaw k'iche'*, third-ranking Quiché lineage, founded by Not Right Now and divided into four segments or great houses after the founding of Rotten Cane.

LUST WOMAN, WAILING WOMAN *Xtaj, xpuch'*, names of two young women sent to the place called Tohil's Bath in order to seduce the gods Tohil, Auilix, and Hacauitz, who appeared there as young men. Today these women take the form of the wailing woman known to Guatemalan Mayans and Latins alike as La Llorona, a freshwater siren who appears along rivers at night and whose icy touch is fatal to men.

MACAMOB One of the volcanoes made by Zipacna; location uncertain.

MACAW HOUSE *Kaqixaja,* name of one of the first four women made by the gods; wife of Dark Jaguar, one of the first four men. Macaw House is also the name of a Cakchiquel patrilineage, otherwise known as Bat House.

MACAW OWL *Kaqix tukur,* third-ranking Military Keeper of the Mat for the lords of Xibalba, one of four messenger owls. This is clearly the so-called Principal Bird Deity of Classic Maya vase paintings, who has the head and wings of a horned owl but the tail of a macaw.

MAKER, MODELER *Tz'aqol, b'itol,* names or epithets for the gods who amass and give form to the materials that make up the earth, plants, animals, and humans. The same gods are also called Bearer, Begetter, and they include Sovereign Plumed Serpent.

MASTER OF CEREMONIES *Nim chokoj,* a title held by one lord in each of the three ruling Quiché lineages and extended, during the reign of Quicab, to the heads of eleven vassal lineages. Master of Ceremonies for the Cauecs ranked fifth among the Cauec lords, Master of Ceremonies for the Greathouses ranked sixth among the Greathouse lords, and Lord Master of Ceremonies for the Lords ranked third among the Lord Quiché lords. The authors of the alphabetic Popol Vuh may have included the current holders of one or more of these three positions. See also Mothers of the Word, Fathers of the Word.

MATASANOS *Ajache,* a tropical fruit (*Casimiroa edulis*), pulpy, thin-skinned, yellow inside and chartreuse outside; called "matasanos" in Guatemalan Spanish.

MATCHMAKER *Mamom,* an arranger of marriages and conductor of marriage ceremonies. An epithet for Xpiyacoc.

MEAUAN The mountain beneath which Hunahpu and Xbalanque defeated Earthquake. Possibly located within the great bend of the Río Negro or Chixoy, north of Rabinal.

METEOR *Ch'ab'iq'aq',* a place of uncertain location, occupied by vassals of the Quiché lords during the reign of Quicab.

MEXICAN PEOPLE *Yaki winaq,* referring to speakers of Nahua, claimed to have been present in the eastern citadel of Tulan at the same time as the Quichés, Rabinals, Cakchiquels, and those of Bird House (Tzutuhils). Their god was called Yolcuat and Quitzalcuat.

MEXICAN SOVEREIGNS *Yaki tepew,* probably identical with the Mexican people (see above).

MIDDLE OF THE HOUSE, MIDDLE OF THE HARVEST *Nik'aj ja, nik'aj b'ichok,* names given by Xmucane to the unripe ears of corn she incenses and then puts in her house, repeating what Hunahpu and Xbalanque did when they left for Xibalba. She calls the ears Middle of the House because that is where

347

she puts them, which is to say at the center of the storage space in the attic; she calls them Middle of the Harvest because the attic is where she will store the ripened ears of corn at harvest time. See also Living Ears of Green Corn, Bed of Earth.

MIDDLE OF THE PLAIN *Nik'aj taq'aj,* name of the god received by Dark Jaguar at Tulan.

MIDMOST SEERS *Nik' wachinel,* diviners whose techniques include gazing into something translucent. The term is applied to Xpiyacoc and Xmucane, One and Seven Hunahpu, and Xulu and Pacam.

MILITARY KEEPER OF THE MAT *Rajpop achij,* title held by the four owls who served as messengers for the lords of Xibalba. Also one of the titles conferred upon the heads of vassal lineages during the reign of Quicab.

MILITARY MINISTER *Uq'alel achij,* one of the titles conferred upon the heads of vassal lineages during the reign of Quicab.

MILITARY WALLS, MILITARY CORNERS *Rajtz'alam achij, utza'm achij,* titles referring to the parts of a stockade and the frontiers of the Quiché kingdom, conferred upon the heads of vassal lineages during the reign of Quicab.

MINISTER *Q'alel,* the title, sometimes prefixed with *ajaw* or "Lord," of the lord who ranked first among the Greathouses and headed one of the nine great houses into which their lineage was divided after the founding of Rotten Cane. He also ranked third among the four lords who jointly ruled the Quiché state from Rotten Cane, coming below the Keeper of the Mat and the Keeper of the Reception House Mat and above the Herald for the Lords. During the reign of Quicab, when Woven was Lord Minister of the Greathouses, the title of Minister was conferred upon the heads of twenty vassal lineages, presumably lineages that were specifically vassals of the Greathouses.

MINISTER FOR THE LORDS *Q'alel ajaw,* one of the titles conferred upon the heads of one or more vassal lineages during the reign of Quicab, when Armadillo Dung was Lord Herald for the Lord Quichés. Presumably these would have been vassals of the Lord Quichés in particular, although Minister is not listed as one of the titles actually held by their lineage.

MINISTER FOR THE ZAQUICS *Q'alel saqik,* title of the lord who ranked second among the Zaquics and headed one of the two great houses into which their lineage was divided after the founding of Rotten Cane. The Zaquics may not have acquired this title until the reign of Quicab, two generations after the founding of Rotten Cane, since it is elsewhere listed as one of the titles conferred on the heads of vassal lineages during the reign of Quicab (p. 190). It could also be that the Zaquics themselves ennobled one or more lineages subordinate to themselves, titling them Ministers for the Zaquics in order to distinguish them from the Ministers created by the Greathouses at this same time.

MINISTER OF THE RECEPTION HOUSE *Q'alel k'amja,* title of the lord who ranked third among the Greathouses and headed one of the nine great houses into which their lineage was divided after the founding of Rotten Cane.

MIRROR SIDE *Chulimal,* a place three kilometers north of Chichicastenango, occupied by vassals of the Quiché lords during the reign of Quicab.

MIXTAM COPAL The type of copal used by Jaguar Quitze to incense the direction of the rising sun. The name is of Nahua origin, meaning "cloudy."

MONKEY HOUSE *B'atz'a,* Lord Minister in the sixth generation of Greathouse lords.

MOTHER-FATHER *Chuchqajaw,* composed of *chuch,* "mother," and *qajaw,* "father," but pronounced as a single word. It carries the sense of "parent," but without any final reduction of the difference between motherhood and fatherhood. The gods known as Maker, Modeler are called mother-fathers, and so are the first four human males and the male heads of present-day patrilineages. See also Mothers of the Word, Fathers of the Word.

MOTHER OF THE RECEPTION HOUSE *Uchuch k'amja,* title of the lord who ranked ninth among the Cauecs (also titled Sovereign Mexican) and headed one of the nine great houses into which their lineage was divided after the founding of Rotten Cane. The fifth-ranking lord of the Greathouses, who headed one of the nine great houses of their lineage, was also titled Mother of the Reception House.

MOTHERS OF THE WORD, FATHERS OF THE WORD *Uchuch tzij, uqajaw tzij,* an epithet for the three Masters of Ceremonies, suggesting that they were ritual heads of patrilineages (see mother-father) and that they may have been responsible for the Word (see Ancient Word) that is set forth in the Popol Vuh itself.

MOUNTAIN-PLAIN *Juyub'taq'aj,* composed of *juyub',* "mountain (or hill)," and *taq'aj,* "plain (or flat)," but pronounced as a single word. It carries the sense of "earth," but without any final reduction of the difference between mountains and plains. In modern Quiché ritual language, mountain-plain is a common metaphor for the human body; in the Popol Vuh the gods conceive humans at the same time they conceive the earth.

NACXIT The lord of a populous domain, somewhere in Yucatán, where Noble Two, Noble Acutec, and Noble Lord go on a pilgrimage. He gives them the emblems of legitimate lordship. His name is of Nahua origin, meaning "four legs."

NANCE *Tapal,* a tropical fruit *(Byrsonima crassifolia),* small, yellow and purple. The tree grows in the margins of the rain forest, in savannas, and on the lower reaches of temperate mountain slopes.

NETTLES HEIGHTS *Chuwi la,* the town labeled on maps with its Nahua name, Chichicastenango, meaning "Nettles Citadel." Formerly a Cakchiquel citadel, conquered by the Quiché lords during the reign of Quicab. Today the inhabitants speak Quiché.

NET WEAVE TRIBE *Amaq' ukin k'at,* the place where the Ilocs gave a home to their patron deity, not far from where the Tams, Cauecs, Greathouses, and Lord Quichés did the same; also the place where the Ilocs were when the dawn first came.

NEWBORN NANAHUAC, SUDDEN NANAHUAC *Ch'ipi nanawak, raxa nanawak,* alternative names for Newborn Thunderbolt, Sudden Thunderbolt. Nanahuac is cognate with Nanahuatzin, the Nahuatl name of a god who throws the thunderbolt that opens up the mountain filled with the corn needed to make human flesh. See Split Place.

NEWBORN THUNDERBOLT, SUDDEN THUNDERBOLT *Ch'ipi kaqulja, raxa kaqulja,* gods whose names refer both to shafts of lightning and to fulgurites (glassy stones formed where lightning strikes sandy soil), conceived as projectiles hurled from the sky. The same gods are also called Heart of Sky, Heart of Earth; with Thunderbolt Hurricane they form a threesome.

NINE DEER *B'elejeb' kej,* Lord Minister in the fourth generation of Greathouse lords, when Jaguar Noble Rooftree was Keeper of the Mat. Another Nine Deer was Lord Minister in the ninth generation. At least the first of these two was apparently born on the day Nine Deer on the divinatory calendar; the second was probably named after the first. Today such a birth date would augur a domineering, articulate, and masculine character with shamanic inclinations, and because of the relatively high number these qualities should be obvious.

NINE DOG *B'elejeb' tz'i',* Keeper of the Reception House Mat in the twelfth generation of Cauec lords, apparently born on the day Nine Dog on the divinatory calendar. Today, such a birth date would augur confusion, weakness, promiscuity, and ill fortune. He was tortured and burned by the Castilians when they took Rotten Cane in 1524.

NOBLE ACUL *K'oak'ul,* first-ranking lord in the second generation of Greathouse lords, perhaps a lord over the Acul people. Like his successor, Noble Chahuh (Chajul), he bears the name of a place in the territory of the Ixil Maya.

NOBLE ACUTEC *K'oakutek,* second-ranking lord in the second generation of Greathouse lords. He represented the Greathouses on the pilgrimage to the lord Nacxit.

NOBLE CALLER *K'oyab'akoj,* Herald for the Lords in the eighth generation of Lord Quiché lords.

NOBLE CHAHUH *K'ochajuj,* first-ranking lord in the third generation of Greathouse lords. Like his predecessor, Noble Acul, he bears the name of a place in the territory of the Ixil Maya, the town known today as Chajul.

NOBLE DOCTOR *K'omajkun,* Herald for the Lords in the fifth generation of Lord Quiché lords.

NOBLE INSCRIPTION HOUSE *K'otz'ib'aja,* second-ranking lord in the third generation of Greathouse lords.

NOBLE LORD *K'oajaw,* first-ranking lord in the second generation of Lord Quiché lords. He represented the Lord Quichés on the pilgrimage to the lord Nacxit.

NOBLE MORTAL *K'okamel,* Herald for the Lords in the seventh generation of Lord Quiché lords.

NOBLE RAIMENT *K'okawib'*, second-ranking lord in the second generation of Cauec lords and brother of Noble Two. According to the Title of the Lords of Totonicapán, the generation of these brothers was already the fourth one (starting with Jaguar Quitze) rather than the second. While Noble Two was on the pilgrimage to the Lord Nacxit, Noble Raiment fathered a child, Jaguar Noble Rooftree, with Noble Two's wife. On his return Noble Two nevertheless recognized this child as his successor in the first-ranking Cauec lordship.

NOBLE ROOFTREE See Jaguar Noble Rooftree.

NOBLE SHORT ONE *K'ok'osom*, Herald for the Lords in the fourth generation of Lord Quiché lords.

NOBLE SWEATBATH *K'otuja*, Keeper of the Mat in the fourth generation of Cauec lords and the object of an attempted assassination. A second Noble Sweatbath was Keeper of the Reception House Mat in the fifth generation of Cauec lords, helping Plumed Serpent to found Rotten Cane. Still other Noble Sweatbaths served as Lord Minister in the fifth, eighth, and eleventh generations of Greathouse lords.

NOBLE TWO *K'okib'*, first-ranking lord in the second generation of Cauec lords. He represented the Cauecs on the pilgrimage to the Lord Nacxit. According to the Title of the Lords of Totonicapán, his generation was already the fourth one (starting with Jaguar Quitze) rather than the second.

NOT RIGHT NOW *Majukutaj*, one of the first four human males and founder of the Lord Quiché lineage.

ONE DEATH, SEVEN DEATH *Jun kame, wuqub' kame*, lords who rank first and second among the rulers of Xibalba, named after two days on the divinatory calendar. In the narrative they are treated as two persons, but one and seven stand for all thirteen possible numbers, occurring first and last among the number prefixes of any given day name. By putting the severed head of One Hunahpu in a tree, they initiate evening-star appearances of the planet Venus that begin on days named Death.

ONE HUNAHPU, SEVEN HUNAHPU *Jun junajpu, wuqub' junajpu*, the elder and younger sons, respectively, of Xpiyacoc and Xmucane, named after two days on the divinatory calendar. In the narrative they are treated as two persons, but one and seven stand for all thirteen possible numbers, occurring first and last among the number prefixes of any given day name. One Hunahpu is the father, by Egret Woman, of One Monkey and One Artisan; later, both One and Seven Hunahpu become the fathers, by Blood Moon, of twins named Hunahpu and Xbalanque. By bringing the face of the deceased Seven Hunahpu back to life, the twins initiate morning-star appearances of the planet Venus that begin on days named Hunahpu.

ONE-LEGGED OWL *Juraqan tukur*, second-ranking Military Keeper of the Mat for the lords of Xibalba, one of four messenger owls. As Andrés Xiloj pointed out, owls stand on only one leg at a time.

ONE MONKEY, ONE ARTISAN *Jun b'atz', jun chuen*, the sons of One Hunahpu and Egret Woman; half-brothers of Hunahpu and Xbalanque. Patron deities of musicians, writers, and artisans. One Monkey (specifically a howler monkey) is named for a day on the Quiché and Chol divinatory calendars, while One Artisan is named for the corresponding day on the Kekchí and Yucatec calendars.

ONE TOH *Jun toj,* a day on the divinatory calendar. The patron deity of the Rabinals, declared by the writers of the Popol Vuh to be equivalent to the Tohil of the Cauecs, Ilocs, and Tams.

"OUR PLACE IN THE SHADOWS" *Qamujib'al,* an epithet for the Popol Vuh, referring to the period before the first sunrise is seen and contrasting with another epithet, "The Dawn of Life." The implication of "shadows" is that the light of dawn and of sunrise were really there (somewhere) all along, but that humans remained in darkness.

PATAXTE *Pek,* the seeds or seed pods of the tree *Theobroma bicolor,* a lower grade of cacao than cacao proper, widely known in Mesoamerica by its Nahuatl-derived name, pataxte. See cacao.

PERSON OF BAM *Winaq b'am,* Herald for the Lords in the ninth generation of Lord Quiché lords.

PETATAYUB A plain where a mountain of shattered stones from conquered citadels was piled up during the reign of Quicab, located somewhere in the vicinity of the town of Tecún Umán, formerly known as Ayutla, on the Pacific coastal plain near the Mexican border. The name, from a Nahua source, means "mat turtle."

PLACE OF ADVICE *Chi pixab',* a mountain where the Quichés and other tribes held a council during their migrations. It is a peak of the Montaña los Achiotes, about seven kilometers west of San Andrés Sajcabajá.

PLACE OF BALL GAME SACRIFICE *Pusb'al cha'j,* the place where the decapitated body of One Hunahpu and the complete body of Seven Hunahpu were buried by the lords of Xibalba. Probably not a place name, but rather a name for the altar where losing ballplayers were sacrificed.

PLACE OF SPILT WATER See Spilt Water.

PLANK PLACE *Chitemaj,* a place of uncertain location, occupied by vassals of the Quiché lords during the reign of Quicab.

PLASTER HOUSE *Saqkab'aja,* the town known today as San Andrés Sajcabajá. Formerly a Caoque citadel, conquered by the Quiché lords during the reign of Quicab. Today the inhabitants speak Quiché.

PLUMED SERPENT *Q'ukumatz,* literally "Quetzal Serpent," Keeper of the Mat in the fourth (p. 186) or fifth (p. 195) generation of Cauec lords, named after the god listed elsewhere as Sovereign Plumed Serpent. For at least part of his reign, it seems, he also held the office of Keeper of the Reception House Mat. He was one of the founders of Rotten Cane and was especially remembered for his demonstrations of shamanic power.

POINT OF THE ARROW, ANGLE OF THE BOWSTRING *Uchi' ch'a, uchi' k'a'm,* epithets for the vanguard lineages sent out to occupy conquered citadels during the reign of Quicab.

POORWILL, DANCE OF THE *Xajoj pujuy,* a dance done by Hunahpu and Xbalanque in their guise as vagabonds.

POPOL VUH See Council Book.

PRAWN HOUSE *Chomija,* name of one of the first four women made by the
gods; wife of Jaguar Night, one of the first four men.

PUS RIVER *Puj ya',* a river that crosses the road to Xibalba. Blood River and
Pus River may have been the names of actual dark (deep) and light (muddy)
rivers that flow from the Guatemalan highlands into the northern lowlands.
For today's Quiché the regions that drop off toward the Atlantic, especially in
the area of Cobán, are still an abode of evil.

QUEHNAY EMISSARY *Lolmet kejnay,* title of the lord who ranked seventh
among the Cauecs and headed one of the nine great houses into which their
lineage was divided after the founding of Rotten Cane.

QUENECH AHAU A people belonging to a group of thirteen allied tribes the
Quichés regarded as having come (like themselves) from the east. The name
is from the Yucatec Maya title *k'inich ahaw,* "sun-faced lord."

QUETZAL *Q'uq',* also known as the resplendent quetzal (*Pharomachrus mocinno*). Confined to localized cloud forest habitats scattered from Chiapas to
Panama, it is the most spectacular bird in the New World, red on the breast
and white under the tail but otherwise bright green with blue iridescence.
The two-foot-long tail coverts of the male were a major item of tribute and a
major feature of lordly regalia throughout Mesoamerica.

QUIBA HOUSE, THOSE OF *Ajkib'aja,* a people belonging to a group of thirteen
allied tribes the Quichés regarded as having come (like themselves) from the
east.

QUICAB *K'iqab',* Keeper of the Mat in the sixth (p. 187) or seventh (p. 195)
generation of Cauec lords. He greatly expanded the Quiché state, destroying
the citadels of neighboring peoples and occupying them with vassal lineages
drawn from the immediate vicinity of Rotten Cane. He ennobled the heads
of many vassal lineages, including those who had served him well in his
conquests, but members of this new nobility later perpetrated a revolt that
reduced his power. Three generations later, while Eight Cord was Keeper of
the Mat, a second Quicab served in the second-ranking lordship, that of the
Keeper of the Reception House Mat. This latter Quicab was probably the
grandfather of the famous warrior known as Tecum Umam Quicab, "Black
Butterfly Grandson of Quicab," who died in a battle with Pedro de Alvarado's
forces before the attack on Rotten Cane took place.

QUICHÉ *K'iche',* the name of a people, a language, a town, and a kingdom. As
a people, the Quiché proper consist of those who descend from Jaguar Quitze,
Jaguar Night, and Not Right Now—that is to say, the Cauec, Greathouse, and
Lord Quiché lineages—and who worship the gods Tohil, Auilix, and Hacauitz.
"The three Quichés" include the Quiché proper, as just described, together
with two further lineages whose god was Tohil, the Tams and Ilocs. This
threesome is said to have been together even since the time of Tulan, and to

353

have shared the same language, which is also called Quiché. Late in the narrative Quiché becomes a place name referring to the vicinity of Rotten Cane, covering Rotten Cane itself, Bearded Place (half a kilometer south of Rotten Cane), and the site of the post-conquest town of Santa Cruz. The name can also be extended to the entire kingdom that was ruled from Rotten Cane.

QUITZALCUAT The god of the Mexican people, also called Yolcuat. The present name, from a Nahua source, means "plumed serpent."

RABINALS *Rab'inaleb',* the people known today as the Achí, who speak Achí (a dialect of Quiché) and whose principal town is Rabinal, on the northeast frontier of what was once the Quiché kingdom. They belonged to a group of thirteen allied tribes the Quichés regarded as having come (like themselves) from the east. One of the Rabinal citadels, Spilt Water, was conquered by the Quiché lords during the reign of Quicab.

RATTLING HOUSE *Xuxulim ja,* one of the tests of Xibalba, possibly corresponding to a position on the Mayan zodiac. Also called Cold House; the present name comes from the sounds of the hail that falls on the house and the cold drafts that come in through its cracks.

RAZOR HOUSE *Ch'ayim ja,* one of the tests of Xibalba, possibly corresponding to a position on the Mayan zodiac. Full of stone knives or blades that move back and forth.

RED BANNER *Kaq laq'an,* Herald for the Lords in the third generation of Lord Quiché lords.

RED ROAD *Kaqa be',* one of four cosmic roads. Red is the color of the east. See also Crossroads.

RED SEA TURTLE *Kaqa paluma,* name of one of the first four women made by the gods; wife of Jaguar Quitze, one of the first four men.

ROAD OF XIBALBA *Ri b'e xib'alb'a,* the road that beckoned to One and Seven Hunahpu when they were on their way to Xibalba and led to their deaths, also called Black Road. As a celestial road it is the Great Rift in the Milky Way; as a terrestrial road it descends into Xibalba from somewhere near Great Hollow with Fish in the Ashes.

ROBLES, DON PEDRO DE Lord Minister in the thirteenth generation of Great-house lords, in office when the Popol Vuh was written. Since his predecessor was still in office in September of 1554, the Popol Vuh must have been written after that time.

ROJAS, DON JUAN DE Lord Keeper of the Mat in the fourteenth generation of Cauec lords, in office when the Popol Vuh was written. His title was recognized by the Spanish; he retained his serfs, was given a reception room in the Royal Palace at Santiago Guatemala, served as a minister of native affairs, and attempted to regain jurisdiction over the towns that had been conquered by the Quiché state before the arrival of the Spanish. He was still in office in 1554; since he was no longer signing documents by November of 1558, the Popol Vuh must have been written before that date.

ROTTEN CANE *Q'umaraq aj,* the citadel built by the Quiché lords after they left Bearded Place, founded by the Keeper of the Mat named Plumed Serpent. At Bearded Place there had been only three great houses or lordly lineages, but after the founding of Rotten Cane the Cauecs divided into nine parts, the Greathouses into nine parts, the Lord Quichés into four parts, and there were also two divisions of Zaquics (not mentioned at Bearded Place). Except for the two divisions of Zaquics, which shared a single palace, each of these lineage segments had a separate palace, making twenty-three palaces in all. It was from Rotten Cane that Quicab greatly expanded the Quiché state, and it was Rotten Cane that was taken by Pedro de Alvarado in 1524. The ruins, labeled on maps as Utatlán (their Nahua name), are located three kilometers west of Santa Cruz del Quiché.

RUSTLING CANYON, GURGLING CANYON *Nu' siwan, k'ulk'u siwan,* on the road followed by One and Seven Hunahpu when they descended to Xibalba. It could be east of San Pedro Carchá, where the Río Cahabón disappears into a system of caves and then emerges again.

SANTA CRUZ Bishop Francisco Marroquín gave this name to Rotten Cane in 1539, but the town that came to be known as Santa Cruz del Quiché was not built on the ruins of Rotten Cane itself but three kilometers to the east.

SCAB STRIPPER *Xik'iri pat,* third-ranking lord of Xibalba.

SCORPION RAPIDS *Jalja ja' sinaj,* an obstacle on the road to Xibalba, encountered shortly before the Crossroads. At the celestial level, Scorpion Rapids would be on the ecliptic a short distance west of the place where it crosses the Great Rift in the Milky Way. That would be in Scorpius, which the Yucatec Maya and the Aztecs both saw as a scorpion.

SERPENTS *Kumatz,* a people belonging to a group of thirteen allied tribes the Quichés regarded as having come (like themselves) from the east. The Spanish, who resettled them near the town of Sacapulas, called them Coatecas, a Nahuatl-derived name with the same meaning as the Quiché name.

SEVEN CANE *Wuqub' aj,* Herald for the Lords in the sixth generation of Lord Quiché lords. Apparently born on the day Seven Cane on the divinatory calendar; today such a birth date would augur good luck in all the affairs of life and a potential career as a dutiful priest-shaman or official.

SEVEN CAVES, SEVEN CANYONS *Wuqub' pek, wuqub' siwan,* an epithet for Tulan, the citadel where the ruling Quiché lineages acquired their patron deities. Numerous Mayan ruins have natural caves beneath them; Rotten Cane has three artificial caves, the longest of which runs to a point beneath the main plaza. See also Tulan and Zuyua.

SEVEN MACAW *Wuqub' kaqix,* a god who falsely claimed to be both the sun and moon during the era of the wooden people; husband of Chimalmat and father of Zipacna and Earthquake. In his earthly role he is a scarlet macaw (*Ara macao*), while his celestial role is that of the seven stars of the Big Dipper. At the request of Hurricane, Hunahpu and Xbalanque bring Seven Macaw down out of his tree, opening the way for the great rain that destroys the wooden people who worshipped Seven Macaw as the sun. In the same way, the period during which the Big Dipper is in descent or below the horizon for most of the night coincides with the hurricane season in the latitudes of Mesoamerica and the Caribbean (mid-July to mid-October).

SEVEN THOUGHT *Wuqub' no'j*, Keeper of the Mat in the eleventh generation of Cauec lords, apparently born on the day Seven Thought on the divinatory calendar. Today, such a birth date would augur an ability to solve problems, a potential for leadership, and a markedly masculine character.

SHIELD DANCE *Pokob'*, a dance performed by the Quiché lords while they were settled at Bearded Place.

SHOOTING OWL *Ch'ab'i tukur*, first-ranking Military Keeper of the Mat for the lords of Xibalba, one of four messenger owls. These owls are able to reach the eastern ball court used by One and Seven Hunahpu and by One Monkey and One Artisan, but in contrast with the falcon that serves as messenger of the Heart of Sky or Hurricane, they are not described as being able to reach the place where the Heart of Sky is located.

SKULL OF ONE HUNAHPU *Ujolom jun junajpu*, an epithet for the calabash, referring to the fact that the calabash tree never bore fruit until One Hunahpu's severed head was placed in it. The calabash was and is used for drinking cacao, and Classic Maya ceramic vessels used for that purpose were painted with scenes from stories like those of the Popol Vuh. See calabash.

SKULL OWL *Jolom tukur*, fourth-ranking Military Keeper of the Mat for the lords of Xibalba, one of four messenger owls.

SKY-EARTH *Kajulew*, composed of *kaj*, "sky," and *ulew*, "earth," but pronounced as a single word. It carries the sense of "world," but without any final reduction of the difference between sky and earth.

SNAKE TOOTH *Chamalkan*, god of the Bat House lineage of the Cakchiquels. The name is of Yucatecan or Cholan origin.

SNATCH-BAT *Kamasotz'*, the kind of bat that inhabits the Bat House of Xibalba; one of them bites off the head of Hunahpu.

SOVEREIGN MEXICAN *Tepew yaki*, title of the lord who was ninth in rank among the Cauecs and head of one of the nine great houses into which their lineage was divided after the founding of Rotten Cane; he was also called Mother of the Reception House.

SOVEREIGN OLOMAN *Tepew oloman*, a people who stayed in the east when the Quiché ancestors migrated westward; possibly the speakers of Pipil (a Nahua language) who once occupied an area lying east of Rotten Cane and west of Copán, in the Motagua valley. Oloman, from a Nahua source, means "ballplayer."

SOVEREIGN PLUMED SERPENT *Tepew q'ukumatz*, a god who belongs to the group variously called Maker, Modeler; Bearer, Begetter; and Heart of the Lake, Heart of the Sea. These gods are on or in the sea in the primordial world, whereas the god or gods called Heart of Sky, Hurricane, Newborn Thunderbolt, and Sudden Thunderbolt are in the sky.

356

SPILT WATER *Mak'a'* or *pamak'a'*, the town labeled on maps as Zacualpa, formerly located two kilometers southeast of its present site. Once a Rabinal citadel, conquered by the Quiché lords during the reign of Quicab. Today the inhabitants speak Quiché.

SPLIT PLACE, BITTER WATER PLACE *Pan paxil, pan k'ayala'*, a high mountain just south of the Pan American Highway and near the Guatemalan border with Mexico, with a large spring on its north side. The place where the Makers and Modelers got the corn and water needed to make the bodies of the first true humans; its interior was filled not only with corn but with a variety of tropical fruits. Today the people of the surrounding region, who speak Mam, reckon it as the origin place of corn. Teosinte, a wild grain that crossbreeds with corn, is abundant on its slopes.

STAGGER *Silisib'*, the place where the tribes (other than the Cakchiquels) pledged themselves to be "suckled" (or to have their hearts cut out) by Tohil in exchange for fire.

STAR HOUSE, THOSE OF *Ajch'umilaja*, a people belonging to a group of thirteen allied tribes the Quichés regarded as having come (like themselves) from the east. The Spanish, who resettled them near the town of Sacapulas, called them Sitaltecas, a Nahuatl-derived name with the same meaning as the Quiché name.

STEVIA *Jolom okox*, literally "head of mushroom," a common aromatic herb named for the shape of its composite flower head. It is probably *Stevia serrata*, called "requesón" in Mexico and "pericón blanco" in Guatemala. The burning of this herb, together with marigolds, constitutes a more modest offering than copal incense.

STONE COURSES, SAND BANKS *Cholochik ab'aj, bokotajinaq sanayeb'*, a causeway crossing a body of water, traveled by Jaguar Quitze, Jaguar Night, Not Right Now, and Dark Jaguar on their migration from Tulan.

STRONGHOLD *Kawinal*, one of the four parts into which the citadel of Thorny Place was divided. Today the ruins of all four parts together are called Cauinal.

SUDDEN BLOODLETTER *Kamalotz*, one of the monsters that ends the era of the wooden people.

SUN CARRIER *Iqoq'ij*, the planet Venus as the morning star, also called the "great star."

SUN-MOON *Q'ijik'*, composed of *q'ij*, "sun," and *ik'*, "moon," but pronounced as a single word. A term encompassing all heavenly bodies that move across the background of the fixed stars.

SWALLOWING SWORDS *Xtz'ul*, a dance in which a pair of performers in small masks wear macaw tails on their backs, shake tortoiseshell rattles, pound themselves on their chests with stones, and put sticks down their throats and bones up their noses. Hunahpu and Xbalanque perform this dance while in their guise as vagabonds.

SWEATBATH HOUSE *Tujalja*, a people belonging to a group of thirteen allied tribes the Quichés regarded as having come (like themselves) from the east. They settled at Sacapulas, where the Quiché name for the town center is *tujal*.

SWEET DRINK *Ki'*, an alcoholic beverage made from maguey, known in Mexico by its Nahuatl-derived name, pulque. *Ki'* can mean not only "sweet" but "poison" as well, which has to do with the fact that pulque changes its character, tasting sweet before fermentation and then becoming bitter and (when drunk to excess) sickening.

TALK HOUSE *Uch'ab'aja*, a people belonging to a group of thirteen allied tribes the Quichés regarded as having come (like themselves) from the east. Under Spanish rule they were resettled near Sacapulas.

TAMAZUL *Tamasul*, the toad that swallowed the louse that carried the message of Xmucane.

TAMS *Tamub'* (singular *tam*), one of the allied groups of lineages called "the three Quichés," the other two members being the Quiché proper—comprising the Cauecs, Greathouses, and Lord Quichés—and the Ilocs.

TAM TRIBE *Amaq' tan*, place where the Tams gave a home to their patron deity, not far from where the Ilocs, Cauecs, Greathouses, and Lord Quichés did the same; also the place where the Tams saw the first dawn.

TEARING JAGUAR *Tukumb'alam*, one of the monsters that ends the era of the wooden people.

TEPEPUL Keeper of the Mat in the fifth (p. 187) or sixth (p. 195) generation of Cauec lords. Another Tepepul was Keeper of the Mat in the eighth generation of Cauec lords, and still others were Keepers of the Reception House Mat in the ninth and thirteenth generations. This last Tepepul was taken hostage when Rotten Cane fell to the Spanish in 1524; he was the son of Nine Dog, the Keeper of the Reception House Mat who was tortured and executed by Pedro de Alvarado. His accession to his father's title was later recognized by Alvarado, but eventually he, too, was executed, having been accused of plotting a rebellion. Tepepul, from a Nahua source, means "big mountain."

THORNY PLACE *Chik'ix*, the citadel of the Quiché lords after they left Hacauitz and before they built Bearded Place. It was divided into four parts: Dry Place, Bark House, Boundary Marker, and Stronghold. The ruins of Thorny Place, grouped around four plazas, are located on the Río Calá or Blanco near its confluence with the Río Chixoy or Negro, about twenty kilometers northwest of Rabinal. They are known today as Cauinal (see Stronghold).

THREE DEER *Oxib' kej*, Keeper of the Mat in the twelfth generation of Cauec lords, apparently born on the day Three Deer on the divinatory calendar. Today such a birth date would augur a domineering, articulate, and masculine character, with possible shamanic inclinations, but because of the low number these qualities would be present in only moderate quantity. He was tortured and burned by the Castilians when they took Rotten Cane in 1524.

THREE GREAT HOUSES *Oxib' chi nim ja*, referring to the alliance, at Bearded

Place, of the Cauec, Greathouse, and Lord Quiché lineages, whose members intermarried.

THRONG BIRDS *Tz'ikin molay,* a migrating flock of Swainson's hawks (*Buteo swainsonii*), which funnel through Guatemala in spectacular numbers on their way from North to South America and back again. After performing a harvest ritual, Hunahpu and Xbalanque encounter these birds on their way to Xibalba.

THUNDERBOLT HURRICANE *Kaqulja juraqan,* an epithet for Hurricane.

THUNDER WOMAN, YELLOW WOMAN *Xtoj, Xq'anil,* names or epithets of the goddess who guards the crops of One Monkey and One Artisan, who is also called Cacao Woman and Cornmeal Woman. *Toj* and *Q'anil* are day names from the divinatory calendar; at present days named *Q'anil* are appropriate for harvesting ripened ears of corn, which is what Blood Moon is about to do when she invokes this goddess.

TOHIL *Tojil,* god of fire-making, thunderstorms, blood sacrifice, and rulership. As an aspect of the one-legged god named Hurricane, he takes the role of a fire drill. Patron deity of the Cauec, Tam, and Iloc lineages; the name Tohil sometimes covers not only Tohil himself but also Auilix and Hacauitz, patrons of the Greathouse and Lord Quiché lineages. Tohil was received at Tulan by Jaguar Quitze, who took him to Tohil's Place for the first dawn. At his temple in Rotten Cane, called Great Monument of Tohil, he received offerings from those who came to pay tribute to the lords of the Quiché kingdom.

TOHIL MEDICINE *Kunab'al tojil,* an epithet given to Concealment Canyon after Tohil was placed nearby on the mountain called Tohil's Place.

TOHIL'S BATH *Ratinib'al tojil,* the unknown place where the spirit familiars of Tohil, Auilix, and Hacauitz were regularly seen bathing during the time when the Quiché lords occupied the citadel of Hacauitz.

TOHIL'S PLACE *Patojil,* the mountain where Jaguar Quitze took the god Tohil and saw the first dawn, located between Santa Cruz del Quiché and San Andrés Sajcabajá in the Sierra de Chuacús.

TONATIUH The name given to Pedro de Alvarado by the Nahuatl-speaking people of Mexico. It means "sun" or, more literally, "he who goes along getting hot."

TORTILLA GRIDDLE *Xot,* a round and slightly concave pottery griddle, used in toasting tortillas; better known by the Nahuatl-derived name comal.

TREE-STONE *Che'ab'aj,* an exact Quiché translation of *te'tun,* the Cholan term for stele in the Classic Maya inscriptions at Copán.

TULAN A town in the east that was like the Classic Maya site of Copán in having a bat as its insignia. The lords of the Quiché, Cakchiquel, and other "mountain people" gathered there, paying tribute and acquiring their respective patron deities. By the time they found their own places to rule, Tulan had been abandoned. The site was probably not called Tulan until after its demise. For its other names see Zuyua and Seven Caves, Seven Canyons.

UNDER TEN *Xelajuj,* a citadel conquered by the Quiché lords during the reign of Quicab, corresponding to what is now the second-largest city in Guatemala.

The city appears on maps as Quezaltenango or Quetzaltenango, a Nahuatl-derived name meaning "quetzal citadel," but it is called Xelajú or Xela in everyday Guatemalan speech, whether in Spanish or in Mayan languages. The ancient citadel, whose exact location is unknown, was on a hilltop in the vicinity of the present city.

UNDER THE TWINE, UNDER THE CORD *Xeb'alax, xek'a'maq,* a mountain named for its location on a measured boundary, specifically the boundary separating lands belonging directly to the lords of Rotten Cane from those of their vassals at Mirror Side. When the heads of vassal lineages were elevated to lordship and assigned to the task of protecting newly conquered territories during the reign of Quicab, their induction took place on this boundary mountain rather than in the citadel of Rotten Cane.

WALKING ON STILTS *Chitik,* a dance done by Hunahpu and Xbalanque in their guise as vagabonds.

WATER HUMMINGBIRD *Tz'ununija',* referring to the green kingfisher (*Chloroceryle americana*). The name of one of the first four women made by the gods; wife of Not Right Now, one of the first four men. A Tzutuhil patrilineage carries the same name.

WEASEL, DANCE OF THE *Xajoj kux,* a dance done by Hunahpu and Xbalanque in their guise as vagabonds. The species in question is the long-tailed weasel (*Mustela frenata*).

WHITE CORNMEALS *Saq k'ajib',* a people belonging to a group of thirteen allied tribes the Quichés regarded as having come (like themselves) from the east. They must have settled in the area of the present town of Salcajá, called *saqk'aja* in Quiché.

WHITE DAGGER *Saqi toq',* the sacrificial knife belonging to the lords of Xibalba and of the ball (containing this knife) they are anxious to use in their game with Hunahpu and Xbalanque.

WHITE EARTHS *Saqulewab',* the Mam Maya, named after their principal citadel, White Earth or *saqulew* (Zaculeu on maps). The ruins of this citadel are five kilometers west of the present town of Huehuetenango.

WHITE RIVER *Saqi ya',* a place two kilometers west of Chichicastenango, occupied by vassals of the Quiché lords during the reign of Quicab.

WHITE ROAD *Saqi b'e,* one of four cosmic roads. White is the color of north on the earthly plane, but the White Road of the sky corresponds to the section of the Milky Way whose width is solid white rather than being split lengthwise by the darkness of the Great Rift. See also Black Road.

WHITE SPARKSTRIKER *Saqi k'oxol,* a being who escapes into the shelter of the woods when the sun first rises, taking along the animals that were petrified by the sun. He/she (the sex is ambiguous) has the title role in the present-day dance drama called "Saqi K'oxol" in Quiché and "La Conquista" in Spanish, playing the role of a daykeeper (or else the dwarf companion of the daykeeper) who forecasts the outcome of the Spanish invasion and later escapes into the woods to preserve indigenous customs. Despite the name, he/she has a red mask and is dressed entirely in red, carrying the stone axe he/she used to strike lightning into the bodies of the first daykeepers. As a being who appears in woods, caves, and dreams, he/she is the keeper of the petrified animals (volcanic concretions that resemble animals).

WHITE VULTURE *Saq k'uch,* the king vulture (*Sarcoramphus papa*), a lowland species, white except for black flight feathers and a naked red head and neck.

WILLOW TREE *Tzolojche',* the town labeled on maps as Santa María Chiquimula. One of the citadels conquered by the Quiché lords during the reign of Quicab.

WING, PACKSTRAP *Xik', patan,* lords of Xibalba who rank eleventh and twelfth in earlier lists (pp. 92, 94) and ninth and tenth in later ones (pp. 117–19). The packstrap is a strip of hide used to protect the forehead when a load is carried with a tumpline.

WOVEN *Kema,* Lord Minister of the Greathouse lords, mentioned in one passage as a contemporary of Quicab, who served as Keeper of the Mat in the sixth generation of Cauec lords (p. 189), and in a later passage as belonging to the tenth generation of Greathouse lords (p. 196).

XBALANQUE *Xb'alanq'e,* a hunter and ballplayer, the younger twin brother of Hunahpu. Their mother is Blood Moon and their fathers, who jointly conceived them, are One and Seven Hunahpu. The astronomical roles of Xbalanque include that of the night or underworld sun and that of the full moon that rose when the sun set on the first day of the present era. His name means "sun's hidden aspect" in Kekchí (a Quichean language).

XCANUL *Xk'anul,* one of the volcanoes made by Zipacna. This is the Volcán Santa María, nine kilometers south of Quetzaltenango.

XCUXEBA See Councilor in the Ball Court.

XIBALBA *Xib'alb'a,* the fearful world beneath the face of the earth, ruled by One Death, Seven Death, and other lords. See also Road of Xibalba.

XPIYACOC, XMUCANE Divine grandparents, older than all the other gods; parents of One and Seven Hunahpu; patrons of daykeepers. To this day the ideal daykeepers are husband and wife, and the divinations with the clearest outcomes are the ones they do together. Among the epithets of Xpiyacoc and Xmucane are Grandmother of Day, Grandmother of Light (though Xpiyacoc is male), and Bearer twice over, Begetter twice over (as if to make them even older than the gods who are simply called Bearer, Begetter). They are also described as midwife and matchmaker, which are specialized subfields of contemporary Quiché diviners (female and male respectively).

XTAYUB Probably a variant spelling of Iztayul. Keeper of the Reception House Mat in the eighth generation of Cauec lords.

XULU, PACAM *Xulu, pak'am,* diviners who tell the lords of Xibalba to throw the ground bones of Hunahpu and Xbalanque into a river, with the result that they become catfish. The names are of Cholan origin, respectively referring to catfish and to something sown. See also Midmost Seers.

YACOLATAM Title of the lord who ranked eighth among the Greathouses and

361

was head of one of the nine great houses into which their lineage was divided after the founding of Rotten Cane. The word, from a Nahua source, means "corner of the mat."

YELLOW ROAD *Q'anab'e.* One of four cosmic roads. Yellow is the color of the south. See also Crossroads.

YELLOW TREE *K'ante',* the madre cacao (*Gliricidia sepium*), a large tree planted to provide shade for cacao trees.

YOKES HOUSE, THOSE OF *Ajb'atenaja,* a people belonging to a group of thirteen allied tribes the Quichés regarded as having come (like themselves) from the east. The yokes are those worn in the Mesoamerican ball game.

YOLCUAT The god of the Mexican people, also called Quitzalcuat. Yolcuat, from a Nahua source, means "ingenious snake."

ZACLATOL The Quiché version of a Nahua term for a mat made of cattail leaves.

ZAPOTES *Tulul,* a tropical fruit (*Manilkara zapota*) sometimes called sapota in English. The tan skin resembles suede; the flesh is chocolate-colored.

ZAQUIC *Saqik,* a lordly lineage divided into two great houses after the founding of Rotten Cane. This lineage, which is not listed among those that came from the east, served as a substitute for the lineage that would have been founded by Dark Jaguar and his wife, Macaw House, who had no children. See also Corntassel House.

ZAQUICAZ *Saqiq'as,* the snake that swallows the toad that swallows the louse that carries the message of Xmucane. It is a thick, black snake that is said to flee when it sees people, making a noise with its belly.

ZIPACNA *Sipakna,* the first son of Seven Macaw and Chimalmat and the elder brother of Earthquake. He claims to be the maker of the earth and has the character of a caiman.

ZIYA HOUSE *Siyaja,* a place of uncertain location, occupied by vassals of the Quiché lords during the reign of Quicab.

ZUYUA *Suyua,* part of the name Tulan Zuyua, referring to a town in the east where the leaders of the Quichés and other "mountain peoples" received patron deities that entitled them to lordship. In Yucatec Maya, the term *suyua t'an,* "twisted (or deceptive) speech," refers to riddles whose answers were demanded of pretenders to lordly positions.

BIBLIOGRAPHY

KEY TO LEXICAL CITATIONS

(AA) Aulie and Aulie 1978.
(AB) Barrera Vásquez 1980.
(AG) García Hernández et al. 1980.
(AM) Molina 1970.
(BS) Sahagún 1950–69, book 11.
(CB) Roys 1967.
(DB) Basseta 1921.
(DL) León 1954.
(DV) Vico c.1550.
(DZ) Zúñiga n.d.
(EH) Haeserijn V. 1979.
(FT) Tirado 1787.
(FV) Varea 1929.
(FX) Ximénez 1985.
(JH) Josserand and Hopkins 1988.

(JM) Maldonado Andrés et al. 1986.
(MA) Alvarado López 1975.
(MX) Maynard and Xec 1954.
(OS) Stoll 1888.
(PG) Guzmán 1984.
(PM) Morán n.d.
(RA) Brasseur de Bourbourg 1862.
(RL) Laughlin 1975.
(RS) Siméon 1977.
(TC) Coto 1983.
(TK) Carmack 1973: chap. 6.
(TT) Carmack and Mondloch 1983a.
(TV) Carmack and Mondloch 1983c.
(TY) Carmack and Mondloch 1983b.
(UU) Ulrich and Ulrich 1976.

Academia de las Lenguas Mayas. 1988. *Lenguas mayas de Guatemala: docu-mento de referencia para la pronunciación de los nuevos alfabetos oficiales.* Guatemala: Instituto Indigenista Nacional.

Alvarado López, Miguel. 1975. *Léxico médico quiché-español.* Guatemala: Insti-tuto Indigenista Nacional.

Alvárez del Toro, Miguel. 1971. *Las aves de Chiapas.* Tuxtla Gutiérrez: El Gobierno del Estado de Chiapas.

Aulie, H. Wilbur, and Evelyn W. Aulie. 1978. *Diccionario ch'ol-español, español-ch'ol.* México: Instituto Lingüístico de Verano.

Aveni, Anthony F. 1980. *Skywatchers of Ancient Mexico.* Austin: University of Texas Press.

Barrera Vásquez, Alfredo. 1980. *Diccionario maya cordemex, maya-español, español-maya.* Mérida: Ediciones Cordemex.

Basseta, Domingo de. 1921. "Vocabulario en lengua quiché." Paleography by William Gates of a manuscript (?1698) in the Bibliothèque Nationale, Paris. In the J. P. Harrington collection, National Anthropological Archives, Smith-sonian Institution, Washington, D.C.

Berendt, C. H. n.d. "Calendario de los indios de Guatemala Kiché." Copy of an anonymous manuscript (now lost) originally in the Museo Nacional de Guatemala. University of Pennsylvania Library, Philadelphia.

Brady, James E. 1991. "Caves and Cosmovision at Utatlan." *California Anthropologist* 18(1):1–10.

Brady, James E., and George Veni. 1992. "Man-made and Pseudo-karst Caves: The Implications of Subsurface Features Within Maya Centers." *Geoarchaeology: An International Journal* 7:149–67.

Brasseur de Bourbourg, Charles Etienne. 1861. *Popol Vuh: Le livre sacré et les mythes de l'antiquité américaine.* Collection de Documents dans les Langues Indigenes de l'Amérique Ancienne 1. Paris: Arthus Bertrand.

———. 1862. *Rabinal-Achi ou le drame-ballet du tun.* Collection de Documents dans les Langues Indigenes 2, pt. 2. Paris: Arthus Bertrand.

Breedlove, Dennis E., and Robert M. Laughlin. 1993. *The Flowering of the World: A Tzotzil Botany of Zinacantán.* 2 vols. Smithsonian Contributions to Anthropology 35. Washington, D.C.: Smithsonian Institution Press.

Bricker, Victoria R. 1981. *The Indian Christ, the Indian King: The Historical Substrate of Maya Myth and Ritual.* Austin: University of Texas Press.

———. 1989. "The Last Gasp of Maya Hieroglyphic Writing in the Books of Chilam Balam of Chumayel and Chan Kan." In *Word and Image in Maya Culture: Explorations in Language, Writing, and Representation,* edited by William F. Hanks and Don S. Rice, pp. 39–50. Salt Lake City: University of Utah Press.

Bricker, Victoria R., and Harvey M. Bricker. 1986. *The Mars Table in the Dresden Codex.* Middle American Research Institute Publications 57:51–80.

Brinton, Daniel G. 1885. *Annals of the Cakchiquels.* Philadelphia: Library of Aboriginal American Literature.

Brown, Kenneth L. 1980. "Archaeology in the Quiché Basin, Guatemala." *Mexikon* 2(5):72–73.

———. 1985. "Postclassic Relationships Between the Highland and Lowland Maya." In *The Lowland Maya Postclassic,* edited by Arlen F. Chase and Prudence M. Rice, pp. 270–81. Austin: University of Texas Press.

Bunzel, Ruth. 1959. *Chichicastenango: A Guatemalan Village.* Seattle: University of Washington Press.

Burgess, Dora M. de, and Patricio Xec. 1955. *Popol Wuj.* Quezaltenango: El Noticiero Evangélico.

Burns, Allan F. 1977. "The Caste War in the 1970's: Present-Day Accounts from Village Quintana Roo." In *Anthropology and History in Yucatán,* edited by Grant D. Jones, pp. 259–73. Austin: University of Texas Press.

———. 1983. *An Epoch of Miracles: Oral Literature of the Yucatec Maya.* Austin: University of Texas Press.

Campbell, Lyle. 1983. "Préstamos lingüísticos en el Popol Vuh." In *Nuevas perspectivas sobre el Popol Vuh,* edited by Robert M. Carmack and Francisco Morales Santos, pp. 81–86. Guatemala: Piedra Santa.

Carlson, John B. 1983. "The Grolier Codex: A Preliminary Report on the Content and Authenticity of a 13th-century Maya Venus Almanac." In *Calendars in Mesoamerica and Peru: Native American Computations of Time,* edited by Anthony F. Aveni and Gordon Brotherston, pp. 27–57. BAR International Series 174. Oxford: British Archaeological Reports.

Carmack, Robert M. 1973. *Quichean Civilization: The Ethnohistoric, Ethnographic, and Archaeological Sources.* Berkeley: University of California Press.

———. 1981. *The Quiché Mayas of Utatlán.* Norman: University of Oklahoma Press.

Carmack, Robert M., and James L. Mondloch. 1983a. *El Título de Totonicapán: texto, traducción y comentario.* Centro de Estudios Mayas, Fuentes para el Estudio de la Cultura Maya, 3. México: Universidad Nacional Autónoma de México.

———. 1983b. "El Títutlo de Yax." In *El Títutlo de Yax y otros documentos quichés de Totonicapán, Guatemala,* pp. 33–137. México: Universidad Nacional Autónoma de México.

———. 1983c. "Títutlo de Pedro Velasco." In *El Títutlo de Yax y otros documentos quichés de Totonicapán, Guatemala,* pp. 139–99. México: Universidad Nacional Autónoma de México.

Carrasco, Pedro. 1967. "Don Juan Cortés, cacique de Santa Cruz Quiché." *Estudios de Cultura Maya* 6:251–66.

Casas, Bartolomé de las. 1967. *Apologética historia sumaria.* 2 vols. Edited by Edmundo O'Gorman. México: Instituto de Investigaciones Históricas, Universidad Nacional Autónoma de México.

Chase, Arlen F., and Prudence M. Rice. 1985. *The Lowland Maya Postclassic.* Austin: University of Texas Press.

Chávez, Adrián I. 1979. *Pop Wuj.* México: Ediciones de la Casa Chata.

Chonay, Dionisio José, and Delia Goetz. 1953. *Title of the Lords of Totonicapán.* Bound in the same volume with Recinos and Goetz, *The Annals of the Cakchiquels.* Norman: University of Oklahoma Press.

Coe, Michael D. 1973. *The Maya Scribe and His World.* New York: The Grolier Club.

———. 1977. "Supernatural Patrons of Maya Scribes and Artists." In *Social Process in Maya Prehistory,* edited by Norman Hammond, pp. 327–47. London: Academic Press.

———. 1987. *The Maya.* Fourth edition. New York: Thames and Hudson.

———. 1989. "The Hero Twins: Myth and Image." In *The Maya Vase Book: A Corpus of Rollout Photographs of Maya Vases,* vol. 1, edited by Justin Kerr, pp. 161–84. New York: Kerr Associates.

———. 1992. *Breaking the Maya Code.* New York: Thames and Hudson.

———. 1994. *Mexico: From the Olmecs to the Aztecs.* Fourth edition. New York: Thames and Hudson.

Coe, William R. 1967. *Tikal: A Handbook of the Ancient Maya Ruins.* Philadelphia: The University Museum.

Coto, Thomás de. 1983. *Vocabulario de la lengua cakchiquel.* Edited by René Acuña. México: Universidad Nacional Autónoma de México.

Craine, Eugene R., and Reginald C. Reindorp. 1979. *The Codex Pérez and the Book of Chilam Balam of Maní.* Norman: University of Oklahoma Press.

Davis, L. Irby. 1972. *A Field Guide to the Birds of Mexico and Central America.* Austin: University of Texas Press.

Earle, Duncan McLean. 1983. "La etnoecología quiché en el Popol Vuh." In *Nuevas perspectivas sobre el Popol Vuh,* edited by Robert M. Carmack and Francisco Morales Santos, pp. 293–303. Guatemala: Piedra Santa.

Edmonson, Munro S. 1965. *Quiche-English Dictionary.* Middle American Research Institute Publication 30. New Orleans: Tulane University.

———. 1971. *The Book of Counsel: The Popol Vuh of the Quiche Maya of Guatemala.* Middle American Research Institute Publication 35. New Orleans: Tulane University.

———. 1982. *The Ancient Future of the Itza: The Book of Chilam Balam of Tizimin.* Austin: University of Texas Press.

Fash, William L. 1991. *Scribes, Warriors, and Kings: The City of Copán and the Ancient Maya.* London: Thames and Hudson.

Forshaw, Joseph M. 1973. *Parrots of the World.* New York: Doubleday.

Foster, George M. 1945. "Sierra Popoluca Folklore and Beliefs." *University of California Publications in American Archaeology and Ethnology* 42, n. 2:175–249.

Freidel, David, Linda Schele, and Joy Parker. 1993. *Maya Cosmos: Three Thousand Years on the Shaman's Path.* New York: William Morrow.

García Hernández, Abraham, Santiago Yac Sam, and David Henne Pontious. 1980. *Diccionario quiché-español.* Guatemala: Instituto Lingüístico de Verano.

Grube, Nikolai. 1992. "Classic Maya Dance: Evidence from Hieroglyphs and Iconography." *Ancient Mesoamerica* 3:210–18.

Guzmán, Pantaleón de. 1984. *Compendio de nombres en lengva cakchiqvel.* Edited by René Acuña. México: Universidad Nacional Autónoma de México.

Haeserijn V., Esteban. 1979. *Diccionario k'ekchi' español.* Guatemala: Piedra Santa.

Hammond, Norman. 1982. *Ancient Maya Civilization.* New Brunswick: Rutgers University Press.

Hanks, William F. 1989. "Elements of Maya Style." In *Word and Image in Maya Culture: Explorations in Language, Writing, and Representation,* edited by William F. Hanks and Don S. Rice, pp. 92–111. Salt Lake City: University of Utah Press.

Heyden, Doris. 1975. "An Interpretation of the Cave Underneath the Pyramid of the Sun in Teotihuacan, Mexico." *American Antiquity* 40:131–47.

Hill, Robert M., and John Monaghan. 1987. *Continuities in Highland Maya Social Organization: Ethnohistory in Sacapulas, Guatemala.* Philadelphia: University of Pennsylvania Press.

Houston, Stephen D. 1989. *Maya Glyphs.* Reading the Past, 7. Berkeley: University of California Press.

Houston, Stephen D., David Stuart, and Karl A. Taube. 1989. "Folk Classification of Classic Maya Pottery." *American Anthropologist* 91:720–26.

Hunt, Eva. 1977. *The Transformation of the Hummingbird: Cultural Roots of a Zinacanteco Mythical Poem.* Ithaca: Cornell University Press.

Hymes, Dell. 1981. *"In Vain I Tried to Tell You": Essays in Native American Ethnopoetics.* Philadelphia: University of Pennsylvania Press.

Ichon, Alain. 1983. "Arqueología y etnohistória en Cawinal." In *Nuevas perspectivas sobre el Popol Vuh,* edited by Robert M. Carmack and Francisco Morales Santos, pp. 237–46. Guatemala: Piedra Santa.

Janson, Thor. 1981. *Animales de Centroamérica en peligro.* Guatemala: Piedra Santa.

Josserand, J. Kathryn, and Nicholas A. Hopkins. 1988. "Chol (Mayan) Dictionary Database." Final Performance Report to the National Endowment for the Humanities. Photocopy.

Klein, Cecilia. 1993. "The Shield Women: Resolution of an Aztec Gender Paradox." In *Current Topics in Aztec Studies,* edited by Alana Cordy-Collins and Douglas Sharon, pp. 39–64. San Diego Museum Papers 30. San Diego: San Diego Museum of Man.

La Farge, Oliver. 1947. *Santa Eulalia.* Chicago: University of Chicago Press.

Laughlin, Robert M. 1975. *The Great Tzotzil Dictionary of San Lorenzo Zinacantán.* Smithsonian Contributions to Anthropology 19. Washington, D.C.: Smithsonian Institution Press.

Lehmann-Nitsche, R. 1924–25. "La constelación de la Osa Mayor y su concepto como Huracán o dios de la tormenta en la esfera del Mar Caribe." *Revista del Museo de La Plata* 28:101–45.

León, Juan de. 1954. *Diccionario quiché-español.* Guatemala: Landivar.

Leyenaar, Ted J. J., and Lee A. Parsons. 1988. *Ulama: The Ballgame of the Mayas and Aztecs, 2000 B.C.–2000 A.D.* Leiden: Spruyt.

Lounsbury, Floyd G. 1978. "Maya Numeration, Computation, and Calendrical Astronomy." *Dictionary of Scientific Biography* 25, n. 1:759–818.

———. 1982. "Astronomical Knowledge and Its Uses at Bonampak, Mexico." In *Archaeoastronomy in the New World,* edited by Anthony F. Aveni, pp. 143–68. Cambridge: Cambridge University Press.

———. 1983. "The Base of the Venus Tables of the Dresden Codex, and Its Significance for the Calendar-Correlation Problem." In *Calendars in Mesoamerica and Peru: Native American Computations of Time,* edited by Anthony F. Aveni and Gordon Brotherston, pp. 1–26. BAR International Series 174. Oxford: British Archaeological Reports.

———. 1985. "The Identities of the Mythological Figures in the Cross Group Inscriptions of Palenque." In *Fourth Palenque Round Table, 1980,* edited by Merle Greene Robertson and Elizabeth P. Benson, pp. 45–58. San Francisco: Pre-Columbian Art Institute.

————. 1989. "The Ancient Writing of Middle America." In *The Origins of Writing*, edited by Wayne M. Senner, pp. 203–37. Lincoln: University of Nebraska Press.

Love, Bruce. 1994. *The Paris Codex: Handbook for a Mayan Priest*. Austin: University of Texas Press.

Lowy, Bernard. 1974. "*Amanita muscaria* and the Thunderbolt Legend in Guatemala and Mexico." *Mycologia* 66:188–191.

Maldonado Andrés, Juan, Juan Ordóñez Domingo, and Juan Ortíz Domingo. 1986. *Diccionario mam*. Guatemala: Centro de Reproducciones de la Universidad Rafael Landívar.

Maynard, Gail, and Patricio Xec. 1954. "Diccionario preliminar del idioma quiché." Mimeograph.

McBryde, Felix Webster. 1947. *Cultural and Historical Geography of Southwest Guatemala*. Institute of Social Anthropology 4. Washington, D.C.: Smithsonian Institution.

Mendelson, E. Michael. 1959. "Maximon: An Iconographical Introduction." *Man* 59:56–60.

Miles, Suzanne W. 1981. "Mam Residence and the Maize Myth." In *Culture in History: Essays in Honor of Paul Radin*, edited by Stanley Diamond, pp. 430–36. New York: Octagon Books.

Miller, Arthur G. 1982. *On the Edge of the Sea: Mural Painting at Tancah-Tulum, Quintana Roo, Mexico*. Washington, D.C.: Dumbarton Oaks.

Molina, Alonso de. 1970. *Vocabulario en lengua castellana y mexicana y mexicana y castellana*. Estudio preliminar de Miguel León-Portilla. México: Porrua.

Morán, Pedro. n.d. "Bocabulario de solo los nombres de la lengua pokoman." Manuscript in the Bancroft Library, University of California, Berkeley. Copy in the Tozzer Library, Harvard University, Cambridge, Massachusetts.

Norman, V. Garth. 1976. *Izapa Sculpture,* pt. 2. Papers of the New World Archaeological Foundation 30. Provo, Utah: Brigham Young University.

Orellana, Sandra. 1984. *The Tzutuhil Mayas: Continuity and Change, 1250–1630*. Norman: University of Oklahoma Press.

Palma Murga, Gustavo, ed. 1991. *Indice del archivo del extinguido Juzgado Privativo de Tierras depositado en la Escribanía de Cámara del Supremo Gobierno de la República de Guatemala*, pt. 2. México: Ediciones de la Casa Chata.

Paxton, Merideth. 1986. "Codex Dresden: Stylistic and Iconographic Analysis of a Maya Manuscript." Ph.D. dissertation in Art History, University of New Mexico. Ann Arbor: University Microfilms.

Recinos, Adrián. 1957. *Crónicas indígenas de Guatemala*. Guatemala: Editorial Universitaria.

Recinos, Adrián, and Delia Goetz. 1953. *The Annals of the Cakchiquels.* Bound in the same volume with Chonay and Goetz, *Title of the Lords of Totonicapán*. Norman: University of Oklahoma Press.

Recinos, Adrián, Delia Goetz, and Sylvanus Griswold Morley. 1950. *Popol Vuh: The Sacred Book of the Quiché Maya of Guatemala.* Norman: University of Oklahoma Press.

Reents-Budet, Dorie. 1994. *Painting the Maya Universe: Royal Ceramics of the Classic Period.* Durham: Duke University Press.

Robicsek, Francis, and Donald Hales. 1984. "Maya Heart Sacrifice." In *Ritual Human Sacrifice in Mesoamerica,* edited by Elizabeth H. Boone, pp. 49–90. Washington, D.C.: Dumbarton Oaks.

Roys, Ralph L. 1954. "The Maya Katun Prophecies of the Books of Chilam Balam, Series I." *Contributions to American Anthropology and History* 12 (57):3–60. Washington, D.C.: Carnegie Institution.

———. 1965. *Ritual of the Bacabs: A Book of Maya Incantations.* Norman: University of Oklahoma Press.

———. 1967. *The Book of Chilam Balam of Chumayel.* Norman: University of Oklahoma Press.

Rubio, J. Francisco. 1982. *Diccionario de voces usadas en Guatemala.* Guatemala: Piedra Santa.

Rzedowski, Jerzy, and Miguel Equihua. 1987. *Atlas cultural de México: flora.* México: Grupo Editorial Planeta.

Sabloff, Jeremy A., and E. Wyllys Andrews V. 1986. *Late Lowland Maya Civilization: Classic to Postclassic.* Albuquerque: University of New Mexico Press.

Sahagún, Bernardino de. 1950–69. *Florentine Codex: A General History of the Things of New Spain.* Translated by Arthur J. O. Anderson and Charles E. Dibble. 12 vols. Santa Fe: School of American Research and University of Utah.

Saler, Benson. 1976. "Cultic Alternatives in a Guatemalan Village." Paper read at the Association of Social Anthropologists, Conference on Regional Cults, Manchester, England. Mimeographed.

Sam Colop, Enrique. 1994. "Maya Poetics." Ph.D. dissertation in English, State University of New York at Buffalo. Ann Arbor: University Microfilms.

Scarborough, Vernon L., and David R. Wilcox. 1991. *The Mesoamerican Ballgame.* Tucson: University of Arizona Press.

Schele, Linda. 1984. *Notebook for the Maya Hieroglyphic Writing Workshop at Texas.* Austin: Institute of Latin American Studies.

———. 1991. "Venus and the Monuments of Smoke-Imix-God K and others in the Great Plaza." *Copán Notes* 101.

———. 1992. *Notebook for the XVI Maya Hieroglyphic Workshop at Texas.* Austin: University of Texas.

Schele, Linda, and Barbara Fash. 1991. "Venus and the Reign of Smoke-Monkey." *Copán Notes* 100.

Schele, Linda, and David Freidel. 1990. *A Forest of Kings: The Untold Story of the Ancient Maya.* New York: William Morrow.

Schele, Linda, and Mary Ellen Miller. 1986. *The Blood of Kings: Dynasty and Ritual in Maya Art.* Fort Worth: Kimbell Art Museum.

369

Schele, Linda, and David Stuart. 1986. "Te-Tun as the Glyph for 'Stela.' " *Copán Notes* 1.

Scholes, France V., and Ralph L. Roys. 1968. *The Maya Chontal Indians of Acalan-Tixchel: A Contribution to the History and Ethnography of the Yucatan Peninsula.* Norman: University of Oklahoma Press.

Schultze Jena, Leonhard S. 1944. *Popol Vuh: Das heilige Buch der Quiché-Indianer von Guatemala.* Stuttgart: W. Kohlhammer.

Shaw, Mary. 1971. *According to Our Ancestors: Folk Texts from Guatemala and Honduras.* Norman: Summer Institute of Linguistics.

Siegel, Morris. 1943. "The Creation Myth and Acculturation in Acatán, Guatemala." *Journal of American Folklore* 56:120–26.

Siméon, Rémi. 1977. *Diccionario de la lengua nahuatl o mexicana.* México: Siglo Veintiuno.

Smith, Mary Elizabeth. 1973. *Picture Writing from Ancient Southern Mexico: Mixtec Place Signs and Maps.* Norman: University of Oklahoma Press.

Stoll, Otto. 1888. *Die Sprache der Pokonchí-Indianer.* Die Maya-Sprachen der Pokom-Gruppe, vol. 1. Vienna: Alfred Hölder.

Stross, Brian. 1983. "The Language of Zuyua." *American Ethnologist* 10:150–64.

Stuart, David. 1987. "Ten Phonetic Syllables." *Research Reports on Ancient Maya Writing* 14. Washington, D.C.: Center for Maya Research.

———. n.d. "The Maya Conception of Ancestral Tollan." Paper delivered at the Mesoamerican Histories Roundtable, Dumbarton Oaks.

Stuart, David, and Stephen Houston. 1994. *Classic Maya Place Names.* Studies in Pre-Columbian Art and Archaeology 33. Washington, D.C.: Dumbarton Oaks.

Taube, Karl. 1987. "A Representation of the Principal Bird Deity in the Paris Codex." *Research Reports on Maya Writing* 6. Washington, D.C.: Center for Maya Research.

———. 1989. "Itzam Cab Ain: Caimans, Cosmology, and Calendrics in Postclassic Yucatán." *Research Reports on Ancient Maya Writing* 26. Washington, D.C.: Center for Maya Research.

———. 1992. *The Major Gods of Ancient Yucatan.* Studies in Pre-Columbian Art and Archaeology 32. Washington, D.C.: Dumbarton Oaks.

———. 1994a. "The Birth Vase: Natal Imagery in Ancient Maya Myth and Ritual." In *The Maya Vase Book*, edited by Barbara Kerr and Justin Kerr, pp. 652–85. New York: Kerr Associates.

———. 1994b. "The Jade Hearth: Centrality, Rulership, and the Classic Maya Temple." Paper delivered at a 1994 Dumbarton Oaks symposium. Photocopy.

Tedlock, Barbara. 1982. "Sound Texture and Metaphor in Quiché Maya Ritual Language." *Current Anthropology* 23:269–72.

———. 1983. "El C'oxol: un símbolo de la resistencia quiché a la conquista espiritual." In *Nuevas perspectivas sobre el Popol Vuh,* edited by Robert Carmack and Francisco Morales Santos, pp. 343–57. Guatemala: Piedra Santa.

370

———. 1985. "Hawks, Meteorology and Astronomy in Quiché-Maya Agriculture." *Archaeoastronomy* 8:80–88.

———. 1986. "On a Mountain Road in the Dark: Encounters with the Quiché Maya Culture Hero." In *Symbol and Meaning Beyond the Closed Community: Essays in Mesoamerican Ideas,* edited by Gary Gossen, pp. 125–38. Studies on Culture and Society 1. Albany: Institute for Mesoamerican Studies, State University of New York.

———. 1987. "Zuni and Quiché Dream Sharing and Interpreting." In *Dreaming: Anthropological and Psychological Interpretations,* edited by Barbara Tedlock, pp. 105–31. Cambridge: Cambridge University Press.

———. 1992. *Time and the Highland Maya.* Revised edition. Albuquerque: University of New Mexico Press.

Tedlock, Barbara, and Dennis Tedlock. 1985. "Text and Textile: Language and Technology in the Arts of the Quiché Maya," *Journal of Anthropological Research* 41:121–46.

Tedlock, Dennis. 1972. *Finding the Center: Narrative Poetry of the Zuni Indians.* New York: Dial. Reprinted 1978, Lincoln: University of Nebraska Press.

———. 1983a. "Las formas del verso quiché." In *Nuevas perspectivas sobre el Popol Vuh,* edited by Robert Carmack and Francisco Morales Santos, pp. 123–32. Guatemala: Piedra Santa.

———. 1983b. *The Spoken Word and the Work of Interpretation.* Philadelphia: University of Pennsylvania Press.

———. 1987. "Hearing a Voice in an Ancient Text: Quiché Maya Poetics in Performance." In *Native American Discourse: Poetics and Rhetoric,* edited by Joel Sherzer and Anthony C. Woodbury, pp. 140–75. Cambridge: Cambridge University Press.

———. 1988. "Mayan Linguistic Ideology." In *On the Ethnography of Communication: The Legacy of Sapir,* edited by Paul V. Kroskrity, pp. 55–108. Other Realities 8. Los Angeles: University of California at Los Angeles, Department of Anthropology.

———. 1990. "Drums, Egrets, and the Mother of The Gods: Remarks on the Tablet of the Cross at Palenque." *U Mut Maya* 3:13–14.

———. 1992a. "Myth, Math, and the Problem of Correlation in Mayan Books." In *The Sky in Mayan Literature,* edited by Anthony F. Aveni, pp. 247–73. New York: Oxford University Press.

———. 1992b. "The Popol Vuh as a Hieroglyphic Book." In *New Theories on the Ancient Maya,* edited by Elin C. Danien and Robert J. Sharer, pp. 229–40. University Museum Monograph 77, Symposium Series 3. Philadelphia: University Museum.

———. 1993a. *Breath on the Mirror: Mythic Voices and Visions of the Living Maya.* San Francisco: HarperSanFrancisco.

———. 1993b. "Torture in the Archives: Mayans Meet Europeans." *American Anthropologist* 95:139–52.

————. 1995. "Visions of the Maya Sky." *Cambridge Archaeological Journal* 5:118–20.

Tedlock, Dennis, and Barbara Tedlock. 1993. "A Mayan Reading of the Story of the Stars." *Archaeology* 46(4):33–35.

Teletor, Celso Narciso. 1955. *Apuntes para una monografía de Rabinal (B.V.) y algo de nuestro folklore.* Guatemala: Ministerio de Educación Pública.

Thompson, J. Eric S. 1930. *Ethnology of the Mayas of Southern and Central British Honduras.* Field Museum of Natural History, Anthropological Series 17, no. 2. Chicago: Field Museum Press.

————. 1960. *Maya Hieroglyphic Writing.* Norman: University of Oklahoma Press.

————. 1966. *The Rise and Fall of Maya Civilization.* Second edition. Norman: University of Oklahoma Press.

————. 1970. *Maya History and Religion.* Norman: University of Oklahoma Press.

————. 1972. *A Commentary on the Dresden Codex.* Philadelphia: American Philosophical Society.

Tirado, Fermín Joseph. 1787. "Vocabulario de lengua kiche." Manuscript in the Tozzer Library, Harvard University, Cambridge.

Tozzer, Alfred M. 1907. *A Comparative Study of the Mayas and the Lacandones.* New York: Macmillan.

————. 1941. *Landa's relación de las cosas de Yucatán.* Papers of the Peabody Museum of American Archaeology and Ethnology 18. Cambridge, Massachusetts.

Ulrich, E. Matthew, and Rosemary Dixon de Ulrich. 1976. *Diccionario bilingüe maya mopán-español, español-maya mopán.* Guatemala: Intituto Lingüístico de Verano.

Varea, Francisco de. 1929. "Calepino en lengua cakchiquel." Paleography by William Gates of a manuscript (1699) in the American Philosophical Society Library, Philadelphia, Pennsylvania. In the Gates Collection, Brigham Young University Library, Provo, Utah.

Vico, Domingo de. c.1550. "Vocabulario de la lengua cakchiquel y kiché." Manuscript in the Bibliothèque Nationale, Paris. Photocopy in the Pre-Columbian Library, Dumbarton Oaks, Washington, D.C.

Whittaker, Gordon. 1986. "The Mexican Names of Three Venus Gods in the Dresden Codex." *Mexicon* 8:56–59.

Ximénez, Francisco. c.1701. "Arte de las tres lenguas 3a3chiquel, quiche y 4,utuhil." Manuscript in the Ayer collection at the Newberry Library, Chicago, Illinois.

————. 1857. *Las historias del origen de los indios de esta provincia de Guatemala.* Introduction, paleography, and notes by Carl Scherzer. Vienna: Academia Imperial de las Ciencias.

————. 1973. *Popol Vuh.* Facsimile edition with paleography and notes by Agustín Estrada Monroy. Guatemala: José de Pineda Ibarra.

———. 1985. *Primera parte del tesoro de las lenguas cakchiquel, quiché y zutuhil, en que las dichas lenguas se traducen a la nuestra, española.* Edited by Carmelo Sáenz de Santa María. Academia de Geografía e Historia de Guatemala, special pub. 30. Guatemala: Tipografía Nacional.

Yadeun, Juan. 1993. *Toniná.* México: El Equilibrista.

Zúñiga, Dionysio de. n.d. "Diccionario pocomchí-castellano y castellano-pocomchí." Manuscript in the Berendt Collection at the University of Pennsylvania Library, Philadelphia. Photocopy in the Tozzer Library, Harvard University, Cambridge, Massachusetts.

INDEX

377

fasting, 47, 55, 150, 156, 158, 192, 193, 294, 329, 330
fer-de-lance, 66, 159, 161, 203, 228, 302, 304, 305
Fireplace, 77, 241, 342, 344
Four Hundred Boys, the, 245; and Hunahpu and Xbalanque, 35, 142, 278; as Pleiades, 35, 246, 278, 288, 342, 344 (*see also* Hundrath); and Seven Macaw, 35, 84; and Zipacna, 34, 35, 81–84, 142, 244, 245, 342, 344
Front of the Monument, 188, 342
Fuego (volcano), 241

Genesis, 211, 289
God, 30, 57, 63, 211, 217, 218, 331
God B, 224, 225, 281
God CH, 240
God GI, 224, 225, 281
God GII, 224, 297, 298. *See also* God K
God K, 224, 225, 297, 298
God L, 251
God M, 253
God Q, 253
God S, 239
Goddess O, 217
Godly Copal, 160, 342. *See also* copal
Gouger of Faces, 71, 235, 342
Granary, 195, 342
Grandmother of Day, Grandmother of Light, 69, 150, 217, 231, 232, 342, 361. *See also* Xmucane; Xpiyacoc
Great Hollow, 36, 38, 51, 54, 126, 133, 157, 255, 342. *See also* Great Hollow with Fish in the Ashes
Great Hollow with Fish in the Ashes, 36, 47, 94, 255, 256, 280, 342, 354. *See also* Great Hollow
great house, 149, 181, 183–85, 195–97, 291, 322, 336, 339, 340, 342, 343, 345, 346, 348, 349, 353, 355, 356, 362
Great Monument of Tohil, 191, 328, 329, 340, 342, 359
Great Rift, 256, 257, 337, 340, 354, 355, 360
Great White Peccary and Great White Coati, 34, 63, 69, 79–81, 215, 216, 243, 244, 342, 343
Greathouses, the, 47, 52, 183, 214, 296, 315, 342, 344, 349, 355, 358; and Auilix, 45, 191, 197, 336, 353, 359; at Bearded Place, 52, 181, 183, 337, 359; and

Jaguar Night, 44, 149, 174, 179, 196, 336, 342, 345, 353; and Noble Acutec, 50, 174, 179, 196, 350; and noble titles, 50, 51, 55, 56, 184, 185, 196, 197, 334, 339, 340, 343, 345, 347–51, 354, 361; and Woven, 189, 196, 361; and writers of the alphabetic Popol Vuh as members, 25
Green Path, 193
Green Road, 116, 193, 272, 273, 340, 343. *See also* Crossroads; Yellow Road
Guardians of the Spoils, 149, 293, 343
Guatemala, 21, 22, 25, 27, 54, 56, 77, 201, 206, 214, 245, 247, 260, 272, 284, 288, 299, 320, 325, 334, 338, 339, 342, 344, 346, 353, 357, 359
Guatemala City, 22, 25, 27, 324
Gulf (of Mexico), 22, 209, 212, 296

Hacauitz: as building, 191, 343; as citadel, 49, 51, 159, 162, 180, 213, 314, 343, 358, 359; as god, 45, 52, 152, 154, 158, 166, 191, 193, 212, 225, 297, 307, 311, 312, 343, 353, 359; as god and blood of deer and birds, 164, 165, 226; as god and as Cholan name, 45, 343; as god and hiding place, 47, 158, 159, 163, 302, 307, 343; as god and Lust Woman and Wailing Woman, 49, 167, 168, 311, 346; as god and as stone, 47, 48, 161, 164–66, 191, 304, 305, 307; as god and tribes embracing (suckling), 49, 164–166, 226, 308; as mountain, 47, 48, 159–62, 170, 172–75, 297, 302, 314, 343. *See also* k'ab'awil; Lord Hacauitz; Lord Quichés, the (and Hacauitz)
Hapsburgs, 27, 195
Heart of Earth, 30, 66, 67, 148, 150, 192, 193, 202, 203, 227, 228, 332, 343, 344, 350. *See also* Heart of Sky; Hurricane; Newborn Nanahuac, Sudden Nanahuac; Newborn Thunderbolt; Sudden Thunderbolt; Thunderbolt Hurricane
Heart of Metal, 227, 228
Heart of Sky, 30, 34, 65–67, 70–72, 77, 81, 86, 127, 148, 150, 192, 193, 202, 203, 222, 223, 227, 228, 233, 234, 244, 342–44, 350, 356. *See also* Hurricane; Newborn Nanahuac, Sudden Nanahuac; Newborn Thunderbolt; Sudden Thunderbolt; Thunderbolt Hurricane

Heart of the Lake, Heart of the Sea, 30, 63, 343, 356. *See also* Bearer, Begetter; Maker, Modeler; Sovereign Plumed Serpent

Herald, 51, 185, 189–91, 193, 194, 197, 316, 332, 343, 345, 346, 348, 350–52, 354, 355; Lord, 185, 196, 323, 343, 346, 348. *See also* Armadillo Dung; Noble Caller; Noble Mortal; Noble Short One; Red Banner

Historia Quiché de don Juan de Torres, 301

Holtun, 296

Honduras, 22, 23

Hot Springs, 189, 343. *See also* Hot Springs Heights

Hot Springs Heights, 188, 343, 344. *See also* Hot Springs

Huehuetenango, 325, 360

Huliznab, 77, 241, 344

Hunahpu, 25; as day name, 37, 39, 43, 238, 239, 351; as mountain, 77, 241, 342, 344; as name in prayer, 150, 342. *See also* Hunahpu and Xbalanque

Hunahpu and Xbalanque, 238–40, 243, 244, 255, 267, 268, 338 (*see also* Hunahpu); and animals, 38, 110–12, 126–30, 268, 269, 276–78; and ball game, 33, 38–42, 111–16, 119–22, 124, 128, 129, 207, 239, 254, 257, 269, 271, 273, 277, 278, 280, 338, 342, 344, 360, 361; and Bat House, 40, 125–27, 356; and Black Road, 116, 273; and Blood Moon, 33, 36, 38, 43, 99, 102, 104, 106, 109, 110, 112, 116, 263, 264, 338, 344, 351, 361; as catfish, 42, 132, 136, 278, 280, 281, 361; and Cold House, 40, 124, 258; and corn plants, 39, 43, 50, 116, 139, 140, 271, 272, 278, 284–86, 346, 347; and Crossroads, 39, 116, 273; and Dark House, 119; and Earthquake, 35, 42, 85–88, 249, 347; and falcon, 39, 114, 115, 270, 271, 338, 346 (*see also* laughing falcon); and the Four Hundred Boys, 35, 84, 142, 278; and Great White Peccary and Great White Coati, 34, 79–81; and hunting with blowguns, 33, 38, 86, 114, 115, 238, 239, 249, 270, 344, 361; and Hurricane, 34, 85, 86, 127, 249, 344, 355; as illusionists, 42; and Jaguar House, 40, 124, 125; and One Death, 279; and One and Seven Death, 42, 113, 115, 119, 120, 123, 124, 126, 131, 132, 135–38, 274, 282, 283; and One Hunahpu, 33, 35, 36, 38, 91, 99, 102, 111, 138, 140, 258, 263, 264, 286, 309, 344, 351, 361; and One Monkey and One Artisan, 38, 42, 93, 104–8, 266, 267, 344, 351; and Place of Ball Game Sacrifice, 43, 138, 141, 259; and Razor House, 40, 122, 123, 258; and road to Xibalba, 39; and Seven Hunahpu, 33, 35, 36, 38, 43, 91, 102, 111, 138, 140, 141, 207, 258, 259, 263, 264, 286, 287, 309, 344, 351, 361; and Seven Macaw, 28, 34, 35, 42, 77–81, 240, 242, 244, 355, 356; and sowing and dawning, 87, 225; and squash as head, 40–42, 120, 127–29, 207, 225, 276–78, 309; as sun and moon, 43, 51, 141, 225, 264, 279, 285, 287, 338, 344, 361; as vagabond dancers and actors, 42, 132–38, 209, 215, 232, 280–82, 285, 336, 344, 353, 357, 360; and White Dagger, 40, 120, 273, 360; and Xibalba, 38–43, 51, 55, 59, 112, 113, 115, 116, 118–41, 207, 225, 239, 240, 254, 258, 259, 273–84, 342, 346, 347, 359–61; and Xmucane, 33, 38, 39, 43, 50, 102, 104–13, 115, 116, 139, 140, 232, 266, 269, 284–86, 346, 347; and Xpiyacoc, 33, 232; and Xulu and Pacam, 42, 130, 131, 278, 279, 361; and Zipacna, 34, 35, 42, 84, 85, 246–48

"Hunahpu Monkey" (song title), 106, 344

Hunahpu Place, 189, 344

Hunahpu Possum, Hunahpu Coyote, 63, 69, 215, 232, 344

Hundrath, 84, 245, 246, 342, 344. *See also* Pleiades

Hurricane, 30, 32, 34, 35, 65–67, 69, 72, 85, 86, 91, 99, 127, 148, 150, 155, 192, 202, 203, 223, 224, 233, 249, 298, 310, 343, 344, 355, 356, 359. *See also* Heart of Earth; Heart of Sky; Newborn Nanahuac, Sudden Nanahuac; Newborn Thunderbolt; Sudden Thunderbolt; Thunderbolt Hurricane

ilb'al, 21, 218

Iloc Place, 213

Ilocs, 45, 47, 52, 149, 151, 152, 157, 159, 161, 162, 180–82, 190, 193, 213, 318, 319, 344, 349, 352, 353, 358, 359

380